Changing

Women in Canada

Edited by Sandra Burt, Lorraine Code,
and Lindsay Dorney

M&S

Reprinted 1990

Canadian Cataloguing in Publication Data
Main entry under title:

Changing patterns : women in Canada

Includes bibliographies
ISBN 0-7710-2853-9

1. Women — Canada — Social conditions. 2. Women — Canada. 3. Feminism — Canada. I. Burt, Sandra D., 1947- . II. Code, Lorraine. III. Dorney, Lindsay.

HQ1453.C48 1988 305.4'0971 C88-093222-8

Printed and bound in Canada

McClelland & Stewart Inc.
The Canadian Publishers
481 University Avenue
Toronto, Ontario
M5G 2E9

Contents

Preface

Although Women's Studies has been taught in Canadian universities and colleges since the early 1970s, there is still a scarcity of good Canadian Women's Studies texts. Many instructors continue to find it necessary to teach from American books, which are often ill-suited to give an understanding of the specific experiences of Canadian women. In 1985, in response to this situation, a group of women who had been involved in teaching Women's Studies in south-western Ontario met to plan the writing of a new, all-Canadian text. The group met regularly for several months, comparing notes and suggestions about what was required to produce a readable and informative book, until, in the early spring of 1986, an editorial committee was established, consisting of the three present editors. Our discussions led us to conclude that we wanted to produce a book that would tell the story of recent changes in Canadian women's lives, set against a historical background. At the same time, we were particularly concerned that it not be merely a collection of previously published articles. This meant asking contributors to use this opportunity to present their new research in the context of reviewing work done in their area of expertise. The chapters that comprise this volume were written in response to that request.

One particularly valuable aspect of the production of this book was an all-day conference meeting of all contributors, held in the autumn of 1986. Each of the contributors had prepared an early draft of her chapter, which was circulated before the meeting and discussed by the group. The meeting gave us the opportunity to integrate the chapters in a way unusual for an edited collection. It became clear, for example, that some topics, such as the status of women in the work force, were being addressed by several authors as aspects of their research. Hence there is no separate chapter on work in this volume. In much the same way we concluded that a separate chapter on women's political participation would simply duplicate material that occurs elsewhere in the book. This integrative treatment of these and other aspects of women's lives reflects our conception of the best approach to Women's Studies as an area of study, teaching, and research. We hope that this volume will present an account of what women have achieved that will inspire those who read it to persevere in breaking the silence about women's contributions to society. Such contributions have long been ignored in patriarchal scholarship.

Introduction

The women's movement has touched the lives of most Canadian women and has transformed the structure of their daily existence. Feminist scholars have integrated these transformations into their work, developing critiques of old perspectives and challenging long-standing assumptions about how the world is, and how it ought to be. Women's Studies brings many of these scholars together, reinforcing their sense of common interest in overthrowing the system of power that has determined women's place in society. That system is controlled by men, and is dominated by the values that men have developed. It is reinforced by the nature of production in industrialized societies.

Since the 1960s women have undertaken a vigorous assault on this system of power, with so much apparent success that a new generation of young women has started to think about post-feminist politics, advancing the argument that measures like pay-equity and affirmative action no longer are necessary. This book challenges women's new-found complacency, for while it celebrates women's achievements, it also documents the persistence of many kinds of barriers to full equality between women and men. This book is also about past constraints on women's opportunities. It shows how fixed assumptions about female nature have affected women in all aspects of their lives, influencing their psychological, physical, and social well-being. It addresses questions of how women have examined these assumptions and initiated changes with increasing success.

One of the most important assumptions challenged by feminists is the belief that women and men should live in separate spheres. No contemporary feminist would support the claim that women should be confined to the private sphere of the home, away from the public world of politics and work. Feminists argue that the public/private dichotomy is contrived, unnecessary, and harmful. Indeed, many feminists maintain that the division of human social life into public and private realms, and the relegation of women to the latter, is a primary source of women's disadvantaged social position. In contrast, advocates of the doctrine of separate spheres believe that the important business of any society is conducted in the public domain where men, and reason, rule and that society's frivolous and insignificant pleasures are enjoyed in the private sphere where women dwell. In patriarchal society the home has provided men with physical and emotional comfort. Yet feminists have shown that the ideology of sanctity and domestic bliss that surrounds the realm assigned to women works to conceal and condone male despotism in the home. That same ideology disadvantages women who need or want to enter the work force to become productive, competitive participants in the labour market. It thwarts their efforts to obtain good child care, restricts their employment opportunities, and condemns them to unequal pay for work of equal value.

Yet, the boundaries between public and private domains, activities, and expectations are not nearly so rigid as allusions to "the public and private dichotomy" seem to imply. They vary historically, culturally, racially, and along class lines, according to a number of factors. Even in societies where quite rigid divisions pertain (at any given time) there may be local variations in the extent to which public institutions intervene in matters one might be inclined to consider private. In preindustrial societies, for example, the division between public and private *labour* was not so rigid as it is in present-day industrialized societies. But women were, nonetheless, primarily responsible for domestic duties and child rearing. By contrast, in societies where boundaries between public and private may seem to be becoming less distinct, this blurring of boundaries often manifests itself in increased public intervention in matters of personal health and sexual behaviour. These are areas that traditionally have been considered to be of private concern.

For example, in her chapter on the history of women in Canada, Jane Errington points out that in pre-Confederation New France, where the family was the basic social and economic unit, home and workplace were most often the same. In that society, Errington tells us, "the division between the public and private spheres, both within the walls of the homes and within the minds of its residents, was ill-defined and sometimes non-existent." (p. 54) Yet by the time of Confederation, women in British North America were expected to confine their activities to the private sphere of the home, and to be the guardians of an entrenched ideology of domestic, family virtues.

It would be a mistake to see a linear historical progression in the development of Canadian thinking about separate spheres, however. As industrialization came to Eastern Canada, so a public/private ideology began to be enforced. But at the same time, settlers moving to the Canadian West found that the patterns of their lives more closely resembled those of the residents of New France, with the boundaries between public and private either indistinct or virtually non-existent. Industrialized Western Canadian cities, by contrast, were to repeat the pattern of separate spheres manifested in capitalist industrial society elsewhere. And feminists both at the turn of the century, with the suffrage campaign, and again since the 1960s (especially in their political activities documented by Sandra Burt in her chapter in this volume) have been working – with significant success – to challenge and shift those boundaries.

Shifts in the boundaries between public and private are not uniformly evident throughout Canadian society. One of the most notable lessons to be learned from Roxana Ng's chapter is that immigrant women in Canada so far have not begun to benefit from these shifts in the same way or to the same extent that white francophone and anglophone Canadian women have benefitted. The discriminatory social mechanisms Ng describes work to ensure that in many immigrant families only the husband and father has reasonable access to the public world of work, social exchange, and commercial transaction. Women are confined to a doubly private world of home and/or ethnic community, partially in consequence of their limited access to instruction in the language of their new community. Hence even those who work outside the home are restricted by the extent to which they can engage in 'public' activities. Much of their work involves, and has involved, performing domestic service in other people's homes, or doing sewing, child minding, and related paid work for other women within their own homes. Such activities – which are also performed by a large number of economically disadvantaged non-immigrant women – show how difficult it is to distinguish clearly between public and private life. Yet one distinction is quite clear. It goes without saying that many immigrant women are linguistically ill-qualified to participate in (feminist) political activities outside their ethnic group.

It is not only with respect to labour-market work and political activity that shifting conceptions of the public and private manifest themselves. The 'medicalization' of society, which Wendy Mitchinson discusses in her chapter on the medical treatment of women, is a process in which matters of health that might seem to be a person's private concern become occasions of public intervention and control. Here we see a process that effectively disempowers women in an area where they have a notable history of wisdom and expertise. Mitchinson points to the success of physicians in gaining a monopoly both over esteem and over health care itself by making a university medical degree a requirement for the legal practice of medicine. Women have long experienced difficulty in gaining admission to medical schools (even though this is changing in recent years). And the traditional male-doctor/female-nurse dichotomy parallels the public/private dichotomy both in the kinds of work done, and the authority and esteem conferred. The outlawing of midwifery in Canada is a particularly striking instance of taking over and placing under public jurisdiction a practice where women's (private) experiential knowledge and skill had shaped their activity, and their participation in other women's lives on an empathetic basis. In the so-called private domain, women's capacity to provide health care for their families, according to their designated role, shifted with the move away from home care to hospitalization after the turn of the century. Childbirth, increasingly, was an event moved away from the home and into hospital.

The point of these remarks is neither to paint a nostalgic picture of pre-medicalized or pre-industrial society nor to underestimate the benefits of progress in the last century. It is, rather, to illustrate that 'public work' was often carried out in the home in the past. It is to suggest, further, that there is no progress without cost. Some of the costs, in this context, are in a diminishing of the personal, familial aspects of health care, and a loss of individual control over one's body. Yet gains in terms of decreased burdens and responsibilities for women, and increased capacity to engage in other activities, must be balanced against those losses and costs.

Many feminists who recognize the advantage of state-run medical insurance programs and welfare nevertheless believe that the costs of making women's gynaecological, reproductive health and the economic security of citizens a matter of public concern may have been too great. The result has been what many feminists describe as a significant loss of control over their sexual and reproductive lives. Wendy Mitchinson details innumerable 'expert' interventions into all aspects of a woman's pre-reproductive, reproductive, and post-reproductive life. These interventions range from advice on how much exercise a prepubescent girl should have, through advanced technological control of childbirth, to hysterectomies and estrogen treatment for menopausal women. Doctors have a long history of offering controlling advice about proper, normal female sexual experience; and controversies surrounding abortion and birth control constitute further evidence that Canadian society has not been content to regard a woman's biology as her own. It is ironic that the public/private dichotomy is perpetuated by drawing an ideological equation between women and the private domain on the basis of women's reproductive, biological function. Yet a woman's biology, which is alleged to provide the reasons for her relegation to the private sphere, is not permitted to remain in her own (private) control. Feminist response to these manifestations of a shift in public/private boundaries is evident, for example, in the growing numbers of women's health collectives, and in campaigns (which seem to promise success) to make midwifery legal once again.

The ideology of public and private is revealed for the artificially constructed mechanism of control that it is when one considers how very few of a woman's allegedly private activities are permitted to remain her private concern. Joanna

Boehnert notes how psychology has constructed ideals of what it is to be a good woman, and has judged abnormal and deviant women who fail to conform to those ideals. Condemnations of this sort range over areas of such seemingly private concern as sexual expression and 'proper' sexual response, ideas of what kinds of activities, education, and occupation are 'gender appropriate,' and how a woman ought to mother her children and interact with her husband or partner. Clearly there are many respects in which the private domain is only nominally private. This point is borne out especially strongly in Rona Achilles's analysis of reproductive technology. The fact that motherhood remains central "to women's identity and self-esteem" (p. 293) attests to the social pressures that a woman feels to fulfill her 'natural' biological role. It is true that new developments in reproductive technology have created the possibility for infertile women (and couples) to have 'their own' children. But one must also be aware, as Rona Achilles points out, of the extent to which these new possibilities may impose pressures on women of a sort that in fact restrict their (private) reproductive freedom and choices.

All of these considerations show how difficult it is to trace a linear progression for women away from confinement within the private sphere. Historically, women's suffrage victory provides an early example of the sometimes limited gains from what seem, at the time, to be major victories. Although in many respects women's achievements in the late twentieth century far exceed what the suffragists envisaged, women have come to realize that suffrage alone was not the solution to inequality. Suffrage rights, which were accorded to women federally in 1918, were one of the earliest and most noteworthy developments in the shifting pattern of Canadian women's lives. In their contributions to this volume, Jane Errington and Sandra Burt examine the circumstances that led to the suffrage victory, revealing in their analyses how both reformist and conservative forces contributed to the final outcome. The campaign for women's suffrage was part of the first wave of feminist activity in Canada, which focused primarily upon improving the quality of life in the private sphere of the home. In the early 1900s there was widespread poverty, uncontrolled economic development, and few government services to take care of the weak and the homeless. And it was women's commitment to the creation of better homes that often took them into public life, as volunteers providing essential food, care, shelter, and counselling, drawing them into political debates and policy-making.

As women cross the mythical boundary between the public and private domains of Canadian society it becomes increasingly clear that neither domain can remain untouched by this movement to and fro. Susan McDaniel gives some indication of changes in family structure and child-raising practices that follow upon women's increased labour-force participation. Both Naomi Black and Sandra Burt show how crucial such issues as sex discrimination and equal pay for work of equal value become in the labour market when women seek to become full participants. The impact of women's voting patterns in federal and provincial elections, and the implications of women's lobbying in matters connected with the Charter show some of the effects women are having on the patterns of Canadian life as they challenge the oppressive implications of the public/private dichotomy.

Shifts in these boundaries are particularly evident in women's changing labour force participation. In 1901, for example, only 16 per cent of Canadian women were working for wages.[1] Most of these early female workers were either domestic or factory workers. Sandra Burt notes in her chapter on public policy how even this minor intrusion by women into what most men regarded then as their sphere was viewed with alarm by many legislators who firmly believed that women belonged at home. Between 1907 and 1951 there was only a gradual increase in the percentage of women in the labour force. Susan McDaniel discusses aspects of this increase. Moreover, this pattern of minimal but gradually increasing labour-force participation was broken from time to time. During World War II, for example, women were actively recruited to fill the jobs left vacant by enlisted servicemen. After the war, these women were sent home from the factories and encouraged to resume their family duties. But it would be a mistake to conclude that the women who stayed out of the paid labour force for these years were devoting themselves exclusively to the care of their husbands and children. Jane Errington points out that there was an active network of women's organizations such as the Young Women's Christian Association and the Women's Christian Temperance Union in Canada even in the early 1900s. These groups were responsible for providing social services before governments took on the task. They helped immigrants find jobs and shelter, set up soup kitchens for the unemployed, provided health care for isolated farm families and for the elderly, worked to relieve the burden of loneliness for prairie families, and generally made Canada a more humane place to live. There are no exact figures on the extent of women's participation in these early voluntary associations, but in 1916 one writer estimated that over 200,000 Canadian women belonged to at least one group.[2] In the 1950s, with the expansion and diversification of the Canadian economy, women began to be viewed as a longer-term, but still low-wage labour supply. By the 1960s, women's labour-force participation started to increase.

At one level, this increase signals a continued blurring of the distinction between the public and the private. For a variety of reasons a growing number of women have rejected the choices made by their foremothers and have moved into the public sphere through their work. But, in spite of this apparent breaking down of traditional barriers, some aspects of a public/private dichotomy have remained in place. The movement of women into paid labour has failed to transform women's and men's traditional roles. The labour force has been and continues to be highly segregated by gender. Women and men usually work in different kinds of jobs with different financial rewards and promotion opportunities. In this segregated labour force, women have been and continue to be the disadvantaged group, partly because affirmative action measures have not been forceful enough. Women generally have held the less prestigious jobs with fewer decision-making opportunities, lower pay, and limited job advancement possibilities. Even today women still, on average, earn only about 60 per cent of men's earnings. Women's jobs are concentrated in the service sector and generally confer little decision-making power. We might conclude that while women have gained access to the public sphere, they have been asked to bring with them the attitudes, skills, and expectations of their private roles.

Another negative development has been the increase in the number of jobs women are expected to accomplish. Susan McDaniel, in her examination of the changing Canadian family, shows how labour-force participation has resulted in extra work for most women. Many of the new recruits to the labour force are married women with children. By 1981, 51 per cent of Canadian married women were working outside the home for wages, an increase from 10 per cent in 1950. There has also been an increase in the proportion of women at work who have young children at home. As recently as 1968, in a special labour-force study conducted by the Dominion Bureau of Statistics, the authors concluded that "the presence or absence of a young child remains, in the aggregate, the most important single attribute affecting a wife's participation in the labour force until age 33."[3] Yet by 1984, 57 per cent of Canadian women whose youngest child was between three and five years old were in the labour force. In that same year, 64 per cent of women with school-aged children were working outside the home, compared with 74 per cent of women with no children.

Women's second-class status in the labour force has persisted for a variety of reasons. Researchers cite employer discrimination, discriminatory job descriptions, a lower incidence of unionization among female workers, and voluntary choices by women to limit their job commitments in order to facilitate child-raising. One compelling explanation, which is derived from the predominance of public/private thinking about women's roles, is called the 'reserve army' thesis.[4] According to this thesis, women comprise a large group of potential workers who normally stay at home, but may be called in to the labour force in times of need. The demand for women's work may be short term as it was during World War I and II, or it may be longer term as it is when the economy is expanding and new workers are required. Until the end of World War II women were viewed as a temporary labour reserve.

As recently as the 1950s and the early 1960s there was little public evidence of women's reactions to these changing social and economic patterns. But by the late 1960s women's responses became more vocal. Women were politicized by the growing rift between idealized versions of life in the home and the real conditions developing slowly after the end of World War II. Labour-force participation, changing family forms, and the spirit of rebellion on university campuses contributed to the emergence of consciousness-raising groups, which gave inspiration to the women's movement. The progress of this movement is charted in Naomi Black's account of some of these events. The 1960s and 1970s were witness to an unprecedented increase in the number of women's groups in Canada, united in their call for action on what were defined as women's issues. In setting up rape crisis centres and transition homes for abused women, largely financed by government grants, women let it be known that they intended to continue to play an active part in the development and administration of programs affecting family life. In addition, they raised the call, muted during the first wave of feminism, for an active role in politics and work. At the same time, as Joanna Boehnert notes in her review of psychology, women began to reject men's diagnoses of their successes and their failures, and new forms of feminist psychotherapy began to evolve in response to widespread demand.

Yet, in present-day society, even as women claim the right and demonstrate their capacity to participate in the public domain, the ideology of the sanctity of the private domain is constantly reinvoked to thwart their efforts and restrict their freedom. Inadequate public long-term care for aged and ailing relatives and spouses reflects the assumption that the provision of such care is women's proper job. Not the least of these systematic social practices which relies on a misguided conception of the sanctity of the private realm is social reluctance to intervene in marital violence. All of these practices demonstrate the force of the radical-feminist claim, elaborated in Lorraine Code's chapter, that the personal is political. Indeed, part of the political impact of women's writing in Canada, traced for us in Shelagh Wilkinson's chapter, is that readers can experience the commonality and specificity of women's personal lives. Such experiences give content to the 'personal is political' slogan. They show how women are disadvantaged in the most minute aspects of their lives.

It is clear that the only division that can be drawn between the public and the private is one that benefits men and disadvantages women. Both in its intervention and in its abstention from intervention in women's lives, the ideology of separate public and private spheres works to constrain women's possibilities. This is why feminist activity is directed toward denying the validity of the boundary that is said to separate the spheres, and revealing the authoritarian power structures it purports to legitimate. From a political, activist point of view, it is of paramount important for feminists to keep in mind how the doctrine of separate public and private spheres has been used–and continues to be used–as an instrument of masculine control over women's lives and interests. In the pre-Charter legal cases Beverley Baines analyses, for example, a refusal to admit women to the practice of law was justified in terms of that dichotomy. More recently, Women's Studies courses at universities have been described by men as useless, and characterized as intrusions into the patriarchal tradition of scholarship. It is for reasons such as these that feminists cannot accept the complacency of the post-feminist argument.

The contributors to this volume offer numerous examples of women's achievements. Their feminist perspectives have provided them with a new understanding of these achievements. Yet, students of Women's Studies may sometimes find it difficult to put this understanding into practice. There are those who reject feminist claims and who may also reject the proposition that a feminist perspective enriches an academic curriculum. Fortunately, however, feminist research is becoming widely accepted as good research, both in the newer feminist publications and in some more traditional journals. Women's Studies programs and Status of Women committees now exist in most Canadian universities, and student groups are active in addressing women's concerns. Thus it is clear that there are many valuable resources to be called upon in our struggles to bring an end to women's oppression.

Chapter One

Feminist Theory

Contemporary feminism, which came into being with the student and civil-rights movements of radical protest in the 1960s, is an active, evolving, politically engaged movement. As such, it has been instrumental in effecting fundamental changes in social practices and institutions. Feminism is also a theoretical project whose purposes are to understand the oppressive social practices that disadvantage women and to think innovatively about women's possibilities. British feminist Juliet Mitchell observes that feminism is "an ideological offspring of certain economic and social conditions. Its radicalism reflects the fact that it comes to prominence at points of critical change. It both abets this change and envisages it with an imagination that goes beyond it."[1] Mitchell's observation points to the close connection between feminist practice, which works to transform material and social conditions, and feminist theory, which develops out of that practice and informs it. Theory is constantly modified by what proves to be effective in practice, and practice is shaped by theory. So any apparent separation between theory and practice in the present discussion is made only for purposes of analysis. This account of changing feminist theories is intended to describe the theoretical context in which the practices detailed in subsequent chapters have evolved in Canadian society.

Feminist theorists start from the realization that, in patriarchal societies, women and men live different lives and have different experiences. Patriarchal societies are those in which men have more power than women, readier access than women to what is valued in the society, and, in consequence, are in control over many, if not most aspects of women's lives. Most known societies are patriarchal to a greater or lesser degree, exhibiting only specific variations in the ways power is manifested. Feminist theorists want to understand this power and privilege differential between women and men. They want to know how the differential came into being, how the oppression of women by men is related to other forms of social oppression such as race and class, and how women's oppression can be overcome. With their goal of developing strategies to eradicate oppression, feminist theorists demonstrate the active nature of their project: the point of studying the situation of women is to work toward changing it.

Feminists differ in their identification of the primary feature(s) of women's oppression, in their designation of central theoretical questions, and in the strategies for change they develop and act upon. Yet, although they may be approached from different angles and with varying estimations of their significance, there are a number of common feminist themes. In particular, feminists endeavour to understand how the social structuring of production, reproduction, sexuality, and socialization, in their shifting manifestations, have determined women's condition throughout history and across cultural, class, and racial barriers.[2]

Production, in this context, includes all the processes that go into producing and distributing food, clothing, shelter, and the other material necessities of human life. This is primarily, but not solely, an economic category, for it also includes political and cultural activity. Reproduction includes not just conception, childbearing, and giving birth but childraising, looking after family needs, and caring for the sick. The boundaries between reproduction and socialization, and those between reproduction and sexuality, are not rigid ones, for women are socialized to use their reproductive capacities in certain approved ways. In patriarchal societies, women's sexuality is strongly controlled by social pressures that define and enforce acceptable modes of female sexual expression. This is why both sexuality and socialization are treated by most feminists as political matters, as will be explained later in this chapter. It will be clear from the account that follows that different ideological orientations within feminism lead women to accord these various structures and activities differing importance. Likewise, the structures identified as oppressive to women have shifted throughout history and have been variously affected by class, race, and culture.

The starting point of feminist theory, then, is in the varied experiences of women, in the concrete situations where they live and are disadvantaged. Theoretical analysis is an integral part of the feminist project, for none of the facts of women's experience speak for themselves. It is for this reason that consciousness raising was so important in the early years of the current women's movement. Women needed to learn from each other how to see and name their experiences of oppression. Theory is still fundamental to the movement, deriving ever more subtle descriptions of the effects of patriarchy, defining the problems that must be faced, and evaluating strategies for change.

Marilyn Frye develops a useful image to show why oppressive social structures are so difficult to see.[3] Frye notes that if one examines one wire of a bird cage, one can neither see the other wires nor understand why the cage is so confining. One might wonder why the bird would not fly around that wire and go free. The same would be true if one were to inspect each wire separately – it would not be apparent why any one wire would constrain the bird. It is only by stepping back to contemplate the entire structure – the interconnected and mutually enforcing system of barriers – that one can see why the bird is trapped. Similarly, one needs to stand back from particular oppressive social practices to see their mutually reinforcing structures; to see, in the case of feminism, how patriarchy is constructed out of a number of practices which, considered singly, may not seem particularly significant or oppressive. Yet together these practices form an intractable structure.

Over the last two decades, there has been a shift in most forms of feminism from an earlier view of women as a caste, class, or group, to a concentration upon differences among women. It is no longer assumed that there is a single, essential 'women's experience' out of which universal analytic categories can be developed. Differences of race, class, and sexual practice have become a primary focus of theoretical discussion. Contemporary feminist theorists face the tasks of accounting for significant differences among the experiences of women and, simultaneously, of discerning common threads and themes that make these experiences specifically women's. It is a matter of developing theoretical tools to understand the samenesses and differences in women's lives: of acknowledging specificity *and* commonality. These are delicate tasks, for experience is always structured and mediated by a complex of material, social, cultural, historical, and even unconscious forces. There is no 'pure, untainted' experience; and the forces that shape it need to be understood. Furthermore, it is as important to account for the absence of women from social practices and institutions as it is to produce analyses of visible oppression. For this, one must learn to see how analyses of social practices often justify, or mask, that absence. Finally, in the performance of these tasks one cannot avoid facing the paradox that gender consciousness is a *necessary condition* for the existence of feminism, even though feminism seeks to eliminate prescribed gender roles.[4] The aim of these endeavours is not only to achieve knowledge about women – to make women visible – but also to understand the gender order, the structures of power that keep women in their place and are stubbornly resistant to change. Many feminists argue that there is a fundamental need for a theory of power if an effective feminist political program is to be developed.[5]

Women grow to womanhood in a world where it is assumed that (to quote Adrienne Rich):

> women are a subgroup, that "man's world" is the real world, that patriarchy is equivalent to culture and culture to patriarchy, . . . that

> generalizations about "man", "humankind", "children", "blacks", "parents", "the working class" hold true for women, mothers, daughters, sisters, wet-nurses, infant girls, and can include them with no more than a glancing reference here and there, usually to some specialized function like breast-feeding.[6]

Patriarchal assumptions about the appropriate 'place' for women to occupy in 'man's world' are so seamlessly woven into the thought structures and social policies of most western cultures that they seem to dictate the 'natural' way for things to be.[7] This is another reason why contemporary feminist theory is continuous with the consciousness-raising practices of the late 1960s and early 1970s. There, women learned to see in their personal and seemingly idiosyncratic experiences the reflection of more generally oppressive practices.

In feminist theory, it would be impossible to take on all aspects of patriarchy at once. Frye's birdcage image stands as a useful reminder, however, that concentration on any one aspect of the structure may cause us to lose sight of the whole. It is important to develop a "doubled vision"[8] so that we can both challenge a particular patriarchal practice and stand outside the structure to see how that practice fits into the whole. We have to see what else needs to be tackled for any practice really to be changed, and how changing one practice might affect the whole social structure.

Biological Determinism: *Ancient Views*

A number of ideas and practices that have worked to maintain women's disadvantaged social position have their roots in the history of western thought. The belief that a woman's nature and all of her possibilities are determined by her biology – specifically her reproductive biology – is one of the most ancient and most persistent of these ideas. It has long been used to justify an entire range of social practices designed to keep woman 'in her place.' Assumptions about 'woman's nature' have not only described what that nature allegedly is, but have also prescribed what a woman should be.

Biological determinism has its best known ancient formulation in the philosophy of Aristotle (384–322 B.C.). Despite vast increases in the sophistication of biological knowledge, which make the 'facts' on which Aristotle based his normative claims look quite naive, views remarkably similar to his still persist. In their efforts to bring about reform, feminists repeatedly find themselves required to counter modern varieties of Aristotelian beliefs to the effect that women are not capable (physically or intellectually) of filling certain kinds of jobs, or that placing children in day care is a violation of a mother's *natural* role.

Woman's place in the Aristotelian scheme of things is defined purely by her essential function, which is believed to be a biological, reproductive one. Her rational capacities are declared to be underdeveloped and inferior in comparison with those of men. Hence, men are to rule over women, in whom the irrational element of the 'soul' tends naturally to overrule the rational element. Aristotle writes:

> the male is by nature superior, and the female inferior; and the one rules, and the other is ruled; this principle, of necessity, extends to all mankind. Where there is such a difference as that between soul and body, or between men and animals . . . , the lower sort are by nature slaves, and it is better for them as for all inferiors that they should be under the rule of a master.[9]

In Aristotle's view, neither women, children, nor slaves can be citizens. As only citizens can participate in the political life of the Greek city state, such participation is denied to women, as well as to children and slaves. Furthermore, as virtue, through which the best human qualities are realized, is achievable only through participation in political activity, virtue, too, in its highest forms, is inaccessible to women (and to slaves and children).

Aristotle maintains that even in respect to their own essential function – the reproduction of the species – women play an inferior part. The male parent contributes the soul to the offspring, that which makes it essentially human; The female parent contributes only crude physical matter in the form of menstrual blood (catamenia). Hers is a passive contribution by contrast with semen, which Aristotle regards as an active substance, "for the catamenia have in their nature an affinity to the primitive matter."[10] This unformed matter, then, awaits insemination by the male parent to endow it with human form and human capacity. Women's contribution to reproduction is merely to provide the material that is to be acted upon and to offer a place of incubation to the future infant. Hence, both with respect to rationality, which distinguishes human beings from other Aristotelian 'natural kinds,' and with respect to reproductive function, women are inferior to men. Their inferior position is biologically determined, according to the natural order of things, and no further explanation for their status is required.

Aristotle's philosophy underpins most western theory about the nature of human beings from classical times up to the eighteenth century. As Beverley Baines shows in her chapter in this book, Aristotelian notions of the biologically determined inequality of women and men can be discerned in the assumptions underlying much of nineteenth and twentieth century legal practice.[11] Yet, it was by no means inevitable that Aristotle should develop the functionalist, biological determinist view that he did. From the earliest days of theorizing about human nature there were well-known alternative proposals, which might have opened up quite different ways of thinking about women and about the relations between women and men. In fact, Aristotle seems to have put forward his position partly in reaction to a startling and innovative proposal about the social relations between the sexes developed by his own teacher, Plato, (427–347 B.C.).

In the *Republic*, Plato has *his* teacher, Socrates, describe an ideal society in which every citizen will perform the function best suited to his or her 'natural' capacities. Future merchants, craftspeople, and tradespeople will receive training appropriate to the acquisition of the necessary skills; and those who are to form the military forces will receive an education designed to make them suitably courageous, yet neither rash nor cowardly. The ruling, guardian class will be responsible for maintaining harmony within the state and governing it wisely. Its members will receive a rigorous training in music and the arts, gymnastics and athletics, mathematics and all of the highest arts of reason.

Remarkably for his time and even for ours, Socrates intends that the guardian class should be composed of both women and men, who will receive exactly the same education. He maintains that there is *nothing* in female nature to prevent this, claiming that "there is no pursuit of the administrators of a state that belongs to a woman because she is a woman or to a man because he is a man. But the natural capacities are distributed alike among both creatures, and women naturally share in all pursuits and men in all–yet for all the woman is weaker than the man."[12] Hence, "[w]omen of this kind . . . must be selected to cohabit with men of this kind and to serve with them as guardians since they are capable of it and akin by nature."[13] Socrates explicitly states, then, that there are no specifically female traits, either biological or psychological, that would naturally exclude women from these pursuits. So that child-rearing will not interfere with the education and other activities of women of the guardian class, Socrates describes a set of social arrangements in which there will be no conventional family structures. Children, who will be born as a result of brief periods of cohabitation in designated marriage festivals, "will be taken over by the officials appointed for this, men or women or both"[14] and raised communally.

It would be a mistake to claim, on the basis of this radical proposal, that Plato was a feminist. He puts forward a view quite different from Aristotle's of how women might live in 'man's world,' but there is little doubt that it is man's world, and it is unlikely that the kind of equality he advocates would be acceptable to twentieth century feminists. The guardians' educational system is modelled upon an extension of educational practices designed for the education of *male* citizens of the Greek polis. The proposal is that women participate equally in men's activities and pursuits, devised and elaborated so as to bring out the best in masculine nature. Women might become guardians, but only by becoming honorary men: by having men make room for them within male-defined structures. Present-day variations on this theme, where women are admitted to business and other high-status occupations on the (often implicit) condition that their 'femininity' not be permitted to count, are only too familiar.

In any case, it is Aristotle's views about women's nature that provide the basis for virtually all of western theory up to the eighteenth century, and offer the rationale for patriarchal social arrangements. Even later Platonists, who were influenced by other aspects of Plato's philosophy, did not take up his views about women or about equality between the sexes. In fact, it was not until the development of liberalism in the eighteenth century that the first serious challenge to biological determinism was articulated.

The Liberal Challenge

Liberal political theory, especially as it developed in Britain and France in the eighteenth and nineteenth centuries, prepared the way for a fundamental challenge to biological determinism. The early liberal feminists' contention that women's inferior social status was to be explained by their lack of education and opportunity, and not by their nature, opened the way for a re-examination of traditional assumptions about 'woman's nature.' As well, the social and economic upheavals that accompanied the Industrial Revolution undermined the idea that women's biologically determined place is in the home. As women began to work in factories, there was a growing separation between the spheres of 'home' and 'work.' In the face of such evidence, it could not be so easily maintained that women were fitted only to perform a biologically determined role. These challenges and alternatives are significant feminist milestones, for they undercut the sense of inevitability that feminists may feel in the face of deterministic arguments. If women's situation can be explained by their lack of education and opportunity rather than by their 'nature,' then something can be done to change it. (More recently, feminists have begun to show that biological nature, too, is affected by environmental and other circumstances.)

The eighteenth century witnessed the growth and spread of liberal, egalitarian political ideals, which challenged fundamental social and political beliefs and inspired the American and French revolutions. In particular, liberal thinking gradually came to replace the view that political authority was based in inherited title, and that rulers, by natural right, stood in benevolent patriarchal relations to their subjects. Thomas Hobbes (1588–1679) and John Locke (1632–1704) argued that society should work as though it had been established by a freely entered contract among free and equal individuals. The role of government was to ensure the personal safety and protect the property rights of those individuals who had demonstrated their capacity to know their own interests by opting into the contract. In an age when people believed that members of lower social orders should simply submit to the greater wisdom of their natural superiors and rulers, these were novel ideas.

The argument that all members of a society are free and equally participating individuals led feminists to argue that equality should be enjoyed by women, too. They could see no reason for it to remain a masculine privilege. Yet this is neither to say that all of the early liberals were feminists, nor that they were united in rejecting biological determinism. Most early male liberal theorists unthinkingly assumed that liberal individuals are male individuals; and there is no doubt that many of them believed women to be inferior beings.

It was to take issue with such assumptions about female inferiority that Mary Wollstonecraft (1759–1797) wrote her famous treatise, *The Vindication of the Rights of Woman*, completed in 1792. It is Wollstonecraft's conviction that, were women to have the same education and opportunities as men, they would be men's equals in every respect. Women appear to be merely emotional creatures, lacking in rationality, only in consequence of their inferior education: they are not so by nature. It is women's rights to education and equal treatment that Wollstonecraft is concerned to vindicate.

Wollstonecraft wrote her *Vindication* largely to refute the position developed by Jean-Jacques Rousseau (1712–1778), in *Emile*, his treatise on education. Rousseau is, in a sense, the liberal individual *par excellence*. In his political writings he is deeply committed to values of freedom, individualism, independence, and equality. He envisages a transformation of civil society into a moral society in which all men are citizens and equals, but women are virtuous wives and mothers. In *Emile*, he advocates an education for young men that would develop their reason to its fullest potential and train them to tame nature and to understand its secrets. Women, in Rousseau's view, are much closer to nature than men because they have a different intellectual character–they are less able to engage in abstract thought, to reason well, and to form universal judgements. But they are well endowed with taste, practical sense, and feeling. Hence, he believes, they should be educated to *complement* men, adorn their lives, raise their children, and obey them. Like nature, women must be tamed, kept in check. In particular, their sexual passions must be controlled so that men can be free of enslavement by female seductiveness.

Like Aristotle, then, Rousseau is a firm believer in biological determinism. A number of issues that have become contentious for twentieth century feminists are foreshadowed in his work. Most present-day feminists reject the complementarity thesis, according to which women and men are declared to be different but equal and complementary, and many are troubled by the notion that women should be the guardians of morals, particularly of sexual morals.

In helping men to control their reputedly more robust natural sexuality, women are required to suppress or deny their own sexual nature. This leads to the paradoxical and oppressive view of woman as both chaste and wanton, thus defined wholly in relation to men, rather than as her own person.

Wollstonecraft takes Rousseau to task on many of these issues. Her arguments in favour of equal education for women occupy the greater part of her treatise: all aspects of women's disadvantaged situation are attributed to the denial of intellectual opportunity to women in patriarchal society. When women are trained to prefer, and are expected to occupy themselves with trivial tasks, they cannot help but appear feebleminded and lacking in rational capacity.

In Wollstonecraft's view, women and men are created alike both in sexual feeling and in rational capacity. Rather than claiming that it is women's responsibility to curb excessive masculine sexual interest and indulgence, she argues that female chastity is impossible without equivalent male chastity, both practised according to a single rather than a double sexual standard. Wollstonecraft plainly regards sexual constraint as preferable to free sexual expression. She believes that reason, equally developed in both sexes, should rule over passion, which is equally strong in both sexes. The passion in which marriage begins should evolve into a rational, passionless friendship where sexuality is carefully controlled. It is her belief that such a relationship between equals can serve as a model for the structure of civil society.

Yet Wollstonecraft does not reject complementarity outright, for she believes in the maintenance of a family structure in which women would have the responsibility for child care. Employment outside the domestic sphere is not one of the primary rights she claims for women. If women are to perform well in the important task of mothering, she maintains, then they must be educated just as men are educated. Otherwise they will be unable to give their children a rational upbringing. Her larger point is that only when women are educated so that they too can be ruled by reason will they be able to share in the opportunities of the new egalitarian society. She clearly expects that most women will enjoy these opportunities in the domestic sphere. Yet Wollstonecraft sees such a clear continuity between domestic and civic life that there is no stark public/private dichotomy in her work. She believes that domestic life is part of civic life and that the same capacities and virtues are appropriate to each.

In later developments of liberal theory, women's potential for intellectual achievement and their right to the franchise came to be recognized as interconnected issues. As the franchise could be claimed only by educated property owners, women had remained effectively disqualified as potential voters. John Stuart Mill (1806–1873) was mindful of these considerations when he wrote

The Subjection of Women. So his arguments in favour of education and equal rights for women are, in this respect at least, directed toward a goal somewhat different from Wollstonecraft's. Nonetheless, like Wollstonecraft, Mill believes that educated women will more likely choose a domestic life than a career. The major change he envisages, apart from their qualifying for the franchise, is that women will be better able to share in their husbands' intellectual pursuits and to raise their children intelligently.

Equality is the dominant theme of Mill's essay: the need for "a principle of perfect equality, admitting no power or privilege on one side, nor disability on the other"[15] to govern the relations between the sexes. Like Wollstonecraft, he believes that women and men are equally rational, intelligent beings, and that the contention that women are not rational simply ignores their lack of opportunity to develop rational capacities. Mill is convinced that society as a whole will benefit if women are given all of the educational opportunities available to men.

Harriet Taylor (Mill) (1807–1858) proposes much more radical social changes when she argues that there should be no laws concerning marriage, and that a woman should retain guardianship of, and take financial responsibility for, her own children.[16] This was a radical challenge to patriarchy at a time when wives and children were regarded by law as the property of the father. Taylor's proposals were intended to ensure that questions of providing for children would be irrelevant in divorce proceedings, and could not be used to tie a woman into an unworkable marriage for fear of losing custody of her children. She contends that a woman should consider carefully how many children to have, rather than having a great many in order to strengthen her ties to the man who feeds her. As well, Taylor believes that if women are not to barter their persons for bread, they must not only be educated, but must be permitted to enter any occupational field they wish. Clearly, Taylor would have applauded many of the successes of present-day feminists in restructuring women's participation in the work force and in bringing about reform in family law. Higher education for women, which is taken for granted as an opportunity today, would have been an unknown possibility when she was writing.

This early liberal emphasis upon equality of opportunity has carried over, if in a different guise, into contemporary feminist thought. And liberal rejection of deterministic explanations for women's situation has become a constant feminist theme. But original formulations of liberal theory require modification for contemporary feminist purposes, because most early liberal theorists take for granted that the interests of women can be dealt with by taking account of the interests of men. Contemporary feminists are aware that analyses of men's social circumstances usually gloss over or obscure women's experiences, and that these experiences require separate analysis.

The Marxist Challenge

Liberal ideology is just one of several sources of present-day feminism. An equally important ideological landmark for understanding the origins of feminist theory is the development of Marxist thought in the nineteenth century. Early Marxism was primarily an analysis of the modes of production and the social relations that accompanied the Industrial Revolution and the rise of capitalism. Although Marxist and socialist thinkers do not concentrate upon developing explicit refutations of biological determinism, their work shows that biology cannot provide the only explanation for social inequality and the oppression of one social group by another. Economic factors are equally, if not more, important. Moreover, despite its apparent classlessness, liberalism is very much a bourgeois or middle-class way of thinking. Marxism, by contrast, is deeply class conscious. In its later feminist formulations, Marxist socialism opens possibilities for analysing the relationship of women's oppression to class oppression.

In the view of Karl Marx (1818–1883), culture and society are rooted in material, economic conditions, and human beings are essentially social beings, shaped by material and social circumstances. This view contrasts sharply with the liberal idea of the abstract, self-realizing individual, freely opting into society. Whereas in liberal thought, one must understand the individual in order to understand society, in Marxist thought, it is necessary to understand society in order to understand the individual. Because Marx regards human nature as essentially historical, he maintains that it cannot be investigated in abstraction from specific historical circumstances. More specifically, human nature cannot be understood in abstraction from the organization of productive activity in society.

Under capitalism, which is the focus of Marx's analysis, the two main classes are the working class (the proletariat) and the ruling class (the bourgeoisie), which owns the means of production. Members of the same class participate in similar kinds of productive activity and live in similar social and material circumstances. These factors work to influence the physical development, as well as the personality, attitudes, and consciousness of members of both classes. The greater health and life expectancy of the ruling class than that of the proletariat is one example of this phenomenon. The ruling class dominates not only the mode of production, but also the development and spread of knowledge and values. Hence it generates perceptions of human nature and social reality that are distorted by its own perspective so as to make the status quo seem the 'natural' way for things to be. It is clear, however, that capitalist social structures are designed to serve the interests of the ruling class. So members of the proletariat who accept the received view as 'natural' are living in a state of 'false consciousness,' which makes it difficult for them to see the world from the perspective of their own class interests.

Marx's theory of alienated labour is of particular significance to feminists. Marx argues that the root cause of such alienation is to be found in the structure of industrial production, where workers have no say in the conditions of their work, or in the design of its products, and are cut off from its final use. As Marx puts it: "The *alienation* of the worker in his product means not only that his labour becomes an object, assumes an *external* existence, but that it exists independently, *outside himself*, and alien to him"[17] In consequence of being constantly engaged in alienated labour, Marx believes, members of the working class are deprived of any sense of participation in the processes in which they spend most of their waking hours. They experience their work as meaningless and unfullfilling, and their place in the social order as insignificant.

One of the roots of alienation is in the division of labour into isolated, excessively specialized tasks. Marx would replace this divisive situation with collective ownership of the means of production, and a reorganization of the labour process to reintegrate mental and manual labour. Alienated labour would be supplanted by the conscious, purposeful activity which Marx calls "praxis." This is a cooperative, social activity which does involve some division of labour, but only through drawing upon the knowledge, experience, and skill of workers themselves. By contrast with alienated labour, praxis would develop in awareness of collective human needs, and of the place of each person's endeavour in the scheme designed to satisfy those needs.

Marx's distrust of biological explanations is apparent in his contention that the division of labour in capitalist society is rooted in the division of labour and of power within the family. Those divisions are based purely on physiological factors: on differences of sex and age. Yet in Marx's view, the enslavement of wife and children within the family is the first form of private property. He regards private property as one of the fundamental social evils: an evil that cannot be excused by spurious appeals to biology. It is an evil, nonetheless, that is peculiarly amenable to perpetuation by capitalist social arrangements.

A more sustained analysis of women's oppression under capitalism is developed by Marx's associate, Frederick Engels (1820–1895), in *The Origin of the Family, Private Property and the State*, written in 1884. In the nuclear family of capitalist society, Engels sees a microcosmic mirroring of the larger, macrocosmic social structure, with the husband in the role of the bourgeoisie, and the wife as the proletariat. Engels attributes the privatization and denigration of household labour to the development of the nuclear family, where "the wife became the head servant, excluded from all participation in social production."[18] The solution he envisages would be for women to end their confinement to the sphere of private domestic labour and to enter the public world of productive work. To make this possible, domestic labour and child care would have to become public, collective responsibilities.

In short, in the Marxist view, women are oppressed under capitalism through a sexual division of labour that serves the interests of men directly. That same division of labour serves the interests of capitalism indirectly, through serving the interests of men. Women are responsible, without pay, for child-raising, cooking, attending to the entire range of family needs, and looking after the sick and the aged, leaving men free to devote themselves fully to productivity in the public sphere. Under such an arrangement, capitalist society need not pay for the reproduction of the labour power upon which it depends.

In the early years of socialist fervour, there was some difference of opinion among socialist women about whether 'the woman question' would be dealt with by the revolutionary changes proposed by socialist thinkers and activists. A contrast of views among leading socialist women illustrates this point. Radical German socialist Rosa Luxemburg, for example, believed that her sex was irrelevant to the issues for which she was campaigning. She saw women's oppression as one of the many miseries of capitalist society that would no longer exist after the socialist revolution. By contrast, Luxemburg's friend Clara Zetkin believed that women's issues had to be dealt with separately, in recognition of women's oppression by both capitalism and patriarchy. Zetkin helped to found the International Socialist Women's Congress, and it is she who, in 1910, declared March 8 as International Women's Day. The day, which is celebrated annually in Canada and throughout the world, was set aside to commemorate a 1909 strike by female garment workers in New York, who struck to protest overcrowded, poorly ventilated, dangerous working conditions, and very low pay. From related motives, Russian feminist Alexandra Kollontai campaigned for a special bureau in the Russian Social Democratic Labour party to devise ways of addressing women's concerns, and argued for the inclusion of a commitment to promoting the liberation of women in the stated aims of the party. She had noted that the Social Democratic Labour party in pre-1914 Russia showed little interest in the circumstances of working class women.[19] Although Kollontai's initial efforts met with little success, she did later manage – at least temporarily – to place women's issues on the agenda of the Bolshevik revolution. Kollontai and Zetkin both realized that patriarchy exerts a kind of oppression all of its own. Its manifestations have much in common with other forms of oppression. But it is feminist focus on the distinctive forms of oppression patriarchy creates that has made the oppression of women visible in its own right.

Today, socialist feminists continue to debate the question whether Engels's scheme to deal with the 'woman question' is the best solution. It is still not clear whether women's participation in the work force and the collectivization of domestic tasks and child rearing can work to end women's oppression. What is clear, however, is that no explanation in biological terms alone can account for women's disadvantaged social position. Material and economic factors are instrumental in perpetuating patriarchal oppression of women. As feminists work to alter these circumstances, campaigning for affirmative action programmes, equal pay for work of equal value, and effective day care, progress is made.

The Freudian Challenge

A third and equally important source of inspiration for modern feminism has come out of the analyses of sexuality and psychosexual development initiated by Havelock Ellis (1859–1939) and Sigmund Freud (1856–1939) in the late nineteenth and early twentieth centuries. It is interesting that this line of investigation should have come to play so significant a role in feminist thought, because Freud himself stated unequivocally that "anatomy is destiny":[20] as clear a statement of biological determinism as one could find. Indeed, Freud and the early Freudians had no doubt that psychosexual development was biologically determined. Hence feminists in the early days of the current movement were highly critical of Freud, arguing that psychoanalysis had become a form of brainwashing designed to keep women quiet, passive, and in their place – especially sexually. The well-adjusted woman, in Freudian terms, was one who had learned to accept her patriarchally defined role of passive dependency in heterosexual marriage, schooling herself to please her husband. Sexual maturity was her goal. Evidence for its achievement was to be found in the ability to achieve vaginal orgasm, to recognize male supremacy in all things, and to be content with her place in life. Kate Millett argues in *Sexual Politics* that the primary effect of Freudian discussions of female sexuality was to convince "the dispossessed that the circumstances of their deprivation are organic, therefore unalterable."[21] In short, Freudian doctrine, literally read, stands as a strong rationalization of women's subservient position in the sphere of sexual relations, arguing that their position is biologically determined, natural. Joanna Boehnert suggests in her chapter on the psychology of women that the intellectual and scientific respect Freud's theories commanded made it seem unnecessary to examine the social and institutional ways in which women's lives were restricted. Freudian explanations of psycho-sexual development seemed to be adequate and definitive.

In view of these considerations, it may seem preposterous to claim Freudian thought as one of the inspirations for contemporary feminist theory. Freudianism does seem to reinstate a form of determinism that can lead women to blame themselves if they are unable to accept their natural place in the world. But psychoanalytic theory, especially since the late 1970s, has been an immensely fertile area of feminist discussion. The very need to criticize Freud's views because of their discrepancy with women's experiences opens a vitally important discussion of aspects of women's lives ignored by most political theory. In its emphasis upon sexuality, primary process, desire, and creativity, psychoanalytic theory addresses private, disorderly, and non-rational aspects of personal experience. It acknowledges the centrality of sexuality in human lives, and creates space for an affirmation of female sexuality, defined and practised in women's own terms. It gives impetus to an examination of the place of sexuality in society, the relation of repression to civilization, and the significance of individual psychic formation in the creation and maintenance of the social order.

Through analyses of the effects of parenting and socialization in the shaping of sexual identity, feminists are now developing critical readings of classical psychoanalytical texts and are exploring the implications of the important distinction between sex and gender.[22] 'Sex' refers to the biological differences in genitalia and reproductive function between male and female human beings. 'Gender' refers to the social and psychological creation of masculine and feminine beings, who are socialized to fulfill a complex set of requirements and expectations about what it is to be a woman – or a man. A pervasive gender-order dictates (with variations across historical, cultural, and racial lines) how one should live one's sexual being. Recognition of this has brought questions about the psycho-sexual construction of masculinity and femininity into a central position in current feminist discussion. Oppressive gender structures contribute centrally to women's inferior status in society. But these are human constructs, and many feminists are showing that they are open to radical reconstruction.

One of Freud's most articulate early feminist critics is Simone de Beauvoir (1908–1986), in her pathbreaking study, *The Second Sex*. This work has had a marked influence on the shape of contemporary feminism: even those who criticize it do so within a frame of reference that de Beauvoir has created. Her observation that "one is not born, but rather becomes a woman"[23] connects directly with later feminist analyses of patriarchally constituted psychological and sexual being. At least as influential is de Beauvoir's characterisation of women as "the second sex," thus designated by virtue of their creation as Other, with reference to the masculine norm. De Beauvoir writes:

> just as for the ancients there was an absolute vertical with reference to which the oblique was defined, so there is an absolute human type, the masculine. . . . Thus humanity is male and man defines woman not

> in herself but as relative to him; she is not regarded as an autonomous being . . . She is defined and differentiated with reference to man and not he with reference to her; she is the incidental, the inessential as opposed to the essential. He is the Subject, he is the Absolute – she is the Other.[24]

Many of the best-known present-day feminist writings amount, in effect, to a set of variations on this theme.

De Beauvoir believes that the relegation of woman to 'otherness' arises out of views about female biology and about women's psychological inability to transcend their biology. Women are commonly portrayed as immersed in the material realm, dragged down by their material being, slaves to the reproduction of the species. Influenced by Jean Paul Sartre's view that conscious beings are distinguished from material beings by their capacity to define themselves, to *transcend* their material being, de Beauvoir maintains that this capacity belongs to men but not to women. In this, primarily, women are Other. Because she seems to accept this pessimistic view of female biology, and of women's psychological inability to come to terms with it, many feminists have taken exception to de Beauvoir's description of what it is to *be* part of the second sex. They argue that her view is fundamentally misogynist and that her evident horror at the 'messier' aspects of female anatomy and biological functioning places de Beauvoir in the camp of male detractors of femininity.

The Second Sex presents a detailed descriptive analysis of the social and psychological processes through which a female baby becomes a feminine woman. It offers a marvellous account of the construction of feminine gender on the basis of biological determinism. De Beauvoir's analysis covers such previously unmentionable aspects of female existence as puberty, menstruation, sexual intercourse, childbearing. The simple fact that so much could be said about what it means to live as a woman in a male-defined social setting astonished de Beauvoir's early readers. Their astonishment alone attests to the pathbreaking character of her work.

It is interesting to note that when she wrote *The Second Sex*, de Beauvoir did not consider herself to be a feminist. She believed that revolutionary socialism would bring an end to the oppression of women along with all other social injustices and that the class struggle had priority over the feminist struggle. Although she remained a socialist throughout her life, de Beauvoir later came to believe that socialist and feminist issues deserved separate treatment, commenting that, "feminists are women – or even men, too – who are fighting to change women's condition in association with the class struggle, but independently of it as well." She declared herself a feminist after all, "because I realised that we must fight for the situation of women, here and now, before our dreams of socialism come true.''[25] De Beauvoir remained politically involved throughout her life. She became a member of the group ''Choisir'' in 1971, to protest against the illegality of abortion in France. In 1977 she became editor of a new radical-feminist journal, *Questions féministes*, devoted to theoretical texts on women's oppression. In this latter capacity, she was closely allied with the new French feminists, discussed later in this chapter, even though she wrote none of the texts now considered pivotal to their thought.

Feminist theory could not have developed as it has since the 1960s had the ground not been prepared by the intellectual and social developments outlined in this section. Even feminists who have taken issue with aspects of these lines of thought have found in them a necessary critical focus. In proceeding, now, to discuss some of the forms feminist theory takes in the late twentieth century, the intention is not to suggest that all was quiet in the feminist world between the early growth of liberalism and socialism, and a resurgence of feminist thinking in the 1960s. Feminist activism in campaigning for the suffrage alone would attest to the falsity of such a suggestion. And the concerted activities of cultural feminists and social reform feminists at the end of the nineteenth and the beginning of the twentieth century were remarkable in their social impact. The activities of Canadian suffragists and Canadian social feminists are detailed by Jane Errington in her chapter in this book. Naomi Black shows, too, how wrong it would be to claim that there was no awareness of feminist issues before the emergence of the contemporary women's movement. But the primary purpose of this chapter is to give an idea of some principal strands of present-day feminist theory. Certain historical movements in which these strands originated have been described in order to locate present-day feminism within a broader scheme of intellectual history. The next task is to examine contemporary feminism in some of its many guises.

Contemporary Theory: *Liberal Feminism*

Contemporary feminist theory draws upon the entire spectrum of ideas, causes, and political agendas discussed so far, adding to and elaborating upon those ideas and events. Against the background of classical liberal theory, contemporary liberal feminists argue for women's rights to enjoy the freedom and equality of opportunity claimed by the autonomous liberal individual. Betty Friedan, who is probably the best known spokeswoman of post-1960 liberal feminism, observes in *The Feminine Mystique*: ''My definition of feminism is simply that women are people in the fullest sense of the word, who must be free to move in society with all the privileges and opportunities and responsibilities that are their human and American right.''[26] Feminism, as Friedan understands it, is less a theory of women's oppression by patriarchy than it is a theory of human rights.

In the liberal-feminist view, sex discrimination is unjust primarily because it deprives women of equal rights to pursue their own self-interest. Justice and fairness require equal opportunities for each individual, regardless of sex. Liberal feminists deplore the informal discrimination in assumptions, rooted in biological determinism, that women are not suited to certain kinds of work, or that they are peculiarly suited to other kinds of work. They oppose the formal discrimination evident in an asymmetry in the legal rights enjoyed by women and men. Liberal feminists maintain that women's inferior social status is not freely chosen, but that discrimination denies them access to equal participation with men in occupations of high social status. Women's relegation to low-paid clerical and service work, for example, and their (often sole) responsibility for childcare and housework diminish their freedom and autonomy in the rest of their lives. Their poverty relative to men often makes it impossible for them to exercise their legal rights or to enjoy their social rights. Women's lack of equality in public life is exacerbated by oppressive sexual standards according to which they are viewed as sex objects, and hence limited in their freedom to move about in society.

Liberal feminists aim to free women from their dependent status in patriarchal society, and their efforts have met with notable success. Sandra Burt gives an account of some of the successes realized by Canadian liberal feminists in her chapter. Yet liberal feminists retain some ideological commitment to the view that political decisions are made within the formal political process – that politics is what takes place in the public sphere. For this reason they have been less stringent than socialist and radical feminists in their examination of the politics of daily life in the 'private' sphere and in their analyses of sexual power and privilege. Liberal feminists argue persuasively that women must be included equally within existing public decision-making structures. Yet they often assume that the structures themselves need no modifications beyond those effected by the inclusion of women on an equal basis.

Friedan believes that the root of all sexist evils is in the "feminine mystique," which defines woman in terms of her femininity and judges her solely according to her performance as a wife and mother. Women, in her view, must claim an identity of their own to shake off its effects. Innumerable women have recognized the force of Friedan's critique and have worked to liberate themselves from the spell of that mystique. As Friedan presents the problem, however, it is specific to reasonably affluent middle-class women in the stability of a continuing marriage. While it is true that all women are constrained by the ideology of femininity, it is by no means obvious that the self-affirmation Friedan urges is equally available to all women in all economic and social circumstances. Like most liberal feminists, Friedan fails to recognize the strength of patriarchal capitalism in sustaining female oppression. Indeed, other feminists argue that oppression is not an individual problem at all. It can be understood only by seeing women against the background of the social and economic circumstances that shape their lives, and it can be eradicated only through collective action. Whether abstract equality, or equality with men, can achieve all that is necessary to increase women's freedom remains a question that admits of no easy answer. Perfect equality, once achieved, might create a new set of problems derived from a requirement to live as equals, but on men's terms. Hence although equality is better than subservience and oppression, many feminists argue that it would be only at considerable cost that a feminist would be a liberal.[27]

Liberal theory can, at best, define an area of public life in which women would have unlimited opportunity. It can offer no indication of how access to that area would, in practice, be realized. Feminists who are not satisfied with what liberalism can offer point out that autonomous, freely participating citizens need wives at home to mind the children and attend to domestic matters. Thus it is difficult to see how liberalism's theoretical ideals could be realized in practice. Liberal theory works with a model of society in which feminist change would merely require men to move over within existing social structures to make room for women. But those structures are defined and constructed to promote masculine well-being, understood according to a narrowly stereotyped conception of masculinity. Liberal feminism poses no serious challenges to that concept, nor to the patriarchal relations that sustain women's sexual and economic dependence.

Contemporary Theory: *Marxist and Socialist Feminism*

Marxist and socialist feminists, in response to liberal feminism, contend that there is no point in arguing for political liberalism unless one can show how people can achieve the economic means and the power to enjoy it.[28] Equality of legal rights will have minimal impact upon actual social inequalities in the absence of more fundamental economic and social changes. Drawing, then, upon a Marxist analysis of class oppression, socialist feminists maintain that the capitalist economic system oppresses women as a group, just as it oppresses the working class as a whole. Within capitalist patriarchal society, however, women are subjected to other forms of oppression. First, within the labour force women's work is alienated labour just as men's work is: women own neither the means of production nor the products of their labour. Second, women in the labour force are commonly in positions subordinate to men whose superiority is by no means apparent: hence they are doubly alienated from realizing their own potential. Third, women who work as housewives are in a still more disadvantaged position. Their lives are characterized by servitude, their labour is accorded no material value, and they are excluded from the 'public' world.

Socialist feminists contend that, under capitalism, women are the primary producers of goods and services for use within the family. Their labour is considered worthless because it has no monetary exchange value, and it is invisible in that public space where exchange value is established. But feminists have differing views as to whether domestic labour is alienated labour in the sense that capitalist productive labour is. Some argue that the menial, non-creative, trivial, and isolating nature of household tasks marks them as alienated labour.[29] Others claim that the household is the only unalienated work space in capitalist society. There, women are convinced of the usefulness of what they do and can see the importance of their labour in sustaining family values.[30] In the home women have more control over the pace and use of their work than office or industrial workers have in their workplaces. Nonetheless, socialist feminists agree that women's labour is undervalued. Some socialist feminists argue that there should be wages for housework; most maintain that women's invisible domestic labour needs to be accorded the esteem due to its vital role in reproducing the labour power upon which economic productivity depends.

These discussions are persuasive in demonstrating how capitalism depends upon women's unpaid, invisible labour. But it would be a mistake to assume that capitalist societies are alone in oppressing women. Notable among socialist feminists who warn against attributing women's oppression *in toto* to the sexual division of labour under capitalism are Michele Barrett and Gayle Rubin. Barrett reminds feminists that the sexual division of labour was not a capitalist creation: capitalism may have refined and elaborated it, but the ideology of a gendered division of labour was there to be elaborated.[31] And Rubin sketches out a spectrum of patriarchal practices that work to oppress, subdue, or denigrate women, yet which do not depend upon a capitalist economic system for their existence. She observes: "No analysis of the reproduction of labour under capitalism can explain foot-binding, chastity belts, or any of the incredible array of Byzantine, fetishized indignities, let alone the more ordinary ones that have been inflicted upon women in various times and places."[32] Nonetheless, with other socialist feminists, Barrett notes significant structural differences between precapitalist and capitalist modes of production, reflected in numerous differences in social arrangements that have direct effects on women's lives. Capitalist society is marked, in particular, by an emphasis upon increased productivity, and by that specialized, and alienating, division of labour into minute, isolated units which is a focal point of Marx's critique.

These latter features of capitalism are pertinent to feminist evaluations of

Engels's claim that the pernicious effects of the sexual division of labour would be nullified if women could enter the public work force as full participants. Socialist feminists point out that entry into the work force is not automatically a liberating experience for women. Many women who enter paid employment simply find themselves doing double duty: they work for wages in the public sphere and continue to do unpaid labour in the private, domestic sphere. Without a radical restructuring of society that would include good, cooperative, and collective arrangements for child care and for the performance of other household tasks, the solution Engels proposes is by no means an ideal one.

Its problems are exacerbated by the fact that, more often than not, women in the work force earn considerably less than men do. Even in the late 1980s women commonly earn sixty cents for each dollar that men earn. Some socialist feminists see in this wage differential a primary cause of women's continued powerlessness and oppression, even as they gain increased access to waged work. The wage differential has often been rationalized by claims that the father's income is the 'family income,' which is equitably shared within the family. This argument is used by employers to support the view that women work only to *supplement* that income. Yet the ideology of liberal capitalist society allows no 'interference' in 'private' family matters to see whether the man's income really is available to all family members. Too often that ideology works to conceal the genuine poverty of women and children. Moreover, the terms of the discussion apply only to women living in traditional heterosexual and patriarchal family arrangements. Feminists have worked to transform many of these unjust practices, and there is growing recognition of the need for wage equity legislation.

Women frequently enter the labour force in temporary, unskilled jobs that give them no security. Some socialist feminist theorists characterize such women as a 'reserve army of labour,' which capitalist society can draw upon at times of need and dispense with (relegate to unemployment) when economic circumstances dictate.[33] Such women are not freed from economic dependence upon men or, for those who have no man, from dependence on social welfare. Adding the fact that, in capitalist society, women 'liberated' from domesticity into the public work place often find themselves engaged, like men, in alienated labour, one can see that Engels did not have the perfect proposal to end women's oppression.

Moreover, just as assumptions about the family wage may mask women's inferior economic status, so assumptions about the class to which 'the family' belongs often conceal a woman's inferior, disadvantaged, or equivocal class membership. A Marxist division of society along class lines does not offer an obvious way of discerning a woman's class membership. A woman might be identified according to the class of her husband or of the man on whom she is dependent, but a divorced, single, or independently employed woman could not be appropriately classified in this way.

Circumstances such as these lead socialist feminists to advocate programmes of social change that would involve alternatives both to capitalist modes of production and to the patriarchal organization of the family and other social institutions. With many other feminists, socialists see in the nuclear family a cornerstone of women's oppression. It sustains women's dependent status, enforces compulsory heterosexuality[34] and perpetuates stereotypes of masculine and feminine gender in members of the next generation. Stereotypical masculine traits seem to be necessary for effective performance in capitalist society; stereotypical feminine traits are needed to nurture men to manhood and to help them fulfill the demands of the masculine role. As Heidi Hartmann observes: "Sexist ideology serves the dual purpose of glorifying male characteristics/capitalist values, and denigrating female characteristics/social need."[35] In sustaining a high level of demand for consumer goods, and inculcating in children the ideology of capitalist society, the nuclear family is an effective agent in perpetuating women's disadvantaged status.

Contemporary Theory: *Radical Feminism*

Radical feminists agree with much of the socialist-feminist analysis of women's disadvantaged social and economic position and their strategies for change are compatible with many of those developed by socialist feminists. But radical and socialist feminists differ on a fundamental question of emphasis. Whereas material, economic, and social oppression are primary for socialist feminists, radical feminists are convinced that the oppression of women is at the root of all other forms of oppression (radical = at the root).

Radical feminism grew out of disillusionment with the politics of the New Left in North America, Britain, and France in the late 1960s. Women in the U.S.A., who were fighting for equality and justice in the civil rights movement and against the war in Vietnam, found themselves treated as subordinate members of organizations in which they were vigorously active. They realized that they were being exploited as sex objects and servants by their male coworkers. Such experiences led Robin Morgan to write that "sexism is the root oppression, the one which, until and unless we *up*root it, will continue to put forth the branches of racism, class hatred, ageism, competition, ecological disaster, and economic exploitation."[36] Sexism, as manifested in patriarchal family arrangements, in gender stereotyping, pornography, wife and child abuse, and rape, became the focus of radical-feminist analysis.

Radical feminists have declared that 'the personal is political,' demonstrating how patriarchal society structures personal experiences and relations in ways disadvantageous to women. The liberal slogan that the government has no place in the bedrooms of the nation, which Canadians (echoing Pierre Trudeau) proudly intoned in the late 1960s, is an improvement upon the view that society can legislate permissible sexual behaviour between adults. But it renders immune to public intervention such damaging and exploitative practices as rape and sexual abuse within marriage and the family. In fact, much of the everyday activity that perpetuates women's oppression takes place within the home, a place protected from political scrutiny by an ideology of sanctity and privacy where the invisibility of women's domestic and child-rearing labour is maintained.[37] Before radical feminists placed it on the public agenda, domestic violence was regarded as a private matter in which the law ought not to meddle. Radical and socialist feminists agree that there is an evident and systematic difference in power between women and men, which is defined in part by men's socially and legally sanctioned control over women's sexual, procreative, and emotional labour. Out of the ideology that supports this control emerges the consequence that when all is not well in the domestic sphere, the woman is held accountable, for she has not been appropriately obedient and submissive. Such power relations need to be overturned if women's oppression is to end.

Many radical feminists maintain that any male-female relation is bound to be oppressive to the woman and conclude that female separatism is the only feasible solution. Notable among these is Mary Daly, who claims that "For men . . . life has meant feeding on the bodies and minds of women, sapping energy at the expense of female deaths . . . It is men who have sapped the lifeforce of women."[38] Daly maintains that women under patriarchy live in a condition of "robotitude," a term she uses to refer to "the state of servitude of women in a phallocratic world."[39] This condition is induced by a system of myths devised by men, but internalized by women to the point where they live unthinkingly by them. Radical feminism, as Daly conceives of it, is a voyage of "woman becoming,"[40] fuelled by "gynergy" (women's energy),[41] and moving toward full self-affirmation in an affirmation of woman-centered values. It is a voyage toward the development of a separate and self-centered women's culture.

Contemporary Theory: *Sexuality and Reproduction*

Although socialist and radical feminism developed out of significantly distinct concerns, these two strands of feminism have remained mutually influential in their later evolution. Many common themes and agendas have come to unite their interests, even though it would be quite wrong to suggest that they are now indistinguishable from one another. One important issue of common concern has been that of women's sexual and reproductive freedom. Feminists have been active, vocal – and notably successful – in claiming women's right to abortion on demand, insisting upon reliable means of birth control, affirming the right to sexual relationships – either lesbian or heterosexual – that refuse the patriarchal norm, and challenging patriarchal control over child birth and raising children.

In *The Dialectic of Sex*, one of the first radical-feminist texts, Shulamith Firestone contends that biological reproduction is the primary source of women's oppression.[42] She believes that women can escape from biological entrapment only by turning to reproductive technology, and by creating communal living arrangements to supplant the nuclear family. So long as women bear children, their biology will be their destiny. Since she wrote this argument, however, the revolutionary promise Firestone saw in reproduction technology has been cast in doubt. Rona Achilles shows in her chapter in this book how such technology threatens women's reproductive autonomy. Firestone urges women to reject the ideology of romantic love that encourages them to live as sex/love objects for men, deluded in the belief that romantic (heterosexual) love is the route to happiness.

Adrienne Rich focuses somewhat differently on women's reproductive activity. She claims that women's experience of motherhood has been obscured and coopted by "motherhood as institution." A complex power structure constituted by the interlocking forces of law, medicine, culture, and professional expertise works to create an "invisible institution" of male control over women's bodies and minds.[43] Yet Rich celebrates women's strength in keeping much of the experience of motherhood for themselves despite the power of institutional control. She is impressed that some women have been able to preserve for themselves "even within the destructiveness of the institution: the tenderness, the passion, the trust in our instincts, the evidence of a courage we did not know we owned."[44] In these strengths she sees women's capacity to resist patriarchal power.

In like vein, Mary O'Brien argues that men endeavour to negate their alienation from reproductive process by appropriating children as their own (giving them a name and a place in the social structure). By these means they claim "ownership of the woman's reproductive labour power in a sense recognizably similar to . . . the sense in which capitalists appropriate the surplus labour power of wage labourers."[45] Yet, O'Brien observes, "Embedded in the child is the alienated reproductive labour of the mother":[46] alienated because patriarchal social institutions do not permit her to call the child her own. In her view, this appropriation needs to be understood in dialectical relation to woman's reproductive consciousness. A woman knows that the child is hers, and it grows with her love, yet she must nurture it to be a labourer or a producer of children in its turn. Out of the strength of female reproductive consciousness, O'Brien sees a possibility for the development of a unified social consciousness that could alter the structures that permit only alienated reproductive and productive labour.

The belief that male-female relations are inevitably oppressive to women has led many feminists to explore alternatives either of the separatist sort advocated by Mary Daly, or of some other variety. Some feminists contend that celibacy is the only solution, for they believe that sexual relations, whether lesbian or heterosexual, always lead to dominance and oppression. Separatist lesbian feminists claim that sexual expression between women is the only acceptable form of sexuality for women who would be free of the exploitative requirements of patriarchy. Separatist feminists contend that male domination is sustained by heterosexuality, which ties women to men socially, economically, and emotionally. The only way to break free from such thralldom, they maintain, is through female separatism. Lesbianism has an impressively subversive political potential in a society where women are defined, primarily, as sex objects for men. Adrienne Rich characterizes compulsory heterosexuality as a "*political institution* . . . [created] to enforce women's total emotional, erotic loyalty to men . . . [It wrenches] women's emotional and erotic energies away from themselves and other women and from woman-identified values."[47] Rich believes that the pain a growing girl experiences in switching her affections from a woman–her mother–to a man attests to the unnaturalness of this choice forced upon women by the patriarchal social order. She urges scholars to explore the continuum of lesbian experience past and present, so that women will realize that heterosexuality is not the only option.[48] Separatist feminists believe that lesbianism offers the basis for a radical restructuring of sexuality through the creation of a woman-culture founded on non-hierarchical, supportive female values.

Contemporary Theory: *French Feminism*

Contemporary French feminism stands as a distinct and original contribution to feminist theory. French feminists are ideologically closer to socialist and radical feminists than they are to liberal feminists. They share with English-speaking radical and socialist feminists an activist origin in the student protest movements of the late 1960s – particularly in the student revolt in Paris in 1968. Yet French feminism has roots in French and German philosophical traditions that are markedly different from those that have shaped feminist theory in the English-speaking world. French feminists are not so much political theorists as intellectuals, in a society where the intellectual can have a significant political role, attacking the arrogant assumptions of entrenched institutions. Perhaps in consequence, their theoretical work focuses on literary and psychoanalytic theory, creativity and sexuality. The reinterpretation of Freud by French psychoanalyst Jacques Lacan has become one of the focal points of feminist writing in France.

Lacan sees the Freudian story of psychosexual development as a story of the 'fall' of human beings from one-ness with the mother into consciousness. That fall is, at the same time, a fall into language, which Lacan describes as the symbolic realm. Language reflects the patriarchal social order. It exists prior to the moment when a child learns it, yet it is the primary mode of expression available to that maturing child. It is through language that the pre-conscious child becomes a conscious human subject. Central to Lacan's discussion is the claim that entry into the symbolic order brings with it an awareness of separation–alienation from mother, self, and world. Men endeavour to overcome that separation through a (phallic) means of mastery, partially manifested in the (patriarchal) power of language. It is through language that a child learns the greater value accorded to maleness in a world where femaleness signifies otherness.

It is small wonder, then, that language both as the subject matter of linguistics and as the substance of literary texts has become a primary concern in French feminist writings. Julia Kristeva, for example, claims that the conception of language itself, as it is studied by linguists, is riddled with political implications. She explores the arbitrariness of meaning, the artificiality of considering 'speaking subjects' out of context, and the power inherent in the application of linguistic labels.[49] Her aim is to understand the overweaning power of masculine rationality, which privileges "reason, order, unity and lucidity, and . . . [does] so by silencing and excluding the irrationality, chaos and fragmentation that has come to represent femininity."[50] Above all (and following Lacan), Kristeva sees in language a means of designating sexual difference: a fundamental difference that feminists should not attempt to deny or minimize. It is a difference that manifests itself "in the relationship to power, language, and meaning,"[51] which is a radically different relationship for women and for men. With other French feminists, Kristeva is critical of feminist efforts to gloss over sexual difference. Rather, she believes, women should affirm and rejoice in their difference. In it they have a means of subverting the patriarchal order. It is a means which they should use to advantage, even if it results in their relegation to a marginal status, beyond the written text and the limits of public discourse.

Femininity, sexuality, and discourse are central topics of analysis in the works of two other French feminists: Hélène Cixous and Luce Irigaray. Characterizing traditional discourse as essentially phallocentric, Cixous speaks "about women's writing: about *what it will do*."[52] She believes that conceptions of 'masculine' and 'feminine' imprison thinkers within oppressive binary oppositions. Yet she, too, maintains that the solution is not to *deny* sexual difference, as advocates of androgyny have done, but to emphasize, write, and celebrate the feminine. Such writing, as she conceives of it, does not "annul differences but stirs them up, pursues them, increases their number."[53] Hence no one 'pair' of differences, such as the traditional male/female dichotomy, is privileged.

French feminists read literary texts, then, to see what is left out: they read the gaps and exclusions in a text as manifestations of power in discourse. Rather than studying modes of production, they look at human artefacts and at what these artefacts say – and do not say – about their creators. They draw upon the potential of the comic, the mimetic, to reveal the arbitrariness of patriarchal assumptions. Irigaray advocates a subversive feminine discourse that displaces (phallocentric) male discourse by writing from the margins.[54] By miming the masculine, this writing reveals the ephemerality of masculine power and makes possible a realization of the power of female sexuality, pleasure, and desire. There is no question, here, that women should try in any way to be just like men. Their strength is in their difference. Since women are designated as different because of their bodies, it is the female body that must be celebrated as a source of disruptive female desire and creativity.

In their analyses of sexuality, feminine creativity, and the relationship between sex and class, contemporary French feminists explore many of the physical and psychological aspects of being female that de Beauvoir analyses in *The Second Sex*. Yet contemporary French feminists differ markedly from de Beauvoir in their celebration of bodily femininity, and the challenges they pose to the thought structures that work to devalue it. They expose standard analyses of the 'human condition' as androcentric and heterosexist. Even the word 'human' itself, they maintain, is inadequate to describe anything other than *men's* theories and inventions. This is but one small manifestation of the entrenched phallocentricity of language and discourse, which needs to be unmasked, ridiculed, and subverted. One commentator remarks that French feminists, fittingly, have "stolen the intellectual tools of patriarchy and, in many cases, [have] turned them against their inventors."[55]

Contemporary Feminism: *Universality and Diversity*

Endeavours to distinguish among separate strands of feminist thought should not be allowed to obscure the significant overlap from one 'kind' of feminism to another. Innumerable common causes unite feminists of seemingly disparate ideological persuasions. Not the least of these is a continuing awareness of and concerted opposition to patriarchy. But one danger in concentrating upon the similarities of the various kinds of feminism with one another lies in the possibility of generating a false universalism. In generalizing about the experience of women, feminists have too often ignored specificities of race, class, culture, age, and sexual preference.

Black feminists have been especially articulate in pointing out how consistently feminist discourse, articulated out of white middle-class experience, has purported to speak for all women, black or white, poor or rich. Women of colour have noted that an analogy commonly drawn by white feminists between the social position of women and of blacks reveals unconscious racism both in its language and in its assumptions.[56] In evoking this analogy, white feminists frequently display an insensitivity, particularly to the enormous power differential between black and white women, manifested in the lower income and the restricted options of black women.

Questions of universality and diversity reflect a second paradox: just as feminism requires gender consciousness, yet seeks to eliminate gender roles, so it urges women to recognize their unity while attempting to account for their diversity. Nancy Cott observes that "The value accorded to 'sexual difference' in feminist theory has increased at the same time that the universality of the claim for sisterhood had been debunked. Ethnic, racial, and sexual diversity among women is stressed more than ever before in feminist theory, but so is the emphasis on how women (as a whole) differ from men (as a whole)."[57] Increasing awareness of the implications of this paradox renders problematic one of the oldest and most persistent of feminist projects: the project of achieving equality for women.

Equality and Difference

Equality has long been a central feminist issue. Few would deny that social justice demands equality between the sexes before the law, with respect to opportunities for education and employment, to property ownership and remuneration for work, and to all matters of human rights. Plato's proposal in the *Republic* merits feminist attention because of the equality of educational opportunity he envisages for women and men. Early liberal theorists' preoccupation with issues of equality was one of the principal inspirations of contemporary feminist thought. And socialist and radical feminists today alternately claim and dispute the value of working toward equality. Yet formulations of the project phrased to accord priority to the achievement of equality *between the sexes* are problematic. They are often interpreted, both by feminists and (albeit for different purposes) by anti-feminists, to mean that women really want to be just like men. It would be a rare feminist who would take this to be the aim of her endeavours to promote women's causes. The scheme Plato outlines in the *Republic* gives some idea of why this would not be acceptable.

The liberal vision of equality is not much better, from a feminist point of view. It provides ready support for the claim that the sexes are equal, but different, and hence should occupy different but complementary places in society. This translates too easily into a belief that women – even enlightened and educated ones – are best suited to be wives and mothers. Mill's belief that an equally educated woman will be prepared – and pleased – to share in her husband's pursuits shows that the equality he envisages is to be understood strictly on male terms. None of these arguments in favour of equality between the sexes has been able to show how the unalike can be treated equally. Yet 'equality' is generally understood to mean sameness of goals, rights, and opportunities.

To express the goal as one of achieving equality with men amounts to approving of men's way of being, and declaring that women want to be like that too. If the question were posed: "Equality with *which* men?" the answer could not be "Oh, of course, with all men." It is unlikely that women are claiming equality with men who are disadvantaged and exploited as a consequence of their race, class, or culture. They do not want equality with coal miners, or with male industrial workers who have been sterilized by the chemicals they work with, or have acquired cancer from pollutants in asbestos mines.[58] Modern (liberal) feminist campaigns for equality with men gloss over the fact that men themselves are not equal under capitalism. To aim for equality with men is to buy into the utopian myth that all men can in fact (not just in theory) achieve success in proportion to their natural initiative, intelligence, and energy.

Now, in this formal, abstract sense, women do want the freedom to achieve such status as *their* initiative, intelligence and energy allow. But in patriarchal, capitalist society, equality is more abstract than it is real. Women are not likely to achieve any liveable form of equality as long as the structures of such societies remain unchanged, simply stretching a little to make space for women. If equality is so construed that neither its rhetoric nor its practice can accommodate relevant differences between women and men, then its value is questionable. As long as putative labour market equality can (even implicitly) require women to conceal evidence of pregnancy, to work until the commencement of labour, or to refrain from having children, then women's relevant differences from the (masculine) labour market norm are not being taken into account.[59]

The question of how differences among people should be taken into account is a difficult one, however, as there is a fundamental moral problem about treating individuals differently. In democratic societies it has long been taken for granted that all should be treated alike and equally. Traditional moral theories emphasize the importance of impartiality and equality in moral decisions. And moral decisions, it is believed, should be made on the basis of reason alone, with no appeal to emotions. So if women's relevant differences from men are in fact to be taken into account in moral- and political-decision making, a way of thinking differently about difference has to be developed.

Some provocative reflection on sexual difference in moral thinking has been stimulated by Carole Gilligan's book *In a Different Voice*.[60] From her analysis of male and female subjects' responses to Lawrence Kohlberg's tests for measuring moral development, Gilligan concludes that there are two moral systems. She designates one as a 'male' moral system, which views the moral domain as a complex of rights and principles to be defended as the bases of decision-making (a defensive morality). It contrasts with a 'female' moral system, which perceives human life as a network of social relationships, where judgements of 'right' and 'wrong' depend upon the kinds of caring that a situation demands. Traditionally, moral philosophers have maintained that moral debate should be about rights and principles. Questions about feelings and caring have been relegated to a realm of sentiment that is not amenable to moral scrutiny.

There is a persistent view in the history of western thought to the effect that it is *reason*, rationality, that distinguishes human beings from other living beings. This view supports the belief that the best realization of human possibilities will be achieved through the cultivation of reason. And the emphasis upon rights and principles in moral theory is a manifestation of this veneration of reason. It is through the use of reason that such principles and rights are discerned. In the historical examples discussed in this chapter, education of the 'reason' is a constant theme. It was in consequence of their allegedly inferior rational capacities that women were deemed inferior to men. Wollstonecraft's claim for equal female access to the domain of reason must be understood in the light of this belief. In moral theory, as Gilligan shows, the claim is that rationally discerned, universal, impartial moral principles constitute the proper 'stuff' of moral judgements. The capacity to act upon such principles is heralded as the mark of achieved moral maturity. Yet it is commonly believed that women are lacking in this capacity.

There is a still more subtle problem about reason for feminists, which is both political and conceptual. In an important discussion of this topic, Genevieve Lloyd argues that the very notion of reason is defined, throughout history, by exclusion of all of those traits traditionally associated with femaleness.[61] This is true of reason both as a distinguishing human characteristic and as a character ideal. Lloyd demonstrates the near-impossibility simply of re-valuing, and celebrating, these undervalued traits to grant them a value equal to that accorded to 'masculine' traits. A much more radical rethinking is required. So, although Gilligan claims that both of the voices she has discerned are available alike to women and men, one must wonder how workable this accessibility could be in practice. The 'different' voice she hears has long been associated with female preoccupations, and devalued accordingly. One might conclude from her work that both voices should be permitted to speak freely and both sets of concerns accorded equal worth. But this does not seem to be a practical possibility so long as all modes of expression and action associated with the female are systematically downgraded, and often suppressed.

Feminists are attempting to transform a set of social structures where it has long been taken for granted that what men do is the normal *human* thing to do, as Simone de Beauvoir's characterization of female Otherness makes clear. 'Humanness' has been defined by what men do. When women think, speak, or act differently, their behaviour is judged deviant because it differs from that male norm. Yet it is worth noting that difference is a symmetrical relation. If women are different from men, then men, by the same token, are different from women; if women speak in a different voice, then men do, too. The different voice in which masculine morality (and rationality) has long been speaking – and drowning out all other voices by calling them 'different' – is itself but one voice among many. It may have legitimate things to say: it has gone to some lengths to ensure that its pronouncements are the only respectable ones. But once one hears other voices, one realizes that to speak in that masculine moral voice is to speak in only one of many possible ways.

Even if it could be shown that there are 'naturally' distinctive female and male voices, this would not legitimate any evaluative conclusions. North American culture emphasizes sameness and conformity to the extent that when differences are noted, they tend to be noted judgementally, as deviant from a norm. An observed difference, in this conformist context, often provides a pretext for condemnation. Indeed, that would be one way of summing up the history of woman's place in patriarchal society: woman has been judged different from man, and *hence* inferior (Other). The consequences have been all of those damaging, exploitative, and oppressive practices that feminists are working to eradicate. So it is no wonder that feminists are concerned to arrive at a workable understanding of difference.

Much feminist thought has concentrated upon de-emphasizing and/or defusing difference, arguing in favour of 'gender-blind' laws, policies, and practices. The claim is that this is the best route to equality. Feminists persuaded by this line of thought claim that taken-for-granted polarities are less stark than they seem to be. They argue that theory should be formulated in terms of difference-in-sameness, sameness-in-difference, moving toward a constant interplay between and among voices. But such a programme would not sit easily with radical feminists, or with French feminists, who maintain that female differences must be asserted and celebrated. It would be unacceptable to socialist feminists who believe that social structures need to be transformed to take relevant differences into account.

Gilligan's work was inspired by a perceived difference between her own experience and the theory she was teaching. She comments in an interview: "I was teaching the theory of adolescent development based on the view that maturity was being autonomous and independent. But I had never experienced that. It was clearly based on the male development cycle."[62] Now Gilligan did not simply note a difference between *her own* experience and the theory she was teaching, and conclude that the difference must be based on gender. She cites evidence in support of her conclusions. But her emphasis upon the discrepancy between her *experience* and the accepted *theory* is particularly feminist.

It has long been assumed, in 'malestream'[63] thought, that if experiences seem to fly in the face of established theory, then so much the worse for those experiences. Theories are granted an authority such that, if certain experiences cannot be explained by the theory, then there must be something amiss with those experiences. But like Gilligan, growing numbers of feminists are asking the revolutionary, subversive question: "What is wrong with this theory that it cannot explain my experience and the experiences of other women?" This is the kind of question feminists are asking as they work to articulate the relation between theory and practice, and to undermine the silencing effects of theoretical, patriarchal power structures.[64]

Lorraine Code

SUGGESTED READINGS

Birke, Lynda, *Women, Feminism and Biology*. Brighton: Harvester Books, 1986.

Eisenstein, Hester, *Contemporary Feminist Thought*. London: Allen & Unwin, 1984.

Eisenstein, Zillah, *The Radical Future of Liberal Feminism*. New York: Longmans, 1981.

Elshtain, Jean Bethke, *Public Man, Private Woman*. Princeton, NJ: Princeton University Press, 1981.

Frye, Marilyn, *The Politics of Reality*. Trumansburg, NY: The Crossing Press, 1983.

Gilligan, Carole, *In A Different Voice: Psychological Theory and Women's Development*. Cambridge, MA: Harvard University Press, 1982.

Grimshaw, Jean, *Philosophy and Feminist Thinking*. Minneapolis: University of Minnesota Press, 1986.

Hamilton, Roberta, *The Liberation of Women*. London: Allen & Unwin, 1978.

Keller, Evelyn Fox, *Reflections on Gender and Science*. New Haven: Yale University Press, 1985.

Lloyd, Genevieve, *The Man of Reason: 'Male' and 'Female' in Western Philosophy*. Minneapolis: University of Minnesota Press, 1984.

Marks, Elaine, and Isabelle de Courtivron, eds., *New French Feminisms*. New York: Schocken Books, 1981.

Okin, Susan Moller, *Women in Western Political Thought*. Princeton, NJ: Princeton University Press, 1979.

Segal, Lynne, *Is the Future Female? Troubled Thoughts on Contemporary Feminism*. London: Virago Press, 1987.

Chapter Two

Pioneers and Suffragists

In 1828, a newspaper editor in Upper Canada commented that "the estimation in which woman has been held in various ages of the world and in different countries may be regarded among the most indicative 'signs of the times' denoting with almost unerring precision the state of civilization or the advancement of the people toward that state . . . As knowledge increased, or as civilization was promoted, the rank of woman was correspondingly promoted and her condition proportionately meliorated." Throughout the ages, Hiram Leavenworth of the *Farmers Journal* continued, woman has always been the subject of "deep intense affection" and essential to the happiness and salvation of man. Now, he asserted, in these progressive and civilized times, woman, by reason of "her delicacy of perception," her "feminine purity and serving dependence," and that "elevation of character which distinguishes and endears her sex" has finally attained her rightful place beside man.[1]

One wonders how Canadian women of Leavenworth's time, and those of an even earlier period, themselves viewed their situation. Only in the past fifteeen years have a few scholars begun to consider the women's point of view and to realize that there is an important story to tell about women in New France and Acadia, in British North America and, after 1867, in Canada. In the exciting process of discovering this history, Canadians, particularly Canadian women, are recognizing an essential part of their heritage – a past that gives meaning to the present and offers a deeper appreciation of their own circumstances.

Our knowledge of the history of women and of the evolution of a women's culture in Canada remains woefully incomplete. The discipline is still in its infancy and is complicated by the need to find new ways of recreating and interpreting the past to unravel the complex experiences of often invisible women. Few women recorded their thoughts or daily activities, and only a minority signed petitions, drew wills, or paid taxes. Traditional histories have avoided this problem of sources by denying that women have a history. Most often, only major actors (always men), 'momentous' political events, or 'significant' social, economic, and political national developments are considered worthy of attention. Even social historians are only now beginning to discover that the working man had a wife, a mother, a sister, a daughter, and often a working woman at his side. Though there remain many more questions than there are answers, the story of Canadian women is nonetheless beginning to come to light. It is now possible to tell at least part of the story and to identify a number of factors and trends that shaped women's experiences.

The following is by no means a thorough history of women in Canada and cannot possibly provide the richness of detail which is necessary for a real appreciation of women's experiences. Moreover, although Canadian women's history is but one part of the larger story of the history of European and North American women, space precludes all but passing reference to those vital links. This chapter will provide only a basic overview of the history of Canadian women from the mid-seventeenth century, when Europeans first arrived, to approximately 1960. It also attempts to take 'women's time' into account, for while the Conquest, the American Revolution, the War of 1812, and Confederation affected *all* Canadians' lives, Canadian women, like women throughout the world, more often measured their lives by the more personal events of birth, marriage, and death, and by the demands of day-to-day existence.

As well, it should be kept in mind that there were, and were seen to be, large differences in the experiences of the mistress and the maid, the wife and the spinster, and the teacher and the working girl. But, as Veronica Strong-Boag and Anita Clair Fellman note, "in some ways, women's lives resemble each others as much or more than they resemble those of the men with whom they are closely associated."[2] All women were in some way or another subordinate to men and this often brought them together.

Subordination did not mean automatic submission, passivity, or loss of all personal autonomy, however. Throughout the last three centuries, Canadian women have taken an active part in shaping their own lives and the lives of those around them. All played an essential role in the establishment and development of their communities, and there were a number of women who pushed beyond the bounds of institutionalized restraints and implicitly – sometimes explicitly – challenged the public and personal mores of their times. Gradually, a common women's culture emerged,[3] which was often perpetuated over a number of generations. It is likely that despite differences of language, location, time, and technology, the peasant women of New France would have had a real understanding and sympathy with the women of mid-nineteenth-century rural Upper Canada and with western farming women of the twentieth-century Canadian West.

For this reason, the early colonial period must be included in any general history of Canadian women. The year 1867 was a watershed in the political development of the country but it heralded little change for the nation's women. While Canadians celebrated union, women's daily lives and expectations continued in their colonial patterns. It was not so much the political but rather the economic and social developments – the transformation from an agricultural to an industrial economy, and the movement from a rural to an urban society – that provided the rough benchmarks in the history of women. Moreover, these developments influenced women's lives at different times and in varying ways, and women's responses to these new situations were patterned by tradition and custom. An appreciation of the post-Confederation history of women, therefore, must be firmly rooted in an understanding of colonial lifestyles and traditions.

New France

European women first made their appearance in what would become Canada in the mid-seventeenth century. In 1637 a few well-educated and relatively wealthy women of the Catholic orders of the Ursulines and Hospitalières landed at Quebec, determined to carry the message of God to the New World. Shortly after Marie de l'Incarnation founded the Ursuline convent in Quebec, the religieuses were joined by lay women who arrived with their fathers, husbands, employers and, after 1663, under the protection of the King, to make a new life for themselves and their families.[4]

From the very beginning, the lives of both lay and religious women in New France differed quite significantly from the lives they would have led in Europe. There is no question that many of the religious, political, and social institutions in the new colony were patterned after those in France. But the economics of the fur trade, the importance of the military, the demands of life on the frontier, and the overabundance of men provided the women of the Ancien Régime with a unique opportunity to exercise considerable influence on colonial life and development. And many women eagerly embraced this chance.

In New France and Acadia between 1650 and 1750 all roads for lay women led to matrimony. The physical dangers of the frontier, the economic difficulties of existence, and the scarcity of women prompted them to become wives and mothers, a role that the government, the church, and tradition encouraged. Particularly in the early years of settlement, French Canadian women married young, often at thirteen or fourteen years of age, bore children, and in the frequent event of widowhood, remarried quickly.[5] Marriage and motherhood did not, however, imply a complete submergence into obscurity or total dependence on and subservience to one's husband.

Women, by reason of their sex, were expected to bear children, see to their upbringing and education, and maintain the home and the garden. Yet dwellings in New France were relatively small, simple, and utilitarian, and childhood lasted only until the child was old enough to contribute to the household economy. In the pre-industrial society of New France, like that in Europe, the family was the basic social and economic unit, and the home and the workplace were often the same. By necessity, women, men, and when old enough, children, worked side by side in the fields and in business. As a result, the division between the public and the private spheres, both within the walls of the homes and within the minds of its residents, was ill-defined and sometimes non-existent.[6] Although women were subordinate to the male head of the household by law, in practice marriage was more like a partnership, with women and men assuming joint responsibility for the family and the household economy.

The lack of clearly defined roles for women and men, the primary importance of the family in New France, and the challenge of frontier society together provided women with a latitude of movement and occupational opportunities largely denied them in Europe or later in British North America. Married women often took an active part in the market-place. Some opened taverns next to their artisan-husband's shop; others acted as launderesses for the local garrison. It was not unusual for wives to accompany their husbands to the fur-trade posts in the wilderness, where a few managed the canteens or became directly involved in trading. And when the need arose, a number of women undoubtedly stood beside their husbands in hand-to-hand combat with the Iroquois.

The fur-trade economy of New France also meant that women who stayed at home carried on the family business in their husband's absence. Some became fur traders themselves; others managed property, oversaw extensive mercantile establishments, or 'minded' the store or workshop. As Jan Noel concludes, the wives of absent fur traders and military men played an invaluable role in the day-to-day running of the colony's economy.[7] Particularly during the early years of the eighteenth century, when New France was more settled and the proportion of women to men was more balanced, a number of widows chose not to remarry, but to carry on family businesses alone and as trustees for their children.[8]

As well as those women who played an active part in the economy, there were others who were influential in its religious and political life. Throughout the seventeenth century, French nuns were one of the most prominent and influential groups in New France, providing religious leadership and establishing charitable services essential to the fledgling colony's survival. The religieuses provided not only leadership for the faith, building missions, hospitals and schools for the colonists, they often also had the ear of the royal administration and helped shape local and colonial policy. By establishing schools for both elite and peasant girls, they "endowed the colony with an educational tradition" that was unique and consciously encouraged women to contribute to their own and to their colony's development. The curriculum of the Ursuline schools for the elite at Quebec and Trois Rivières, for example, though apparently weak in housekeeping skills, emphasized the importance of needlework because this skill would enable women to produce trade items for the fur trade. These schools also taught elite women the "requisite skills for administering a house and a fortune."[9] The schools for the popular classes taught basic literacy and provided an education suitable for 'a young lady,' a curriculum that some influential Frenchmen felt was potentially disastrous, for it encouraged girls to move to the towns, causing a "depopulation of the countryside."[10]

The presence of self-reliant, strong, religious women in positions of prominence and influence symbolized the colony's acceptance of women's active participation in all aspects of colonial life. Even the law was forced to recognize the favoured position that women gradually attained. Women who were insubordinate to authority or who committed adultery were dealt with much less harshly than women or men offenders in Europe. Property law carefully protected the rights of a woman as well as her children. Under the Custom of Paris, the foundation of law in New France, a widow was frequently appointed guardian of her children; she also inherited equal shares with her children in her husband's property and often managed the family business until the children came of age.[11]

In hindsight, the French society that was painstakingly established on the Canadian frontier in the seventeenth and eighteenth centuries seems to have been remarkably progressive for women. The relative openness and freedom that most women experienced did not protect them, however, from the trials and miseries of pioneer life. Disease, and endless physical toil only added to the burdens of frequent pregnancy and childbirth. Although apparently healthier and better fed than their sisters in France, the women of the new colony also faced the problems and tensions resulting from enforced separation from their husbands and families, early widowhood, and the periodic calamities of Indian and European wars. In the latter half of the eighteenth century, all French colonists found themselves in a particularly devastating situation.

In the 1750s, with the expulsion of the Acadians by the British, the women of the Maritime region were uprooted, often separated from their families, and forced into exile. In 1760, after the British Conquest of Quebec, a number of women in New France were also forced to abandon their homes and to return to a France in which they were strangers. Most stayed in Quebec after the capitulation, however, and having survived the bitter conflict, the heart-ache, and the deprivation of the British-French colonial wars, discovered that British rule threatened not only the way of life of French society as a whole, but also the unique place that women had attained within it.

Little is known about how the first few years of British rule changed women's place in Quebec society. By the turn of the century, however, although the civil code remained, the arrival of increasing numbers of English-speaking settlers from the thirteen American colonies and from Britain helped to provoke a radical change in Quebec society. Morever, the expulsion of the Acadians, the Conquest, and shortly thereafter the American Revolution signalled the introduction into Canada of what would become a new and quite divergent view of women and their 'properly appointed' roles.

Families of New Englanders moved to the recently vacated lands of Nova Scotia in the 1760s. In 1784, British-American loyalist families fled north after the American Revolution, and in Upper Canada were joined by an increasing number of restless Americans in search of land and expanded opportunities. By 1800, this northward migration was augmented by the arrival of a few immigrants from Britain, whose numbers substantially increased after 1815 and the conclusion of the Napoleonic Wars. Like their French Canadian sisters, most of the English women who came to Canada at the end of the eighteenth and in the first half of the nineteenth centuries came as wives, mothers, or daughters. They had to confront a wilderness frontier and were part of a pre-industrial rural economy, but these women had quite different expectations and experiences than did the women of an earlier New France. Those who arrived in the Maritimes and north of the St. Lawrence and the Great Lakes tried as much as possible to recreate the patterns and traditions of their old homes – whether in the Old World or the Anglo-American community. As well, the rapid development of British North America after 1815, and the gradual acceptance of the Protestant Victorian view that a woman's proper place was in the home, soon imposed restrictions and limitations on English women's lives that had not existed in the Ancien Régime.

Pre-Confederation Canada

The years between 1790 and approximately 1850 were a time of transition for Canadian women. In the early years, the settlers of Upper Canada and the

Maritimes were preoccupied by establishing viable British communities. The family remained the most basic and important social, economic, and political institution, and family members were bound "together in a single body in a common enterprise of subsistence" and survival. Women were a necessary part of this unit and contributed materially to "the corporate family economy." In addition to looking after the affairs of the home and the garden, women were also responsible for "almost every aspect of social reproduction,"[12] including the medical, spiritual, and educational welfare of the family and community. As well, some women found themselves managing property, opening a tavern, and, if widowed, running the family business.

Such an extensive role for women was from the very beginning under attack, however. Under British common law, women, particularly those who were married, were subordinate to men. Moreover, as Mary Ryan notes in her work on American pioneering communities at the same time, the frontier society and the interdependence of family members it encouraged was, "by definition, temporary" and "doomed to extinction within the space of two generations."[13] By 1820, Upper Canadian and Maritime colonies were relatively secure and increasingly developed. Frontier practices and attitudes were perpetuated by newly arrived immigrant and old settlers who were moving to the backcountry. But in the older parts of the colonies the economy was becoming diversified, and society as a whole was increasingly institutionalized and stratified. As a result, although British North America was still pre-industrial, the division of labour on the basis of sex became more exact, as distinctions began to be drawn between public and private spheres of activity. As these distinctions became more defined, women throughout North America were increasingly confined within the physical and psychological limits of the private world of the home and the hearth.

This was not just a linear progression developing over time. From the beginning of this period, there were a number of women who, because of their wealth, training and high position in society, had already accepted the 'dictates of domesticity' or what American historian Barbara Welter has called "the cult of true womanhood."[14] Like most new arrivals, Elizabeth Simcoe, wife of the first Lieutenant-Governor of Upper Canada, Anne Powell, wife of the Chief Justice, and Hannah Cartwright, wife of one of the colony's leading merchants, and other wives, daughters, and mothers of the newly formed colonial elites, attempted to recreate the patterns of their old lives. For these women who were attached to influential and prominent colonists, the patterns of the old thirteen colonies and Britain rested on the acceptance of two separate and distinct spheres of life for women and men. A woman was presumed to be emotionally, intellectually, as well as physically different from a man. By virtue of her sex, she was most suited to be a wife and mother.

Her natural sphere of endeavour and influence was, therefore, within the home, which was now expected to be a haven and sanctuary from an increasingly volatile and hostile world. It was a woman's special responsibility, these gentle folk of wealth and standing believed, to guard the home and make it a place of virtue for the family and thus the foundation of a virtuous and civilized nation. Having embraced such beliefs, it is not surprising that members of the upper class of colonial society actively resisted the levelling endemic to frontier existence and tried to impose their acceptance of a hierarchy of class and sex on those around them.[15]

From the very beginning, therefore, women in British North America were subject to two conflicting views of a woman's place – a climate that persisted throughout the century. Yet even this interpretation, of two lifestyles and expectations existing simultaneously, must be qualified to recognize the diversity, contradictions, expectations, and also the commonalities that existed within and between each group. Increasingly throughout the first half of the century, women of all levels of society lived in male-dominated households and their character and indeed their very existence was defined by the significant men in their lives – father, husband, or son.

The vast majority of women in Canada at this time were wives or widows, mothers, or young girls waiting to attain such 'exalted' and 'natural' positions. "To be female and alone" was "to be confined to the lower ranks of the social order."[16] For elite women, a good marriage was particularly essential to secure or to better their own status in society and the future status of their children. For these women, occupational opportunities outside marriage were very limited. This is perhaps best illustrated by the story of Anne Murray Powell's three daughters in early Upper Canada.

The youngest Powell girl, Mary, married at the age of twenty-seven. The middle daughter, Eliza, apparently popular and well loved although a spinster, conformed to social expectations by serving her parents and her sister within their households, as a companion, nurse, and general help mate. But the plight of the oldest daughter, Anne, highlights the severe restrictions of upper class colonial society after 1800. Perhaps the most intelligent and stubborn of the three, Anne's repeated wilfulness brought her into repeated conflict with her family. And, as Kathryn McKenna notes in her work on the Powell family, Anne's refusal to accept the social norms of her class eventually resulted in complete ostracism.[17]

Most women in British North America did not have the financial means to stay at home indefinitely, patiently awaiting marriage. They either married young or were obliged to support themselves from an early age. The most accessible and, in the first half of the nineteenth century, quite respectable means of self support was in domestic service. Women of 'good character' and 'sober and steady habits' who were willing to work were in constant demand. Young girls and widowed women easily attained posts as maids, cooks, laundresses, and farm help. But most girls did not expect to spend their lives in service. They married or remarried quickly, leaving their mistresses and masters to find a replacement. Unmarried or widowed women of some means, skills, or training found even a short time of drudgery as a servant unappealing. Particularly in the early years of the century, it was quite respectable for a single woman to open a boarding house or tavern or a millinery and hat shop. Some women took their goods on the road and toured the British colonies as itinerant peddlars. The choice of a number of widows not to remarry, but rather to carry on their husbands' businesses, though relatively unusual, was also socially acceptable, as attested to by the appearance in the colonial press of notices from women running saddleries and taverns, who hoped that their deceased husband's customers would continue to patronize them.[18]

As the century unfolded, an increasing, though still relatively small number of single and widowed women of some education took up teaching. Initially, these women, many recently arrived from Britain, opened up academies for young girls to teach the daughters of the upper and middle levels of society their three Rs and all those matters "necessary for a person of their sex" and rank–needlework, housekeeping, embroidery, French, and penmanship. With the growth of the public school movement after 1840, the acceptance of women as teachers became institutionalized. Public trustees quickly realized the economic and social benefits of hiring women teachers to work under male supervisors. Women, it was asserted, were "ideally suited to the instruction and governance of the young . . . By the law of nature and revelation," women, who already had "a position of subordination and dependence"[19] could best instill these qualities in their students. More importantly, trustees soon found that women could be employed at substantially lower wages than men, and they encouraged unmarried women to take up their duties in the growing number of public schools.

The feminization of the teaching profession after the mid-century provided colonial women with an occupational option in a world that was becoming progressively closed. The nature of their involvement in teaching, however, reflected the quickly solidifying attitudes towards a woman's role in the workplace, an attitude that would prevail for the next hundred years. Women did, and it was asserted, *should* have subordinate positions, and they required and deserved less wage for equal work. This view was readily learned by Canadian children, who were daily exposed to "this powerful symbol of women's inferior position in society."[20]

It was not just in teaching that the nature of women's work changed radically. Between 1820 and 1860, as British North America developed economically and became socially more stratified, economic opportunities for single and married women outside the home constricted. Many in rural areas continued to work in partnership with their husbands on the family farm. In colonial towns and cities, however, not only did fewer women engage in 'male' occupations in the marketplace, but their involvement in even those occupations traditionally reserved for women lessened. The midwife, for example, once the only and fully accepted help for the pregnant woman was disappearing, fast being replaced by trained, male doctors, as Wendy Michinson discusses in her chapter on the medical treatment of women.

By the time of Confederation, the transition from pioneering communities to a stratified Victorian society was largely complete. All women were expected to remain within the private sphere of the home, and those who could not were allowed to pursue only those endeavours that were considered natural extensions of a 'true woman's' place–teaching, nursing, and domestic service. Fewer and fewer women were running businesses; rather, they were at home, pursuing 'woman's work.' By example, they were to protect the hearth, the family, and the children of the nation from the evils of the public world. Ironically, as the ideology of domesticity became increasingly entrenched, the industrialization of British North America was simultaneously encouraging the complete division of public and private spheres and forcing a growing number of unskilled women into the factories as poorly paid wage labourers.[21]

It must be noted that, although they were expected to remain in the private sphere, some women in British North America did become involved, to a limited degree, in the community at large. Between 1800 and 1860, middle and upper class women, like their sisters in the United States and Great Britain, organized and joined various Bible and charity societies. The need for such organizations was increasingly evident to colonial elites after 1820, as thousands of immigrants and destitute and unemployed residents began to move to the towns and villages of British North America. For women like Eliza Powell, Christian duty and traditional involvement in church affairs, their high rank in society, and a fear of growing social disorder encouraged, even demanded that they protect their families by looking after the deserving poor, orphans, destitute mothers, and unlettered and ungodly families.

Organizations such as the Female Benevolent Society of Kingston, Upper Canada, the Dorcas Society, and various Orphan's Home and Widow's Friends Societies were formed to give help to the needy. Although often, but not always subsidiary to male organizations, these women's groups did provide many of the colonies' earliest social services.[22] As well, they provided some wealthy women with contacts outside the home, with opportunities to learn and to practise leadership skills and with a sense of community that was exclusively female. Through such activities there evolved a distinct woman's culture and a consciousness of women's concerns that crossed class lines. The givers of charity, those women of the upper levels of society who were attempting to preserve and strengthen the family, most often concentrated their attention on the plight of homeless, needy, and abandoned women and children. Nonetheless, these group activities were limited and were considered to be of secondary importance to a woman's primary duty to her own family.

By 1867, when the older colonies united, the public/male, private/female dichotomy was seemingly entrenched. Yet, as women moved into the Canadian West with their husbands and fathers, the pioneering cycle of Canadian life was perpetuated. In the West, however, the old ideas were reshaped by the new conditions of settlement, the isolation of frontier existence, and the new technology at hand.

Confederation Canada

Canadians and, later, American and European immigrants were propelled west between 1867 and 1920 by the accessibility of land and opportunities and by their own rising ambitions and expectations. Women were an integral part of this migration and played a vital role in the settlement and establishment of a new society. This was not the first time that women had played a significant role in the development of the West. Before the arrival of white women in the Red River and the Hudson Bay Company lands, the fur trade had been largely dependent on the labour and co-operation of native people, particularly native women. Indian wives had provided white fur traders with an essential personal link between the indigenous and the European commercial cultures. Native women, until well into the nineteenth century were "remarkable economic partner[s]," whose skills and "wilderness know how" materially aided the Europeans' physical and economic well-being.[23]

The arrival of the first white women in 1811 had little initial impact on the practice of mixed marriage or on white-Indian personal and trading alliances. But as their numbers increased, white women added a new and divisive element to the fur-trade society. They brought with them expectations and assumptions of a genteel life and Victorian attitudes towards race and family, which encouraged these wives of Hudson Bay factors and traders and Protestant clergymen to demand that European-Canadian social customs and mores prevail.

The influx of Ontario farmers and entrepreneurs and their wives and daughters reinforced the growing belief in Anglo-Saxon racial and social supremacy and added another level to the existing social order, one based on a sedentary, pioneer, farming lifestyle. The new women in the West worked beside their husbands in the fields and contributed to the family economy by tending the garden, raising chickens, and often taking sole responsibility for the dairy, as well as coping with the demands of the household and the children. Gradually, these women also "set about to reproduce the traditions they had left behind, the missionary societies, the bible classes . . . temperance organizations, women's institutes and the less formal networks through which medical knowledge and the craft skills of domestic life were shared."[24]

Life in the Canadian West was quite different from that in rural Ontario. Particularly during their first years, farming families were often distant from each other and from the convenience of schools, shops, and close neighbours. Such isolation made new emotional and physical demands on farm women. After 1900, as a national market system, a wheat economy, and mechanization encouraged cash cropping and increased specialization, the role of the farm wife changed quite radically. Larger farms and larger farm households all encouraged a sharper division of labour based on sex. Many of the tasks once considered a woman's responsibility became too extensive to remain part time. As Majorie Cohen notes, "As long as any aspect of production involved the farmhouse, it remained within the female domain, but outdoor activities gradually became the preserves of men."[25] For example, the founding of cheese factories and creameries, the increased size of herds to meet new market demands, and the introduction of new machinery to separate and process milk all encouraged male farmers to assume responsibility for the dairy, which traditionally had been controlled by women.

Nonetheless, Prairie wives continued to contribute to the overall economy. In addition to working in the home, a number of women after the turn of the century also took (or were forced to take) employment off the farm, supplementing the household economy with wages earned from working as teachers, shop clerks, or as employees of the growing service industries of the region. Despite this diversification of occupational activity, the primary role of married women in the Canadian West continued to be as partner of their husbands. They also continued to share a distinct sense of rural, western farming identity that was quite different from that of the East. This became evident toward the end of the century as women began to pressure first for increased involvement in the political process and then for the right to vote.

Not only married women were on the move west. Single Canadian and immigrant women joined this migration in growing numbers, attracted by the demand for farm help, domestic servants, teachers, and wives. Yet, between 1870 and 1920, as the Canadian economy became industrialized and urbanized, women were also drawn to the growing towns and cities of the new nation, where factories, shops, and mills promised adventure, greater personal and economic independence, and relief from the seeming monotony and drudgery of farm life. As Susan McDaniel shows in her chapter, the effects of this movement from farm to city were felt particularly strongly by women. Those who remained on the farms found that their traditional activities outside the farm house were increasingly marginalized. The women who left the farm, either with their families or on their own, found new opportunities in the cities but also new restrictions. The realities of city life and factory work also brought new insecurities and new demands on women's time and skills and raised apprehensions in the minds of many Canadians about the future of the family. Both women and men became alarmed that the family unit was disintegrating before the industrial onslaught.[26]

Industrialization did provide young, single, and widowed women, particularly in Ontario and Quebec, with an attractive occupational alternative to domestic service, which throughout the period continued to employ most women workers. Even the least skilled girl had hopes of securing what seemed to be a well-paid job, which, with its set hours, allowed her to leave the demands the workplace at the end of the day. But work in the factories, the burgeoning service industries, the stores, the telephone exchanges, and the textile and needle trades also entailed long hours, unhealthy working conditions, and boredom. There was no protection from arbitrary pay cuts, periodic speed-ups, or demands for more production or layoffs. Women workers soon discovered that the industrial system, and the male workers within it, erected almost impenetrable barriers to attaining either skills or advancement. A general acceptance of scientific-management techniques and specialization of tasks meant that a heirarchy of occupations and responsibilities was increasingly institutionalized. After 1900, the economy expanded and women could now find work as clerks, stenographers, typists, telephone operators, nurses, and workers in a variety of factories. Women were carefully relegated, however, to subordinate positions, to well-defined 'women's work,' which often demanded patience and dexterity, or to semi-skilled and unskilled tasks. Men established and managed the new businesses, which were creating increasingly restricted and poorly paid work ghettos for women.[27]

A large proportion of the female work-force seemed unconcerned about the implications of many of these developments. Few expected to stay in the workplace for any length of time. Work provided the single girl with a wage, perhaps some training, and an opportunity to contribute to the family income. Work outside the home was expected to and usually did end upon marriage, and few women appeared to have any personal commitment to their jobs. Attempts by a few concerned women to organize segments of the female work force met with resistance not only from male co-workers, unions, and employers, but also from many women. There were exceptions to this. Women telephone operators in Toronto organized and struck for better wages and hours in 1907; women needleworkers unionized, and some women were admitted as members of skilled craft unions.[28] But the weakness of the union movement in Canada before World War I and the prevailing assumption by women and men of all classes that a woman's true work was as wife and mother, together deterred the transient female work force from organizing and agitating for better wages and conditions. Their very presence in the workplace in such numbers seemed to be revolutionary.

By the turn of the century, there were a few Canadian women who challenged quite vehemently both their domestic roles and their limited place in the work-force. Choosing to pursue a career rather than, or perhaps in addition to marriage, some daughters of middle and upper class families, like their counterparts in Europe and the United States, began to demand entry into universities and into the new professions. Augusta Stowe-Gullen, Emily Stowe, and Amelia Yeomans, for example, breached the walls of male exclusivity in the medical profession. A few others pursued legal careers. Most middle class women, however, continued to gravitate to teaching or to the new professions of the progressive age, particularly nursing and social work. Yet, to the discerning few it was evident that, even in the so-called professions, women were relegated to the bottom rungs or were segregated because of their sex. Women medical candidates in the 1870s met firm resistance from established schools and had to go for their training to the United States or, eventually, to attend special women's medical colleges affiliated with some Canadian universities. This segregation carried over into later medical practice. The few women doctors in Canada became obstetricians or entered mission work, where ''their unique nurturing instinct'' was utilized.[29]

Most women attracted to the medical profession were encouraged to train as nurses, an occupation that most people, certainly doctors, believed was far more suited to their nature. Within institutions, nurses almost always played a subordinate role. Only the few public health nurses had any independence from the tyranny of constant supervision, submission to doctors' orders, and the rigid moral code that prevailed in a hospital. Nurses, like teachers, discovered that the mystique of femininity, which regulated their lives, also meant lower wages. Attempts by the growing numbers of nurses and teachers to gain some semblance of control over their own work and training by forming professional organizations were adamantly resisted. It was only after World War II that the Federation of Women Teachers of Ontario and nursing associations gained any control over the admission and certification of their members.[30]

Despite the continuing segregation of work by sex and the continuing subordination of women, rapid industrialization between 1900 and 1920 ushered in the 'new woman' – a woman who was increasingly educated, apparently independent (many claimed they were far too independent), and unquestioningly in the public workplace. A few Canadian women dared to suggest that this 'coming out' was but the first step towards attaining full political and economic parity.

The Reform Movement

Canada's industrial development furnished a number of women with outlets for their skills and energies in addition to the home and the workplace. Improvements in transportation and communications, the growth of cities, and the availability of new consumer goods provided by the coming of industrialization heralded an age of national growth and excitement. Yet, the expanding economic horizons also brought with them social and economic tensions and problems, which seemed to jeopardize the nation's continued physical and moral development. Canadians of all classes were concerned about the presence of 'alien' immigrants, the growing crime rate, and the visible poverty that plagued Canadian cities; and the antagonism between the interests of owners and workers threatened the very foundations of the nation. This new awareness of society's ills was accompanied, however, by an optimistic belief that by identifying and classifying problems, by organizing like-minded citizens and, where necessary, by enacting legislation to redress specific ills, the world and the nation could be reformed to ensure progress and the continuance of a moral, civilized, virtuous society.[31]

The progressive-reform impulse that gripped North America between the years 1880 and 1920 sanctioned an increased activism and awareness among Canadian women. Across the country, but particularly in the cities, thousands of upper and middle class women, increasingly educated, with their children in schools and new labour-saving devices and servants in their homes, joined the movement to reform. They were propelled out of the isolation of their homes by a sense of religious duty and a spirit of expanding opportunity, which combined with their growing apprehension about the state of Canadian society and their special place within it. First at the local and then the provincial and national levels, Canadian women came together to redress a host of social ills, campaigning for, among other things, temperance, religious instruction, improvements in the workplace, better housing, facilities for single women, and state-run public health and child welfare programs. Eventually, their activities compelled them to press for direct involvement in the political life of the nation.

Many of the first of these women's organizations were denominational. Methodist, Presbyterian, Baptist, Congregational, Catholic, and Anglican women established women's auxiliaries, institutes, and missionary societies to spread the word of God and, in some cases, make provision for the needy.[32] These groups were soon joined by a number of secular, although still religiously motivated organizations, which took their mandate from parent organizations in Britain and the United States. In 1870, the first Canadian branch of the British Young Women's Christian Association was established in St. John, followed shortly by the appearance of local YWCAS, which provided housing, domestic training, and religious instruction for young girls in Montreal and Toronto. Over the next twenty years, other groups coalesced and joined the forces of reform. The Anglican Girls' Friendly Society, the Dominion Order of the King's Daughters, and the Fédération Nationale Saint-Jean-Baptiste in Quebec were among the most prominent.

The Girls' Friendly Society (GFS), a branch of a British organization, was established in Canada in 1882. With its primary objective to provide shelter and support for single immigrant girls in a family-like setting, this Anglican group sponsored "labour bureaus, adult education classes, lunch rooms, recreation centres, vocational homes and sick funds."[33] In 1886, the American-inspired Dominion Order of the King's Daughters (DOKD) was also organized to assist young single girls in Canada's cities. A broadly based Protestant group, the DOKD, like the YWCA and the GFS, attempted to guard the spiritual, social, and personal integrity of the working girl. After the turn of the century, the Fédération Nationale Saint-Jean-Baptiste provided Catholic francophone lay women in Quebec with similar services. Founded in 1907, the Fédération was a loose alliance of some twenty-two women's groups, which had emerged to address specific problems created by the industrialization of the province. Unlike the YWCA, the GFS or the DOKD, the Fédération, although concerned about individual girls, primarily concentrated its efforts on broad social and economic issues affecting all Quebec women–housing, child welfare, working conditions, the need for vocational education for women, and prohibition.[34]

The largest, and perhaps the most influential women's organization of the time was the Women' Christian Temperance Union (WCTU), founded in Owen Sound, Ontario, in 1874. Formed expressly to stop the liquor trade, it had attracted thousands of members by the time it became a national union in 1883. Inspired by temperance movements in the United States and men's organizations in Canada, the women of the WCTU believed that alcohol was the root of all society's ills. It caused crime, poverty, sexual immorality, and most insidiously, it invaded the nation's homes and destroyed the lives of innocent women and children. The only solution, the WCTU declared, was complete prohibition, legislated by the state. The liquor trade was not the only target of the WCTU, however. The struggle to preserve and strengthen a moral society also prompted members to form Protestant missions, to agitate for stronger drug laws and anti-tobacco legislation, and in the end, to demand female suffrage.[35]

The vast majority of those whom Vernonica Strong-Boag refers to as "club women" believed that they not only had a right but an obligation to participate in the public sphere. As mothers, it was their particular responsibility to preserve the sanctity of the Canadian family. They held that "those special nurturing qualities which were common to all women,"[36] when organized and aimed at society's ills, would not only improve men and their actions in the public sphere, but would also bring society back to its virtuous roots in the family. Thus, most women reformers were essentially conservative. But, as a result of their participation in reform organizations, many Canadian women gained valuable leadership and organizational skills and gradually began to act independently of their men. A new interdependence among Canadian women and a respect for their own abilities developed, which reinforced their collective confidence and encouraged a growing public assertiveness. These middle class women, by their very participation in organized reform, were also challenging "the private/female and public/male dichotomy." Yet, they did so only because they believed it was absolutely essential to infuse the public world with a domestic, female morality.[37] Most continued to accept the middle class belief that women were best suited to be wives and mothers. It was to protect this view of the world and to ensure the continuance of the family and, thus, of the race and civilized society that an increasing number of women become involved in national affairs.

Most Canadians gradually accepted women's participation as agents and promoters of social reform, particularly as the "social feminist"[38] impulse that was embraced supported the public view of a woman's rightful place being in the home. There *were* a number of citizens, mostly men but also a few women, who feared this new woman, who was organized, forceful, and increasingly vocal in pressing her concerns. By her very presence in the public arena and her unseemly demands for recognition as the nation's conscience, the new woman, some argued, was challenging, indeed threatening the family and those traditional values she was claiming to strengthen. This attitude was particularly evident in Quebec. Nationalists like Henri Bourassa and conservative Catholic clerics generally considered that French Canadian feminists and the Fédération were tainted by foreign, alien, Anglo influences. Although all three groups, Quebec feminists, nationalists, and the church, were committed to preserving the family, they were divided on how best to achieve this. The nationalists and the church were agreed, however, that active Quebec women were a particular threat to traditional authority and social values, and clerics and nationalists in Quebec and ultra conservatives throughout the country mounted vehement attacks on the new woman.[39]

In the early years of the reform movement, few reform-minded women advocated a revolutionary change in the social or political order or desired any involvement in politics. Even after the turn of the century, they were divided over the question of female suffrage. In the 1880s and 1890s, only a few in Canada were so radical as to assert that "the insidious distinction of sex is an arbitrary and artificial one, having no foundation in reason or common sense."[40] There were only a handful who, like the members of the Toronto-based Dominion Women Enfranchisement Association (DWEA), demanded equality and the vote as a natural right. Most women involved in reform recognized and welcomed the innate differences between the sexes. And most of the nation's mothers began to agitate for the vote only after it became clear that the reforms so necessary to their society's regeneration would not be enacted without it.

By the early 1890s, several of the female reform organizations had active support across Canada. The WCTU had almost 10,000 members, scattered throughout the countryside and in the nation's towns and cities. The Girls' Friendly Society, the Dominion Order of the King's Daughters, the YWCA, and the missionary societies all continued to attract new members. These numerous associations were diverse in their goals, membership, and philosophy. Some were specifically religiously motivated, while others carried on the traditional nondenominational charity function of the earlier women's groups. A few, like the Aberdeen Association and the Women's Art Association, had been established to promote culture, art, and patriotism among Canadian women. Others, like the WCTU, had been formed to redress specific social ills. These differences in purpose and intent were offset, however, by considerable duplication of ideas, methods, problems, and members among the many organizations. By 1893, the growing self-awareness and self-confidence of women, together with their realization of the need to expand their scope, prompted the creation of one national body to bring the various national associations into cooperation and common action.

Under the strong influence of Lady Ishbel Aberdeen, wife of the Governor General, the new National Council of Women of Canada (NCWC) became a clearing house and a strong lobbying group for women's reform activities across the country. Declaring itself non-partisan and non-sectarian, in an effort to defuse the potential conflicts arising from differing religious and political beliefs, the NCWC also asserted its commitment to "the homes and the Nation . . . the family and the State." Its intention was to extend "feminine influence over the operation of Canadian society" and to promote "national enthusiasm and affection." The formation of the NCWC "set the stage" for "feminine nationalism, reform and ambition,'' and for the first time, gave the Canadian women's movement a sense of national unity and group identity.[41]

The formation of a national organization did not resolve, however, the varied and, at times, conflicting views women of various regions of the country and of differing income levels held towards the issues of the day. Most 'club' women lived in the nation's cities and their proposed reforms were, not surprisingly, concerned with urban problems. Women in the Canadian West did share the national desire for prohibition and concern for the problems presented by the arrival of large numbers of immigrants. Indeed, the WCTU was particularly strong in the West. As farmers' wives, however, living on the political periphery of Canada, rural western women did not share many of the eastern concerns for municipal and factory reforms. Many members of the women's auxiliaries of the United Farmer's Associations of Manitoba, Saskatchewan, and Alberta distrusted the intentions of the urban-based, middle class reform groups, believing that they were but appendages of the industrial, political interests of the East. The growth of western cities and the increasing diversity of classes, races, and occupations in the West tended to exacerbate such division among Canadian women. As Carol Bacchi has pointed out, ''although these women managed to cooperate for several female-oriented goals, ultimately they identified with their class rather than their sex.''[42]

With their commitment to middle class values, the city women's thrust for reform also tended to ignore the real, daily problems of large numbers of women who worked in factories and shops. Such organizations as the YWCA, the WCTU, and increasingly the NCWC, were concerned only that working girls be protected from the immoral, unhealthy, and seemingly unwomanly aspects of the workplace. With their distrust of labour and labour organizations and their view of women as future mothers, not members of the work-force, middle class women advocated piecemeal reform of the physical and moral environment of the workplace. Although their proposals did include better hours and wages, the establishment of nurseries to care for the children of the working woman, and new safety and training regulations, the progressive impulse accepted without reservation the hierarchical organization of the social and economic order and that the needs of women were essentially different from those of men. For the most part, equal pay and questions of promotion and advancement for women within the system – issues that many working girls considered essential – were not considered.[43]

The Suffrage Movement

These differences in concerns and, indeed, in ideas about how women could best achieve the necessary reform of society became evident when a number of women extended their activities from the social to the political realm. Initially, the call for female suffrage was sounded by a small number of women. Before the turn of the century, most women involved in the auxiliaries, missionary and charitable societies, and groups like the YWCA and the GFS believed that moral suasion and the justness of their causes would ensure reform. It became increasingly clear, however, that though women's concerns and suggestions for change were often applauded, politicians, legislators, and businessmen were not inclined to provide legislative support. Gradually, during the late 1880s and the 1890s, women across the country began to realize that while petitions, pamphlet campaigns, mass meetings, and even the newly granted right for some women to vote at the municipal level raised Canadians' awareness of national problems, they did nothing to redress them and ensure economic and social justice. The answer, it seemed, lay in getting the vote, so that through women's voice in the democratic process, Canadian society could be saved.[44]

The battle for women to get the vote was by no means a triumph of equality, of women's rights broadly defined, or the union of Canadian women for a great cause. Even at the height of the campaign, just before and throughout World War I, a number of women vocally disapproved of the proposal, asserting that politics was no place for a mother. Those who supported the campaign did so for a variety of reasons and chose a number of different vehicles to press their claims. For the 'club' women of the East and the cities, suffrage was merely the means to ensure the success of various reforms, particularly prohibition, protection of women in the workplace, and care of the nation's children. The female preoccupation remained the home and the family. Working women who supported the cause did so to promote the practical concerns of equal pay and equality in the workplace. For the farm women of the West, though no less committed to reform, the vote also came to be viewed as a means of placing particular regional interests on the national political agenda.[45] And the few women of Quebec who actively campaigned for female suffrage did so cautiously because of constant pressure from the church and public opinion to abandon their cause.

The movement for the vote, like that for reform, began at the local and provincial levels. Between 1880 and 1900, most municipalities granted the franchise to all property owners, regardless of sex, thereby affording first unmarried and then married women the means to promote their reform ideas in the community and the school system. Canada's problems, however, were national in scope, and a number of women began to agitate for the franchise provincially and then nationally. The first suffrage organization, the Toronto Women's Literary Club, founded in 1876, was a small group of middle class, educated, professional women, who lobbied not just for the vote, but also for the opening of schools and universities to women. It was not, however, until the WCTU endorsed the suffrage campaign in 1893 and the Dominion Women's Enfranchisement Association (DWEA) was founded in 1889 that the issue really entered the public sphere.

Between 1895 and 1910, suffrage or political-equality leagues were formed in each province with branches in all major urban areas. Farm associations in Ontario and the West and some labour groups, including the Toronto Labour Council and the B.C. Federation of Labour, supported women's demands for the vote, and increasingly, members of the press supported the cause. Yet, even after the National Council of Women endorsed women's suffrage in 1910 (after a heated debate and only by a vote of seventy-one to fifty-one) there was little unity among women on if or how this reform could be achieved. While the middle class 'club' women worked within provincial and national branches of the NCWC and the DWEA (renamed the Canadian Suffrage Association in 1907), western farming women most often chose to combine their efforts within the Grain Growers' Associations of Manitoba and Saskatchewan and the United Farmers of Alberta.[46]

The WCTU was one of the few, perhaps the only organization that managed to bring diverse and potentially conflicting groups of women into common action. In large part this was because its primary objective was prohibition. The demand for the vote, although a key concern, was merely the means to attain social and political reform. The WCTU, because of "its appeal to women's maternal role"[47] and its avowed purpose to strengthen the home and the family, was able to galvanize support from both men and women who remained fearful of the social and political upheaval that might result when women were granted the vote. Moreover the WCTU developed skilled leaders through their battles against the liquor interests, and were able to provide much of the leadership of the suffrage movement. One of the best-known activists for suffrage and for women's rights in general, Nellie McClung, got much of her inspiration and early training in the WCTU. As her biographer, Veronica Strong-Boag, concludes, "Nellie McClung represents that generation of women who were active in both the reform and the feminist communities. As such, she was in the mainstream of turn-of-the-century feminism."[48]

It was in the West–Manitoba, Alberta, and Saskatchewan–that women first received the provincial franchise in 1916. Within the next six years, all of Canada's provinces, with the exception of Quebec (where women did not receive the vote until 1940) had granted women the vote and also what many Canadians considered was the even more contentious right of running for public office. The provincial franchise did not ensure the triumph of prohibition or other national reforms, however, and the suffragists now concentrated their attention on the Ottawa campaign. The federal government had assiduously avoided the question for some time. But in 1917, political necessity and the demands of wartime policies finally prompted the Borden government to take action.

The Military Voters' Act of 1917 and the Wartime Elections Act were blatant attempts by the new coalition government led by Borden to ensure its success in the crucial upcoming national election. The first act granted the vote to all British subjects, female and male, who were actively participating in the Canadian armed services. The second disenfranchised conscientious objectors and naturalized Canadians born in enemy countries and enfranchised women who had close relatives serving in the armed forces of Canada or Britain. The intent of this partial female enfranchisement was to ensure that the views of men in the service could be heard, if only through their next of kin. There was certainly no assumption by the government that women had a natural right to participate in political affairs. It was not until March 1918, when Prime Minister Borden introduced the Women's Franchise Act, followed two years later by a new Dominion Elections Act, that all women were granted the right to vote. Yet even after Agnes Macphail of Ontario was elected to the House of Commons in 1921, Canadian women were still denied full participation in Parliament. Only after the Judicial Committee of the Privy Council confirmed that women were 'persons' in 1929, was that last institutional bastion of male prerogative, the Canadian Senate, at least in theory, forced to open its doors to women. As Beverley Baines shows in her chapter on women and the law, the decision in the Persons case rested solely on evidence that women were not specifically excluded from Senate membership in the British North America Act.

The victory at the federal level and the judgement in the Persons case did not resolve the question for all Canadian women. Those in Quebec, although able in the 1920s and 1930s to vote for representatives to the House of Commons and to participate at the municipal level, were denied this right provincially. In the early years, the Fédération Nationale Saint-Jean-Baptiste, the English-speaking Montreal Local Council of Women, provincial chapters of the WCTU, and various affiliates of the NCWC campaigned for equal political rights for women within the province. Fierce resistance from influential Quebecers and the church forced the Fédération to abandon its support of female suffrage in 1922.[49] A few courageous French Canadian women nonetheless continued to agitate as members of the Montreal Council of Women. Unfortunately, however, throughout the 1920s, the women of Quebec were divided along class and cultural lines. This was particularly true after 1927 when a second francophone organization, L'Alliance Canadienne pour le Vote des Femmes du Québec, was established. Over the next few years, many activities, representatives, and membership and educational campaigns were duplicated by the two groups, and as a result, efforts to pressure the government and the Quebec people to obtain the vote were weak and uneven.

It was not until the end of the decade, when Thérèse Casgrain became president of the Provincial Franchise Committee that the feminist movement in Quebec became a force to be reckoned with. Reorganized into the League of Women's Rights and with a strong leader, Quebec women made suffrage a critical issue in the public press and in the National Assembly. In 1940 the new Liberal Government of Premier Godbout, despite renewed and intense resistance, finally gave women the vote and the ability to hold provincial office.

The triumph of Canadian women in gaining full political rights did not bring with it equality. As Sandra Burt shows in her chapter on public policy, the exercise of female franchise did not initiate revolutionary changes in the political process. With few notable exceptions, provincial legislatures, the Senate, and the House of Commons have remained male preserves. Getting the vote and being recognized in law as equal participants in the political affairs of the nation were significant and necessary victories, but they did little to change the place of women in the home and in the workplace or to alter community attitudes about the 'other' sex. In the 1920s, women found these battles much more difficult to fight, and indeed, they have yet to be won.

The War Years

There is no question that the outbreak of war in 1914 and the manner of Canada's participation in it were instrumental in securing many progressive reforms, including female suffrage. Canadians expected that this momentous battle for the Empire and for Justice would be the beginning of a new and better era of national and global development. And, throughout the war years, there seemed to be indications that a new era of real equality was at hand for women.

Particularly after 1916, as the economy was fully mobilized to meet wartime demands, women moved in large numbers into the nation's factories, replacing the men who were fighting overseas or had transferred to war industries. Throughout 1917 and 1918, women became an essential part of Canada's wartime labour force. To meet new demands, the Imperial Munitions Board encouraged employers to accept women workers, who received wages 20 to 30 per cent lower than a man's for the same work.[50] Industry, it seems, welcomed their new employees.

The presence of so many women in the workplace was accepted by Canadians as part of the great patriotic effort. But public opinion held that only single women should be so engaged in industry and only on a temporary basis.

At the end of the war, women would move back into the home to resume their real work as wives and mothers. And in 1919, though some women did continue to work in the industries that had employed them before the war – textiles, tobacco, appliance, and service industries – many found themselves unemployed, forced out of their workplaces by returning men.

The end of the war did not herald a new, enlightened age. Indeed, an immediate post-war depression and mounting social and labour unrest prompted a new conservatism in Canadian society. Women, rather than being "beneficiaries of a reorganized and updated capitalist order" continued to be subject to "inequality in the workplace . . . merely modernized [in] its forms."[51] As in the pre-war years, most working women continued to be in domestic service. Nevertheless, a perceived shortage of servants prompted the governments to establish training programs in the domestic arts for young girls and to promote the immigration of single women as domestic workers.[52]

Certainly, there were some changes in circumstances and attitudes as a result of the war and industrialization. Women's magazines, clerics, employers, and the middle class now accepted that single women had a valid role to play in the paid work-force. But women in the work-force were still underpaid and relegated to the least skilled and most mundane tasks. For the most part, it continued to be assumed that girls would only work for a limited time. Marriage automatically meant the end of a 'career' and the new matron was expected to retreat to the home to look after her husband and children. Perhaps unconsciously aware that many girls might not welcome leaving the work-force, the media and the schools began to stress that homemaking was a career in itself, demanding skill and determination. In the 1920s, motherhood was raised to the level of a profession, one, it was asserted, that was essential for the development of the nation.[53] And as the prosperous 1920s gave way to the terrible 1930s, women found themselves under increasing pressure to embrace this 'new' profession of homemaker and leave the public workplace to men, who now more than ever needed to earn a wage.

After the federal victory for suffrage, what has come to be known as the first wave of feminism lost much of its drive and receded from the public political arena. But discrimination in the workplace and the prevailing social acceptance of real differences between the sexes did arouse some women activists in the 1920s and 1930s to try to redress the balance. At both the provincial and federal levels, representatives such as Agnes Macphail, Nellie McClung, and Mary Ellen Smith joined with other social and economic reformers to enact protective legislation for women and children, at home and at work. In the 1920s, most provinces passed married women's property acts and minimum-wage legislation for women and took measures to protect the nation's children. The NCWC, the YWCA, professional organizations like the

Federation of Women Teachers' Associations of Ontario (FWTAO) and nursing associations and other groups did continue to work quietly, but their activities received little public attention. For many working class women, the continued acceptance of Victorian, middle class values and of the primary virtue of motherhood by many of these groups failed to address the real concerns of the workplace.[54] For some working class women, the answer lay in political parties of the left; others turned to unionism.

In 1902, the Socialist Party of Canada had been the first political party to admit women as full members and since that time, all the various tendencies within the Canadian socialist movement had championed the cause of women's suffrage.[55] The impact of this support seems to have been negligible on the final decision to grant women the vote, but it did open the door for women's participation in political parties of the left. After the 1921 federal election, a growing number of women began to assume "an auxiliary or supportive role" within the traditional structures of all political parties. As well, a number of women remained influential within the Progressive farmers organizations, while still others continued to support socialist platforms. By the 1930s, some working class women, rejecting "both the conventional feminist mode of moderate social reform as well as the traditional partisan model of women as ancillary political workers and primary social and fund raising organizers"[56] established women's committee in the new Co-operative Commonwealth Federation, the forerunner of the New Democratic Party, to promote leadership training and other programs that assisted Canadian women. Even today, however, at both the provincial and federal levels, the number of women candidates and sitting members is grossly unrepresentative of the female population.

In the 1920s, many working class women concluded that a rather more direct and more immediately effective means of gaining economic equality was through unionism. Despite opposition from employers and working men, such groups as the International Ladies Garment Workers Union of America (ILGWU), the Amalgamated Clothing Workers of America (ACW), and the Industrial Union of Needle Trades rallied their constituents.[57] Through a number of well-publicized strikes, such as that in 1924 by the ACW against the Society Brand Clothing Company in Montreal or, in 1931, when the ILGWU of Toronto walked out for better wages, the working woman's concerns were brought to the attention of the public. Economic gains were limited at best, however. It was not until the outbreak of World War II that the aspirations of women workers to achieve real equality seemed about to be fulfilled.

As in the first war, between 1939 and 1945 women took an integral part in the great patriotic effort, a part co-ordinated this time by the national government.[58] In 1942, the National Selective Service registration identified Canadian women as part of a large labour reserve, and shortly thereafter the government began to draw selected groups of women into war-related industries. First young girls, then married, childless women, and, finally, women with children were recruited into all aspects of Canada's industrial war effort. From the outset it was clear that this policy was only to meet the wartime emergency. Women did receive some training through various government-sponsored programs for specific jobs, but the training was designed to meet the immediate needs of industry, not to enhance women's labour skills.[59] The tasks women performed in the munitions industry, for example, were sex-linked, demanding the dexterity, acceptance of repetition, and patience deemed 'natural' to women. The temporary nature of their employment was quickly brought home to women at the end of the war when government-sponsored facilities for child care closed and the tax concessions granted to married women came to an abrupt halt. Married women were clearly expected to return home; single women were expected to marry and make a home to raise their children. And though many women resisted, it was clear that that long-hoped-for new day of equality was not at hand.

Throughout the 1940s and 1950s, ideas of femininity, of fundamental differences between the sexes and of a 'woman's place' persisted and were actively espoused by that stratum of middle class women who had embraced maternal feminism at the turn of the century. But the war had given a significant number of women, for a time at least, economic independence and personal autonomy. While their husbands were overseas, many had worked and maintained the family single-handedly. Others had joined the services and had taken an active part in the war effort in Europe. Economic prosperity in the 1950s and a quiet new self-confidence in their own abilities encouraged a growing number of women to question and to challenge society's expectations.

After 1950, more and more girls completed high school, attended university, and demanded admittance to professional programs. Women's occupational organizations, like the FWTAO and nursing associations renewed their efforts to gain control over training and certification of their members. An ever-growing number of women entered the work-force, including married women who often chose to work part time as well as to raise a family. And, increasingly, middle class women became directly and actively involved in the political process.[60] Problems of inequality persisted, however. In the 1950s, women worked in rapidly expanding work ghettos within factories, service industries, and offices. They sought part-time work not only from choice, but also to provide the family with sorely needed income to make ends meet. Part-time work also gave employers a way to improve productivity and profits without the expense of a full-time worker's benefits.[61] Throughout the economy, women's wages were, and still are, well below those of men performing comparable tasks. In addition, although more girls were in school, they were usually directed into those fields considered appropriate for their sex and their overall numbers continued to be well below those of boys. And throughout the post-war period, society's ambivalence and, at times, outright hostility, particularly towards married women working, was evident in the lack of social and legislative support available to them. Nonetheless, the groundwork of education, increased affluence, and awareness resulted in a growing self-confidence and a rise in personal expectation during the 1950s, which laid the foundations for a new wave of feminism to emerge in the 1960s.

The Voice of Women (VOW), founded in 1960 to oppose nuclear-weapons testing and proliferation is considered by some to be the first self-conscious women's group in English Canada of the second wave of Canadian feminism, as Naomi Black discusses in her chapter on the second wave. Despite internal political divisions, which appeared in 1963 after the Pearson government decided to allow BOMARCS on Canadian soil, and an apparent lack of public credibility, the VOW did provide leadership training for future status-of-women activists.[62] It also illustrated the political tensions and opposition that any campaign for women's rights could and did generate in Canadian society. Middle class women in Canada, increasingly frustrated by lack of opportunities and the basic institutional inequalities in national life, continued to demand action throughout the early 1960s. By February 1967, they had successfully pressured the federal government to establish a Royal Commission to study the status of women in Canada. The commission did not solve the problem; however, it did provide women with a forum to articulate their grievances.

By 1967, although the division between the private and public spheres persisted, advanced industrialization, changes in the structure of the family, and rising expectations among all Canadians blurred and complicated an easy distinction between women's and men's roles. While many Canadians continued to assume that a woman's real work was still as a wife and mother, economic necessity, ambition, and personal circumstance continued to force and to encourage both married and single women to work.

To a casual observer, it might also have seemed that the history of women in Canada had come full circle. The women of New France and early nineteenth-century British North America too had been responsible for looking after the home as well as taking an active part in the marketplace. There were significant differences in the two situations, however. For the first time, a significant proportion of women in Canada in the 1960s was questioning the very basic tenets of a paternalistic, male-dominated society. And although divisions based on occupation, class, and location persisted, there now existed a sense of unity among an increasing number of Canadian women, one that would have been impossible in the eighteenth or nineteenth centuries. In 1967, women, as they had done for hundreds of years, presented radically differing solutions to their problems. Nonetheless, most were agreed that traditional assumptions of a woman's place and a woman's work had to change.

Jane Errington

SUGGESTED READINGS

Armstrong, Pat, and Hugh Armstrong, *The Double Ghetto: Canadian Women and Their Segregated Work*, 2nd. edition. Toronto: McClelland and Stewart, 1984.

Gorham, Deborah, "The Canadian Suffragists," in Gwen Matheson, ed., *Women in the Canadian Mosaic*. Toronto: Peter Martin Associates, 1976.

Griffiths, Naomi, *Penelope's Web*. Toronto: Oxford University Press, 1976.

Kealey, Linda, ed., *A Not Unreasonable Claim: Women and Reform in Canada, 1880s–1920s*. Toronto: Women's Educational Press, 1979.

Light, Beth, and Joy Parr, eds., *Canadian Women on the Move, 1867–1920*. Toronto: New Hogtown Press and OISE, 1983.

Prentice, Alison, and Susan Mann Trofimenkoff, eds., *The Neglected Majority II*. Toronto: McClelland and Stewart, 1985.

Strong-Boag, Veronica, and Anita Clair Fellman, eds., *Rethinking Canada: The Promise of Women's History*. Toronto: Copp-Clark Pitman, 1986.

Trofimenkoff, Susan Mann, and Alison Prentice, eds., *The Neglected Majority I*. Toronto: McClelland and Stewart, 1977.

Chapter Three

The Canadian Women's Movement: The Second Wave

In the 1960s, no one expected the women's movement to re-emerge. In prosperous postwar Canada, women seemed to be doing well in both economic and political terms; their remaining problems looked like temporary disadvantages. Women were increasingly getting the education needed for better-paying work, and public opinion supported their right to work and to get equal pay (legally guaranteed since the 1950s). Even in Quebec women had been enfranchised for almost a generation. There were still few women in the federal Parliament, but the tradition of having one woman in the cabinet seemed secure, while local women politicians like Ottawa Mayor Charlotte Whitton were highly visible and vocal – often objecting to any specific concern for the status of women.

When something most often called the women's liberation movement gained media attention late in the decade, first in France and the United States, it was as part of a student movement radicalized by racism and imperialism: women were to be 'liberated,' like minorities and colonial dependencies. The newly visible feminism was initially interpreted as simply another, relatively unimportant part of an era of activism. In Canada the burning national issue was linguistic-cultural: a question of national unity played out in federal-provincial conferences and royal commissions. The Canadian student revolt was late and muted and, like it, the 'new' women's movement was seen as an American import. In Canada, as elsewhere, there was general astonishment when feminism proved able to tap massive discontent among even the most privileged women.

The renewed activism among women continued throughout the 1970s, and continued also to receive a real and increasingly favourable response. A significant minority of Canadian women were even willing to call themselves 'feminists' – 42 per cent in a poll taken for *Weekend* magazine in 1979, 5 per cent more in one taken for *Chatelaine* in 1986 – and by 1986 some three-quarters of Canadians agreed that 'the feminist movement' had had a positive rather than a negative effect on Canadian society.[1]

Looking back, we can see that feminist stirrings were unexpected for the same reason that they occurred: during the 1950s and 1960s, women's domestic obligations and their self-images had remained virtually unchanged while their activities had altered drastically. Most importantly, women had retained responsibility for the household and family at the same time as their participation in the paid labour force had increased massively, reaching the previous wartime peak in 1967. Nevertheless, throughout their lives women continued to put success in marriage and child-rearing high among their goals. They also continued to perform, and expected to perform, the large majority of necessary domestic tasks. Even by the mid-1980s, there was general agreement in Canada only that husbands of women in the paid labour force should 'help' with the housework; the very wording showed whose task housework still was.[2] The result of all this was, unsurprisingly, growing strains and tensions for women.

More specifically, by the 1960s Canadian women had two sorts of grievances that fuelled the women's movement. An old set, identified as feminist in an earlier era, related to the areas where women were basically the same as men but were treated in a different, disadvantageous manner, in effect excluded from men's rights and privileges. There was still more outright discrimination than most people realized, including explicit or implicit refusals to allow women to hold family property or citizenship or Indian status on the same terms as men. Where the barriers were officially down and women shared in 'male' activities, they did it without the rewards men could expect. Feminists were to identify a 'glass ceiling' that stopped women at a certain level: they could vote, but few would become lawmakers and none would become premiers; they could graduate from university and even from professional schools, but they could not expect to be judges or surgeons; they could work for pay, but it would be for less pay than men received, and they were unlikely to become rich by their own achievements.

Furthermore, the few women who succeeded in public life found they had to do it the men's way, hiding their feminine qualities, neglecting or concealing their private lives, dressing for success, learning the conflictual 'games mother never taught us.' Respondents to a poll posed to 'successful' Canadian businesswomen complained that there was too much pressure on women to be good at everything. They agreed emphatically (72 per cent) that "to get ahead in this world a woman has to be twice as good at what she does as a man is," but 82 per cent of them wanted a daughter they might have to be "as interested in pursuing a career as getting married and raising a family." Men did not have to respond to such multiple, conflicting expectations.[3]

The second, new set of grievances was therefore related to women's specific qualities, characteristics that they valued and thought society appreciated insufficiently. Women wanted to stay different without being disadvantaged.

More positively, they wanted credit for their valuable female qualities, as well as protection from their vulnerabilities in a male-dominated world. Women's situation in relation to the combination of paid labour and domestic responsibilities crystallized the old and the new demands: they were not compensated for their 'double shift' of paid and unpaid work, they were not protected against violence in or out of the home, and their socially valuable tasks of public and private nurturance were unrecognized.

These conditions produced individual dissatisfactions, felt by individual women even if largely unvoiced. In the aggregate, the resulting grievances implied an image of a more desirable society – one in which women were treated as well as men but also one in which public life had changed because women were equally active in it. For most Canadian women, their continued commitment to home and family life was a value they cherished and which they thought society ought also to cherish. A society in which women were equally influential would be one that took women's preferences and experience seriously, and that was transformed by the result.

The basic situation of Canadian women was shared by women throughout the industrialized world. This goes a long way towards explaining why the revolt of the women students did not die down in the early 1970s like the activities of the male-dominated organizations from which they broke away. In addition, as the organizational history of contemporary women is gradually pieced together, the immediate causes of the postwar feminism emerge as different in each location. Its successes and failures – and the form they took – were related to the history of women and of the women's movement in each specific place. Canada's newly visible feminist activism inherited the situation and the goals of its predecessor groups, which are described in Jane Errington's history of early Canadian women in this book. This occurred in part because of the survival of these groups and their role in producing a 'second wave' of feminism. For that and other reasons, the long-held goals of the Canadian women's movement were reinvigorated to respond to the conditions of women's postwar lives.

It was not a 'rebirth of feminism.' Feminism and women's groups had not simply died off at the successful end of the suffrage campaigns. As we begin to uncover the history of women in the interwar and early postwar years, it becomes clear that, as might be expected, women like Nellie McClung and Helen Gregory MacGill moved with their customary energy to make use of the new instruments of influence for which they had fought so hard. After enfranchisement, organized women were engaged in fewer concentrated campaigns, had less publicity and less success, but their activity never stopped. In the 1960s, with the appearance of new groups, the pace quickened and the visibility increased. The notion of a second wave catches what was happening, reminding us that in social change, as in oceans, calmer patches are followed by new and stronger peaks of activity. The second wave also implies the image of a tide pouring in, each wave going further up the beach, with a continuity of organizational and individual efforts over time and a hope of progress.

The Components of the Second Wave

It is now clear that women's liberation groups were not always the first active in feminism's second wave. Two different sorts of new women's organizations began independently at much the same time, towards the end of the 1960s: those which grew out of the student movement and also liberal-feminist groups which were organized specifically to pressure for government action in relation to the status of women. These latter groups were often similar in membership, structure, and beliefs to the women's organizations of the first wave; in Canada they were, initially, mainly coalitions of surviving first-wave groups. They were, nevertheless, something new, founded in response to the situation of women in the 1960s. Over time, they developed new policy goals and, sometimes, new feminist analyses. Established women's movement policies, such as opposition to pornography and to violence against women, support of reproductive freedom and of peace, and the quest for equal pay, all acquired new importance in ways compatible with the analyses made by the members of women's liberation.

The groups which called themselves women's liberation brought into Canadian feminism for the first time a large infusion of younger women, students, or ex-students. These in turn brought with them, from the student movement, a significant commitment to a Marxist or at least an economic, class-oriented analysis of women's situation; they were to identify themselves as Marxist or socialist feminists. Distrust of government and a belief in revolutionary change was accompanied by organizational novelties: small non-hierarchical 'cells' and 'consciousness-raising' through small-group discussion. All these were new to the Canadian women's movement. But the women's liberation slogan "the personal is political" had close affinities to the views of nineteenth- and twentieth-century social feminists who thought politics should be cleaned up the way houses were.

In Canada, the second wave of feminism made its first appearance, unrecognized, with the establishment in 1960 of the Voice of Women, followed by the 1966 reorganization of a large number of existing Quebec women's organizations into the Fédération des femmes du Québec and the Association féminine d'education et d'action sociale. In the same year, 1966, a Committee for Equality for Women was organized to obtain a government enquiry into the status of women. Its achievement, the establishment of the Royal Commission on the Status of Women (RCSW) in 1967, was the first success of the second wave of Canadian feminism. At that point in time the women's caucuses that were to become the Canadian women's liberation movement were in the process of forming.

The second wave of feminism also saw, in Canada as in all countries, numerous new women's groups, mostly small and local, which emerged to express the interests of specific categories of women. Women's caucuses and groups were revitalized within unions, religions, and political parties. More marginalized groups of women began to organize, including, in Canada, groups of Indian and non-status Indian women focusing on the issues related to women's right to Indian status; black women who formed a national congress; lesbian mothers co-ordinating the legal tactics for retaining custody of their children; farm women voicing their concern about the survival of the family farm and their own status in it; and wives of armed services members claiming the right to speak out politically in their own interest.[4] As the 1970s advanced, there were also more and more new women-organized, more-or-less feminist service or cultural groups for women, often the successors to the women's liberation movement: rape crisis centres, health centres, and abortion referral services; transition houses for battered women, hostels for homeless women and for teen-age mothers; women's centres and women's studies programmes; women's magazines, journals, and presses; women's music and arts centres and companies. Such groups and institutions continue to appear and disappear, often with short life-spans.

In the context of this book, our interest is in those parts of the second-wave movement which can be seen as influencing the treatment of women by Canadian society and, more specifically, by governments. These were the counterparts and often the causes of the government attitudes and activities detailed in the chapters by Sandra Burt and Beverley Baines; they are the better recorded parts of the movement. But it is important to remember that the vitality and importance of feminism were crucially dependent on the myriad small groups that influenced both individuals and the larger society simply because they existed.

In addition, any comprehensive account of the women's movement – which is not attempted here – will have to include some discussion of the resistance to the second wave of feminism by conservative women. In Canada, this backlash has been slow to emerge, and in the late 1980s it is only beginning to become significant. Groups like the anti-abortionist REAL Women and Alberta's AFWUF are related to the feminism they attack.[5] Furthermore, they, too, responded to the surviving inequities in the treatment of women; they, too, in their misinformed defence of a traditional family that no longer exists, attempted to obtain recognition and reward for the distinctive abilities and activities of women.

Royal Commission on the Status of Women

In general, it makes sense to date the second wave of feminism from the appearance of new women's organizations in the 1960s. Even though the first among these resembled their predecessors, they survived and changed into something unarguably part of a new era. In Canada, the group that seems to have been the earliest, the Voice of Women, picked up in 1960 the feminist pacifism of the interwar period. Voice of Women was formed in response to a newspaper column by Lotta Dempsey asking desperately whether women couldn't do something to deal with international conflict and the threat of war. Hundreds of women wrote in and thousands eventually joined a grass-roots organization whose activity over the next decades extended from anti-nuclear vigils to international conferences and protest marches. To their great pride, Secretary of State for External Affairs Howard Green gave the group credit for Canada's delay in joining the missile alert at the time of Cuban Missile Crisis. Guided by scientist Ursula Franklin, Voice members presented to the government thousands of baby teeth documenting how strontium-90 in fall-out from nuclear testing had got into the food chain and into the bones of children; this demonstration played a role in producing the 1963 test-ban treaty. Other campaigns, ranging from knitting for the children of North Vietnam to boycotting war toys, mobilized a large number of women at the community level, and helped to shape public opinion about Cold War and environmental issues.[6]

Voice of Women showed a familiar pattern of membership–married women with children – and motivation – concern for family well-being and therefore for a safe, peaceful, and now non-nuclear world. Initially, this group did not look like anything new, but over the years it steadily became more political and more feminist. Many of its members went on to be active in other second-wave groups and in mainstream politics. Representatives of Voice of Women were important in the series of events, beginning in 1966, that produced a Royal Commission on the Status of Women and, later, the national women's organization formed in 1972 to pressure for implementation of the commission's recommendations. This was the National Action Committee on the Status of Women (NAC), an umbrella group, which by 1986 could claim to represent five million women in more than five hundred organizations.

After the founding of Voice of Women, the next important surge of feminist organization took place in Quebec. The Fédération des femmes du Québec, established in 1966 as a follow-up to the twenty-fifth anniversary celebrations of the enfranchisement of women in Quebec, drew together most of the existing women's groups, including some anglophone ones. At the same time, the Association féminine d'éducation et d'action sociale consolidated and reactivated two of the other, older, more Catholic women's groups, which focused on the interests of housewives and of women working in family businesses. By the mid-1960s, a significant number of the existing francophone groups were realigned, and ready for action. The two large coalitions were in close and friendly contact, linked also with Voice of Women: suffragist Thérèse Casgrain was the chief organizer of the Fédération and of la Voix des femmes, the Quebec branch of Voice of Women, as well as second national president of Voice of Women.[7]

It is a pattern of continuity and overlap, which makes it look as if there was no break between the first and second wave of the Canadian women's movement. Yet there was. To begin with, the push that produced the Royal Commission was itself something unprecedented.

The campaign for the Royal Commission on the Status of Women began publicly in 1966, when Doris Anderson wrote in a *Chatelaine* editorial:

> Reluctant as I am to suggest one more be added to the groaning shelfful of past Royal Commissions, I believe it's time we had a study on the status of women in Canada today.

Anderson justified the request by the level and nature of women's participation in education and the work force and concluded, reassuringly:

> what we don't need in a commission is an all-woman witch-hunt. We do need a forward-looking commission composed equally of impartial men and women prepared to take a cool twentieth-century approach to our problems. Because these questions affect us all – men, women and children, and for our own collective good, we should set about getting some answers.[8]

Under Anderson's leadership, *Chatelaine*, the largest of Canada's popular women's magazines, had come to incorporate a fair amount of feminist content; she had rejected the offered serialization of Betty Friedan's *The Feminine Mystique* on the grounds that *Chatelaine* had already covered most of the same subjects.[9] In this editorial she was deliberately supporting an initiative spearheaded by Laura Sabia, who in 1966 was president of the Canadian Federation of University Women. Successful city councillor in St. Catharines, Ontario, unsuccessful provincial candidate, and popular radio talk-show host, Sabia was a charmer and a rabble-rouser, endlessly energetic as a campaigner and organizer, following in the line of the women like Emily Murphy who energized the first wave of Canadian feminism.

The thirty-two-member Committee on Equality for Women Sabia drew together was made up of representatives of the large voluntary and professional women's organizations, including the most vocal and consistent campaigners for woman suffrage.[10] These groups had continued to be active, if relatively unnoticed; for instance, the National Council of Jewish Women had an early involvement with promoting birth control and the Business and Professional Women's Clubs had been important in producing the equal pay legislation of the 1950s. Their attitudes can be inferred from their ready response to Sabia's appeal; in the same year, their counterparts in the United States had explicitly refused suggestions that they become publicly involved in issues of women's equality.

The Committee on Equality for Women could reasonably claim to represent the organized women of Canada. Although the Fédération des femmes du Québec did not participate actively in drawing up a presentation to the Prime Minister, Thérèse Casgrain and Réjane Laberge-Colas (first president of the Fédération and later, first woman to be appointed judge in a Canadian Superior Court), joined the delegation to Ottawa. The women's groups of all three political parties also supported the brief, as did a considerable number of women's professional and service groups; there were some sixty observers accompanying the five women who made up the official delegation. That support of women meant support of national unity should have been obvious; that the second wave of feminism was going to be federalist was also clear.

The Pearson government nevertheless virtually ignored the group's first mildly posed request. Laura Sabia was provoked into what the *Globe and Mail* reported as an "ultimatum to the Government: establish a royal commission or face the consequences":

> "We're tired of being nice about trying to get an official enquiry into women's rights in Canada," Mrs. Sabia said. "If we don't get a royal commission by the end of this month, we'll use every tactic we can. And if we have to use violence, damn it, we will."[11]

Sabia threatened to march two million women on Ottawa, which got her the headlines she needed. In terms of specific timing, her group was responsible for the establishment of the Royal Commission. But we may wonder whether Prime Minister Pearson (who, with his customary adroitness, had evaded any face-to-face meeting with the women's delegation) was more than embarrassed by such hollow threats.

Pearson's eventual action probably responded to the same inter-related patterns of women's education and work that explain the second wave of feminism. From the perspective of the government, women's lesser rewards and lesser opportunities to participate in the expanding economy translated into a lesser contribution to national growth. Doris Anderson made this point in her 1966 editorial: "Perhaps we should pause in our breast-beating about the brain drain to the United States," she wrote, "and consider whether we are using all of our own mental resources."

In addition, there were political reasons to placate women whom the 1966 approach to the government showed to be dissatisfied. In Cabinet, the Honourable Judy LaMarsh put up a lonely but highly visible fight on behalf of women and a commission of enquiry. In Parliament, the New Democratic Party, urged on by their only woman M.P., Grace MacInnis, used the issue of a women's commission as yet another handy weapon against a government that lacked an absolute majority. By 1965 Canadian women were voting at approximately the same level as men and participating in campaign activities almost as frequently; women's votes might possibly be swayed.

The request for a royal commission was ideally suited to the double purposes of getting the necessary information about fully integrating women into the work-force while appeasing and possibly defusing any feminist activism. This was a period of numerous royal commissions in Canada, most conspicuously the Royal Commission on Bilingualism and Biculturalism (1963–71). It is a truism of Canadian politics that one way to deal with insistent claims is to "royal-commission them to death." "There was a general consensus in editorials all across the country that the Commission would be pigeon-holed and forgotten," wrote Florence Bird, the American-born Chairman of the Commission: "It was also often suggested that the Commission was a political gimmick to allow women to let off steam and to appease Judy LaMarsh and Laura Sabia's cohorts."[12]

As occasionally happens, the Royal Commission on the Status of Women turned out to be far more dynamic, even progressive than might have been expected. For instance, Jeanne Lapointe, a Quebec academic selected for cultural (and political) reasons and for her experience with the Parent Commission on education in Quebec, was transformed by the experience into an active radical feminist. The unprecedentedly extensive public hearings held by the RCSW in fourteen cities over a period of ten months had a major impact on the media and on the public, and also on all the members of the group.

Most importantly, Elsie Gregory MacGill, past president of the Canadian Federation of Business and Professional Women, first Canadian woman to be an aeronautical engineer, was effectively the vice-president of the RCSW. Born in British Columbia, she could be seen to have a regional significance and to represent both women in business and women in science, a counterpart for the Quebec/education, Prairies/farm, and Maritimes/law roles of commissioners Jeanne Lapointe, Lola Lange, and Judge Doris Ogilvie respectively.[13] MacGill was an ardent, committed, and highly effective third-generation feminist and it was really she who educated the commissioners. Later she was to be active in NAC and other organizations founded in the 1970s to implement the RCSW's report. The royal commission thus inherited, from both founders and participants, the active tradition of the Canadian women's movement. It passed on that tradition through successor organizations and through the document they took as their agenda, the 1970 report of the Royal Commission on the Status of Women.

Canadian Women's Liberation

The key period for the second wave of the Canadian women's movement was the years 1967 to 1970. The activities of the royal commission in this period resulted in a significant increase of public awareness of women's situation. The same period produced women's liberation and radical feminism in Canada. These latter groups, which drew substantial public attention, can take much of the credit for directing attention to such crucial women's issues as equal pay, abortion, and violence against women. The groups themselves were crucial in the cooperative efforts that got such issues both onto the agenda for public policy and into the consciousness of individual women.

At the time of the Committee for Equality's project for a royal commission, the future members of women's liberation still identified with the student left. But they had become aware that, within their own movement, they were exploited as quasi-secretarial help and as sex objects, while the men who ran that movement failed to respond to a plea for liberation at home. In addition, they were unable to persuade the male students that the oppression of women was a valid political issue. Like their foremothers, they were faced with the refusal to allow women a voice in politics–in their case, revolutionary politics. Finally, following earlier precedents, they organized autonomous, women-only groups that could work for both women and society as a whole.

By 1967, Toronto housed one of the five women's liberation groups in North America; in 1968 a Feminist Action League appeared at Simon Fraser University, then a Women's Caucus in Vancouver. In 1969 similar groups were established in Regina, Saskatoon, Winnipeg, Ottawa, Kingston, Guelph, Hamilton region, Halifax, Sudbury, Thunder Bay, and Edmonton; Montreal Women's Liberation began in the fall of 1969 among students and faculty at McGill and Sir George Williams universities. In a student movement that was continental, the Canadian groups do not seem anything special to American historians. But their grievances were articulated somewhat differently, and the Canadian segments of the movement were indeed significantly different.

The 1967 document "Sisters, Brothers, Lovers, Listen . . . " shows just how Canadian the members of women's liberation were. The piece's authors, the women's caucus of the Toronto student organization, the New Left Caucus, still hoped to persuade their comrades to recognize the significance of sexism. They continued to focus to some extent on the history that the Canadian student activists shared with the antecedents of women's liberation in the United States: "male chauvinism" in the student movement was compared to "a civil rights organization with a leadership of southern racists." But the women reluctantly went on to consider secession; "if we are really serious about changing our role, then we better start doing it – no one is going to do it for us." And they ended with an image drawn from Lord Durham and used by Egerton Ryerson and Mackenzie King: "We are going to be the typers of letters and distributors of leaflets (hewers of wood and drawers of water) no longer."[14]

They also tapped Canadian traditions in other ways. Although "Sisters, Brothers . . . " voiced the resentment felt by the student-activist women who found they were expected to make coffee, not policy, women who were part of the Canadian women's liberation groups agreed that they did not leave with the same anger as their U.S. counterparts. In this, they saw an echo of the history of the Canadian reform movement. Groups such as the Grain Growers of Alberta had supported women both in their suffragism and in their desire for separate, single-sex organizations. For the Canadian second wave, Manitoba suffragist Nellie McClung became a heroine once more. Later, Canadian feminists were to be more selective about their history, so that the pacifist and socialist strands in Canadian suffragism were often preferred to the more patriotic and gender-oriented ones; Nellie McClung was then criticized for nativism and for her support of the Canadian entry into the First World War.[15] But feminist attention to these individuals and issues in itself differentiated the Canadian movement from the American one.

In Quebec, the situation of feminists in the student movement was both similar to and different from that of those in the rest of Canada, with nationalism playing a crucial role. The anglophone sector of the movement was the first to make its appearance, and the student feminists at Sir George Williams and McGill universities then encouraged establishment of the first francophone group, le Front pour la libération des femmes du Québec. But the very name of the French group indicates its context: it was a response to the marginalization of women in the independentist Front pour la libération du Québec. The first public action of Toronto Women's Liberation had been, in 1968, an intervention in a winter bikini contest, protesting the marketing of women as sex objects. In contrast, the first public action of the feminist Front was a protest in 1969 against governmental repression of trade-union and other leftist-nationalist activity in Montreal.[16]

Many feminist issues were shared between Quebec and the rest of Canada; the priorities and the action were not. In 1970, women's liberation groups all across Canada joined in an Abortion Caravan that ended in Ottawa on Mother's Day with a demonstration that closed up Parliament, as women chained themselves to the Visitors' Gallery. The same day, the Front had its own pro-choice demonstration in Montreal; they had refused an invitation to join the caravaners on the grounds that they denied the legitimacy of the federal regulations. Challenging present and future governments of Quebec to serve women better, they placed their feminist efforts squarely in the context of independentism.

The effects of Quebec nationalism thus extended even to reproductive rights, the issue that most transcended the differences within the women's movement. In 1968, the McGill Student Society had produced the widely distributed *Birth Control Handbook*, illegal until the 1969 reform of the Criminal Code that permitted advertising and sale of contraceptives. The Front helped to translate and distribute the handbook and, with Montreal Women's Liberation, staffed a follow-up abortion referral service. But in 1970 the francophones in women's liberation in Quebec expelled the anglophones, dividing up even the referral services. The struggle for independence, central among leftist issues in Quebec, meant that linguistic barriers were symbolic of Quebec identity: anglophone feminists were seen as representatives of the federalist 'colonizers.' Furthermore, autonomous, women-only feminist organizations faced practically insurmountable obstacles, for they seemed to deny the priority of the national struggle. The Front survived only into 1971, producing the first issue of its important newspaper, *Québécoises deboutte!* Its successor, the Centre des femmes, struggled on for three years (1972–75) active mainly in abortion referral and in producing further issues of the newspaper.

Marxist and socialist feminism in Quebec, closely related to the strongly nationalist and well-organized union movement and to the independentist Parti Québécois, was effective only within those mainstream groups; from the early seventies, all had status-of-women committees. Their major achievements were, under the Parti Québécois government, reforms in family and related law and a policy tolerating free-standing abortion clinics. The Front commun of public service unions also succeeded, in 1979, in obtaining generous paid maternity leave for its female members.

In anglophone Canada, the pattern was different, in that women's liberation and its successors succeeded in cooperating with other feminist groups, including those of the first wave. In this case, Canadian issues and Canadian nationalism served to unify the different segments of the women's movement. Within the student movement – which shaped the founders of women's liberation – there was increasing hostility to the American war resisters who came to Canada and expected to lead the left opposition. "The problem the Canadian left faces is not the draft," stated a 1969 pamphlet of the Toronto Women's Liberation Group; "It is American imperialism."[17] In the 1960s, that included the cultural imperialism represented by the American intellectuals who came to fill the faculties and swell the student bodies of the expanding Canadian universities.

Such views made women's liberation converge somewhat with the Voice of Women. Socialist feminists shared from the start Voice's opposition to the Vietnam War; as both groups became more nationalist, they protested Canada's complicity in the process through arms sales and membership in NATO and NORAD. Both also came to share the general nationalist response to American cultural and economic as well as political influence. Possibly even more importantly, Voice of Women – as well as the surviving first-wave groups – had in common with women's liberation the Canadian feminist conviction that women were more able than men to protect Canadian values, including the equal treatment of women and active resistance to American influence.

In addition, the different women's groups became more similar as Voice of Women became more explicitly feminist and less concentrated on anti-nuclear issues. Peace and environmental concerns were close: both related to the world in which children were to live. Voice of Women found itself asking for a moratorium on exploration of the North until the environmental issues were investigated, worried about dumping of radioactive substances, and calling for Canadian withdrawal from NATO and NORAD as well as refusal of nuclear weapons. Environmental concerns included concerns for the social and political climate, and for the possible influence of women there. Halifax Voice made an investigation of the employment of blacks in Halifax and in 1972 Toronto Voice started a daughter group called Women in Political Action to assist women to become active in conventional politics. Women had commonalities across language and culture, and Voice had a Quebec branch, so Voice became a supporter of bilingualism, biculturalism, and Quebec's special identity. These are all leftist – and women's liberation – issues.

At the same time, liberation groups turned towards direct services for women. Class analysis of women's oppression made the middle class liberationists set up organizations devoted to the needs of poor and needy women much as their foremothers had. Their analysis of femininity as an ideology and interest in reproduction as an analogue to production directed their attention to education, child care, and the family – 'women's issues.' Job-training and referral were obvious needs of working class women. In addition, women's liberation groups became involved with health-care and with referral services related to reproduction, as well as with hostels and counselling services for the predominantly female victims of public and family violence (battery, incest, rape). In spite of a primary goal of political education, they found themselves engaged in the long-established tradition of feminist philanthropy.

Radical Feminism

Meanwhile, Voice of Women continued to campaign against the sale of war toys. How more effectively could mothers make known their opposition to war? and how more effectively could they influence the social conditioning of sons as well as daughters? The concern with sexual stereotyping was, of course, shared by the liberal-feminist groups who critiqued textbooks and mass media for their image of women as dependent and inferior. But Voice of Women's commitment to notions of women's specificity aligned them less with liberal feminism than with the groups calling themselves 'radical feminist,' which grew out of women's liberation, beginning in 1969 in Toronto and much later in Quebec.

There were ironies here, for radical feminists were heterodox in their life styles and in their views of the family, explicitly theoretical in their analyses, and committed to the liberationist procedures of consciousness-raising. They were very different from the wives-and-mothers of Voice of Women. Indeed, it was from radical feminism that women often moved to feminist lesbianism. Yet radical feminists shared with Voice of Women the central assumptions that women were the crucial agents of social change, and that men and male values were responsible for what was wrong with society.

In general, the Canadian women's liberation groups in their first years disliked and rejected the very term 'feminist,' associating it with an ideology "in which the critique of the family usually takes precedence over the critique of capitalism."[18] Proudly socialist and proudly nationalist, members of women's liberation initially felt that 'feminism' identified an American movement that, unlike the Canadian, promoted a sort of sex war between men and women. Later, they developed the notion of socialist feminism, and Canadian socialist-feminist academics did important work on the concept of 'reproductive' domestic labour. Here was a basis for more convergence among women's groups, for the household was always central to the analyses made by radical feminism. In fact, Bonnie Kreps, who had been active in New York Radical Feminists, seems to have started the first radical-feminist group in Canada in 1969, by walking out of a Toronto Women's Liberation meeting which refused to accept that "women were oppressed in the household."[19]

For the radical feminists, liberation was related to asserting the uniqueness of women's situation; their earliest goal tended to be obliteration of gender roles as a basis of oppression. In Canada, a major target was the conditioning of children into (aggressive) men and (submissive) women; the logic produced campaigns to allow girl children to wear comfortable jeans instead of seemly skirts to school. Such concerns clearly have affinities to VOW's campaigns against war toys as part of the process of socialization to male violence. Like Voice of Women and like much else in the Canadian women's movement, Toronto's New Feminists started from an insistence on the uniqueness and unique value of women's experience, and on the absolute right of women to define it for themselves and to reshape society accordingly. Voice and the first-wave survivors made such claims in the name of their own families and society; radical feminists spoke for women as a group; all called for a drastically reformed society responsive to women's values and priorities.

Toronto New Feminists seem to be the only radical-feminist group in English Canada to have left records, including a newspaper; they voluntarily dissolved in 1973. In Quebec an important radical-feminist paper, *Les Têtes de pioche*, was influential beginning in 1976. Certainly, radical-feminist groups or fragments must have existed elsewhere. They seem to have begun and continued in a pattern of political cooperation with other women's organizations. Like the Canadian women's liberation groups, they had connections with the National Action Committee on the Status of Women and, like them, they co-operated in lobbying campaigns such as those connected with the inclusion of 'sex' in human rights codes. More recently, groups such as Women Against Violence Against Women, most often associated with Take-Back-the-Night marches protesting street violence, were clearly radical feminist in orientation, as was the group attempting to organize the Feminist Party of Canada beginning in 1979. The strong coalitions against pornography also seem to have had radical-feminist inspiration, as do many elements of Women's Studies in Canadian universities. The impact of radical feminism can be recognized by an insistence on the primacy of gender as a basis of women's oppression, and usually also by the rule that no men can participate in the group.

But these last are, as we have noted, views shared by many elements of the Canadian women's movement over time, in both first and second waves. In general, a high degree of overlap and relatively amiable co-existence are major characteristics of the second wave of the Canadian women's movement. They produce (and are in part produced by) the over-all umbrella of the National Action Committee on the Status of Women and the overlapping coalitions within it, as well as by the relationship all groups share with the federal government. At a provincial level similar patterns of mutual toleration and cooperation exist, at least in public. For instance, in 1976, the British Columbia Federation of Women, essentially a socialist-feminist group, was able to organize a massive demonstration and lobbying effort at the provincial parliament to protest when the Social Credit government cut off funding to women's groups.

Quebec, of course, is always an exception. Even when cooperation within the province is possible, groups find it hard to work across linguistic boundaries and even harder to collaborate with the necessarily federalist national women's groups. It is remarkable that the Fédération des femmes du Québec and the Association féminine d'education et d'action sociale have been members of NAC during most of its existence.

After the Royal Commission

The Royal Commission on the Status of Women reported in 1970. The National Council of Women and the Fédération des femmes du Québec had been given advance access to the *Report* so that they could prepare summaries in English and French for wide distribution. Four underlying principles were stated in the introductory section; they encompassed the double set of demands of the second wave.

The first principle was "that women should be free to choose whether or not to take employment outside their homes." It recognized women's double role, noted the validity of both sectors of it, and gave women the right to autonomous decisions about their own choices. It also obligated society to make the considerable changes that would make such choices realistically possible. The same social obligation, as well as the desirability of major change in men's domestic responsibilities, was implied in principle two: "the care of children is a responsibility to be shared by the mother, the father and society." Principle three was that "society has a responsibility for women because of pregnancy and child-birth, and special treatment related to maternity will always be necessary," a recognition of women's biological specificity and its value. Treatment of women exactly as if they were men was not acceptable. Finally, the *Report* specifically noted in principle four the existence of discrimination and the need for affirmative action to conteract its consequences: "in certain areas women will for an interim period require special treatment to overcome the adverse effects of discriminatory practices."[20]

Guided by these principles, the commissioners wrote 167 recommendations, whose implications were radical indeed. The majority of the recommendations dealt with direct or indirect discrimination against women. Some went further.

For instance, they recommended a national day-care act committing the federal government to contribute to both operating expenses and capital costs. They also recommended adoption of the principle of equal pay for work of equal value (replacing the existing regulations, which provided only equal pay for equal work). And they recommended that abortion be permitted "by a qualified medical practitioner on the sole request of any woman who has been pregnant for twelve weeks or less."[21] None of these measures has yet been fully adopted, although there is limited federal and provincial legislation related to equal pay for work of equal value, and in January 1988, the Supreme Court ruled the federal abortion law unconstitutional.

Those who had been active in demanding the RCSW remained active in the follow-up period. Impatient when the government did not produce immediate responses to the Royal Commission Report, they turned the Committee on Equality for Women into a National Ad Hoc Committee on the Status of Women in Canada. It met during 1971, adding a number of new groups, including both the liberal-feminist Manitoba Action Committee on the Status of Women, Toronto Women's Liberation, and Toronto's radical-feminist New Feminists.[22] This group presented a substantial brief to the government, then early in 1972 became the continuing umbrella organization, the National Action Committee on the Status of Women (NAC).

NAC dropped the optimistic 'ad hoc' from its title because the government would not fund ad hoc groups, and money was wanted, first for "Strategy for Change," the national conference which inaugurated NAC in the spring of 1972, and then for continuing funding (on which NAC still depends, its constituent groups making only token contributions). As the continuation of the Committee on Equality for Women, it precedes the emergence of women's liberation in Canada.

The Strategy for Change conference set a pattern for cooperation as it inaugurated NAC, with Voice of Women president Helen Tucker in the chair, Elsie Gregory MacGill as keynote speaker, Toronto New Feminists running the workshops, and over five hundred women from more than forty groups present. A group of militants protested what they viewed as excessive moderation. But although a radical caucus finally presented a minority report calling, among other things, for all-women media crews, the whole conference agreed to endorse all of the RCSW recommendations, except the proposal for Status of Women Councils appointed by the government.

NAC quickly became and remained an almost all-encompassing umbrella group, which included through indirect affiliation a considerable number of organizations that did not belong directly. For the 1984 federal elections, the group was able to pull off the considerable coup of sponsoring a public, nationally televised debate on women's issues between the leaders of the three major parties. The group had sufficient acceptability as representative of Canadian women that, in the mid-1980s anti-feminists began to challenge it.

The Impact of the Second Wave

Second-wave feminism in Canada is clearly distinctive. There seems to be no equivalent elsewhere to the way in which the National Action Committee on the Status of Women was able to incorporate into its membership – as it still does – first-wave survivor groups, representatives of women's liberation, the new pressure groups organized around the RCSW recommendations, and the many sectoral women's groups, as well as the cultural and service inheritors of women's liberation.

If we sort out the elements of NAC's membership in the ideological terms most commonly used to discuss feminism, we can say that the organization managed to accommodate groups whose ideologies ran the gamut of feminist belief from liberal through Marxist and socialist to radical, as discussed by Lorraine Code in the first chapter of this book. Putting it another way, we can say that NAC members ranged along almost all of the possibilities of equity feminism, which extends existing belief systems to include women. They were, by and large, groups that were separate from corresponding male or mixed groups because those organizations failed or refused to incorporate into their agendas the demands made by women. NAC members also included, however, organizations that subscribed to social-feminist beliefs extending women's domestic values to public life.[23] These included the first-wave groups described in Jane Errington's chapter; they also included radical feminists, a second-wave category entirely novel in its analyses and actions.

This variety of feminisms, however described and classified, can be found in every country. What is unique to Canada is their ability to cooperate in institutional terms, if only intermittently and incompletely. This account of the first years of the second wave suggests how the Canadian context – the situation of women, the history of women and the convergence of feminist goals and beliefs – created clusters of compatible new and old organizations.

Analysis of their impact is another and even more difficult task. As Sandra Burt points out in her chapter on public policy, the commission contributed to a significant transformation in the federal government's treatment of women's rights. All assessments agree that the legal standing of women in Canada has been much improved since 1967, particularly in regard to citizenship and immigration and to family law and family property law as well as the law concerning sexual assault (under which heading rape is now included). Legal regulation of workplace access and conditions is much improved, though equal pay legislation has been disappointing in its impact and government training schemes have made only minor adjustments to the necessity of retraining women, especially in relation to non-traditional trades for women (the ones that can expect to expand in the near future). In 1985 the situation of native women was finally equalized in law, when those married to non-Indians were given back status for themselves and their children. The Canadian Forces have lifted their bar against women in combat roles.

In addition, the government cleaned up the sexist language it had previously used, began to increase the role and number of women in the Civil Service, and put in place a fairly substantial bureaucracy directed towards status of women. In 1985–86 the Women's Program of Secretary of State had a budget of over thirteen million dollars to provide project and operational funding to women's groups; the Minister Responsible for the Status of Women had a rather smaller budget for the same purpose, as did Status of Women Canada which reports to the Minister. The government has made something of an attempt to appoint women to federal boards and commissions (women even appeared on the governing body of Air Canada and at the head of the board of Canadian National Railway as well as, also for the first time, as head of the national granting agency for the arts, the Canada Council). The party in power during most of the seventies, the Liberal Party, successfully ran a number of women in safe ridings, appointed a more substantial number of women senators (including Thérèse Casgrain and Florence Bird, chairman of the RCSW, and the first black senator, Anne Cools), and appointed a woman Governor General (former cabinet minister Jeanne Sauvé) as well as the first woman member of the Supreme Court of Canada (Bertha Wilson; the second, Claire L'Heureux-Dubé, was appointed by the Conservative government in 1987). The 1984 election that saw a Conservative sweep nevertheless saw twenty-seven women M.P.s elected, including the former head of the Federal Advisory Council on the Status of Women and the former head of the Fédération des femmes du Québec, while the very large incoming cabinet included no fewer than six women, at least three of them in significant positions.

By 1987, most of the RCSW Recommendations related to legal inequalities had been implemented on the federal level. In the meantime, discussions and disputes about the equality provisions of the Charter in the early 1980s had clarified feminists' perceptions of their goals in relation to government: equal administration of law, equal laws (no laws treating women in a discriminatory fashion), and also no laws that indirectly had a discriminatory impact on women. After the 1984 *Report* of the Royal Commission on Equality in Employment, a one-person enquiry by Judge Rosalie Silberman Abella, the term "structural discrimination" was available to make it clear that even without intending it, existing policies and procedures could disadvantage women. The logical consequence was positive acts of remedy, an extension of the RCSW's notion of "special measures." In the mid-1980s, governments began affirmative action in a limited and gingerly fashion, mainly voluntary and slow to take effect.

The remaining major area of government inaction was in regards to abortion, as might have been predicted. It is significant that the RCSW disagreed internally on this matter, with three commissioners objecting to liberalization and Elsie Gregory MacGill asking for more radical measures. It is also significant, and probably an achievement of the second wave, that in 1982 some 72 per cent of the Canadian population polled declared themselves in favour of making abortion an affair affecting only a woman and her doctor.[24] In 1988 there was general support of the 5–2 Supreme Court decision declaring the federal legislation on abortion unconstitutional under the Charter of Rights. But, in three provinces, it was impossible for women to obtain abortions, and governments were under pressure to pass new, possibly restrictive, legislation.

At the end of the 1980s, it was not easy to evaluate all this, difficult to see the causes and more difficult still to make judgments about the outcome. Let us close with an example that illustrates the contradictions that feminists encounter: the integration of women into the Canadian armed forces.

In 1987 Sheila Hellstrom became Canada's first woman (Brigadier) General. "I am not a woman officer," she told reporters. "I am an officer first, who just happens to be a woman." Feminists were bound to realize that General Hellstrom had previously been disadvantaged as a woman in the military, whatever she believed. They also realized that she was promoted in part because of the insistence of the women's movement on, not just equal treatment, but positive measures to advance women. At the same time many feminists are also pacifists, who want equality for women in order to bring peaceful, domestic considerations to bear on public policy. "The main reason for the lack of women at senior levels in the Canadian Forces," commented Major (Res.) Doris Guyatt, "is the Canadian Forces policy that has denied women the opportunity to serve in combat roles and, consequently, the opportunity to gain the operational experience necessary to progress to the top."[25] It was also in 1987 that the Canadian Forces began the steps necessary for integrating women into combat roles. This, like General Hellstrom's promotion, could count as a victory for the women's movement. But if these changes removed discrimination, what did they do for women's hopes of changing society by their participation in public life?

The answer to that question, eventually, will be the answer to the question of the impact of the second wave of feminism on Canadian life.

Naomi Black

BRIEF CHRONOLOGY OF THE SECOND WAVE

1960	Voice of Women; Quebec branch 1961
1961	Planned Parenthood of Canada
1966	La Fédération des femmes du Québec L'Association féminine d'éducation et d'action sociale The Committee for the Equality of Women in Canada
1967	The Royal Commission on the Status of Women Toronto Women's Liberation
1968	Feminist Action League, Simon Fraser University; Women's Caucus, Vancouver 1st edition of McGill *Birth Control Handbook* Indian Rights for Indian Women Birthright
1969	Montreal Women's Liberation starts at McGill and Sir George Williams universities
1969–1970	Women's Liberation groups in Regina, Saskatoon, Winnipeg, Ottawa, Kingston, Guelph, Hamilton region, Halifax, Sudbury, Thunder Bay, Edmonton
1969–1971	Le Front pour la libération des femmes du Québec; *Québécoises deboutte!* no. 1.
1969–1973	Toronto New Feminists
1970	Abortion Caravan organized by Vancouver Women's Liberation (February 14–May 10) *Report* of the Royal Commission on the Status of Women
1971	National Ad Hoc Committee on the Status of Women Ontario Committee on the Status of Women
1972	"Strategy for Change" Conference (Toronto) and founding of National Action Committee on the Status of Women (NAC) Women for Political Action Le Centre des femmes (-1975) –remaining issues of *Québécoises deboutte!*
1973	Federal and Ontario Advisory Councils on the Status of Women Le Réseau d'action et d'information pour les femmes (Montreal) First national lesbian conference, YWCA, Toronto; first Canadian lesbian journal "Long Time Coming" (Montreal) First national conference of black women

1974	Canadian Association for the Repeal of the Abortion Laws (CARAL – after 1980, Canadian Abortion Rights Action League).
	Native Women's Association of Canada, l'Association des femmes autochtones du Québec
1975	Canadian Association of Women Executives
	National Association of Women and the Law
1976–1979	"Les Têtes de pioches" published by radical feminists in Quebec
1976	L'Association des femmes collaboratrices
	Lesbian Organization of Toronto
1977	le Coop-femmes (Montreal)
	Women Against Violence Against Women (WAVAW)
	Pluri-elles; in 1978, becomes *Des luttes et des rires des femmes*
1979	Feminist Party of Canada
1981	Canadian Congress for Learning Opportunities for Women
	AFWUF (Alberta Federation of Women United for the Family)
1983	Canadian Coalition Against Media Pornography
	REAL Women (Realistic Equal Active for Life)

SUGGESTED READINGS

"The Decade," a special issue of *Canadian Women's Studies/Les cahiers de la femme* 2, no. 2, 1980.

Demers, Jeanne, et Line McMurray, *Femme scandales, 1965–1985*. Montreal: La nouvelle barre du jour, 1987.

Fitzgerald, Maureen, *et al.*, eds., *Still Ain't Satisfied! Canadian Feminism Today*. Toronto: Women's Educational Press, 1982.

O'Leary, Véronique, et Louise Toupin, *Québécoises deboutte! Une anthologie de textes du Front de libération des femmes (1969–1971) et du Centre des femmes (1972–1975)*. Montreal: Les éditions du remue-ménage, 1982.

Prentice, Alison, *et al.*, *Canadian Women: A History*. Toronto: Harcourt Brace Jovanovich, 1988. Especially chapters 14 and 16.

The Clio Collective, *Quebec Women: A History*. (Translated by Roger Gannon and Rosalind Gill.) Toronto: Women's Educational Press, 1987. Especially chapters 14 and 15.

Women Unite! An Anthology of the Canadian Women's Movement. Toronto: Women's Educational Press, 1972.

Chapter Four

The Changing Canadian Family: Women's Roles and the Impact of Feminism

Understanding the family and recent changes in the family is fundamental to understanding the position of women in Canada in the present, in the past, and in the future. Women's place in society is inextricably intertwined with the family, not because of women's biologies, but because of the social roles women play, the ways we are constrained and provided opportunities through these roles, and by the prevalent images of both the family and of women held by Canadians. Sorting out these complexities is not an easy task, but is essential to understanding women's changing patterns in Canada.

In Canadian society, the family, whatever form it takes, is expected to meet needs for affection, understanding, emotional support, and solace from a possibly harsh world. Considerable flexibility is necessary in defining the family in Canada today, since it takes many forms and varies across ethnic groups. Essentially, for the purposes of this chapter, family is whatever people living in families commonly think of as family. In many parts of the world, such as in India, for example, the individual's emotional needs may be met through friends, religious commitments, civic duties, or from a more extended family group than generally exists in Canada. The range and intensity of needs to be met by the family here may explain why the family is a place of conflict. Conflict can result, for example, from the dual function of the family as an agent of society and as a source of emotional support to the individuals within it. Although these conflicts are experienced by most members of families at some time, they tend to be particularly pronounced and poignant for women, who are often caught between the private and the social expectations of the family.

The family is considered the most basic of social institutions – the organized ways society meets its basic needs. Society's needs of the family include giving birth to new members, teaching them how to behave appropriately, inculcating ethical and moral principles shared by society, producing and/or distributing goods and services, and maintaining social order. These needs, needless to say, often conflict with each other. Further conflict arises when what is needed by society differs from what is needed by individuals within a family.

Family membership is a dominant fact of life for most of us and an important vehicle for becoming a person–developing an identity, belonging to a group, acquiring a sense of values, caring for others as well as oneself, and passing on traditions as well as wealth. In this process, the family is closely tied with other social institutions–religious, economic, political, legal, and educational. Thus, the family becomes the place where many of the beliefs and values of society converge and are passed on to the next generation.

The family is both idealized and ideologized. It is touted as the bedrock of society. Images abound of the ideal family, which range from the extended family of days gone by; the 'Father Knows Best' family; the family we think we remember from childhood; or the family as sanctioned by the Bible, the Koran, or the Torah. It is seldom, if ever, the family in which we actually live. These idealized images of the family can lead to longing for what is lost, even if what we long for many never have actually existed. Some have referred to this as the "world we have lost syndrome."[1] The power of idealized images is such that we can long for Mom's apple pie and times gone by, even if Mom never made apple pie and our adult lives are far better than our childhoods ever were! It is as if we mourn for something that few people actually experienced, but we feel somehow as if it is only we who missed out. The mass media, and advertisers in particular, are adept at selling nostalgic images of family life.

Given the conflicts that are built into the modern family, the expectations of society and of individual family members, the interconnections of the family with other social institutions, the ideologies and the images of the family, both true and fictionalized, it is hardly surprising that considerable confusion exists about the changing roles of women in the family. Explanations of women's social roles tend to be surrounded by considerable vested interest, muddled thinking, and out-and-out misrepresentation. So, it is hardly surprising that women's roles in the family are seen with less than clear vision. In this confusion, it becomes tempting to simplify everything by attributing all contemporary change in the family, whether bad or good, to feminism and to what are seen by some as women's selfish needs.

Few people living in Canada in the late twentieth century can be unaware that there have been changes in the family, if only because they are regularly discussed and analysed by the mass media. Unfortunately, in many of these discussions as much misinformation as information is generated. To get the 'hook' the media needs to sell their programs or articles, the extent of these changes is often exaggerated. Alarm is raised about what is happening to the family, laments offered about what we have lost, or women's growing self-awareness is blamed for the 'demise' of the family.

In discussing recent changes in the Canadian family, myths, misunderstandings, and misconceptions must be dispelled by relying on the best and most recent data and research available. It is not possible, of course, in a single chapter to discuss all aspects of the changing Canadian family. Several books have appeared recently which analyse aspects of family change more completely than can be done here.[2] Here, only the more salient changes will be highlighted. Discussion will focus on the implications of these changes for women and on the roles played by women in bringing them about. Issues such as socialization of children or of women at various stages of the life cycle are beyond the scope of this chapter.

Three of the most basic changes that have occurred in the Canadian family since the mid 1960s are the decrease in family size, the increased labour-force participation of married women and mothers, and the increase in marital dissolution through divorce and separation. These trends are not independent of one another, but intertwined, and have been accompanied by large scale socio-economic changes.

In this chapter some of the confusion about women and the family is stripped away to show the ways in which feminism may have positive effects on the family, to examine the changes occurring in the Canadian family, and to explore the implications of these changes for women.

Declining Family Size

We have moved from a time of baby boom from the mid 1940s to early 1960s to a period of baby bust in the 1970s and 1980s. The number of births per woman, on average, has fallen from a high of 3.9 in 1959, the peak of the baby boom, to 1.7 in the early 1980s.[3] The Canadian birth rate is now at an all-time low (with the Quebec birth rate the lowest in Canada), and is expected to remain at a very low level for some time. The fertility decline has been sufficiently pervasive in Canada that it includes a precipitous decline in family size among native people as well, whose traditionally high birth rates have been replaced by a pattern more similar to that of all Canadians. This trend toward smaller families parallels a similar trend in most western industrialized countries.

An exclusive focus on the recent drop in the Canadian birth rate obscures the longer-term historical trend. When long-term trends are analysed, it is not the current low levels of birth that are striking, but the exceedingly high birth rates of the baby boom era. The Canadian birth rate has been declining since

1851.[4] The average number of births per woman in 1937, for example, was 2.6. The baby boom period produced the largest generation known in history. It may be that the long-term downward trend in fertility is simply resuming as the conditions that fostered the baby boom alter.

To understand how women's family roles and reproduction are bound to the needs of society, some of the factors behind the baby boom must be considered. Contrary to popular belief, the baby boom was not solely the result of lonely soldiers returning to hearth and home. Rather, a convergence of late and early childbearing with an overall increase in family size produced increased fertility. Women's roles were redefined as more family-centered than in the 1920s and 1930s. In the post-war period, women returned to housework and motherhood, leaving the jobs in the labour force they held during the war. Wilson cites the efforts of the Parliamentary Sub-committee on Postwar Problems of Women as having an important role in elevating the status of housework and family life for women in postwar Canada.[5] Parallelling this concerted and deliberate effort, which may not have succeeded impressively, was the appearance of women's magazines singing the praises of motherhood, of family, and of the joys of making meatloaf. The propaganda of the day pictured women at home and strong families as hedges against another war or as ballast in the Cold War. Economic expansion in the post-war period enabled male workers to be paid a family wage, meant to support a family. It is not surprising then, that women married in record numbers and focused their attention on building families.

The baby boom era, however anomalous, may have produced the conditions responsible for today's low birth rates, as well as for women's increased self-awareness. Competition in the 1960s and 1970s among the members of the huge baby boom generation was fierce for the attention of teachers, for university places, for jobs, even for mates. "This generation has experienced high unemployment, high dissatisfaction with the existing system and high educational and societal drop-out rates."[6] The post-war years also produced a group of dissatisfied and frustrated full-time mothers, who followed social expectations but felt unrewarded and depressed. Friedan expressed these feelings in her 1963 book, *The Feminine Mystique,* whose implications for the development of feminist theory Lorraine Code discusses in her chapter. Friedan focused on "the problem that has no name," that is, that women's work at home is not considered work by society, so its accompanying frustrations, as well as rewards, go unrecognized.

The convergence of economic problems and women's growing dissatisfaction with their socially prescribed familial roles may explain, in large part, the current low levels of childbearing. It is not that women do not want children – most do – but that they find it difficult to be mothers of large families given the constraints of having to work to support families, inadequate day care options, limited extended families, and the escalating costs of raising children. The pattern of change in childbearing suggests that economic factors are as important as social factors in explaining smaller family sizes. The proportion of large families, where there are six or more children, has dropped from 40 per cent in 1876 to less than 5 per cent in the mid-1980s.[7] This decline is particularly pronounced in Quebec, where the traditionally high birth rate was known as 'cradle revenge,' against the English-speaking majority in Canada. The decline is also dramatic among native people. The decline in fertility among younger women suggests that couples may be postponing childbearing until they feel they can afford it. The increase in the proportion of married women and mothers who work outside their homes, discussed later, further attests to the importance of economic factors in women's lives in the 1980s, with clear consequences for childbearing.

Two recent trends suggest that women's changing self-images also play a role in reducing family size. One is that voluntary childlessness is increasing among Canadians. Women may appear to be voluntarily childless as they postpone births for longer periods. However, the long-term postponement of births can result in inadvertent voluntary childlessness, as women become accustomed to a child-free life style or subsequently find that they are unable to have a child. Nonetheless, Statistics Canada projects that as many as 16 per cent of all young Canadian women at present may ultimately forgo maternity.[8] The previous record of childlessness, 21 per cent, occurred among women who were in their prime reproductive years during the Depression. The rewards of motherhood for women may not be as large as they once were, or were perceived to be. Alternatively, of course, the causes could be economic. Both partners now often have to work full-time to make ends meet; babies are very costly in both money and time; and day care opportunities are limited.

A second social factor important in the decline in family size has to do with the satisfaction derived from having children. It used to be thought, and still is by some, that fulfillment in life, particularly for women, was not possible without children. Wendy Mitchinson discusses the extent to which the medical profession subscribed to this belief in her chapter. However, new evidence suggests that children may not be essential to life satisfaction. Singh and Williams for example, have discovered that having children has little effect on life satisfaction,[9] while Glenn and McLanahan and Spanier and Lewis have found that having children has a negative effect on marital happiness, especially for women.[10] Canadian women may no longer see themselves as lifelong mothers and wives, with childbearing and childrearing the central part of their lives.

The trend toward postponing births and having fewer babies means that a much smaller proportion of women's lives is devoted to childrearing. Gee and Kimball have calculated that women born 1951–1960 spend an average of 23.6 years married with no children at home.[11] This compares with no years spent in this life stage by Canadian women born 1841–1850, 12.2 years for women born 1901–1910, and 18.1 years for women born 1931–1940. Clearly, the life patterns of women in Canada have been transformed. It is as if childbearing has become streamlined, making more time available to women for other activities.

Recent work by Grindstaff challenges the conventional belief that women limit their education and labour-force participation to have babies and find fulfillment in the domestic realm.[12] His findings reveal that childbearing, particularly early childbearing, diminishes women's future economic and social options and opportunities. Women's lost opportunities, both to themselves and to society, may be the price that society pays for reproducing itself, according to Grindstaff. Canadian women, in postponing childbearing, forgoing it altogether, or having smaller numbers of children, may be voting with their wombs that they think the price society asks of them for having children is simply too high to pay. Women may not want to forgo childbearing or larger families at all, but find that the social support system for having children is inadequate.

The declining birth rate and the emergence of smaller families is often seen to be the consequence of women's enhanced reproductive choice, yet this is not entirely the case. While some women have had the choice to postpone or opt out of childbearing, many continue to face unwanted pregnancy, most notably the poor, young, immigrant, differently abled, and physically and mentally abused women. Any assumption that childbearing has become a choice for all Canadian women overlooks women's continuing quest for reproductive control. The abortion debate in Canada and the way policy-makers have dealt, or not dealt with it, highlights many of the issues involved in women's campaign for choice in reproduction. The media, in focusing on well-to-do couples agonizing over the decision about whether or not to have a child, have lent support to the misconception that childbearing is now a clear choice for all women. Rona Achilles, in her chapter, lends support to the contention that reproductive choice is often influenced by class, race, and economic factors, so that it is not clearly a 'free' choice.

Women's Increased Labour Force Participation

Shifts in childbearing patterns and family size have been accompanied by the dramatically increased participation of married women and mothers in Canada in the labour force. Prior to the Second World War, married women generally did not work outside their homes, except in family businesses or farms. Family was women's central vocation, as is discussed in Jane Errington's chapter on history. Marriage alone was sufficient reason for an employer to fire a woman employee until recently in Canada. The past half-century has seen a dramatic change in women's work-force participation as shown in Table 1. In 1931, the discrepancy in labour-force participation between single and married women was wide. In 1988, most women in Canada now work, whether married or not. Most dramatic has been the change in the participation of women with families. Eichler notes that women more often work throughout their lives now, whether they are married or mothers or not.[13]

Table 1
Shifts in Labour Force Participation of Women in Canada

	% who work *of Single Women*	*of Married Women*
1931	43.8	3.5
1951	58.3	11.2
1961	54.1	22.0
1971	53.5	37.0
1981	64.6	50.5

SOURCE: Adapted from Statistics Canada Census data.

Before the implications and consequences of the increased participation of wives and mothers can be understood, the reasons for the changed pattern of economic activity among married women need to be examined briefly. A 1979 National Council of Welfare study found that family income was a crucial variable in whether women worked. The lower the family income, the higher the probability that wives work.[14] In families where both husband and wife work, the wife often works for economic reasons, as Luxton discovered in her classic study in Flin Flon, Manitoba.[15] The dual earner family is emerging as the most common form, because families often cannot live on one income.

Economic pressures have taken on new meaning in the 1980s, with high unemployment, factory shutdowns, increased interest rates, and inflationary prices for essential goods and services. Increasingly, women work at the same time that their more highly paid, more often unionized husbands are being laid off or cannot find employment. Women, as they did during World War II, come into the paid work-force when needed and are encouraged to leave when economic conditions warrant.

The majority of married women in Canada now work, but this reality has not been fully assimilated into the thinking of employers or even of women themselves. A surprising number of studies have focused on whether women with young children should work, whether they feel guilty about working, and whether their marital situation is compromised by their work. That these questions are raised at all points out the assumption that working husbands or fathers do not feel any such divided loyalty. Nonetheless, most Canadians seem to feel that, ideally, mothers with small children should not work outside the home. The presence of young children at home continues to deter women from working in the paid work-force. Yet, in 1981, 45 per cent of all women with children under three years old worked.[16] Clearly, public attitudes are lagging behind the realities of women's lives.

Working mothers with young children at home face dilemmas both at home and at work. They continue to hold chief responsibility for childcare and housework, even if they work also outside the home. This is a 1980s pattern of work outside the home with a 1950s division of labour at home. Inadequate child care options, inflexible school hours, and the unsympathetic attitudes of most employers all add further problems for the working mother. At work, a woman with children, particularly young children, is often perceived as having divided loyalties between home and work. While marriage and children for a man are seen as assets in motivating him to work harder, for women they tend to be seen as liabilities or distractions. A woman with children is seen as a risk for permanent employment, for a job with responsibility, and for promotions. She may be made to feel guilty about 'leaving' her children to work, even if she is working to support them. Combining family and work or career poses challenges to women, challenges that most of us must face, since most women, including most feminists, work and have families, too.

The increased participation of married women in the work-force parallels changes in housework. Tasks that used to be done at home (baking bread, making clothes, and so on) have been taken over by industries. The time spent by women in housework, however, has not necessarily decreased because expectations have also increased. Housewives now seldom work with other women in performing these tasks as they once did, increasing the isolation of the woman at home. Breadmaking and washing, for example, used to be done by groups of women who enjoyed each other's company while working. Now bread is bought and clothes are washed by machines in the home or laundromat by women at every socio-economic level, with the result that the services provided by housewives are even less valued by society than before. Women at home might seek paid work, in part, to be with other people and to reduce their alienation. Recent research, however, questions this motivation, since so many women work in boring, isolating and low-paying jobs.[17]

It is not surprising that there is a minor rift between women at home and women who work outside their homes over what should be on the political agenda for women. Even though the extent of this rift may be exaggerated by politicians eager to splinter the potential political power women could have if we acted *en bloc*, there is some truth that housewives and women working in paid employment have different interests. In the late 1980s in Canada, the group REAL (Realistic, Equal, and Active for Life) Women formed to lobby for the interests of traditional homemakers.

Women's changing work-force patterns have brought about and have been accompanied by changes in family structure and the way the family is seen. Some of these changes are paradoxical. The increased work-force participation of married women both reinforced and undermined the idea that marriage may be women's best economic option. Reinforcement resulted from the realization that women's labour is worth less than men's, even men doing comparable work. Women seeking paid employment are often channelled into women's job ghettoes, sometimes called pink-collar ghettoes, characterized by poor pay, low status, and minimal opportunity for promotion. Such poor conditions are especially evident in the ghettoized labour of immigrant women, described by Roxana Ng in her chapter. Graphic evidence is thus provided for what women have been told for decades: the answer for women facing exploitation and low pay at work is to find a man and settle down. When women still earn, on average, sixty to seventy cents for every dollar earned by a man, marriage to a man whose earnings are higher might be seen as women's best option for economic security. Economic inequality between women and men may force women's silent acceptance of their need to marry. Westoff, a leading American demographer, puts it succinctly, "Women have traditionally offered child-bearing and domestic services in exchange for the protection, security and status deriving from men's economic position."[18] This trade-off may continue to have appeal to some women faced with the alternative of low pay, long hours, and poor conditions in the work place.

At the same time, increased labour-force participation undermines the idea that marriage is women's best economic bargain. Until recently in Canada, married women were, by law, under the control of their husbands and families. Their options and rights were limited, and any money they earned was considered their husbands'. With more married women working outside the home, even for low pay and few benefits, the consideration of women and women's earnings as family 'property' is called into question. When women find work while their husbands face unemployment, traditional roles in the family change. Men are no longer the sole breadwinner for many families today in Canada. In sectors of the economy and regions where unemployment is chronic, women frequently assume the breadwinner role. Some credibility is gained from this shift, although too often at the price of abuse from a resentful husband and/or the poverty of supporting a family on one inadequate, woman's income. Women with jobs and incomes of their own, of course, also have the option to leave a marriage if they so choose.

The increased participation of married women in the work-force calls into question the 'separate but equal' doctrine. This is a traditional view of the family, which holds that men and women do different tasks but are held in equal regard by society. Women who work for pay find that their jobs are often extensions of the work they do at home – child care, food preparation, and so on. Women do this work for considerably less pay and less prestige than men receive for their work. The message to women is clear – their work relative to men's, both at home and outside the home, is undervalued by society. Both the Wages for Housework movement of the 1970s and the pay-equity discussion of the late 1980s make it clear that women's work subsidizes the economy. Wages for housework could, according to economic analysts, bankrupt the country by paying women fairly for the work they already do.[19] Similar statements have been made about pay equity. Fairness aside, argue the pundits, Canada cannot afford to pay women what they are worth. The message is clear – the Canadian economy runs on women's work, which is systematically underrewarded, undervalued, and performed out of good will.

Women's increased participation in the work-force highlights the inequitable division of labour at home as well. Despite all the hype about shared work at home, it is women who continue to do most of the housework, whether or not they hold a job. This, of course, is even more the case in single-parent (typically mother-led) families, where mothers must do everything. Women now often do a double day of work or even a triple day if they have children. When domestic work is shared in two-parent families, it is seldom shared equally. In 1975, Meissner found that husbands of wives who go out to work increase their share of work at home by an average of one hour per week.[20] Recent studies provide little evidence that this has changed.[21]

Also highlighted by the changed work-force patterns of married women is that child care is considered the private responsibility of individual families. The family in Canada is perceived as virtually self-contained, responsible for itself and its children. This privatized view of the family takes its toll on its members and on society in terms of overlooked violence, assumed economic responsibility of family members for each other, and perhaps undisciplined children. Inadequate facilities for child care result from the assumption that it is the mother's responsibility to care completely for her own children. If she works in order to feed them, she is made to feel guilty and selfish. If she chooses to seek welfare to stay home with the children, she is considered lazy and dependent. Some of the issues involved in child care options will be discussed later on in this chapter.

Women who work and also have families are regarded with some suspicion in the workplace, as mentioned earlier. Recognizing this, many women are forced into the untenable position of 'choosing' a family or a career, but not both. The choice is actually an empty one, since the rewards of each are separate and cannot be compared. Yet the notion of choice conveys to women the idea that they must decide one way or the other and, as a result, must 'pay the price' for this choice. Thus, women's poorer wages in comparison to men are 'justified' by our 'choosing' work, knowing its problems, rather than our more 'natural' vocation of motherhood. Employers see themselves as justified in paying women less than men because women made the 'choice' to accept less pay when they 'decided' to work. If they choose motherhood, they are assumed to have made the choice knowingly, and cannot expect equal consideration in the workplace.

IDEA OF "CHOICE"

Marital Dissolution

Many Canadians see increasing rates of marital dissolution as a fundamental change in the Canadian family, one that largely accounts for the dramatic increase in single-parent families. Levels of public awareness of this trend are impressive, although the level of public knowledge about it less so. Statistics Canada estimates that the divorce rate among Canadians rose by 82 per cent in the ten-year period between 1972 and 1982.[22]

Divorce-trend analysis poses a number of challenges, which have implications for how divorce trends are interpreted. One problem in analysing divorce trends is a conceptual one. The point of legal divorce never coincides with the point of actual separation. Thus, divorce rates can rise and fall with changes in the legal grounds on which divorce is possible, since divorce can be postponed almost indefinitely. Between 1968 and 1969, for example, there was almost a doubling of the number of divorces granted to Canadians.[23] The liberalization of the legal grounds for divorce in the amendments to the Divorce Act of July 1968 explains this increase better than substantive change in popularity of marriage. Couples who had been long separated decided in late 1968 and 1969 to legalize their marital situation by applying for divorce. A smaller surge in divorce rates in Canada occurred between 1972 and 1975. This, too, seems attributable to changes in the legal code, which, in effect, gave legal sanction for divorce to those who had been separated. The 1986 changes in the divorce law reduced the minimum time allowed between separation and application for divorce. Another small surge in the divorce rate is likely. Reliance on divorce rates as an indicator of marital dissatisfaction, therefore, can be misleading. Changes in the divorce law, however, do not cause divorce; they merely enable those whose marriages have dissolved to legalize their situations. People do not take on lightly a formal dissolution of their marriages, as the process involves considerable personal pain and anguish.

The divorce rate in Canada is high and has increased, yet Canada's rate of divorce is far from being the highest in the world. Canada's increasing divorce rate parallels similar increases in divorce in most countries of the developed world, so conditions unique to Canada are not likely responsible for the increase. Divorce is more common among couples in which one partner was previously divorced. Thus, as second or third marriages increase, the divorce rate will likely increase. Divorce statistics may be 'inflated' by the same people reappearing.

Too often, the increase in divorce rates is equated with an escalation of marital unhappiness, for which women's changing roles are cited as contributing factors. Wilson argues that "it is erroneous to conclude that the rising divorce rate is indicative of the disintegration of family life in Canada. Two-thirds of divorced women and three-quarters of divorced men remarry."[24] Eichler adds that "there is a fair amount of research which suggests that unhappy marriages are not necessarily unstable, and that happy marriages are not necessarily stable."[25] The reasons for divorce are extensive and varied, ranging from an increasingly secularized view of marriage to overly hasty marriages made because of premarital pregnancy. This strongly suggests that divorce, although very painful for those experiencing it, might provide an opportunity to start anew. Rather than necessarily indicating a decline in family values or of interest in marriage, the high rate of divorce might be an indicator only of the poor first matches people make, who then reaffirm their faith in family and marriage by trying again.

Women who are divorced have a lower probability than divorced men of remarrying. This may be because divorced men seek younger single women to marry, while divorced women, because of our social norms, have a more limited selection of potential mates. Divorced women more often have responsibility for the children of the dissolved marriage, which can affect their prospects for remarriage. The most profound difference between the divorce experience of men and of women is their altered financial circumstances, however. Contrary to public belief, fewer than 5 per cent of women receive alimony after divorce.[26] With childcare responsibilities (and limited day care facilities), limited job opportunities and, all too often, inadequate or non-existent child support, divorced women often find themselves among the ranks of the poor. A 1986 report of the National Council on Welfare of Canada found that families headed by women (most single-parent families) run over four times the risk of poverty as families headed by men.[27]

One result of the increasing divorce rate is that the ranks of the poor are becoming filled by women, often mothers with dependent children. Although men may lose close contact with their children as a result of divorce, the economic implications of divorce for men are far less severe. Eichler and Chesler find that men's real incomes actually rise after divorce, while women's incomes decline substantially.[28] Many divorced women, even middle-class women, find themselves facing welfare. In part, and somewhat paradoxically, this results from society's changing views of marriage. It used to be that wives were legally regarded as their husband's exclusive sexual property. Despite the drawbacks to this, wives then had something with which to bargain in court. If their husband's adultery led to the divorce, women could often win alimony and child-support payments as the 'wronged wife.'

Divorce 'reform,' intended to make divorce more equitable and fair, and changes in family law have led to a different perception. Women are no longer seen by judges as 'wronged' dependent wives, but as equal partners who, because of the presumed strides women have made in the work place, are now able to support themselves and their children. Alimony payments are now less likely to be awarded by the courts, and child-support payments are generally smaller. Even women with limited job skills and no work experience are now assumed by judges as capable of self support as heads of single-parent families. Eicher finds, "the courts are therefore moving towards an assumption that self-support after divorce is the expected course of action for the wives as well as the husbands."[29] Although this seems egalitarian, it overlooks women's real wage and job prospects, as well as the demands and expense of child care.

In situations where courts award child-support payments, "apparently up to 75 per cent of support payments are at some point defaulted on, while average child support payments are very low."[30] Canadian courts have made little attempt to enforce court-ordered child-support payments. In a society that claims to value women as mothers and to put a high premium on reproduction and children, one cannot help but wonder what the poverty of divorced mothers suggests. Possibly it is as Pogrebin has argued, that women who are not under male control are viewed with suspicion and punished economically for their 'unwillingness' to conform.[31] Needless to say, the anguish of divorce is made worse by the poverty divorced women so often experience. This, without doubt, has consequences on divorced women's ability to parent.

A new trend in child custody is evident in Canada as part of an attempt to make family laws more equitable. Courts increasingly are granting fathers custody of their children. This may seem fair at first glance, but closer inspection reveals a bias in these new court decisions. Chesler's study of mothers' challenges for custody in the U.S. between 1960 and 1981, found that 87 per cent of the fathers awarded custody were not involved in child care at all prior to the divorce, and 67 per cent paid no child support.[32] Fathers' rights groups in Canada have been increasingly successful in winning custody battles. A particularly insidious aspect of the new trends in child-custody cases is that mothers contesting custody are often in a no-win situation, according to Chesler.[33] If they were stay-at-home mothers, they often lost custody because they had limited incomes; if they were working, they lost custody because they were away from home too much. Mothers, most amazingly, even lost custody for 'deserting' abusive marriages, for 'interfering' with incestuous relationships of the fathers with their children, and for having other relationships, after their divorces had become final. This is a case of how what seem to be egalitarian reforms in law and policy lead to inequality.

A second trend has been toward mandatory joint custody. While this, too, seems egalitarian, it, too, may not be. Implementing court-ordered joint custody for parents who cannot get along or do not wish to live in physical proximity to each other poses challenges. Mandatory joint custody is now viewed by many women's groups as retrogressive. The different economic resources of women and men may relegate women to permanent subservience to their ex-husbands who can make the major decisions about the children because of their greater economic resources and their continued legal control. Eichler cites studies that indicate that mandatory joint custody can work well in cases where the couples might have worked out voluntary joint custody anyway.[34] The relative merits of joint custody and sole custody are not obvious to many women. Women who are offered the Solomon's choice of the demands of their own sole custody, joint custody, or father custody, seem to prefer to have sole custody, no matter how difficult the financial burdens. The other alternatives, they argue compellingly, are so weighted in favour of the father (despite the public image of the poor, hard-done-by divorced father), that women's and children's interests are overlooked.

The number of marriages in Canada that involve at least one previously married spouse is increasing. In 1980, 26.5 per cent of all marriages involved a previously married partner.[35] The phenomenon of remarried families with children – the so-called 'blended' family – is so new that terms have not yet been developed for the possible relationships. Eichler has estimated that 120 different family types are possible, assuming that husband and wife have only one previous marriage.[36] Clearly, research on these new family types is needed; research that does not assume that the only proper family is a traditional nuclear family. One striking aspect of the blended family, whatever future research shows, is that biological roles and social roles in the family are not the same, and that the two are becoming increasingly divergent. This, without doubt, has profound significance for women, about whom it has been incorrectly assumed that biology is destiny.

Challenges on the Family Front

In the late 1980s, many challenges to the family and women's roles have emerged, some of which may bring about a new appreciation of the family in society. Only a few of these can be discussed here.

There was a time, not too long ago, when what went on in the family was considered private – nobody's business but one's own, and perhaps God's or the parish priest's. This, of course, was not really true, particularly when it is understood that the family is doing work on behalf of society, but this is the way it was seen. The distinction between the public world and the private world was 'discovered,' established, and maintained by men and the partriarchal system. Rowbotham sums it up:

> This difference in the sexual division of labour in society means that the relationship of men as a group to production is different than that of women. For a man, the social relations and values of commodity production predominate and home is a retreat into intimacy. For women, the public world belongs to and is owned by men. She is dependent upon what the man earns but is responsible for the private sphere, the family.[37]

This split between the private and the public, artificial as it is, is maintained by the 'separate but equal' doctrine – the idea that women and men are equals who exist in separate spheres doing functionally interdependent tasks. As pointed out by numerous modern feminist critiques of this doctrine, there is much that is separate about the realms of women and of men, but little that is equal. Nonetheless, the notion that women and men exist in separate spheres, one private and one public, tends to preserve the traditional division of labour within the family and the labour force, which is rationalized as biologically based. Further, and this is emphasized by most of the dominant sociological theories of the family, a functional fit is maintained between the family as a social institution and the requirements of an industrial, capitalist economy. Women who work in the home are both secondary sources of labour and consumers, with this latter role becoming vastly expanded in recent times. Men, then, are freed through women's domestic and emotional labour, to be hard-working and productive. As Rowbotham suggests, "the family under capitalism carries all the rags and bones and bits of old iron not used by the commodity system."[38]

It is not surprising, given this patriarchal view of the family, that men view family as a retreat from industry, a "haven in a heartless world" as Lasch has called it.[39] There is some truth in Smith's statement that the family is a place where:

> people are stored when they are not at work, where they are maintained,

> serviced, fed and cleaned, where they are psychologically repaired and the injuries of daily routine and tensions generated on the job made good, and where the next generation of employees is produced and trained for their future occupational roles.[40]

Given this view of the family, and the tightness of fit between the economic system and the family, women's work at home can be seen as essential to the smooth running of the capitalist system. This work is so essential that it is done by women whether they work outside the home as well or not. Should women's performance of this work be impeded by pressures of paid work, marital dissolution, or other factors, the family is thought to be in disarray. What this may mean is that women's unpaid, unrecognized, and unrewarded labour on the home front is no longer as fully devoted to the service of the economy and of men as it once was. Women increasingly are questioning, sometimes without knowing it fully, why we are asked to provide these services on the homefront for the 'compensation' of vulnerable dependency on a man who might leave us at any time and on a system which provides little reward.

The separation and isolation of the family works against women in hiding the violence we face on the intimate frontier. Although some progress has been made by the women's movement in bringing family violence into public awareness, violence against women at home is still viewed by police, judges, doctors, lawyers, and, indeed, large segments of society as either resulting from a domestic dispute, in which societal agents have little right to intervene, or precipitated by the woman herself, in which case she is thought to be 'getting what she deserves.'[41] Abused women who seek help from the police, hospitals, and courts are still often disbelieved, because the experience of the woman facing domestic violence does not fit the idealized image of the family. The private nature of the Canadian family permits women's pain to go unheard, unseen, and unheeded by the public authorities. Campaigns to improve public recognition, such as that taken recently by the Ontario government, help, of course, but do not solve the problem.

Incest and rape within marriage also go largely unacknowledged, despite the growing number of women and girls who have brought their painful experiences to the attention of those they thought would help and despite the greater availability of shelters and assistance. All too often the woman's or girl's experience is reconstructed, under the influence of a therapist or member of the helping professions, to become more consistent with the prevailing societal images of the family and of women. This doubly victimizes women, first by the violence itself, which often has life-long effects, and second by the denial of her version of the experience. This can be crazy-making to the woman who knows clearly what she experienced yet is obliged to accept a reconstructed version of that experience. The privacy accorded the nuclear family prevents investigation of the woman's experience and ends up hiding the harshness of that experience, even to the woman herself. Fortunately, as Joanna Boehnert shows in her chapter, some feminist therapists are beginning to move away from such prejudicial methods of reconstructing women's experience.

Women, spurred on by feminist analyses of the artificial distinction between the private and the public on family-related issues, have increasingly been making public their concerns about and experiences in the family. At first, women were accused of shrillness and/or of over-reaction. But in the 1980s, there has been greater credence given to the criticism that the traditional patriarchal family is not private, that violence and exploitation within the family costs everyone, and that the patriarchal family can be a nightmarish institution where violence and sexual abuse go unnoticed and unpunished. The present-day women's movement has used as its rallying message 'the personal is political.' In the realm of family, women are increasingly seeing their personal lives as having political components. Feminists envision a family form in which humanity is valued above roles, different abilities are tolerated, and gender-specialization is less rigid.

The view that the Canadian family is in crisis often blames feminism for the changes occurring in the modern family. The right-wing political agenda, of which the family-in-crisis view is a fundamental component, holds that women's familial and reproductive roles are political. The intent is to bring women's sexuality and reproduction back firmly under the control of men and patriarchy. The irony is that this agenda is carried out under movements that call themselves pro-family.

Perhaps the most striking example of this is the contemporary abortion debate in Canada, but issues of day care and the new reproductive technologies are also important in this regard. The abortion debate is particularly salient to the agenda of the New Right because the issues involved are not discussed openly in Canada by politicians. Rather, there is a strong tendency, evidenced in the 1984 federal election, for candidates to separate their personal (supposedly moral or ethical views) from their public stances. Abortion and women's roles have become politically contentious issues, covered in the cloak of morality and privacy. This may be a clever hedge against decisive action by legislators on these issues. Legislative inaction and the repackaging of abortion as an essentially moral issue have obscured the overt political dimensions of abortion and the ways in which the New Right would like to redefine women's roles.

Encroachments on women's legal access to abortion have been increasing in Canada. Several provinces now have no legal abortion facilities at all. In those that do, there has been a reduction in the number of hospitals with functioning therapeutic abortion committees and a reduction in the numbers of doctors willing to perform therapeutic abortions.[42] This has resulted from local pressure by groups calling themselves 'pro-life' and/or 'pro-family' on doctors and hosptials in their own communities. Women's roles are being politically redefined as maternal by these groups without any recourse to national debate or to legislative change. These groups, sometimes without being fully aware of what they are doing, often cite their opposition to any regulation or interference with the family, yet by their actions they are making motherhood compulsory, thereby making state control over reproduction and women's roles complete.

Eichler argues, given the agenda of the "pro-family movement, that it must be seen as detrimental to the well-being of the majority of Canadian families."[43] Its agenda includes denial of equal opportunities for women, compulsory heterosexuality, banning of contraception and abortion, eradication of day care, and denial of the existence of wife abuse, marital rape, and incest. In short, the movement might be more appropriately called, as Eichler suggests, a "Movement for the Restoration of the Patriarchal Family."[44]

Paralleling the 'pro-family' movement in Canada and working in conjunction with it are groups that claim to represent the interests of women at home such as REAL Women. The position of REAL Women essentially is anti-abortion, anti-equal pay, anti-day care, anti-no-fault divorce. Their agenda also includes restoration of the traditional patriarchal family in which women have few choices and few rights. The concern and the challenge to feminists posed by groups like REAL Women is that these groups seem (or claim) to have the ear of numbers of politicians who think that groups like this represent a significant number of Canadian women, or who simply like the idea of the restoration of partriarchy for their own reasons. There is growing concern among Canadian social scientists and feminists who do research on women and the family that feminist research funding, which was never large, may be cut further by the lobbying of groups such as these.

The new reproductive technologies may well represent another challenge to the small gains women have made in changing the traditional patriarchal family and its confining familial roles. Rona Achilles's chapter addresses these matters specifically. These technologies are still being developed and legislation has by no means kept pace. However, some things are already clear about the new technologies.[45] They are being developed or controlled by the same medical and scientific elite that gave us the Dalkon shield, the drug D.E.S., and the birth control pill whose damaging side-effects on women have been amply documented and publicized. Second, infertile women are being used to develop the technologies, as experiments essentially, without sufficient knowledge of long- or even short-term consequences. Third, the availability of reproductive technologies may force some women into a painful and absorbing quest for motherhood, rather than to finding fulfillment in other realms. The degree to which societal coercion may be evident in the new reproductive technologies is also being addressed by critics and concerned observers. The advent of new reproductive technology, like the advent of the birth control pill, has the potential for freeing women to choose reproduction, but it also has the potential, as we know all too well from past experiences, to place our reproduction and our social roles under further control by patriarchy.

Biases in Research on the Family

It has been recognized for several decades that theory, research, and data collection in social science are biased against women, against discovering the truth about our lives and our patterns. Not surprisingly, the time (1960s and 1970s) when these sexist biases were made an issue coincided with the increased involvement of women in intellectual work and in higher education. Spurred on by real social problems, an increasingly critical social science emerged. By 1985, the Social Sciences and Humanities Research Council of Canada adopted guidelines for developing sound non-sexist research.[46] In 1986, a Task Force on the Elimination of Sexist Bias in Research submitted its report to the Social Science Federation of Canada.[47]

Sexist bias, or the unintentional or deliberate misrepresentation or distortion of women's and men's behaviour in theory and research can take many forms and is both pervasive and invisible. Andocentrism – the assumption that men's experiences are more representative of human experience than are women's – is one example. Social science has failed, given the pervasiveness of sexist biases, to provide useful tools to women to better understand ourselves and the society in which we live. Work is typically defined as what men do – exchange labour for a wage. Unpaid work, most often done by women at home, on the farm, or in the family business is not seen as work and therefore is often not included in the concept of Gross National Product.

In analyses of women in families, sexist biases become particularly strong. We may wish to think that biases about women being primarily wives and mothers may have become outdated, but recent work provides compelling evidence to suggest that not only have things *not* improved much in family research, but that new ways of being sexist have been discovered.[48] Examples include a study that asks, as the title of the article, "Do adolescents believe the employment of wives is a threat to marital relationships?"[49] In posing the question in this way, the researchers are revealing their strong suspicion that the employment of wives may undermine marriages. Another example would be the many studies that focus on women's family/work role conflicts and the few that ever ask men whether they experience such conflicts. Yet another example would be the common practice of asking only one member of a family, usually the wife/mother, how the family operates and how various members behave, feel, and think. The assumption here is that family life is the domain of women, so women can speak authoritatively about family experience, not only for themselves but for all members of their families.

Sexist biases work against a clear understanding of women's roles in families in many ways, including the assumption of a natural differentiation by sex in families, the assumption of one reality within families, the androcentric view of society, and the power of labels. One prevalent sexist bias is the assumption that there is a biologically based, functional differentiation within families that accounts for the differences in opportunities and talents of women and of men. This assumption can be self-fulfilling. If a woman believes herself to be limited by her biology, she may act within those limits, thereby curtailing her opportunity. Alternatively, if it is believed that women, because of biology, are capable of less than men, society could expect, ask, and provide less to us. Those in power tend to attribute aspects of a situation they wish to maintain to 'nature' (this observation was made by Roland Barthes[50]) thus rendering the structural power imbalance apparently unchangeable. This tendency is accelerating in the latter part of the twentieth century in North America with the propagation of sociobiology, an attempt to explain all human social behaviour as biologically determined.

The assumption of natural differentiation within the family works to dichotomize human experience into male/female and thus emphasizes and exaggerates the differences between men and women rather than the similarities. The view that women are the natural reproducers and childcarers and men are producers of goods and services keeps women from being producers and shunts us out of high-paying jobs, professional work, and other kinds of work that might give us power. Women are seen as suited to work that is an extension of our 'natural' function, such as child care, nursing, or typing. Research tends to focus on male issues, and away from female issues except when they are seen to be consistent with the bias, such as women's role conflict. As Oakley has suggested, "A way of seeing is also a way of not seeing."[51] The sexist interpretation that argues that because women give birth and men do not, that there is a biological basis for the economic and social limitations under which women struggle, is particularly insidious. This is one aspect of biological determinism, whose effects Lorraine Code discusses in her chapter on feminist theory. Although studies have shown repeatedly that women do more of the child care and house work than men do, there may be nothing 'natural' about this, as evidenced by the fact that it is changing at present, has changed in the past, and varies enormously across societies. The danger, of course, is that in accepting the belief that this division of labour is natural, we may be blinded to changes that are occurring and, importantly, to the possibility of innovative changes that may benefit both women and men in the future.

The assumption of one reality within the family may seem to be in contradiction with the assumption of natural differentiation. Eichler states, however, that these obviously contradictory assumptions "happily co-existed for many decades." Eichler goes on to argue, compellingly, that these two biases are actually mutually supportive:

> *Because* we have assumed that there is a natural functional differentiation between spouses we have not bothered to ask individuals to what extent these assumptions are true . . .
>
> *Because* we assume that family members share one reality we often find it sufficient to ask only one family member about family circumstances . . . Because we ask, in general, one-sided questions of only one member of an entire familial unit, we can maintain both fictions.[52]

Bernard's 1973 analysis of 'his' and 'her' marriages was among the first to reveal the one-family bias.[53] In contrast to prevailing myth, Bernard discovered that married men benefit impressively from marriage: they live longer, are happier and healthier than men who remain unmarried. Married women, on the other hand, despite recurrent images of marriage as woman's ultimate fulfillment, suffer more often from depression, unhappiness, and general ill health than do unmarried women.[54] Clearly, popular beliefs about a single reality in the family require reassessment, as do contemporary myths about the happy carefree bachelor who tries to avoid marriage and the miserable 'spinster' who pines away looking for a husband.

Since Bernard's path-breaking research, evidence of both subjective and objective differences in the family experience for women and for men has accumulated. For example, for many married men, marriage and family tend to be assets as well as incentives to work hard. For married women, on the other hand, marriage and family tend to be liabilities and the justification for lower-paid jobs or lack of promotion, as we have seen. Divorce, as well, is a radically different experience for men and for women. A Canadian study found that divorced men were much less likely to have money problems than divorced women, and much more likely to remarry.[55] A recent American study has found that men's average incomes increase by some 73 per cent after divorce while women, who more often have custody of the children, experience a decline of some 25 per cent in their living standard.[56] Eichler cites numerous examples of widely discrepant subjective responses from husbands and wives on who makes the decisions, on marital happiness, on marital expectations, and even on numbers of children they have.[57]

An androcentric bias runs through most research and theory on the family. Although it takes different forms, androcentrism essentially holds that what males do is generally representative of all human experience. The behaviour of women is either analysed in male terms, compared to a male standard, or rendered invisible or meaningless.

An example of androcentric bias is the use of tools developed by men, which are then applied to women without ever actually studying women. Studies of male-only samples which are generalized to all people would be one example. Two well-publicized examples of this include Kohlberg's study of the stages of moral development, which was based entirely on males, and McClelland's study of need-achievement, which also included only males in the sample.[58] When compared to the male standard, women may appear to be lacking in both moral development and achievement motivation. Both Joanna Boehnert and Lorraine Code discuss in their chapters how Carole Gilligan's recent work has challenged these entrenched views. Similarly, women have more often been chosen as the subjects of studies of family dynamics, childbearing, and child care.[59] It is concluded that men are not particularly good in these areas, when, in fact, questions have seldom been put to men about family and childbearing. This kind of research might be called what the distinguished British biologist, C.H. Waddington, referred to as the "Conventional Wisdom of the Dominant Group," or the evocative acronym "COWDUNG."[60]

Quantitative analysis of data, even when not appropriate to the data, is another example of androcentric bias. Called "the machismo factor in social research" by Wilson, this has also been termed "physics envy," by male social scientists who feel emasculated when their methods are compared to those used in the harder (significantly termed) natural sciences.[61] Quantitative methods allow for control of data (in this case people) from which the researcher remains distant, a distinctly masculine approach. Demographic analyses of family change, including marriage and divorce rates, family composition, and birth rates, provide an extreme example of how quantitative analysis removes the problem from its context. Vickers suggests that use of quantitative methods tends to remove human behaviour from its context, "mathematics as a language for the expression of feminist reality is often the most context-stripped of all."[62] What is needed is a feminist methodology that involves respondents in the process of understanding what is happening to them, rather than equating them with atoms. Steps taken to develop such a methodology include action-oriented research strategies and an interactive interviewing technique, which gives credence to respondents as people rather than as only data.[63]

One further example of how androcentric bias prevents us from understanding our family patterns as women is the inappropriate use of cultural relativism. Examples of this include the widespread overlooking or acceptance of violence against women in our homes (as well as on the streets and at work) as a private and even subcultural phenomenon. Institutionalized sexism, in this case, goes so far as to enlist the legal and medical professions to justify and excuse partriarchal violence against women by arguing that the source of the problem lies with the woman who 'asked for it,' either by her behaviour or by her mental or emotional 'problems.'

The power to label gives those in a dominant position in society the capacity to categorize and discuss the experiences of those who have less power. This bias, like the others discussed here, distorts what we know about women in families and about women generally. The very name by which adult human females are known, 'women,' had to be reclaimed by us, in defiance of the dominant group's preferred usage of the term 'girls.' The term 'lady' can still control women who were taught to take special care in how we behave and are seen by others. Most distorting, perhaps, are the images held of the family by society as caring, loving, sharing, of family as the bedrock of society, of family as a 'haven in a heartless world,' of family as women's place where women 'build nests' for the happiness of men, children, and ourselves. Supported by religion, art, literature, and the media, as well as by professionals such as social scientists, counsellors, lawyers, and doctors, these images are sufficiently powerful to overwhelm women's reality. Some families may be all this, but familism tends to deny that family can have negative aspects, too.

The mass appeal of familism and the widespread propagation of nostalgic family images rests on the assumption that there is no better alternative to the family. This creates the impression that people in families, particularly women, should not be unhappy or try to change the family because there is no real alternative to the family as we know it. Feminist analysts of the family have argued that family images, combined with the legitimacy and privacy of the family in our society, can mask the oppressive relations engendered by the economic dependency of women and children in the patriarchal family.[64] Families, after all, are supposed to be centres of loving and caring, not oppression. Barrett takes this one step further with her insight that "the family sucks the juice out of everything around it, leaving other institutions stunted and distorted."[65] Sharing and loving might be more widespread if the family did not claim them for its own.[66] Socialist and Marxist feminists, among others, have taught us that caring and sharing among people in a non-familial situation might be preferrable to living with false images in the patriarchal nuclear family.

Taking Stock
Women's Family Patterns in the Future

We have seen, in this chapter, how the family in contemporary Canada is central to the lives of women, yet it is not all it can be. The patriarchal family as a social institution may be imbued with too many expectations, too many false images to enable us to thrive within it. Yet, as women, it is often important to us, whether we are feminists or not, to have a good family life.

Changes have occurred in the Canadian family over the past few decades and will, no doubt, continue to occur in the future. The family cannot be a static institution. But change, as we have seen, may not be unwelcome. The decline in family size among Canadians appears to be part of a world-wide trend, yet we have seen that women seldom opt out of child-bearing altogether. Although families are no longer as large as they once were for a variety of reasons, having children is still important to the vast majority of women. Motherhood is an option now as never before, yet it is an option most women want. While some alarmists may worry that women are forsaking their traditional roles as mothers, it seems more likely that motherhood continues to be an important, if not always dominant feature of women's lives, but in an altered form. Smaller families and the decreased portion of women's lifetimes spent in childrearing both result from and provide greater opportunities for women to be people as well as mothers. It seems clear that small families are here to stay.

The dramatic increase of married women and mothers in the paid work force is another salient change in Canadian society. Out of economic necessity, the dual-earner family is becoming the norm among Canadian families today. Although often difficult to balance, given the division of domestic chores within the patriarchal family, mothers who work are saying that both activities matter. Women work to support their families and themselves. An unfortunate aspect is that working mothers are paid so little, on average, and offered few benefits and opportunities in the work-force because of the widespread, mistaken belief they are not working out of necessity. One change that the future must hold is a more equitable sharing of child care and domestic responsibilities among spouses. Enhanced recognition of the value of women's work to the economy is another. It is untenable to think that women can continue forever carrying a double or triple work load without calling out for substantial change.

Divorce, although an important recent change in the Canadian family, may not be a sign of disenchantment with family. Prohibition of divorce does not guarantee marital happiness or even that the marriage will stay together. Increases in the divorce rate might instead indicate a dissatisfaction with traditional family expectations and constraints. It can be a vote for a new kind of family – one that is more egalitarian, flexible, caring, and giving. Since most divorced people do remarry, this seems to be strong evidence that they are searching for something marriage and family provide. There is no hint that marriage in Canada will go out of style, yet the variety of marriage types is likely to widen allowing couples a flexibility to be and become themselves more, regardless of rigid social expectations.

Only some of the challenges to the Canadian family of the 1980s have been explored here. The family has emerged on the political agenda of the New Right as well as on the feminist agenda. On the right wing, the patriarchal family is lamented to be in decline. The challenge for the right wing is to restore it by stemming the tides of change in women's work-force participation, in availability of contraception, abortion, and divorce, and in shifting patterns of domestic division of labour. On the feminist front, these changes are welcomed and encouraged as signs that the family is alive, well, and capable of changing as the world changes. These changes further allow for human mistakes and different human needs, but do not suggest that the family is being abandoned.

The Canadian family and women's place in it have been changing and continue to change. Consistent with the action-oriented perspective characteristic of feminism, it is our hope that these changes evolve in a way that enables the family to emerge from its patriarchal form into a flexible institution. Such a modern family would encourage each of its members to care about and for each other as other human beings with whom they are sharing their lives, rather than as people bound into roles by social convention.

Many changes have occurred in the Canadian family other than these discussed here. Some social psychologists, for example, have suggested that socialization of children in the family in less gender-specific ways is one such change. Every book on gender roles, of which there are many, focuses on socialization, as do many contemporary magazine and newspaper articles and TV programs. Whether, in fact, changes are evident in socialization patterns is not clear. Other analysts focus more on socialization by the schools, the media, and the work force. They suggest that family roles might change as a consequence of changes occurring outside the family. This, too, is being studied and debated among experts. The roles of older women in families as grandmothers, of women as widows and as caretakers for the elderly members of their families are now being explored as Canada's population ages. The effects of family changes on people's self-images and expectations are being examined. All these are important issues but beyond the scope of this chapter. Our hope is that readers will seek further information on these and related family issues that could not be discussed here.

Susan A. McDaniel

SUGGESTED READINGS

Eichler, Margrit, *Families in Canada Today: Recent Changes and Their Policy Consequences*. Toronto: Gage, 1983.

Grindstaff, Carl, "The Baby Bust Revisited: Canada's Continuing Pattern of Low Fertility," *Canadian Studies in Population* 12, no. 1, (1985): 103–10.

Luxton, Meg, *More Than a Labour of Love: Three Generations of Women's Work in the Home*. Toronto: Women's Educational Press, 1980.

McDaniel, Susan A., "Abortion Implementation in Canada as a Woman's Issue," *Atlantis: A Women's Studies Journal* 10, no. 2, (1985): 74–91.

O'Brien, Mary, *The Politics of Reproduction*. Boston: Routledge & Kegan Paul, 1981.

Smith, Dorothy, "Women, the Family and Corporate Capitalism," in Marylee Stephenson, ed., *Women in Canada*. Don Mills: General Publishing, 1973.

Statistics Canada, *Current Demographic Analysis, Fertility in Canada: From Baby Boom to Baby Bust*, written by A. Romaniuc. Ottawa: Ministry of Supply and Services, 1984.

Wilson, S.J., *Women, the Family and the Economy*, (2nd. edition). Toronto: McGraw-Hill Ryerson, 1986.

Chapter Five

Legislators, Women, and Public Policy

When we consider the changing patterns of Canadian women's lives, it is important to look beyond the choices made by women to the laws that at different times have both constrained and liberated them. The laws that make up the public policies of governments affect our lives in many ways, from our options for work and the rewards for our labour to the quality of life in the home. In Canada, these laws have been made almost exclusively by men and generally have reflected men's assumptions about the 'natural ordering' of society, about what women and men are capable of achieving. Over time these assumptions have changed, and this chapter traces the transition. Most significant in the transition is the gap, which developed soon after Confederation, between legislators' understanding of women's roles and the reality of Canadian women's lives. While women's increased political activity in the 1970s and 1980s has visibly narrowed this gap, current policies still have more to do with what legislators think women ought to be doing than with the needs and aspirations expressed by women themselves. This chapter examines some of the reasons why this gap has persisted over time.

Public Policy from 1867 to Women's Suffrage

In 1867 most women and men accepted the view that there was a sharp distinction between the private sphere of the family and the public sphere of politics and business, and the men holding elected office were no exception. Legislators believed that women by nature were suited to the private sphere and men by nature were suited to the public sphere. Women's roles were fairly inflexible and men's roles rather more flexible. Women were defined in terms of their relationships with men, and legislation was framed in the context of what Lisa Peattie and Martin Rein call a "discourse of social roles, interpersonal responsibility, and commitment," which focused on "family ties, home-making, masculinity and femininity in love and marriage."[1] It was a discourse of inequalities, which celebrated men as providers and leaders and women as care-givers and followers.

The belief in separate spheres was written into the legislation of the time. It was widely believed in the nineteenth century that a woman's primary responsibility was to care for her family, and that she should devote herself to the procreation and raising of children. To this end, the 1892 amendment to the federal Criminal Code prohibited the sale, display, or advertisement of birth control devices and this amendment remained in force until 1969. It was based on the view that sexual intercourse should take place only within marriage, where the wife was the property of her husband and should bear many children for him.

Early legislation also designated the husband/father as the head of the household, with the power to decide the fortunes of all family members. This was a reversal of the practice in New France described by Jane Errington in her chapter. She points out that in the eighteenth century, many women who settled in New France participated in the economic activities of the colony and enjoyed liberal property and guardianship rights. By Confederation this freedom had disappeared, and from 1867 until the turn of the century, the husband was in charge of family finances and controlled any wages his wife might earn. He also held the exclusive right in the family to own and sell property or sign contracts. Even guardianship rights were vested in the father by the terms of the 1867 British North America Act. Although in Ontario after 1887 a mother could apply to the courts for guardianship, the general practice was for the father to have absolute legal authority over his children. In addition, according to the federal 1881 Act respecting Naturalization and Aliens, married women took on the citizenship of their husband upon marriage. Divorce was rare in those days, and in all provinces but Nova Scotia divorce laws were written in the framework of inequality. Men seeking divorce had to prove that their wife had committed adultery. For women seeking divorce, the husband's adultery alone was not sufficient, and evidence of cruelty, incestuousness, or some other crime was required.

In this early thinking about women's and men's roles, it was assumed that men would support their families financially in return for their right to rule as masters in the home. In fact, as Jane Errington notes in her chapter, men often failed to fulfil their obligations. Slowly, both levels of government decided to intervene to protect women from the consequences of this failure but without disturbing the distribution of roles or power in the family. This intervention was extraordinary in the political climate of the late nineteenth century in Canada, for this was the era of the negative state, when it was generally believed that the government that governs least governs best. The bulk of legislation was outside the realm of what were then widely considered to be women's concerns such as health, education, and welfare. At the federal level, members of Parliament were legislating territorial settlement, defence, customs, and the Criminal Code. At the provincial level, legislators were concerned with roads, schools, industrial development, and organizing the municipalities. That both levels of government were prepared to break this pattern and provide welfare to needy mothers underlines their commitment to preserving what they referred to as the "pure Christian home," which provided "the only safe foundation for the free and enlightened state."[2]

The new laws protecting women did nothing to alter women's status. Legislators adhered firmly to the principle that the wife owed allegiance to her husband, and provided some financial relief only to women with children who had been left without a husband, through death or desertion. Divorced women were not eligible for funds. Furthermore, if a deserted wife committed adultery, her support was stopped. In some cases, such as in Newfoundland after 1872, the government itself paid the relief. In others, such as in British Columbia after 1901, the husband was ordered to make payments to his wife. In 1869, the federal government passed a law which imposed a fine on a man who failed to provide for his wife, and in 1913 this was amended to include providing for his children. In this same spirit of looking after women who had lost the male provider in the family, the first pensions in Canada were granted to women. Beginning in 1868, the federal govenment awarded pensions to a small number of widows of men who had performed great services for Canada. In 1914, with the granting of $100 to the widows of volunteers who had defended the government in the Fenian Raids, the federal government began the practice of providing for the widows of servicemen. All pensions ceased if the widow married again. These relief payments never matched living expenses, but alleviated the worst cases of poverty.

In their concern for the continued strength of the family, legislators also began to pass laws that gave women slightly more power over family finances. These laws were not intended to make women independent or equal, but to provide them with some economic security in case of their husbands' death or desertion. Between 1872 and 1922 in English Canada, although not until 1940 in Quebec, property laws were changed to allow that the person who purchased the property was the owner. By 1897 in English Canada and 1931 in Quebec, a wife employed outside the home was allowed to retain her wages. Another early concession granted to married women was the right to be treated as joint owner of the homestead in the Homestead Exemption Act of 1878. This act was limited in its impact since it applied only to those parts of Canada that were then administered by the federal government, namely those lands that had not yet been given provincial status. The legislators who spoke in favour of this measure pointed out that the family, and not the individual, was the basis of Canadian society. The homestead act "recognized the fact, although the law generally treated the head of the family as the absolute proprietor of the property which he controlled, that this property was also the product of the industry of his wife and children, that they had some interest in it which the law ought to recognize and, in some measure, to protect."[3]

This mode of reasoning sometimes led politicians to take unusual actions which seemed, at first glance, to challenge the belief in separate spheres. In 1883, for example, the prime minister, Sir John A. MacDonald, sought the franchise for propertied widows and spinsters. But he was not concerned about equality rights. Rather, he believed that women would vote for his party in the next federal election, and that women would also use their vote to "strengthen the defences against the eruption of an unbridled democracy."[4] This was an early declaration of the gender gap in Canadian politics. While MacDonald's early attempts at women's suffrage failed, his arguments re-emerged thirty-five years later when votes for women became a reality.

Because women in the nineteenth century were valued primarily as wives and mothers, governments took some action to safeguard the purity of young girls before they married. Chastity laws were passed in an attempt to eradicate prostitution. The separate incarceration of female convicts became the practice in the 1870s, and female reformatories were the scene of crusading attempts to purify the inmates. The morality crusade also led the federal government in 1910 to prohibit any contact between female immigrants (many of whom were brought to Canada for marriage to frontier men) and the ship's crew during passage. But while the state was prepared to defend the interests of innocent young women, it was also concerned with protecting men from what it considered to be the mercenary schemes of evil women. Women were viewed as both victims and seductresses, and the 1886 amendments to the Criminal Code provide a good example of this double image. The amendments punished seducers of young women between the ages of twelve and sixteen, but the onus of proof was on the accuser. The amendments decreed that one witness to the act of seduction was insufficient, and that the defendant was a competent witness for the defence. Men were protected from unscrupulous women, but women found it nearly impossible to win convictions against unscrupulous men.

In this early vision of women's proper roles there was some allowance for women to participate in the labour force, but this participation was seen to be class specific and temporary. In this respect, the laws reflected women's perceptions, for as Jane Errington points out in her chapter, most women at the turn of the century expected to make a good marriage. Working-class girls were actively recruited for domestic service, for they were needed to keep the middle-class family alive and well. It was assumed that these young girls were merely putting in time as domestic workers before marriage. The federal government went so far as to advertise for female domestics both in Canada and abroad, and in 1881 there were 800,410 households in Canada employing 49,345 servants.[5] But the thought of women taking part in industrial labour was unacceptable to the early law-makers. In the *Report* of the Royal Commission on the Relations between Capital and Labour, women's presence in the economy was described as an unfortunate corollary of industrial expansion.[6] There were even some formal attempts to limit the extent of women's work. Nova Scotia and Ontario passed laws in the late 1800s restricting women from mining underground. Quebec and Ontario established minimum wages and maximum hour restrictions in the 1880s for women in some industrial occupations. All provinces excluded women from hazardous jobs. These regulations may have afforded some protection to women, but they also demonstrated women's lack of control over the manner of their participation in the labour force and kept them out of some of the better-paid jobs. They reinforced the paternalistic treatment of women by governments and did nothing to break down the principle that women were both different from and unequal to men.

There were some exceptions to the prevailing notion of separate spheres. In the West in particular, women who had taken risks side by side with men were less willing than their central-Canadian sisters to sit back and be controlled by these same men. On the whole, however, there were few challenges by women to legislators' judgements about the pattern of their lives until the twentieth century.

Public Policy from the Franchise to the 1940s

By the turn of the century, the agreement between women and men on appropriate roles for women had begun to break down. This was most apparent during the struggle for women's suffrage rights, when women sought entrance to the public sphere through the vote. Suffragists "demanded for women a kind of power and a connection with the social order not based on the institution of the family and their subordination within it."[7] While it is true that most suffragists saw the vote as a means of safeguarding peace in the home, there was a small group of working women who sought equality rights in the labour force. Manitoba, Saskatchewan, and Alberta were the first provinces to grant women voting rights in 1916, with British Columbia and Ontario following in 1917. The federal government also enfranchised some women in 1917 with the Wartime Elections Act, which gave the vote to close relatives of members of the armed services. In the same year the Military Voters Act gave the vote to women who were themselves in active service. By 1918 the federal government had granted full female suffrage in federal elections. In the same year

Nova Scotia granted female suffrage, followed by New Brunswick in 1919 and Prince Edward Island in 1922. Quebec women did not gain the right to vote in provincial elections until 1940. With the vote, women were allowed into the public sphere and for the first time since the emergence of the notion of separate spheres, were offered "a relationship to the larger society that was entirely and explicitly outside the boundaries of women's familial relations."[8] However, most women and men were convinced that women would use the vote only to improve the quality of life in the home. One member's speech in the federal House of Commons in 1918 during the debate on women's suffrage captures this attitude well: "Here I approve, but with the understanding that the exercise of these rights will not go to lengths where woman will be diverted from her function, from her natural and sacred duty."[9] Furthermore, at the federal level at least, the suffrage legislation was passed by a government convinced that votes for women would guarantee its re-election.

In the wake of the suffrage victory, women's rights in the home were strengthened. Between 1917 and 1923 most provinces enacted equal guardianship laws, which gave mothers equal rights with fathers to the custody, control, and education of children. Divorce laws were made less discriminatory. Adultery alone was accepted as grounds for divorce for either the husband or wife, although property settlements still did not recognize the housewife's contribution to family assets. Citizenship laws were amended in 1931 to allow a woman who was a British subject before marriage to retain her British citizenship after marriage to a person classified as "alien."

The participation of women in the labour force became more acceptable in this post-suffrage period. The change in thinking was partly due to the need for labour in the rapidly expanding Canadian industrial economy. But it was a policy still based on separate spheres, and women in the labour force were expected to be single, to work in different jobs than men, and to receive lower wages. This was obvious during World War II when, in the face of labour shortages caused by men's participation in the armed services, the federal government reluctantly recruited women to work. It was a case of single women first. "Government officials publicly expressed a reluctance to draw upon those people in the female labour reserve whose mobilization would disrupt the traditional family system."[10] Nevertheless, by 1944, the need for female labour in the war industries was so great that even married women with children were called out. To facilitate their participation in the war effort, day nurseries were set up in some industries, and tax concessions were offered to make women's earnings more attractive. As soon as the war was over, however, married women with children were expected to return home. The nurseries were closed and the tax concessions cancelled. It was obvious that the "large-scale employment of women was not supposed to last."[11]

During the first half of this century, these and other changes in the working patterns of Canadian women led to another series of protective laws, for governments felt responsible for safeguarding the reproductive capabilities of single women who, they now conceded, could play a limited role in the developing industrial economy. In order to develop guidelines for this new policy, most provinces set up commissions to investigate women's work. The Nova Scotia Commission of Inquiry into the hours of labour, wages, and working conditions of women employed in industrial occupations was typical. The commission was made up of three men and one woman and its report, presented to the Nova Scotia government in 1920, was based on open hearings and a survey of employment practices. In its deliberations, the commission was guided by the principle that "if we are to have a healthy virile race, it is of primary importance to preserve the homes and conserve the health, morals and efficiency" of working women.[12] The commission recognized that there was "a striking disparity between wages paid to men and their hours of labour,"[13] but did not try to remove this inequality. The commission accepted the principle that the labour of women and men is different and therefore unequal.

At the time there was generally little concern for the unequal wages paid men and women. Even J.S. Woodsworth, then leader of the Co-operative Commonwealth Federation – a party committed to social justice – rose in the House of Commons in 1926 to complain about the wages paid to married men, but not about the even lower wages paid to single women. Ten years after the Nova Scotia Commission's *Report* was tabled, women still were earning on average only 39 per cent of men's earnings. But the concern for women's childbearing potential did lead to some reform proposals. The commission called for minimum wages and maximum hours of work for women, together with the adoption of standards essential "to the health and morals of these women."[14]

Most provinces acted on these proposals, and minimum-wage laws for women were passed in the early 1900s, considerably in advance of minimum-wage laws for men. British Columbia was the first province to pass a Women's Minimum Age Act in 1918. The act stipulated that experienced women would not be paid less than the living wage. Between 1918 and 1922, all provinces but Prince Edward Island and New Brunswick passed minimum-wage legislation for women. Alberta was the one province that had a minimum wage for both women and men. In each case the legislation established a minimum-wage board, which was to determine the amount needed to sustain a single woman. Farm labourers or domestics were not covered, and this meant that only about one-half of the women in the labour force were protected. In most cases, the acts gave the cabinet the power to decide if the wage boards' recommendations should be followed. A study of the Ontario board has shown that "co-operation with employers was made a goal in itself, as important as the goal of ensuring that women's wages would meet the cost of living."[15] At best, these laws alleviated only the worst instances of exploitation. They did nothing to advance the principle of equal pay for equal work – and working women were beginning to make this demand, as Jane Errington notes in her chapter in this book. Telephone operators in Toronto struck for better wages and shorter hours in 1907, but this and other calls for justice were ignored.

In the same spirit of protecting women's reproductive capabilities, there was legislation restricting the lifting of weights. In 1920 the federal government amended the Criminal Code to provide penalties for male employers who tried to take sexual advantage of female employees under twenty-one who were "previously chaste."[16] These protective laws were a mixed blessing for women. While they undoubtedly moderated some of the harsh conditions in the labour force, they did not really guarantee healthy working conditions or a decent living wage. At the same time, they further reduced women's access to employment. They were enacted by a paternalistic government which gave little thought to the ambitions or proposals of working women themselves, but was concerned, as in earlier times, with protecting women's reproductive functions, and with keeping young working girls pure for marriage.

The gradual admission that some women might need the income from working outside the home coincided with the realization that the traditional family unit was not always a success. In spite of this concession, most legislators were still convinced that marriage was woman's calling in life. They continued to view the family as women's proper sphere, and in order to make it easier for single mothers to stay at home, the provinces introduced the notion of the mothers' allowance, then called mothers' pensions. Manitoba was the first province in 1916 to enter "into inadequate homes as the active agent of middle-class values."[17] The program provided a small subsidy, which would permit working mothers to stay at home for at least part of each day. The first mothers' pensions were not distributed to all mothers. While there were some provincial variations in requirements, generally the applicants had to be needy widows with two or more children. Some provinces allowed wives of insane men to apply. Most provinces disallowed divorcées or unmarried mothers, for this was not a move to sanction marital breakdown. These mothers' pensions were designed to reduce infant mortality rates and the incidence of juvenile deliquency, and were instigated by the belief that "if the present and next generation of widows' children are to be conserved for the nation, a mothers' allowance is the present practical solution."[18]

Women in the Developing Welfare State

The welfare state took a firm hold in Canada in the period following the end of World War II. It brought governments into areas of legislation such as employment and income security, which formerly had been regarded as outside the scope of public policy. Twenty years earlier, the famous feminist Nellie McClung had said that "more and more the idea is growing upon us that certain services are best rendered by the state, and not left to depend on the caprice, inclination, or inability of the individual."[19] This philosophy ultimately became popular in the 1940s, and women played a significant role in the welfare state that emerged. With the creation of the welfare state, the boundaries of the public sphere widened and those of the private sphere narrowed. Governments seemed ignorant of the impact these changes would have on women's lives. They passed a series of measures to encourage women to continue to stay at home and raise healthy future workers for the rapidly expanding economy.

Some of the earlier relief measures that had been developed to assist needy single mothers became part of a universal program of benefits. Mothers' allowance is a good example. By 1940 all provinces but New Brunswick and Prince Edward Island provided mothers' pensions, although the amounts paid to women varied widely from province to province. In 1942, for example, average monthly benefits were $39.19 in British Columbia, but only $13.77 in Saskatchewan, one of the provinces hardest hit by the post-war depression.[20] In 1944 the federal government stepped in and took over the program. The means test was dropped and the allowance was sent to all mothers with children aged sixteen or younger.

This family-allowance program was one of the first in the federal government's growing package of income-security measures. It helped to set the tone of the welfare state, underscoring the fact that "the Welfare State is not just a set of services, it is also a set of ideas about society, about the family, and–not least important–about women, who have a centrally important role within the family, as its linchpin."[21] The federal government's motives in making family allowance a universal program were linked to the needs of the expanding economy. Canada needed healthy workers to fill the increasing number of available jobs, and women were urged to stay at home, have babies, and raise them to become strong and productive workers.

In his speech to the House of Commons justifying the introduction of family-allowance payments, Mackenzie King, the Liberal prime minister, noted: "This measure proceeds upon the assumption that children are an asset to the state." He went on to argue that: "Properly nourished children become active, productive members of society, and there is no doubt that this is the only way in which a strong and healthy citizenry can be built up."[22] Family allowance cheques, payable to the mother, would make it easier for women to stay at home and raise these citizens. Clearly, the value of women's labour in the home had changed from the time of Confederation. Whereas the nineteenth century mother was viewed as the moral guardian of the nation, the twentieth century mother was viewed as the producer of workers for an expanding economy. The language of social purity and morality, which dominated legislative discussions about women's roles in the early 1900s, was replaced by the language of healthy babies, strong soldiers, and better workers.

At the same time, the need for more workers also led to greater acceptance of the possibility that women without children might work outside the home. In the egalitarian spirit of the post-war years, governments slowly adopted some equal-rights legislation for women with paid jobs. For, once governments with liberal principles had accepted the possibility that women could be members of the paid labour force, it was difficult to deny them the rights being extended to male workers. Most employees were under provincial jurisdiction, and there was a series of provincial legislative initiatives in the 1950s to improve equal opportunity for women at work. Slowly, beginning in 1951 in Ontario and ending in Newfoundland in 1970, the provincial governments passed equal-pay legislation, which generally was worded to guarantee women and men in both the public and private sectors the same pay for similar or essentially similar jobs. Unfortunately, these initiatives were too weak to have much effect since then, as now, the labour force was highly segregated by gender and few women actually worked in the same jobs as men.

In 1954 the federal government finally decided that it should know more about women's labour force participation and established a Women's Bureau in the federal Department of Labour. According to the 1951 census, 24 per cent of Canadian women were then members of the paid labour force. Governments knew very little about these women, and the Women's Bureau was designed to "promote a wider understanding of problems peculiar to women workers and the employment of women." The bureau, in keeping with the spirit of labour legislation for women in this period, was to help women "to make a more effective contribution to the development of Canada."[23] The bureau struggled to carry out its mandate with one director and only two staff members. Even with this small staff, the bureau played a vital role in informing governments, civil servants, and the public about the nature of women's work outside the home, and in its first year undertook a survey of married women working for pay in Canada.

The bureau also played a role in preparing the federal equal-pay legislation, introduced in 1956. This legislation had most of the flaws of the provincial laws and did not go very far in guaranteeing true equality for women workers.

It applied only to federal works or businesses, or corporations performing work on behalf of the government, and limited equal pay to "identical or substantially identical work." The aggrieved employee was required to complain in writing to the Minister of Labour, who might then ask a fair wage officer to make an inquiry, a cumbersome procedure which was rarely used. In spite of these limitations, the federal and the earlier provincial equal-pay laws were significant landmarks in the legislative history of women's rights. First, they recognized the possiblity that women and men might hold similar jobs in the public world. Second, they established the principle that when women and men were performing similar work they should receive the same rewards. The earlier presumption that women and men were different and, therefore, always unequal was being replaced by the notion that they might, in some cases, be the same and therefore equal. The boundaries of policy-making for women had begun to shift. But the movement was gradual, and marked by important setbacks. The Canadian Bill of Rights, which became law in 1960, guaranteed women and men equal treatment before the law, where they were in equal situations. Litigation based on the Bill of Rights demonstrated quickly how few instances there might be in which such equal situations would be judged to exist, as Beverley Baines demonstrates in her chapter.

The principle of equal treatment was applied unevenly and primarily in the public sphere. The 1969 amendments to the Criminal Code illustrate how far governments were from legislating in the spirit of equal rights in the home. These amendments permitted the sale of contraceptives and made it legal for doctors to perform abortions in hospitals where a therapeutic abortion committee had given its approval. The committee was instructed to make its decision on the basis of the medical need of each case. Women seemed to be on the brink of winning control away from men over reproductive rights. However, the abortion amendments had two consequences, neither of which protected the rights of individual women. First, they moved the issue of abortion to the local level, thereby institutionalizing unequal access to abortions and at the same time removing some pressure from federal politicians to change abortion laws. Second, they failed to remove men's control over women's reproductive rights, since the therapeutic abortion committees were made up primarily of male doctors. The federal government had not yet come to terms with the growing conflict between its laws for women in the public sphere, where individual rights were becoming more important, and its laws for women in the home, where the preservation of the family was still the dominant theme.

On other measures, particularly those requiring new thinking about women's and men's roles, governments' performances remained poor. Indian women by law were still unequal to Indian men; rape laws still favoured the accused at the expense of the accuser; property distribution on dissolution of marriage rewarded men and penalized women; day care provisions were woefully inadequate; government-run pension programs discriminated against housewives; and there was unequal pay for women and men working in different but equally valuable jobs.

The Success of the Equal Opportunity Principle

Two events in 1970 signalled a transition in legislators' thinking about women's roles: maternity leave provisions became part of the Canada Labour (Standards) Code, and the *Report* of the Royal Commission on the Status of Women was published. While the *Report* was not implemented in its entirety, it nevertheless unleashed forces which contributed to the development of a new view of women by legislators. In the legislation of the 1970s and 1980s, the concept of the working mother was recognized; there were improvements in women's equality rights in the public sphere; and there was better protection for women from sexual harassment and wife-battering.

With the introduction of maternity-leave provisions, the traditional view that women must be mothers first and workers in the labour force second began to disintegrate. The 1970 legislation provided pregnant women with eleven weeks of paid leave and automatic job reinstatement at the same level of pay and seniority at the end of the leave period. The legislation was far from perfect. The payments made by the unemployment insurance program were lower than the wages earned before the leave. If pregnancy and unemployment coincided, the applicant was refused benefits. Because the benefits were part of the unemployment package, the cost of maternity was borne by taxpayers rather than employers. Nevertheless, the legislation was significant since it was national, and across all of Canada the message was clear that the employment cost of child-bearing, although not child care, was a community responsibility rather than an individual woman's burden.

In keeping with this new philosophy of welcoming women more fully into the public sphere, both levels of government enacted a series of equal-opportunity laws for women. As a first step, governments tried to remove discriminatory practices from existing laws. At the same time, they progressed rapidly to establish women's formal legal equality. In 1981 the federal government ratified the United Nations Convention on the Elimination of All Forms of Discrimination Against Women. In 1984 a federal parliamentary task force was set up to identify discriminatory laws. In 1985 the task force issued its report with eighty-five recommendations, and in 1986 the government tabled

Toward Equality, its response to the report. *Toward Equality* affirmed the federal government's commitment to legal equality rights for women. Finally, in April 1985, the equality rights provisions of the Charter of Rights and Freedoms came into effect. Section 15 of the Charter guarantees the equality of women and men before and under the law, and their right to the equal protection and benefit of the law. Provincially, the pattern was similar. In 1969 British Columbia became the first province to make discrimination in the employment of women illegal under its Human Rights Act. By 1975 all provinces but Prince Edward Island and Newfoundland had similar legislation.

The early equal-opportunity laws were based on the philosophy that discrimination against women in the labour force was a human-relations problem, a consequence of "evilly motivated conduct."[24] Individuals who felt that they had suffered discrimination had to take their case to either a provincial or a federal human rights commission, and the onus was on the individual to demonstrate her case. By the late 1970s, it was recognized that women's access to jobs was limited by systemic barriers such as height and weight restrictions in job descriptions. Governments started to put in place affirmative action programs, which would remove these factors and increase women's access to jobs formerly held primarily by men. For the most part, these programs have been voluntary and limited to government employees. They have had only minimal impact on employment practices.[25] In 1979 the federal government set up the Affirmative Action Directorate of the Canada Employment and Immigration Division. It contacted over 1,400 employers "to encourage them to participate in a voluntary affirmative action program. As of July 1984, only seventy-one companies had agreed to do so."[26] In addition, a national industrial training program was established to try to prepare more women for non-traditional jobs. The Treasury Board was put in charge of an affirmative action program in the public service, but it has been slow to implement this program.

Today, the principle of affirmative action has been accepted by both levels of government because it merely affirms that women and men should be treated equally when they are the same. It improves women's access to the public sphere but requires them to behave like men and compete equally on men's terms for jobs which men have created and defined. Most provinces now have a version of affirmative action in place. In 1986 the federal government took affirmative action one step further and passed Bill C-62, which requires federally regulated and Crown companies with over 100 employees to report to the government on their adherence to the principle of fair competition. But only the reporting is mandatory. There are no provisions to enforce compliance with fair-competition practices. In addition, the success of this program is dependent on the watchdog talents of the Canadian Human Rights Commission. With its backlog of roughly 1,500 cases, the Commission is not able to act quickly on complaints.

Equal pay for work of equal value laws have been less common, for they challenge the traditional notion that women's work is less valuable than men's, by legislating the principle that women are different but equal. They incorporate the argument advanced by many feminists in the 1980s (described by Naomi Black earlier in this book) that women should be allowed to remain different from men without being economically penalized for their differences. In 1977 the federal government passed the Canadian Human Rights Act, which established the principle of equal pay for work of equal value in the federal public service. On the face of it, this was a great leap forward for women. However, the federal guidelines for equal value were poorly written, and the program has had only limited effectiveness. In 1984 the federal government also implemented a national Equal Pay Program to ensure that employers under federal jurisdiction adopt the principle of equal pay for work of equal value. The success of this program has not yet been determined. In 1975, Quebec affirmed the equal value principle, and in 1986, Manitoba imposed it on all public sector employees. Ontario introduced a bill covering both public and private employees in 1986 and this became law in 1988. The Ontario legislation applies to all firms with more than 100 employees, and wage adjustments come into effect between two to four years from the date of proclamation of the act. If these programs are applied effectively, they will change significantly our perceptions of women's and men's worth.

However, these programs to redress imbalances in the labour force have not been very effective to date. In the 1987 *Report* of the Neilson Task Force, the following observation was made about the federal government's program of equal opportunities for women:

> In spite of the existence of several government programs directed at the achievement of equal pay/value and employment equity/affirmative action goals, the significant wage gap between men and women employed on the same full-time, full-year basis has remained virtually unchanged since 1978, according to a variety of detailed and comprehensive studies as recent as the Abella and MacDonald Commissions.[27]

As the Abella Commission on Equality in Employment recognized, one of the keys to labour-force equality for women is improved access to affordable, reliable day care.[28] In 1984, 52 per cent of mothers with children under age three were working outside of the home, and 80 per cent of these mothers were forced to use unlicensed day care. The Canadian Commission for the International Year of the Child estimated that in 1979 over one million Canadian children were left at home alone or with siblings while their parents were at work.[29] The lack of day care has affected women in different ways. Low-income women, who must work to survive, have responded either by working part-time or by making do with less than adequate child care. Middle class women have been "made to feel guilty by the idea that they might be damaging their children if they went out to work."[30] At the same time, the scarcity of reliable, affordable day care has reinforced class differences in our society, with full-time nannies looking after the children of professional women, and very often no one caring for the latchkey children in working-class homes.

One of the recommendations of the Royal Commission on the Status of Women was the setting up of more status of women offices within governments. Gradually, an extensive bureaucratic group has been assembled at the federal level, and the provinces have adopted part of the federal package. The commission also recommended that the federal government provide financial support to women's groups. In 1973 the federal Cabinet approved the creation of the Women's Program within the Secretary of State. Its budget has been used primarily to support women's groups, and in 1987 this budget reached $12.7 million.

In the 1970s, the federal government also rediscovered its earlier mandate of legislating for morality. In 1979, when the government adopted a Plan of Action as part of its strategy for the United Nations Decade of Action, three of the five areas selected for action were morality issues. The plan included action on rape, sexual harassment, wife-battering, women in the media, and pensions. The concern for protecting women had been transmitted to governments by women's groups, and it continues to be a central issue in women's struggle to control their lives. Yet, one cannot help but be somewhat suspicious of the government's motives. The switch in focus from equal pay for work of equal value and affordable, accessible day care to rape and wife-beating reduced the pressure on federal finances and on federal-provincial renegotiation of social service funding.

Since the election of the Conservatives in 1984, there has been little movement federally to accelerate the pace of reforms. In the spirit of improving the legal equality of women, the government's statutes have been brought into line with the Charter of Rights and Freedoms. In the early years of the administration, the recommendations of the Cook Task Force on Child Care were placed aside in favour of more study by a new Parliamentary Task Force on Child Care. In December 1987, the government announced its National Strategy on Child Care. This strategy provides for an increase of 200,000 spaces in both non-profit and commercial childcare facilities, as well as an increase to $4,000 in the childcare expense deduction. It does not, however, guarantee the availability of accessible, affordable, high-quality childcare.

The issue of pensions for housewives has been ignored in favour of extensions of the spouses' allowance for widows and the adoption of equal benefits for women and men retiring under similar circumstances. In negotiations leading to the Meech Lake Accord, women's concerns about possible conflict between the Accord and equality rights provisions in the Charter were ignored.

Looking back on the period from 1970 to 1988, it can be seen that there has been increasing acceptance of the principle of equal opportunity for women in the public sphere. Nevertheless, the pace of change has been slow, and women's concerns are still low on the governments' priority lists. Women's demands in the 1970s and 1980s for the application of private-sphere values to public-sphere life have been ignored. There has been little action on issues that would alter the traditional distribution of roles in the private sphere, beyond a resurgence of concern for the morality of husbands and wives and a more equitable splitting of family assets on divorce. The very fact that day care still is regarded as a 'women's issue' attests to the continued belief by law-makers that the household is primarily the woman's responsibility. This means that, on the one hand, women are now expected to compete equally with men and on men's terms for positions in the public sphere, be it the economy or politics. On the other hand, women are also expected to provide most of the care of the family, either by doing the work themselves or by hiring someone to replace them.

Explaining the Pattern

In the years following Confederation, legislators viewed the family as they viewed society – as a hierarchical structure, with men at the top. But while women were legally inferior to men, by custom and later by law men had certain obligations to fulfil towards women. It was a feudal arrangement, based on man's presumed natural superiority. This view, which feminists now call patriarchal, has gradually been transformed for a variety of reasons. There is convincing evidence from our history that women themselves have contributed to the transformation. The work done by the few women who have been elected to public office, the activity of women's groups, working both independently and inside institutions, and the pressures exerted by women working in government bureaucracies have had an impact on the increasing acceptance of equality rights. There is evidence, too, that the pattern of laws would have been very different if women had been more actively involved in writing and implementing our laws.

Women are relatively new to the world of politics and are still quite far removed from political and economic power.[31] In terms of the governing side of politics, women's experience in Canada, as throughout the world, ''ranges from total exclusion to selective inclusion, from discrimination to paternalism, from rejection to condescension.''[32] While the participation rates of women and men in mass-based political activities are becoming more similar, a gap has remained at the higher levels of politics where power is concentrated.

Women have been active in politics in the sense of working for political parties or for specific candidates for a very long time. When Canadian survey data on political participation were first collected in the 1960s it was found that about the same proportion of women as men were helping out the parties at election time. In addition, about the same proportion of women as men turned out at the polls on election day. However, the similarity in the political behaviour of women and men breaks down as we move from activities such as voting or political campaigning to activities such as seeking elected office or the leadership of party organizations. In 1919 it became legal for women to be federal candidates, but between 1919 and 1972 women never held more than 5 per cent of the seats in the House of Commons.[33] After 1972 the percentage of women seeking election increased, and more women ran in their own right rather than as a replacement for a husband (legislator) who had died. In the 1984 election, the percentage of women in the federal House increased dramatically to 10 per cent. It is not clear how much of this increase can be attributed to unexpected Conservative victories in ridings that had not traditionally returned Conservative members, since women are more likely to be nominated in such 'lost cause' ridings.[34] Provincially, the record is somewhat better. In 1983, 12 per cent of the members in the legislatures of both British Columbia and Manitoba were women, although the figure was only 2 per cent in Nova Scotia.[35]

In other words, while Canadian women have been active politically, particularly since the end of World War II, their activity has been concentrated in the support positions that keep the political system running smoothly. This has meant that women have not been making the important decisions either in the political parties or in government. From the time that women won the right to seek elected office, they have had a voice in the legislatures, but it has been muted by their minority status and their distance from powerful cabinet posts. This may be significant for policy decisions. In Finland, for example, it has been noted that women in the legislature, regardless of their views on feminism, are more likely than men to introduce feminist or humanitarian reforms directed to solving the problems of deprived groups.[36] In Canada, a review of the Debates in both the federal and provincial legislatures reveals how frequently female legislators have brought the needs and perspectives of women to the attention of their male colleagues. A forceful reminder of the significance of the female presence came in 1980 when the Ad Hoc Committee on the Constitution was working to ensure that women's equality rights remain in the Constitution. The members of the committee were supported almost exclusively by the female members of Parliament. Reflecting on her Charter experience, one committee member observed that "Parliament, with 282 men, all of them concerned and all of them trying to put our views forward, will not do it like 141 women and 141 men. So that there's a combination of they do not and they cannot. Forget about will not!"[37]

The first women elected to public office found themselves surrounded by men and struggled to bring women's points of view into the legislatures. Many of these early female legislators were members of reform parties committed to social change and improved welfare policies. Irene Parlby is a good example. She was first elected in the 1919 provincial election of Alberta, as a member of the United Farmers of Alberta. She was named minister without portfolio in the cabinet, and used her position to press for legislation on child welfare, support for deserted wives, and the joint guardianship of children.[38]

At about the same time (in 1921) one of Canada's best known feminists, Nellie McClung, was elected to the Opposition bench in Alberta as a Liberal. She often broke party lines to vote with the government on issues that she felt would benefit women. She tried, unsuccessfully, to liberalize the divorce laws in the province, to change the naturalization laws so that a woman marrying an alien would not be disenfranchised, and to alter the Married Women's Property Act. When she was defeated in the 1925 provincial election, she left political life to work in women's organizations.[39] In British Columbia, Mary Ellen Smith, a Liberal elected provincially in 1916, also became a minister without portfolio. She was active in promoting concern for public health and education and is best known for working for mothers' pensions and a minimum wage for women.[40]

The history of Quebec female legislators did not begin until 1940, when women in that province were first given access to elected office. It was twenty-two years after that, in 1962, when the first woman, Claire Kirkland-Casgrain, was elected to represent the Liberals in the provincial legislature. Her record in office for advancing the cause of women's rights is impressive. One of her most significant victories was a civil-rights bill in 1964, which changed Quebec women's legal status. The 1964 bill gave Quebec women the right to be legal guardians of their children, a reform the other provinces had adopted in the early 1900s. It also provided that women could sign leases or enter into business transactions without their husband's consent. Quebec women were experiencing their own Quiet Revolution.

At the federal level, the first woman M.P. was Agnes Macphail (elected in 1921), who represented the United Farmers of Ontario. She therefore operated outside the boundaries of the established parties, and her impact was limited to the role of critic. She was an untiring champion of women in the labour force, and regularly reminded her male colleagues that not all women were provided for by men. Grace MacInnis (also in opposition as a member of the NDP) stands out for her work as an advocate of women's rights in the labour force. Among other things, she worked diligently for maternity leave provisions, pointing out in 1970 that the International Labour Organization had supported maternity leave as early as 1919. She stressed that pregnancy is not women's "burden alone, but the burden of society,"[41] and was one of several women who brought a new perspective on women's roles to the legislative arena.

These are only some examples of the early work done by women in the legislatures to advance the cause of other women. Some of these early female legislators have supported the notion of separate spheres. In the House of Commons, Martha Black made a strong defence of women's special place in the home in 1936 when she noted that: "By the nature of our being we must be home-makers, we have to bring up our children in the service of the world, otherwise where would the world be, where would all the smart men in the House be?"[42] But even this defence of women's separate roles led Black to request that one member of the newly established National Employment Commission be a woman. On the whole, however, women's contributions to legislative deliberations have contributed to the recognition of the legitimacy of women's claims.

The granting of votes to women may have had some impact on the pattern of policy as well. This was the view of Helen Gregory MacGill in 1939, when she reviewed the laws affecting women and children in British Columbia. She explained the passage of the Equal Guardianship Act of 1917, which gave mothers equal custody rights with their husband over children, in the following way. "As naturally as daylight follows darkness, with the recognition of the rights of women as citizens came justice to the married mother in regard to her children."[43] However, after 1918, the political parties generally ignored the 'women's vote' when it became obvious that women were not voting in a block. It was not until 1984 that indications of a possible gender gap led to a national debate on women's issues in the federal election campaign in that year. This debate was precipitated by Gallup polls of 1983, which indicated that women were more likely to support the Liberal party by about 10 per cent.[44] A more recent example of the new-found strength of women voters came in 1987, when the federal Conservative government declared its intention to concentrate on women's issues in an attempt to improve its standing in the polls. While it is true that much of this recent interest in women's issues is mere posturing by the political parties, the concern for women's political allegiance has at least forced the parties to take note of women's concerns.

Women's voices have been raised to governments through their voluntary group memberships as well, and both Jane Errington and Naomi Black discuss the political action of these groups in their chapters. The lobbying efforts of Canadian women's groups have been a significant force affecting policy. Until recently, little was known about the political work of early groups like the National Council of Women or the Women's Christian Temperance Union. Early accounts of these and other groups classified them as charitable and social organizations. The work of feminist historians has shown that they were also very active politically, pressing governments for welfare, labour, and equal-rights legislation.[45]

Most of the newer groups, such as the National Action Committee on the Status of Women, support political action. A national survey of women's groups, conducted in 1984, revealed that 76 per cent of the 144 groups participating in the survey had tried to influence government policy at least once in the preceding ten years. Among their successes, these groups can include fairer asset splitting at divorce and improved sexual assault laws. However, women's groups have also met with many failures. In the 1984 survey, only 19 per cent of groups that had tried to influence governments reported success, and a surprising 25 per cent of them described public officials as hostile.[46] Women's groups have been restricted in their effectiveness by several factors. One factor is that many of them rely heavily on government funding. This puts them at the mercy of government programs, places them under government control, and has restricted their freedom to act as lobbyists. The role of critic is compromised by this financial tie. Another factor is that many groups, such as the Canadian Congress of Learning Opportunities for Women (CCLOW), are committed to democratic practices within their organizations. This means that membership agreement is sought on important issues. In the high-powered world of pressure politics this consensus approach is often a disadvantage since it is time-consuming and expensive.

In addition, women's groups are not all agreed on what should be done for women, or how reforms should be accomplished. The most publicized disagreement has been on the abortion issue, where anti-abortion and pro-choice groups compete for government approval. Less well publicized has been debate on issues such as pensions, censorship, affirmative action, and child care. There is no consensus, even among groups committed to equality rights for women in the public sphere, on how these issues should be resolved. The spectrum of opinions has been altered dramatically, as well, by the recent emergence of groups that argue for a return to the traditional family values and life-style of the nineteenth century. In the face of these differences of opinion, governments have been content to proclaim, as they did at the turn of the century, that they need more information about what women really want.

It has been suggested that this record of limited successes was finally broken in 1980 with the emergence of the Ad Hoc Committee on the Constitution. This was a new, single-issue group which emerged when it became clear to a small number of feminists in Toronto and Ottawa that the existing women's groups might not succeed in ensuring that sex equality rights would be written into the new Charter, which was to become part of the Constitution. The Ad Hoc Committee ultimately adopted hard-sell pressure tactics to convince the federal and provincial justice ministers to support a sex equality clause in the Charter. At the same time, the committee was prepared to combine the consensus style of decision-making with the less democratic practices of most successful interest groups. In addition, the committee learned how to use personal contacts to bring pressure to bear on politicians. Committee members phoned friends working in government and solicited their help. The use of non-governmental funding also gave the committee independence from government. One of the most significant lessons learned during the Charter negotiations was that political decisions in Canada are made within the framework of federal-provincial relations. The members of the Ad Hoc Committee mobilized supporters in all of the provinces and forged an alliance with the federal government when it looked as if the provinces would destroy the federal bargain on equality rights for women. Finally, there was a willingness to compromise. Women on the Ad Hoc Committee later admitted that they presented two sets of demands to the federal government. Publicly, they pressed for the resolutions that had been adopted by the conference they organized in February 1981. Privately, some of their members pressed the Justice Minister to agree to a shorter list of what they felt were attainable demands.

One can only be cautiously optimistic about the future potential of groups adopting the Ad Hoc Committee's model. While it is true that the women on the committee learned how to work in the federal-provincial framework of policy-making, the Charter success may not be replicated easily. The Ad Hoc Committee was working with a government already committed to the issue in question–equality rights for women. There was no disagreement in principle. In addition, the support from Canadian women was almost unanimous–a rare occurrence in political life. On issues involving transformations in the distribution of power between women and men in both the public and the private spheres, even well-orchestrated tactics such as those used by the Ad Hoc Committee will probably fail. There is already some evidence that governments are not prepared to act on women's demands when these demands conflict with their own agenda.

Women's voices have been heard as well within the bureaucracies of government since 1956 when the Women's Bureau in the Department of Labour was established federally, and given the resources devoted to these offices, women might have expected a significant change in their fortunes. In the 1970s, the number of voices increased dramatically with the establishment of a network of status of women officers. But the voices of these officers have been muted by several factors. They lack financial resources, are constrained by their role as advisers to government, and are frequently invisible within large departments.

At the federal level, since 1971 there has been a minister responsible for the status of women. The minister is assisted by Status of Women Canada, which began as part of the Privy Council Office and became a separate central agency in 1976. The funding of women's groups is controlled by the Women's Program in the Secretary of State. In addition, advisers on women's issues were appointed in the departments of Justice, Employment and Immigration, and Health and Welfare. In 1973 the government also appointed an Advisory Council on the Status of Women, to give advice on women's concerns. An overview of the government's record following their establishment generates a mixed review of their success.

Ten people have been appointed as minister responsible for the status of women since 1971. They have shared some common characteristics. All have had to combine this portfolio with a significant other cabinet post and all but two have been men. It is a post that women in government have tried to avoid, on the grounds that the portfolio lacks the necessary resources to be effective, and out of fear that they would be marginalized in a post far removed from the centre of government decision-making.

The power of these ministers has been constrained by a set of variables. There has been strong Cabinet resistance to any change in women's status. Bryce Mackasey encountered this resistance when he tried to introduce government support for day care in the early 1970s. Judy Erola found it on the issue of equal pay for work of equal value.[47] Without the support of Prime Minister Pierre Trudeau who, while he was not a feminist, was committed to justice for all, their achievements would have been even less impressive. They were constrained as well by the lack of support staff. The problem of funding first became publicly apparent when, in 1968, the Women's Bureau in the Department of Labour was the subject of parliamentary debate which focused on the director's lack of authority and funds. Size has also been a problem. The Office of the Co-ordinator was too small in the beginning, although it has now expanded to what the bureaucrats call forty-three person years. Conflicts between the minister and her/his status of women advisers have also served to weaken the significance of this portfolio. Such conflicts were common during the early days of the ministry, and sapped the energy of those involved.[48]

In addition, ministers have tended to view their responsibilities for women through the perspective of their other portfolio. This has had the effect of limiting the scope of reforms. For example, Bryce Mackasey was minister of labour while he held the women portfolio. Most of his contacts with women's issues were through the Women's Bureau in the Department of Labour rather than the Office of the Co-ordinator on status of women.[49] When Marc Lalonde held the post he even proposed to reorganize the Office of the Co-ordinator and make it part of his other portfolio, the Department of Health and Welfare.[50] This move would have weakened the co-ordinator's position as a ministry adviser and as a co-ordinating officer. This points to the potentially negative consequences of linking two portfolios. On the positive side, ministers who have another powerful portfolio in addition to their status of women responsibilities sit on important cabinet committees where they can, if they wish, advance the cause of women's rights.

The status of women officers have played an important part in presenting the reality of women's lives to the government. They have also served as a liaison between government and the growing number of women's groups. However, they too have been constrained by a set of factors. There is a history of weakness *vis-à-vis* other government departments. There has also been friction between status of women departments, and the ministries within which they operate.[51] In addition, there has been too little co-ordination either among the various status of women departments or between these departments and the other ministries. There is a formal mechanism for cooperation. The Office of Co-ordinator was first established as part of an inter-departmental committee assigned the task of considering the recommendations of the Royal Commission on the Status of Women. The co-ordinator was to "be responsible for the interdepartmental examination of the report and drafting of the necessary Cabinet documentation."[52] According to Freda Paltiel, the first woman appointed co-ordinator, that early attempt at cooperation was a success.[53] But, over time, the pattern of inter-departmental consultation and cooperation has broken down.

There is good evidence that status of women concerns are not taken seriously by all civil servants. This problem must have been obvious to government officials as well, for in 1976 an inter-departmental committee, chaired by the assistant secretary to the cabinet's Social Policy Committee, met to consider mechanisms to integrate status of women concerns in government policy. This was the preliminary to the cabinet decision that it would consider each cabinet decision in light of its impact on the status of women. The committee recommended that a standing interdepartmental committee chaired by the co-ordinator, Status of Women, should monitor the implementation of this policy. It also recommended that in "each department and agency of the federal government a structure shall be established or designated which will be responsible for implementing the integration of status of women policy concerns.''[54] It stressed that the people in these status of women structures should be knowledgeable in the working of their department overall, and not just in the status of women. This was a clear call for the integration of status of women concerns in the regular operations of government.

The proposal was not implemented. In the recent Neilson Task Force *Report*, a similar proposal has been formulated. The study team observing status of women programs noted that there was no evidence that ''all departmental policies and programs being developed are systematically reviewed to determine their impact on women.'' They noted as well that there was still insufficient co-ordination, and proposed that within each department an assistant deputy minister be assigned responsibility for status of women.[55]

In spite of the efforts of female legislators, women's groups, and female bureaucrats, male domination of the legislatures has persisted, and women continue to press for reforms from positions that are, on the whole, outside the centres of power. This has meant that women still lack control over the decisions that so obviously affect their daily lives. However, even within the framework of a gender-based explanation of policy it must be recognized that other factors interacting with gender have set the limits for policy debate and action. The most significant of these other factors is the nature of the economic system within which the dialogue between government and groups takes place. It is clear from the preceding review of legislation that men's ideas about women's roles have changed as the needs of the economy have changed. Throughout the period in which women took note of their political system and sought policy decisions that would favour them, our economic system has been capitalist. Marxist-feminist scholars in particular have noted the link between capitalist thinking and the pattern of laws affecting women. They stress the impact of industrial capitalism in its changing forms in the nineteenth and twentieth centuries on the decisions reached by legislators.[56]

There are several reasons why capitalism might be expected to contribute to the perpetuation of segregated gender roles. At the very least, the willingness of governments to adopt equality measures is related to their faith in free-market forces. The more a government is committed to the law of supply and demand, the less willing it is to intervene in the economy and enact pay equity measures or government-funded day care. The Liberal party federally, since the mid-1900s, has been prepared to legislate for equal opportunity. The Conservative party has been more reluctant to interfere with market forces. Neither party has been prepared to work outside the boundaries of the competitive market economy. The impact of capitalism can be seen in other ways. First, women in the home reproduce the workers needed for economic development. Second, women provide a reserve pool of cheap labour, which can be pulled from the home, at little cost to the employer, in times of economic necessity. Third, women in the home have been perceived as consumers of the goods the capitalist state produces. Finally, women perform, unpaid, the job of domestic servants, sustaining the work force and getting it ready for work. Regardless of whether one accepts the Marxist-feminist arguments, there is convincing evidence that economic forces serve as one more constraint on government policy.

Another factor which interacts with gender and capitalism is the set of priorities established by the party in power. Each political party in Canada operates according to a different set of principles, and women's rights fit more comfortably in some party platforms than in others. There are several examples of this in Canadian history. Suffrage for women was a Liberal policy in British Columbia and Quebec. In Alberta, minimum wage legislation, resisted by the Conservatives, was brought in by the United Farmers of Alberta. Status of women officers were appointed by the Parti Québécois in Quebec. At the federal level, concern for individual rights dominated the government agenda during the Trudeau era. Under Trudeau's leadership, while there was little movement from the notion that women are the natural guardians of the home, there was a dramatic shift from the language of political obligation to the language of individual rights. Within the government's new rights package, women's claims were given some space. This is clear from policy directives circulating within government in the 1970s. In 1971, in a situation report prepared by the Privy Council Office Briefing Team for the Priorities and Planning Committee, there were indications that the government was at least concerned about changes in attitudes on gender roles.

That 1971 report listed for consideration: the increasing socio-economic power of women; changes in women's images of marriage, work, and the family; increased resistance to women in the male work world; and increased diversity in sexual expression.[57] This was followed in 1972 by a memorandum to the cabinet from Trudeau, in which he included the equalization of opportunities for women in his list of government goals. However, there were clear limits on how far this notion of the just society was to go. It did not include rewriting the rules for relations in the private sphere, but concentrated on equal opportunities in the public world of paid labour. Women were to be integrated "into the development process as equal partners with men."[58]

Perceptions of gender roles, the nature of the economic system, and the government's priorities all affect legislators' perceptions of what should be done. In addition, there are more immediate structural constraints that limit their discourse. In Canada, the most significant structural characteristic of the political system is the division of powers between the federal and provincial levels. Federal-provincial relations have had a profound impact on the pace of reform in areas such as child care, divorce, and even the definition of women's rights. Because the two levels of government, either for financial or constitutional reasons, share responsibility for most of the social service package in Canada, co-operation between them is essential. That co-operation is often hard to obtain.

Canada is a country of great regional diversity. The special status of Quebec, with its separate language and culture, is best known, but the other provinces also differ significantly from one another in economic development, patterns of settlement, and culture. In his review of the Canadian welfare state, Keith Banting concludes that "the evolution of federalism is the institutional feature that has had the greatest impact on income security in Canada."[59] He goes on to argue that in "comparative terms federalism is clearly a conservative force in welfare politics."[60] In the area of policies for women, the impact of federalism has been mixed. In the early 1900s, the western provinces were innovators in the area of women's rights, establishing a pattern that the other provinces generally followed. In the 1980s, with complicated funding arrangements in place, the provinces often are unwilling to reopen discussions of social security to include, for example, child care, out of the fear that other programs might be cancelled.

Conclusion

This overview demonstrates the boundaries within which successive governments have been prepared to operate when legislating for women. These boundaries have shifted gradually over time (and the policies reflect this gradual transition) but they have always been set within the dichotomy of public and private roles. In the early days of Canada, the natural position for women was in the private role of wife and mother. The state was prepared to legislate to facilitate women's ability to carry out this role. Then it was not even the case that women were separate but equal, since the wife was in a clearly subordinate legal and economic position in the family. Over time the restriction of women to the private role has weakened, although the functions of that role have remained almost exclusively women's concern. Slowly, with the development of the welfare state, equal opportunity for women in the public sphere began to dominate the discourse of the state.

Until the end of the 1960s, it was possible for equal opportunity in the public world to co-exist with patriarchal relations in the private world. By the 1970s, that co-existance was challenged by women's groups demanding radical transformations in the distribution of roles in both public and private spheres, and transformations as well in the structuring of these roles. Governments' response to the challenge has been guarded. There is little reason to believe that, without a strong commitment from within government to breaking down traditional gender roles, the concept of separate spheres will cease to define future boundaries for action, or that creative new definitions of these roles will evolve and reflect more fully women's experiences and understanding. That commitment is unlikely without the proportional representation of women in both federal and provincial legislatures.[61]

Sandra Burt

SUGGESTED READINGS

Bashevkin, Sylvia, *Toeing the Lines; Women and Party Politics in English Canada.* Toronto: University of Toronto Press, 1985.

Brodie, Janine, *Women and Politics in Canada.* Toronto: McGraw-Hill Ryerson, 1985.

Burt, Sandra, "Voluntary Affirmative Action: Does It Work?" *Relations industrielles* 41, no. 3, (1986), 541–50.

Canada, Department of Labour, Women's Bureau, *Women in the Labour Force: Earnings of Men and Women.* Ottawa: Ministry of Supply and Services, 1979.

Dranoff, Linda Silver, *Women in Canadian Law.* Toronto: Fitzhenry & Whiteside, 1977.

Findlay, Sue, "Facing the State: The Politics of the Women's Movement Reconsidered," in Heather Jon Maroney and Meg Luxton, eds., *Feminism and Political Economy.* Toronto: Methuen, 1987.

Hamilton, Roberta, and Michele Barrett, eds., *The Politics of Diversity.* Montreal: The Book Centre, 1987.

Kome, Penney, *The Taking of Twenty-Eight: Women Challenge the Constitution.* Toronto: Women's Educational Press, 1983.

Wilson, Elizabeth, *Women and the Welfare State.* London: Tavistock Publications, 1977.

Chapter Six

Women and the Law

Throughout this century, Canadian women have asserted their claims to sex equality in a significant number of legal cases. Unfortunately, some of these legal challenges were never included in the case law reports and so their stories are lost. However, when the known cases are collected together, they reveal a remarkable diversity. During the early decades of this century, there were cases involving the admission of women to the legal profession, the capacity of women to be police magistrates, the eligibility of women for appointment to the Senate, the validity of a will bequest to the mother who had "given birth in Toronto to the greatest number of children" in a particular ten-year period, and the dissemination of information about birth control. More recently – as recently as the decade immediately preceding the adoption of the Canadian Charter of Rights and Freedoms – there have been cases about Indian status, matrimonial property, reproduction, employment, sports teams, prostitution, rape, abortion, and pornography.[1]

These cases have been litigated at all of the levels of the court system, from courts of first instance, where the decisions are usually made by a single judge, to the highest court of appeal, where as many as nine judges decide the case. Not every case went to every level of court, but most were appealed at least once and many went to the highest court of appeal. Although the Supreme Court of Canada is now the highest court of appeal, one case – the Persons case – went to what was then, but is not now, an even higher court, namely the Judicial Committee of the British Privy Council.

In virtually all of these cases the courts rendered decisions that lagged behind the changing patterns of women's lives. Some people, including some judges, defend this juridical lag by explaining that it is not the function of the courts to make (or change) the law. However, this explanation is not persuasive because it does not reflect the way in which the courts actually decided these cases. When these cases are examined, it becomes apparent that the judges were never asked simply to apply an existing law to a particular fact situation.

Instead, they were always asked to decide between competing versions of the law. They responded by resolving these controversies and in so doing always made, and in some cases changed, the law.

There is a more compelling explanation of the lag between these judicial decisions and the changes in women's lives, which becomes clear through an analysis of the two clusters of cases conventionally characterized as sex equality cases, namely, the 'persons' cases and the Canadian Bill of Rights cases. Perhaps surprisingly, given their sometimes diverging outcomes, all of these cases are consistent with the same theory of equality. According to this theory, alikes must be treated alike or equally, while unalikes must be treated unalike or differently. This view has also informed legislators in their formulation of public policy, as Sandra Burt shows in her chapter in this book. Less surprisingly, perhaps because it can be traced at least as far back as Aristotle, the validity of this theory remains unchallenged.

Instead, the Aristotelian theory of equality, discussed more fully by Lorraine Code in her chapter on feminist theory, is regarded as controversial only in its application to women and men, when the question whether women and men are alike or unalike is posed. Aristotle himself answered this question by arguing that "the male is by nature superior, and the female inferior; and the one rules, and the other is ruled; this principle, of necessity, extends to all mankind."

Canadian judges have not hesitated to follow where Aristotle led. Most of the judges in the cases that follow were as gender-biased as Aristotle. When women won their cases, they won only because the judges found some basis for treating women like men. Although there may be some occasions when doing so is better than not doing so, nevertheless, treating women like men is no less gender-biased than is defending male supremacy. Gender-bias, not judicial function, explains why Canadian courts have rendered decisions that have lagged behind the changing patterns of women's lives.

Under these circumstances, it is not surprising that some women turned to the legislatures for redress. Indeed, Canada recently opted for a generalized type of remedial legislation in the form of the Canadian Charter of Rights and Freedoms. The Charter contains two sex equality provisions. One is Section 15 which provides that:

> (1) Every individual is equal before and under the law and has the right to the equal protection and equal benefit of the law without discrimination and, in particular, without discrimination based on race, national or ethnic origin, colour, religion, sex, age or mental or physical disability.
> (2) Subsection (1) does not preclude any law, program or activity that

> has as its object the amelioration of conditions of disadvantaged individuals or groups including those that are disadvantaged because of race, national or ethnic origin, colour, religion, sex age or mental or physical disability.

The other is Section 28 which provides that:

> Section 28. Notwithstanding anything in this Charter, the rights and freedoms referred to in it are guaranteed equally to male and female persons.

These provisions suggest that it should be easy to predict that the courts can no longer render legal decisions that lag behind the changes in women's lives. Unfortunately this prediction is premature. There has been considerable disagreement over the meaning of the Charter's sex equality provisions, and the task of resolving such disagreements rests solely with the courts.

The Early 'Persons' Cases

The 'persons' cases were aptly named because they were about whether women were included in the legal interpretation of the word 'persons.' There were five such cases, and all five had already been decided by 1930.

Not surprisingly perhaps, the three earliest of the 'persons' cases were initiated by two women who wanted to become lawyers; Mabel Penery French initiated the first case in 1905 in New Brunswick and the second in 1911 in British Columbia, and Annie Macdonald Langstaff initiated the third case in 1915 in Quebec.[2]

These women were obliged to launch three cases because it was, and is, the provinces that have the jurisdiction to regulate lawyers. The New Brunswick, British Columbia, and Quebec regulations about admission to the practice of law were surprisingly similar. None of these regulations explicitly denied women admission, nor did they explicitly restrict admission only to men. Rather, in New Brunswick and British Columbia, the regulations referred to the admission of 'persons' and, in Quebec, to 'candidates.' There were three cases because each time one of these women applied for admission, the judges refused her request.

By the time that Mabel Penery French and Annie Macdonald Langstaff applied for admission in their respective provinces, they had already completed the required courses of study to become lawyers. Mabel Penery French had also "fully satisfied" the Barristers' Society of New Brunswick of her "moral character, habits and conduct," and, by 1914, Annie Macdonald Langstaff had become the first woman to graduate from the Faculty of Law at McGill University. But, despite their evident qualifications, both were denied the right to practise law solely because they were women.

This denial was more suspect than surprising. By 1905, several women had already been admitted to the practice of law in Ontario.[3] The first woman lawyer in Ontario – indeed, in the whole British Empire – was Clara Brett Martin, who was admitted eight years before Mabel Penery French initiated her first case. Clara Brett Martin, too, had to fight for admission. Although she never went to court, she fought the Law Society of Upper Canada for six years. Ultimately she won, but only after the Ontario legislature passed two statutes: one, in 1892, admitting women as solicitors and the other, in 1895, admitting women as barristers.

While Clara Brett Martin was the first woman lawyer in Canada, she was by no means the first woman lawyer in North America. Margaret Brent became the first woman lawyer in North America when she arrived in the American colonies in 1638. The first woman admitted to a state bar in the United States – Arabella Mansfield – was admitted in 1869 in Iowa. And in 1879, the American Congress passed legislation allowing women to practise in the federal courts, including the United States Supreme Court.[4]

Given these precedents, the applications of Mabel Penery French and Annie Macdonald Langstaff were neither novel nor radical. Yet when their cases got to the courts, they lost; and they lost resoundingly. Fourteen of the fifteen men who sat as judges in their cases refused to admit women to the practice of law. Ten of the fourteen put their reasons, such as they were, in writing. Although their reasons varied somewhat, all were completely consistent with Aristotle's defence of male supremacy, as the following case-by-case analysis reveals.

Mabel Penery French's first case began with representations from three lawyers. First the president of the Barrister's Society presented all of the previously decided British and American legal cases and other pertinent information without arguing either for or against her admission. Then two other lawyers presented arguments clearly supporting her admission. Both argued that the previously decided British cases were not decisive; and one of the two, the recorder for the City of St. John, also argued that since the previously decided American cases were about evenly balanced, they should be ignored.

According to him, only the real merits of this case mattered, and he based his argument on the recent trend to increasing the vocations open to women. At this point, the Chief Justice intervened and argued that admitting "this young lady" as an attorney would, in a few years, make her "eligible to be appointed to the bench." In response, the recorder was not prepared to admit that as a necessary sequence. But even were it so, he noted, "worse things might happen."

This case is particularly striking because none of the lawyers argued against Mabel Penery French's admission. That did not stop the five-man New Brunswick Supreme Court from unanimously refusing to admit her, however. Nor did it stop the Chief Justice from exceeding the limits of acceptable judicial reasoning when he wrote, "If I dare to express my own views I would say that I have no sympathy with the opinion that women should in all branches of life come in competition with men. Better let them attend to their own legitimate business."

Traditionally, judges do not express their own personal views. So the Chief Justice's statement was, if nothing else, a forthright admission of male bias. Indeed, his statement was the most forthright admission of male bias offered by any judge, not only in this case, but in all of the cases to follow.

Lacking the Chief Justice's gall, the four remaining judges relied on more traditional legal reasoning. They concentrated on interpreting the word 'persons' as used in the New Brunswick lawyers' statute. Their task was not easy because, as they themselves acknowledged, the word 'persons' was "sufficiently comprehensive to include both sexes." Moreover, as one of them also acknowledged, Mabel Penery French "undoubtedly would be included in that word as used in many statutes." Nevertheless, they decided that the same was not true of the New Brunswick lawyers' statute, apparently because the context demanded otherwise.

By context, they did not mean the recent trend to increasing the vocations open to women. To the contrary, one of the two judges who provided written reasons characterized the admission of women as a "radical change," one which the court was in no way bound to make. The other emphasized that "the remedy in this case is with the legislature and not with this court." With these words, he – and the many other judges who have echoed him in subsequent cases – were warning women not to rely on the courts to implement the changing patterns of their lives.

Instead, what these judges meant by context was the historical context. Specifically they meant the previously decided British and American legal cases, or what is usually referred to as the 'common law.' Although they both agreed that the 'common law' excluded women from the practice of law, they differed over which of the 'common law' cases were actually decisive. While one judge relied on "the British authorities, and also some of the authorities in the United States," the other characterized the British authorities as "useless" and relied only on two of the American cases. In one such case, the American Supreme Court had refused to admit Myra Bradwell to the practice of law in Illinois because:

> the civil law, as well as nature herself, has always recognized a wide

> difference in the respective spheres and destinies of man and woman. Man is, or should be, woman's protector and defender. The natural and proper timidity and delicacy which belongs to the female sex evidently unfits it for many of the occupations of civil life. The constitution of the family organization, which is founded in the divine ordinance as well as in the nature of things, indicates the domestic sphere as that which properly belongs to the domain and functions of womanhood.

Simply by quoting this passage with approval, one of the New Brunswick judges added the constraints of nature and divine ordinance to those of history and outright male bias as the bases for treating women as inferior to men.

Since the judiciary had, to a man, adhered to Aristotle's defence of male supremacy, Mabel Penery French wisely refrained from appealing to another court. She turned instead to the provincial legislature where her argument did prevail. In 1906, after the legislature had passed a law admitting women to the practice of law, she became a lawyer in New Brunswick. Although it might appear from these facts that the legislatures are more willing than the courts to move forward on the question of women's rights, such is not always the case.

When Mabel Penery French applied to transfer her practice of law to British Columbia six years later, it was as if time had stood still. Although the British Columbia judges knew that she had already been admitted in New Brunswick, they were unanimous in denying her the right to become a lawyer in their province. Again, it was because she was a woman and again it was because the judges relied on arguments based on the historical context. One judge even harkened back to "the Mirror of Justice, a work issued at the time of William the Conqueror" for the quotation that "femmes ne poient estre attorneys." Not surprisingly, therefore, this judge concluded that "The context of our Act refers to a profession for men, and men alone." French appealed the first judgement she received in British Columbia, but at the Court of Appeal, where her case was heard by three judges, she was again denied admission.

In these British Columbia cases, a new argument was raised about the use of the pronoun 'he' in the Legal Professions Act. This pronoun had also appeared in the New Brunswick lawyers' statute, but the lawyers there had simply argued that a mere pronoun was not sufficient to exclude women. In British Columbia, however, her lawyer offered a more constructive pronominal argument. First he pointed out that a provision in another British Columbia statute–the Interpretation Act–extended words importing the masculine gender to women. Then he applied this provision to the Legal Professions Act, arguing that these two Acts, when read together, expressly gave women the right to be lawyers, even if they had no such right under common law. None of the British Columbia judges agreed with this argument. As one put it, echoing the words of one of the New Brunswick judges, the Interpretation Act should "not be used to bring about so radical a change." To a man, therefore, the British Columbia judges also subscribed to Aristotle's defence of male supremacy. Again Mabel Penery French turned to a provincial legislature for legislation admitting women to the practice of law. She was admitted in the same year.

Three years later, Annie Macdonald Langstaff was not so fortunate. Although she worked for a law firm until she retired in 1965 at the age of seventy-eight,[5] she was never admitted to the practice of law. Not only was she denied admission by two Quebec courts, but also the Quebec legislature refused to amend the Bar Act to admit women to the practice of law until 1941. By 1941, however, admission to the Bar required an undergraduate degree as well as a law degree, and, while Langstaff had a law degree, she did not have an undergraduate degree. So, although she could work for a law firm, she could never appear in court nor, technically speaking, call herself a lawyer.

Annie Macdonald Langstaff's case differed from those of Mabel Penery French in only three respects. First, unlike either French or the Ontario lawyer Clara Brett Martin, Langstaff was not only married but was also separated from her husband. As one historian has argued, "In a Province that did not grant divorce and that 'protected' its women to such an extent that husbands' authorizations in writing were required before they could contract any obligations, the fact that Annie Langstaff was separated from her husband set the seal on her lost cause."[6] But her cause was lost as much because she was a woman as because she was married or separated. In the words of the trial judge, "to admit a woman, and more particularly a married woman, as a *barrister*, that is to say, as a *person who pleads cases at the bar before judges or juries in open court and in the presence of the public*, would be nothing short of a direct infringement upon public order and a manifest violation of the law of good morals and public decency."

He belaboured this point by picturing a woman lawyer questioning a complainant in a rape case: "No woman possessing the least sense of decency could possibly do so without throwing a blur upon her own dignity and without bringing into utter contempt the honour and respect due her sex." Given his example, it would have been most peculiar had he singled out married women. Their sense of dignity, decency, honour, and respect was surely less vulnerable than that of unmarried women, at least when it came to questioning the complainant in a rape case.

Second, Annie Macdonald Langstaff's case differed insofar as the Quebec judges relied not only on the previously decided British and American cases, but also on the civil law tradition in France. They did so because, as one of the appeal judges put it, "La loi française, comme la loi anglaise, était alors à l'effet que la profession d'avocat était interdite aux personnes du sexe féminin." Nor did it trouble the Quebec judges that, unlike Britain, France had recently passed a special law admitting women to the practice of law. Since Quebec had not passed a similar law, they simply held that until that happened they would not have to admit women to the practice of law.

Her case differed in a third and final way because, on appeal, one of the five judges dissented. In doing so, he did not rely on the argument that vocational opportunities for women were increasing. Nor did he rely on the Interpretation Act argument about applying masculine pronouns to women. Instead, the dissenting judge offered a completely new argument in which he focused on the Bar Act.

Specifically, he focused on the fact that the Bar Act did not expressly exclude women. But the significance of that omission was not clear until he contrasted it with another fact, that: "Dans beaucoup de nos lois, quand on a voulu exclure la femme de certaines situations, de certaines charges, on l'a mentionné formellement." Nevertheless, once it was clear that there were laws that explicitly excluded women and some – for example, the Bar Act – that did not, it also followed that, "Si le législateur avait voulu dire qu'une femme ne pourrait être avocat, il l'aurait dit." With these words, the dissenting judge signified that, unless there was an express provision to the contrary, women and men should be treated alike. In other words, unlike the other fourteen judges in these three cases, he did not subscribe to Aristotle's defence of male supremacy.

Neither did four of the five judges who decided the next 'persons' case. This case, which was decided two years later in 1917, did not involve the admission of women to the practice of law. Rather, it involved a prostitute named Lizzie Cyr, alias Lizzie Waters, who was convicted of the crime of vagrancy and sentenced to six months hard labour. Not surprisingly, given her sentence, Lizzie Cyr appealed her conviction on various grounds, two of which raised sex equality issues. But to say that Lizzy Cyr raised two sex equality issues is not to say that she argued for sex equality. To the contrary, she defended sex inequality.

She argued that only men could be convicted of vagrancy because the provision that made vagrancy a crime used only masculine pronouns. Now, given that Mabel Penery French and Annie Macdonald Langstaff had already made the opposite argument and lost, Lizzie Cyr should have won this argument. But she lost, too, simply because the five judges who heard both of her appeals invoked the Interpretation Act argument that words importing the masculine gender included women. The message was clear: the Interpretation Act worked against women, applying only when burdens (such as vagrancy convictions) but not benefits (such as lawyering) were at issue.[7]

Lizzie Cyr raised a second sex inequality issue involving Alice Jamieson, the police magistrate who initially convicted her. Alice Jamieson was one of two women–the other being Emily Murphy–who had been appointed as police magistrates in Alberta. Indeed, when Emily Murphy was appointed as police magistrate for the City of Edmonton on June 13, 1916, she may have been the first women in the British Empire to receive such an appointment. However, although defence counsel objected to Emily Murphy's appointment from time to time, it was Alice Jamieson's appointment as police magistrate for the City of Calgary in December 1916 that was actually challenged.[8] Most likely this was because Alice Jamieson almost convicted Lizzie Cyr without giving her lawyer the opportunity to present his defence argument.

On appeal, Lizzie Cyr's lawyer argued that Alice Jamieson was "incompetent and incapable of holding the position of police magistrate" because she was a woman. While the first judge to hear this appeal entertained "serious doubt whether a woman is qualified to be appointed to that office," he refused to act on his doubt. Surprisingly, the Alberta Court of Appeal also refused to uphold Lizzie Cyr's appeal on this issue, and did so without relying on the Interpretation Act. Instead the Court offered two other arguments, both of which merit consideration. One was a new argument about the recently passed Alberta equal suffrage statute. The other was a more novel and detailed version of the argument advanced by the dissenting judge in Annie Macdonald Langstaff's case.

When Lizzie Cyr's lawyer interpreted Alberta's equal suffrage statute as excluding women from being police magistrates, he completely ignored the intention behind this legislation. In 1916, Alberta had become the second province, after Manitoba and almost simultaneously with Saskatchewan, to pass women's suffrage legislation. However, the Alberta legislation was the most comprehensive. It provided that, in some twenty-four statutes, "Women shall be upon an absolute equality with and have the same rights and privileges and be subject to the same penalties and disabilities as men." But as Lizzie Cyr's lawyer pointed out, the police magistrates' statute was not among the twenty-four. This, he argued, meant that women could not be police magistrates.

Fortunately this argument was completely rejected by the Alberta Court of Appeal. According to the Court, Lizzie Cyr's lawyer had totally misunderstood the purpose of the equal suffrage statute. Instead of excluding women from the statutes that were not mentioned, as he had argued, the Court held that the purpose of the equal suffrage statute was one of "wiping out the *expressly enacted disqualification of women*" in the statutes that were mentioned.

The other argument the Alberta Court of Appeal offered was even more novel. In this argument, the Court canvassed the historical context in considerable detail and then came to the following conclusions. First, there were "well-established facts" showing "that women had on many occasions held high and important public offices in England, some of a judicial character." Second, where their capacity to do so was questioned, it was answered with "a decision favourable to the existence of the capacity." Third, no British legal case disqualified women from holding public office until the middle of the nineteenth century. Fourth, the British cases decided after that time were not "strictly" binding because of the "different conditions" in Alberta. Fifth, "at a very early stage" in Alberta law, "it was recognized that women should be put in a new position" such that, "In all the early ordinances . . . there is evidence that it was considered necessary if women were not to vote or hold public office that it should be so expressly stated." Finally, since the relevant Alberta statute did not expressly exclude women, therefore, women could be police magistrates.

This argument was significant for four reasons. It meant that Alice Jamieson, who was neither plaintiff nor defendant nor even represented in this case, and Emily Murphy, who later initiated the Persons case, could continue to sit as police magistrates. It meant that women and men were treated alike and, in this respect, was one of only a few cases in which this outcome occurred. Further, it meant that this outcome could be achieved without challenging – indeed was consistent with – the historical perspective so favoured and yet so perversely interpreted by other Canadian judges in sex equality cases. Finally, this argument was significant because it was totally ignored only eleven years later when the Supreme Court of Canada decided the Persons case.

The Persons Case

The Persons case was initiated in 1927 by five women from Alberta – Emily Murphy, Nellie McClung, Louise McKinney, Irene Parlby, and Henrietta Muir Edwards.[9] Their case raised the question of whether women were eligible for appointment to the Senate. The answer depended on how Section 24 of the British North America Act, 1867, was interpreted. Section 24 provided that "qualified persons" were eligible for appointment to the Senate. However, the federal government refused to interpret Section 24 as making women eligible. According to the federal government, women were not persons.

This was a strange position for the federal government to take in 1927, particularly as between 1916 and 1922 (or 1925, if Newfoundland is included) women became eligible to vote in elections for the federal House of Commons and all of the provincial legislatures, except Quebec. Indeed, for some time prior to 1916, women had been eligible to vote in various school and municipal elections. For example, women with property, whether married or single, were eligible to vote for school trustees in Ontario as early as 1850 and in municipal elections in British Columbia as early as 1873.

Moreover, between 1916 and 1925, women had become eligible to sit as members in the federal House of Commons and in all of the provincial legislatures, except New Brunswick and Quebec. In Alberta the first two women legislators, Louise McKinney and Roberta Macadams, had been elected in 1917, followed by Nellie McClung in 1921. In British Columbia, Mary Ellen Smith had been elected in 1918; in Saskatchewan, Mrs. M.O. Ramsland had been elected in 1919; and in Manitoba, Edith Rogers had been elected in 1920. As well, in March 1921, Mary Ellen Smith had been appointed to the cabinet in British Columbia–the first woman cabinet member in the British Empire–and in August 1921 Irene Parlby had been appointed to the cabinet in Alberta.

So why in 1927 did the federal government take the retrograde position that women were not 'persons' for the purposes of eligibility for appointment to the Senate? According to the lawyer for the Crown in the Persons case, it was because the crucial date was not 1927, but rather when the B.N.A. Act, 1867, was first passed. He argued that, in 1867, women did not hold public offices of any kind in the provinces that were then joining the Canadian federation. Nor could they hold any public offices under the British common law. Of course, his argument totally ignored the Alberta Court of Appeal's considered decision to the contrary eleven years earlier.

So did the five Supreme Court of Canada judges who first decided the Persons case. Indeed, all five simply agreed with the arguments offered by the lawyer for the Crown. It has since been said that one of these five "rejected the common law rule excluding women from government."[10] However, what he rejected was not the common law rule itself but rather the contention that the judiciary could change it. Nor was his rejection significant. Not only did it merely echo the position of the judges in the earlier cases involving Mabel Penery French and Annie Macdonald Langstaff, but also all four of the other Supreme Court of Canada judges in the Persons case took exactly the same position.

Fortunately, the Supreme Court of Canada did not have the last word in the Persons case. The decision was appealed to the Judicial Committee of the British Privy Council. While waiting for the Judicial Committee's decision, one of the five women who had initiated the case – Emily Murphy – wrote a friend: "Going to win, Dear? You bet!"[11] Emily Murphy was right. On October 18, 1929, the five-man Judicial Committee decided that women were eligible for appointment to the Senate under Section 24 of the B.N.A. Act. It decided, in other words, that women were 'persons.'

The Judicial Committee's decision was certainly surprising by British standards. In effect, the decision meant that "Six decades of precedent stating that women could not be included in the term 'persons' were swept aside."

Indeed there had been a British case on this point just seven years earlier, in 1922. In that case, Margaret Haig, Viscountess Rhondda, had sought a seat in the House of Lords. Even though she was a peeress in her own right, however, the House of Lords had denied her a seat simply because she was a woman. Surprisingly, just two years before Viscountess Rhondda was denied the right to sit in the House of Lords, the British Parliament had passed a law which provided that "A person shall not be disqualified by sex or marriage from the exercise of any public function."

Notwithstanding this law, it was a further forty years after Viscountess Rhondda's case was decided before British women were admitted to the British House of Lords. By contrast, in Canada the first woman – Cairine Wilson – was appointed to the Senate in 1930, just one year after the Judicial Committee's decision in the Persons case.

What is most surprising, however, is that the meaning of the Judicial Committee's decision is still controversial. According to one interpretation, "what had changed was . . . the conception of women and women's position in public life held by judges."[12] Most other commentators have been more cautious.[13] According to one, the Judicial Committee's decision only "opened a very small door for women to creep through."[14] To resolve this controversy, it is important to explain what the Judicial Committee actually said.

In the first place, unlike the Alberta Court of Appeal, the Judicial Committee never denied that the common law excluded women from holding public office. To the contrary, the Judicial Committee acknowledged the common law exclusion by referring to it as a "relic of days more barbarous than ours," which excluded women "probably due to the fact that the deliberative assemblies of the early tribes were attended by men under arms, and women did not bear arms." Then, having exposed this rationale for the anachronistic and irrelevant notion that it was, the Judicial Committee simply said that "The appeal to history . . . in this particular matter is not conclusive." With these words, the Judicial Committee discredited the common law exclusion.

The members of the Judicial Committee also did what none of the previous judges had been prepared to do. They changed the law. Even the Alberta Court of Appeal judges had stopped short of changing the law and had insisted that they were just following in the tradition of the early ordinances. By contrast, therefore, it could be said of the members of Judicial Committee, and only of the Judicial Committee, that "in practice, if not in theory, they accepted the view so emphatically denied by their predecessors . . . that the law was the instrument of the judges rather than the judges the instrument of the law."[15]

The Judicial Committee's view made complete sense because the law it changed – the common law exclusion of women from holding public office – originated as judge-made law. So, as judges had been the ones who initially made this law, why should subsequent judges not be the ones to change it?

Although the Judicial Committee had changed the law, it had not changed the "conception of women and women's position in public life held by the judges." This distinction was initially acknowledged by the Supreme Court of Canada when one of the judges stated that "we are, of course, in no wise concerned with the desirability or the undesirability of the presence of women in the Senate, nor with any political aspect of the question submitted." But the Judicial Committee members also acknowledged the same distinction when they said that they were not "deciding any question as to the rights of women but only a question as to their eligibility for a particular position."

There is even more explicit evidence that the Judicial Committee did not change "the conception of women and women's position in public life held by the judges." This evidence derives from what it said and did not say about the interpretation of the word 'persons.' The word 'persons,' according to the Judicial Committee, "*may* include members of both sexes." But it did not say that it *must* include members of both sexes. Instead it said that "the burden is upon those who deny that the word includes women to make out their case." Were such a case to be made out, however, then it could not be said that the Judicial Committee had changed "the conception of women and women's position in public life held by the judges."

Nor could the Judicial Committee resist making out just such a case. Indeed, it made out two such cases from two other sections of the B.N.A. Act, albeit not from the Senate sections. While none of the Senate sections explicitly excluded women, sections 41 and 84 referred specifically to men. Accordingly, the Judicial Committee concluded that such references were "expressly used when it is desired to confine the matter in issue to males."

Furthermore, the members of Judicial Committee used sections 41 and 84 as the basis of comparison with Section 24. In their words, "If Parliament had intended to limit the word 'persons' in section 24 to male persons it would surely have manifested such intention by an express limitation, as it has done in sections 41 and 84."

In the end, the Judicial Committee offered the same qualified interpretation of the word 'persons' as had the Alberta Court of Appeal judges in the case of Lizzie Cyr and Alice Jamieson and as had the dissenting judge in Annie Macdonald Langstaff's case. According to all of these judges, the word 'persons' only included women if they were not expressly excluded.

Nevertheless, even this qualified interpretation was an improvement over the interpretation it had displaced. It was better that the word 'persons' be interpreted as including women unless they were expressly excluded than to interpret it as excluding women unless they were expressly included. As Mary Eberts wrote, "These opposite attitudes . . . have a significant bearing on whether women will have to seek legislative permission to do something or just do it and put the burden on their opponents to stop them."[16] But the more inclusive interpretation was not all that the Judicial Committee might have decided. It should have decided that the word 'persons' *always* includes both sexes.

This argument is not merely of historical interest. Although the National Defence Act currently uses the word 'persons' to describe military service personnel, women are nevertheless excluded from combat and combat related military service. Since the source of their exclusion is not the National Defence Act itself but orders issued under the authority of the Chief of the Defence Staff, there is always the possibility that judges might refuse to characterize the exclusion of women as an express limitation. However, were the judges to decide otherwise, then the word 'persons' in the National Defence Act would not include women. Such a decision would have more than economic and employment consequences: it would affect women's rights and responsibilities as citizens. For, as one commentator has noted, "risking one's life in battle is the most extreme act the state can ask or demand of its citizens."[17] As well, it would confirm the argument that the Judicial Committee did not change "the conception of women and women's position in public life held by the judges" when they decided the Persons case.

In the sixty years since the Persons case was decided, there have been no further 'persons' cases whose stories are known. However, we can draw some conclusions from the five stories we do know. We know that nineteen of the thirty judges who decided these five cases were not prepared to include women in the word 'persons.' As none of these judges ever suggested that the word 'persons' did not include men, it is clear they subscribed to Aristotle's defence of male supremacy. The remaining eleven judges were prepared to include women in the word 'persons' only under some circumstances. For them, sometimes–but only sometimes–women and men were to be treated alike, or equally. Not one of the thirty men who decided these five cases was prepared to argue that the word 'persons' must always include both sexes.

The Canadian Bill of Rights Cases

Although we have as yet no comprehensive study of the cases that were litigated by women in the years since 1930, during the 1970s a new cluster of sex equality cases arose in the context of the Canadian Bill of Rights.[18] In theory, the Canadian Bill of Rights guaranteed sex equality. This guarantee was enshrined in Section 1 (b), which provided that:

> Section 1. It is hereby recognized and declared that in Canada there have existed and shall continue to exist without discrimination by reason of race, national origin, colour, religion or sex, the following human rights and fundamental freedoms, namely, . . .
>
> (b) the right of the individual to equality before the law and the protection of the law.

Despite the wording of Section 1(b), there are several good reasons for arguing that the Canadian Bill of Rights never guaranteed sex equality to women.

One reason is historical and dates back to the time the Canadian Bill of Rights was passed by the federal parliament in 1960. At the committee hearings that preceded passage, the then Minister of Justice, who was supposedly defending the legislation, in fact did precisely the opposite. At one point he offered to withdraw Section 1(b) completely. Then he changed his mind, saying, "I do feel that the expression . . . would not be interpreted by the courts so as to say we are making men and women equal, because men and women are not equal: they are different."[19] Although his words were only part of the legislative history and, by tradition, should not have been taken into account when the judges were deciding the sex equality cases, they nevertheless indicate the framework in which this legislation was formulated.

Another reason to doubt the guarantee of equality is coverage. As a federal law, the Canadian Bill of Rights could only cover claims involving other federal laws and not claims involving provincial laws. For example, many employment laws are within the area of provincial legislative responsibility and, as such, are not covered by the Canadian Bill of Rights. Under these circumstances, therefore, the Canadian Bill of Rights was unable to cover all of the possible claims for sex equality that women might make.

But the most important reason is the judiciary. In effect, the judiciary denied every claim in which women relied on the guarantee of sex equality in the Canadian Bill of Rights. Although there were at least five lower court decisions that were favourable to women, every one of these cases was reversed–either on appeal or in a later case on the same issue–by a higher court. Thus, from the perspective of women, the judiciary effectively emptied the guarantee of sex equality in the Canadian Bill of Rights of any meaning.

This happened even though women did not launch any sex equality cases until after the Canadian Bill of Rights had proved effective in a race equality case. In 1970, a male Indian named Drybones used the race equality provision in the Canadian Bill of Rights to challenge a federal law, the Indian Act, which made it an offence for an Indian to be intoxicated off a reserve.[20] Drybones ultimately litigated his case in the Supreme Court of Canada and won, meaning that the law which he had challenged was no longer enforceable.

By contrast, the laws upholding female inequality always remained enforceable whenever women challenged them, even though they used the same argument as Drybones. Drybones had argued that the law he had challenged treated Indians more harshly than non-Indians. Similarly, when women used the Canadian Bill of Rights to challenge various laws, it was always on the grounds that these laws treated women more harshly than men. Even so, in the sex equality cases, the judges always found reasons for upholding the laws even though they treated women more harshly than men.

In the earliest of these cases, brought in 1970 and 1971, several women challenged the prostitution provision, or what was then known as the vagrancy provision, in the criminal law because it was being applied only to women and not to men.[21] At least one trial judge agreed that the prostitution law violated the sex equality provision in the Canadian Bill of Rights, but he was overruled in a subsequent case by a higher court judge. According to the higher court judge, prostitution referred to "activities which can only be engaged in by females." It followed, therefore, that the law could treat women more harshly than men, at least in the context of prostitution.

None of these prostitution cases was ever appealed to a provincial court of appeal, possibly because the federal government changed the law in 1972. This change was supposed to make the prostitution – or soliciting, as it is now known – law applicable to men as well as women. But at least one Ontario judge refused to do so, albeit without making any reference to the Canadian Bill of Rights. Fortunately, in a subsequent case, the Ontario Court of Appeal indicated their displeasure with the view that men could not be prostitutes. Thus this particular issue, at least, is unlikely to be troublesome in the future.

The prostitution cases were followed by three cases which were ultimately decided by the Supreme Court of Canada. Two of these cases were brought by Indian women – Jeannette Lavell and Yvonne Bedard – and the remaining case was brought by Stella Bliss.[22] Not surprisingly, all three of these women used the same argument as Drybones. After all, Drybones had won in the Supreme Court of Canada, and although his argument had not worked in the earlier prostitution cases, those cases had not gone to the Supreme Court.

Jeannette Lavell and Yvonne Bedard even challenged the same statute as Drybones had, namely, the Indian Act. Specifically, they challenged the section that deprived them of their Indian status when they married non-Indian men. In Yvonne Bedard's case, this section had also stopped her from returning to her reserve when she subsequently separated from her husband. But the Indian Act denied Indian status only to Indian women who married non-Indian men; it did not deny Indian status to Indian men who married non-Indian women. Jeanette Lavell and Yvonne Bedard both argued that the Indian Act violated the sex equality provision in the Canadian Bill of Rights because it treated women more harshly than men.

Similarly, Stella Bliss challenged a section of the Unemployment Insurance Act on the grounds that it treated women more harshly than men. That section denied unemployment insurance benefits to otherwise qualified women simply because they were about to give birth or had just given birth. Although some women qualified for pregnancy benefits during that time, others – including Stella Bliss – could not qualify because they had not worked long enough. However, Stella Bliss had worked long enough to qualify for unemployment insurance benefits and so, shortly after giving birth, she applied for these benefits. No one at the Unemployment Insurance Commission disputed her evidence that she was capable of and available for work. Nevertheless, she was denied unemployment insurance benefits – solely because she had been pregnant. In other words, Stella Bliss was treated more harshly than any man who might apply for unemployment insurance benefits.

All three women should have won their cases on the bases of their arguments. However, the Supreme Court of Canada issued a single decision ruling against both Jeannette Lavell and Yvonne Bedard by a five to four majority in 1973. Then, in 1978, a unanimous seven-man Court also ruled against Stella Bliss. Of the three men who sat on both cases, one wrote the majority judgement both times and the other two agreed with him both times. In the Lavell and Bedard case, the Court ruled that it was permissible to deny Indian status to Indian women who married non-Indians because that had been happening "for at least one hundred years." In the Bliss case, the Court ruled that it was all right to deny unemployment insurance benefits to pregnant women because "any inequality between the sexes in this area is not created by legislation but by nature." In these two cases, the judges relied on history and on nature, respectively, to justify the harsher treatment of women, just as they had done more than forty years before in the 'persons' cases.

But just as history and nature were spurious justifications in the 'persons' cases, so were they in the Canadian Bill of Rights sex equality cases. In the case of Jeannette Lavell and Yvonne Bedard, the historical justification was spurious for two reasons. First, there is evidence that it was not Indians who originated the idea of denying Indian status to Indian women who married non-Indian men.[23] Second, what the historical justification protected was simply the sex-based stereotype of powerful men (whether Indian or white) and subordinate women (whether white or Indian). In Stella Bliss's case, nature was a spurious justification because it could only dictate that a pregnant woman would give birth and not that certain social arrangements, such as the denial of unemployment insurance benefits, must necessarily follow.

Clearly, the judges subscribed to Aristotle's defence of male supremacy. Fortunately, the federal Parliament did not continue to do so. In 1983, the federal Parliament repealed the offending section of the Unemployment Insurance Act and in 1985 repealed the offending section of the Indian Act. But the situation has not been finally resolved, at least with respect to the 1985 changes to the Indian Act, as six Indian chiefs from Alberta have challenged the validity of these changes.

Some men also brought sex equality cases to court under the Canadian Bill of Rights.[24] However, they did not argue that women were more harshly treated than men. Had they done so, they would have lost before they had begun. Instead these men argued that women were given special benefits not available to men, and that doing so violated the sex equality provision in the Canadian Bill of Rights. The judges did not agree. In each case the judges were able to rationalize women's special need of that benefit and ruled that this special treatment did not violate the guarantee of sex equality in the Canadian Bill of Rights.

Several unpalatable conclusions followed from the judicial decision-making process as manifested in the Canadian Bill of Rights sex equality cases. First, the bill was ineffective in protecting the equal rights of women. However limited the arguments had been in the Cyr and Persons cases, at least the outcomes of those cases were acceptable. The Canadian Bill of Rights sex equality cases were, by contrast, unrelieved by a single favourable judgment. Second, in the Canadian Bill of Rights cases, the judges seemed unconstrained by the tenets of consistency. In the cases brought by women, the judges rationalized and upheld laws that treated women more harshly than men; while in the cases brought by men, they rationalized and upheld laws that ostensibly benefited women. Third, a clear majority (nine out of thirteen) of the Supreme Court of Canada judges who decided these cases subscribed to Aristotle's defence of male supremacy. Consequently, it seemed obvious that the judiciary did not believe that the Canadian Bill of Rights guaranteed sex equality to women.

The Canadian Charter of Rights and Freedoms

The message from both the 'persons' cases and the Canadian Bill of Rights sex equality cases seemed clear as constitutional negotiations preceding the adoption of the new Charter began. As the proposed Charter of Rights and

Freedoms contained a sex equality provision, it was important for women to ensure that it was drafted properly. Yet women's choices were limited. On the one hand it was clearly necessary to avoid replicating the unpalatable outcomes of the Canadian Bill of Rights sex equality cases. On the other hand, while the outcomes of the Cyr and Persons cases were clearly acceptable, their underlying arguments were much less reliable. In Aristotelian terms, it seemed as if the choice lay between perpetuating the defence of male supremacy or subscribing to the theory that women were like men.

When the federal government finally decided to patriate the Canadian constitution and to add to it a Charter of Rights and Freedoms, the Canadian Advisory Council on the Status of Women became one of the first organizations to lobby actively for changes to the proposed Charter. Early in the summer of 1980, its president, Doris Anderson, commissioned a series of studies on the impact of the proposed Charter on women. The results of these studies were to be made public at an Advisory Council conference on Women and the Constitution scheduled to take place immediately before the First Ministers meeting in September 1980. The conference was subsequently rescheduled because of a translators' strike. When it was finally held in May 1981, the purpose of the conference had been eclipsed by the intervening events.

The first event occurred when the Advisory Council presented their brief to the Special Joint Committee of the Senate and the House of Commons on the Constitution of Canada on November 20, 1980. Immediately preceding the Advisory Council's presentation, the National Action Committee on the Status of Women made its presentation. When the National Action Committee's president, Lynn McDonald, finished speaking, one of the co-chairmen of the Special Joint Committee, Senator Harry Hayes, made the following unsolicited comment: "We want to thank the National Action Committee on the Status of Women for being present today and for your brief. We appreciate your coming and as a matter of fact we are honoured. However, your time is up and I was wondering why we do not have a section in here for babies and children. All you girls are going to be working and we are not going to have anybody to look after them."[25]

Although the "stark chauvinism" of his words may have helped "sensitize the committee to the concerns of the women appearing before it,"[26] what really mattered were the briefs presented by such women's groups as the Canadian Advisory Council on the Status of Women, the Canadian Committee on Learning Opportunities for Women, the National Action Committee on the Status of Women, the National Association of Women and the Law, and the Native Women's Association of Canada. The influence of these presentations was specifically acknowledged by the minister of justice, Jean Chrétien, in February 1981.

By then the second event was under way. It had begun on January 5, 1981, with yet another postponement of the Advisory Council's conference, which prompted Doris Anderson's resignation as president. She said that she was resigning because Lloyd Axworthy, the federal minister responsible for the status of women, had pressured the other members of the Advisory Council into cancelling the conference. Doris Anderson's resignation hit the press. As Chaviva Hosek wrote, "the political costs of cancelling the conference turned out to be high. The women's movement suddenly had a heroine, a villain and an event, all of which symbolized its exclusion from the constitutional process. The media had a field day. The complex issues involved were reduced to a dramatic fight between a woman and a man."[27]

The day after Doris Anderson resigned, a small group of women met and decided that the conference should go forward on February 14–15 as scheduled, despite the Advisory Council's cancellation. These women formed what became known as the Ad Hoc Committee of Canadian Women on the Constitution. Within three weeks, they organized a two-day National Conference on Women and the Constitution that 1,300 women from across Canada attended in Ottawa.

After the conference, the Ad Hoc Committee continued to lobby for changes to the proposed new Charter. Initially it concentrated on strengthening the proposed sex equality provision, Section 15, as did the National Action Committee and the National Association of Women and the Law. These lobbying activities resulted in the creation of a new sex equality provision, Section 28. On April 23, 1981, the House of Commons approved the inclusion of Section 28 in the Charter. According to one commentator, Penney Kome, Section 28 "became the law of the land only because of one of the most impressive lobbies in recent history."[28] Penney Kome attributed the success of this lobby to three factors:

> One is solidarity: organized women, from Women's Institutes to the Feminist Party, agreed on what they wanted and got it. Another is the grass-roots nature of their support: they were able to demonstrate that they had vast, non-partisan backing among the women in Canada. The third and perhaps most important reason was surprise. Their movement was spontaneous and therefore swift, thrown together at more or less the last moment. It caught opponents off-guard.[29]

This massive lobby worked for Section 28 because Section 15 did not offer a strong enough guarantee of sex equality. Section 15 was, and is, still subject to the limitations clause in Section 1. In other words, whatever protection Section 15 might guarantee, Section 1 could remove it if a government were to persuade the courts that there was a reason for doing so. But Section 28 is different; it prevails "notwithstanding anything in this Charter." So Section 28 should prevail over the limitations clause in Section 1. Thus Section 28 has more potential to guarantee sex equality than has Section 15.

The third and last event occurred in November 1981 when the prime minister and nine of the ten provincial premiers finally agreed to patriate the constitution. In doing so, they also agreed to add a new provision to the Charter. This provision, Section 33, became known as the override provision. When invoked, the override provision protects the continued existence of laws that would otherwise violate one or more of the rights and freedoms contained in the Charter; and it does so for up to ten years. When the override provision was announced on November 5, it clearly applied to most of the rights and freedoms in the Charter. But no reference was made to whether it applied to Section 28. It turned out that all ten First Ministers had forgotten about the existence of Section 28! By November 9, however, the Prime Minister had decided that the override provision should apply to Section 28.

The women's lobby was devastated by this decision but not deterred. First they lobbied the federal government to exempt Section 28 from the override provision. The federal government agreed to do so, but only on condition that all nine of the provincial premiers also agreed. So the women's lobby then set out to persuade all of the provincial premiers through a combination of telephone calls, telegrams, and letters, as well as through personal contact. The Saskatchewan premier was the last holdout. Finally, on November 23, 1981, the Minister of Justice, Jean Chrétien, announced in the House of Commons that he(!) had obtained the agreement of all nine provinces to exempt Section 28 from the override provision.

Together, these events reveal how some politicians – both federal and provincial – responded negatively to women's claims for sex equality. In that respect, very little seemed to have changed since the passage of the Canadian Bill of Rights in 1960. Without the intervention of a large women's lobby, women's constitutional rights would have been much weaker than they currently are. In other words, it would have been folly for women to rely too heavily on the legislative process.

The intervention of the women's lobby did secure two sex equality provisions in the Charter. Probably one of the members of the Ad Hoc Committee best captured the value of both of these sections when she said that Section 28 "would have been a helluva lot to lose, but it's not a helluva lot to gain."[30] These sections were not "a helluva lot to gain" because they do not explain the meaning of sex equality. That meaning is no more self-evident from these Charter provisions than it was from the Canadian Bill of Rights sex equality provision. The Charter does not preclude the gender bias that permeated most of the 'persons' cases and all of the Canadian Bill of Rights cases. This puts an enormous burden on women before they even begin to litigate the Charter sex equality cases.

The Charter Cases

In 1988 it is still too early to know how the judges will interpret the sex equality provisions in the Charter because there have been very few decisions. Although the Charter came into effect in April 1982, the implementation of Section 15 was delayed for three years, ostensibly to give the federal and provincial legislatures time to bring their laws into conformity with it. Section 15 was the only section to be treated this way. Since very few legislative changes were made by the time that Section 15 finally came into effect in April 1985, the delay mainly served to stave off litigation for that three-year period. Nor have there yet been any significant decisions under Section 28.

Still, there have been some cases involving Section 15(1). In May 1985, a woman successfully challenged the Yukon change-of-name law because it denied married women the right to change their names; and in December 1985, a married woman successfully challenged the Ontario vital-statistics law because it denied her the right to give her child her surname. In 1986, a twelve-year-old girl successfully challenged the Ontario single-sex sports team law. Women have initiated other Charter sex equality cases, but the decisions are not yet available. Men have also relied on Section 15(1), although they have seldom initiated their cases. Instead they have used Section 15(1) as a defence when charged with such criminal offences as statutory rape and, in one case, in a paternity suit. Two men have successfully challenged the Nova Scotia family-benefits law because it granted welfare benefits only to single mothers.

Only one of these cases has the imprimatur of the Supreme Court of Canada. This is the case of Justine Blainey, the twelve-year-old girl who challenged the Ontario law about single-sex sports teams.[31] Her case arose in the fall of 1985 when the Ontario Hockey Association denied her the opportunity to become a regular member of a minor hockey team. Since she had already played in four exhibition games with the team, the team's coach had been able to assess her ability. According to the coach, Justine Blainey not only had the talent and the physical strength to be a regular member of the team, she was also well accepted by her male teammates. Nevertheless, like many other women before her, she was disqualified solely on the grounds of her sex.

Justine Blainey turned to the Ontario Human Rights Commission for help. The Commission administers the Ontario Human Rights Code, which provides that it is wrong to use sex as the basis for denying services, goods, and facilities. Unfortunately, the Code also contained another section which affected Justine Blainey's case. This was Section 19(2), which specifically protected the continued existence of single-sex sports teams. Given Section 19(2), therefore, the Ontario Human Rights Commission had to advise Justine Blainey that they were unable to help her.

Others might have given up at this point, but Justine Blainey did not. She decided to challenge the validity of Section 19(2) of the Ontario Human Rights Code in court. She cast her challenge in terms of sex equality, arguing that Section 19(2)–that is, the single-sex sports team law–violated her right to sex equality under Section 15(1) of the Charter. More concretely, she argued that she would "not have as great a challenge on the girls' teams as she would have on the boys', nor would she have as many games or practices." As well, were she "to play on another women's team suitable for her capabilities," that "might mean that she would be playing outside her own age group and would have to play at greater distances from home." In Aristotelian terms, Justine Blainey asked the court to treat girls, or at least some of them, and boys as alike for the purposes of playing hockey. But the trial judge just could not do it.

It was not a question of the evidence. The judge conceded that there were "individual females such as Justine" who "may be able to compete in hockey with men for a short number of years." But for him, the answer did not rest with what some "individual females" could do. Rather, what mattered was that "females generally cannot compete successfully with men in hockey because of physiological differences." Unfortunately he did not follow this argument through to its logical conclusion. And so he left unanswered the question: Why do we need a law (the single-sex sports team law) to do what physiology (apparently) already does?

Had he answered this question by stating that we need such a law because physiology does not always work, then he would have undermined his own starting point. If physiology does not always differentiate women and men, then it is not enough to point to it to justify a law which does differentiate them. Something else must weigh into the justification. Indeed, there is even some hint of what that might be when he also referred to Justine Blainey's claim as "jeopardizing" the existence of voluntary sports teams. But he never explained how the competition of women athletes would "jeopardize" men's teams. So his remark served only to invoke the stereotype so aptly identified in 1916 by Nellie McClung when she wrote, "People still speak of womanhood as if it were a disease."[32]

Fortunately, Justine Blainey decided to appeal the trial judge's decision to the Ontario Court of Appeal. Three judges heard her case. By a two to one majority, they decided that "it is females who are being denied the right to participate in athletic activities by reason of section 19(2). There is no evidence that males are being denied the right to full membership and participation in athletic organizations.'' In other words, Section 19(2) ''permits the posting of a 'no females allowed' sign by every athletic organization in this province.'' Accordingly, they held that Section 19(2) of the Ontario Human Rights Code – the single-sex sports team law – violated Justine Blainey's right to sex equality under Section 15(1) of the Charter.

The Ontario Hockey Association immediately sought leave to appeal the decision of the Ontario Court of Appeal to the Supreme Court of Canada. In June 1986, however, the Supreme Court of Canada refused to hear the case. That meant that the Supreme Court of Canada avoided making any explicit pronouncement about the meaning of the sex equality provision in Section 15(1) of the Charter. It also meant that there could be no further challenge to the Ontario Court of Appeal's decision. Justine Blainey had finally won her case.

But what exactly had she won? Unfortunately it is easier to explain what she had not won. After her case, we still do not know whether girls can play on boys' teams. Indeed we do not even know whether Justine Blainey herself can play on the team that wanted her. This is because the Ontario Court of Appeal did not rule that the Ontario Hockey Association had to let her play hockey. Instead, what the Court of Appeal ruled was that the Ontario Hockey Association could not rely on Section 19(2) of the Ontario Human Rights Code to keep her from playing. This difference is significant. It means that if the Ontario Hockey Association were to find other reasons for keeping Justine Blainey, and other girls, off the boys' hockey teams, they might continue to do so.

That is precisely what the Ontario Hockey Association proceeded to do. After the Supreme Court of Canada refused their appeal, the Ontario Hockey Association again denied Justine Blainey's application to play hockey on the boys' team that wanted her. Thus they forced her to go back to the Ontario Human Rights Commission to initiate another complaint. This time, however, Section 19(2) could no longer impede her progress. All she had to do was to show that by refusing to let her play, the Ontario Hockey Association was discriminating against her on the basis of her sex. It took months – eighteen more months, in fact – before the Ontario Human Rights Commission ruled that she was eligible to play on the boys' team. The Commission also ruled against boys playing on girls' teams.

However, a ruling from a human rights commission is not as powerful as a court order. In the absence of a further court order, therefore, after Justine Blainey's case we still know very little about the legal meaning of sex equality, even in the context of sports teams.

While single-sex sports teams no longer have the automatic seal of approval that Section 19(2) of the Ontario Human Rights Code used to give them, we still do not know whether single-sex sports teams are ever consistent with sex equality, and if so, under what circumstances. For example, since the Ontario Human Rights Commission has ruled that Justine Blainey is eligible to play hockey on the boys' team that wanted her, what implications does that ruling have for university sports teams? Does it mean that male students are also eligible to compete for and win places on the women's basketball or field hockey teams?

In other words, does sex equality mandate integrated sports teams? Were Aristotle to put aside his defence of sex *in*equality and promotion of male supremacy long enough to answer this question, he would have to give an affirmative answer. For Aristotle, that girls could compete successfully for places on boys' hockey teams would have to mean not only that girls and boys were alike, but also that they must be treated alike, or equally. So it would follow that were girls eligible to play on boys' teams, then boys would have to be eligible to play on girls' teams.

But this conclusion exposes the limits of Aristotle's theory of equality from the perspective of women. All of the evidence is that integrated sports teams continue to disadvantage women.[33] For every woman who can compete successfully for a place on a previously male team, there are many other women who will be displaced by men who successfully compete for positions on previously female teams. Therefore, while integrated sports teams may be consistent with Aristotle's theory of equality, they are not consistent with – indeed, they simply impede – women's claims to sex equality.

The better remedy would be to allow women to compete for places on previously male teams while not allowing men to compete for places on women's teams. However, this remedy would be more preventative than curative. It would prevent some of the disadvantages of rigorously sex-segregated sports teams, but would not cure the long-run inequities caused by the chronic underfunding and second-class status of women's teams. As a result, some commentators have suggested that we must redefine what we think of as 'sports.'[34] If they are right, and our experience suggests that they are, then it is premature to speculate about the best remedy.

It is not too premature for the courts to reject the validity of Aristotle's theory of equality, however. To the contrary, it is long past due. Aristotle's theory of equality is not sophisticated enough to respond to the problems of sex equality. In the context of sports teams, for example, Aristotelian theory forces us to choose between treating women and men as alike or unalike and, hence, to choose between sex-integrated or segregated sports teams. According to the Aristotelian view, we cannot choose to have both; we cannot choose to treat women and men as sometimes alike and sometimes unalike, nor can we choose to integrate some sports teams and not others. Thus the Aristotelian view restricts equality claims to those who are alike and condemns unalikes to inequality. It fails to allow for the possibility that women and men could be unalike and equal, a possibility contained also in the principle of equal pay for work of equal value, as Sandra Burt shows in her chapter in this book.

Although Aristotelian theory fails to explain treating unalikes equally, others have. There are feminists whose theories about the meaning of sex equality have the potential to elucidate the meaning, purpose and effect of treating unalikes equally. In particular, the theories of feminists such as Carol Gilligan, Catharine MacKinnon, and Mary O'Brien[35] draw on the realities of women's experience to explain the meaning of sex equality. Accordingly, their theories have the potential to explain how sex equality might involve treating unalikes equally. Thus an understanding of these theories should be required of Canadian judges who are seeking to explain the meaning of sex equality under the Charter.

This is especially important in view of the fact that so few of our judges are women. According to a recent report, only 52 or 6 per cent of the 796 judges appointed by the federal government are women, and only 39 or 4.6 per cent of the 846 judges appointed by the provincial governments across Canada are women.[36] The first woman to sit on the Supreme Court of Canada is Madame Justice Bertha Wilson who was appointed in 1982, just before the Charter came into effect. Madame Justice Claire L'Heureux-Dubé became the second woman to sit on the Supreme Court of Canada when she was appointed in 1987. The Canadian judiciary remains overwhelmingly male.

Until more women are appointed as judges, it really matters that male judges begin to listen to what feminists are saying about sex equality. Unless they do, there is every reason to assume that the bias of past sex equality decisions – that is, the gender bias of the Aristotelian theory of equality – will continue to prevail. Unless they do, in other words, the likelihood that future judicial decisions will really accomplish sex equality objectives under the Charter remains bleak.

Beverley Baines

SUGGESTED READINGS

Abella, Judge Rosalie Silberman, *Equality in Employment: A Royal Commission Report*. Ottawa: Canadian Government Publishing Centre, 1984.

Atcheson, M. Elizabeth, Mary Eberts, and Beth Symes, with Jennifer Stoddart, *Women and Legal Action: Precedents, Resources and Strategies for the Future*. Ottawa: Canadian Advisory Council on the Status of Women, 1984.

Bayefsky, Anne, and Mary Eberts, *Equality Rights and the Canadian Charter of Rights and Freedoms*. Toronto: Carswell, 1986.

Boyle, Christine, Wayne MacKay, Edward McBride, and John Yogis, *Charterwatch: Reflections on Equality*. Toronto: Carswell, 1986.

Sub-committee on Equality Rights of the Standing Committee on Justice and Legal Affairs, *Equality For All: Report of the Parliamentary Committee on Equality Rights*. Ottawa: Canadian Government Publishing Centre, 1985.

Canadian Journal of Women and the Law

Doerr, Audrey, and Micheline Carrier, *Women and the Constitution in Canada*. Ottawa: Canadian Advisory Council on the Status of Women, 1981.

Dranoff, Linda Silver, *Women in Canadian Law*. Toronto: Fitzhenry & Whiteside, 1977.

Dymond, M.J., *The Canadian Woman's Legal Guide*. Toronto: Doubleday Canada, 1987.

Kome, Penney, *The Taking of Twenty-Eight: Women Challenge the Constitution*. Toronto: Women's Educational Press, 1983.

Smith, Lynn, Gisele Cote-Harper, Robin Elliot, and Magda Seydegart, *Righting the Balance: Canada's New Equality Rights*. Saskatoon: The Canadian Human Rights Reporter, 1986.

Chapter Seven

Immigrant Women and Institutionalized Racism

Immigrant women have always been part of the Canadian historical landscape. The contributions of our pioneer gentlewomen, such as Catherine Parr Trail and Susanna Moodie, are well known and are discussed by Jane Errington in her chapter. Less visible is the fact that, in order to develop Canada as a colony and preserve white supremacy, working-class women from Britain were recruited into Canada as wives and domestic workers.[1] Much of their contribution to nation-building has been erased from history. As a result of the postwar boom and the relaxation of immigration policy, many non-white immigrants came to Canada. While immigrant men integrate relatively quickly into Canadian society through their participation in the labour force, many immigrant women, especially if they do not speak English, become marginal members of society. Together with native women, they become the most disadvantaged and invisible groups in our society.

This chapter focuses on the contemporary situations of immigrant women. Commonly, native and immigrant women's difficulties in Canada are attributed to cultural differences and problems of adjustment. On closer examination, however, we find that while it is true that these women come from different social and cultural backgrounds, their situations, especially if they are non-white and non-English speaking, are similar. This commonality has to do with how their experiences are shaped by the legal, economic, and social processes in Canadian society and has little to do with their ethnic and racial origins.

This is not to say that their cultural heritage and backgrounds are unimportant. Certainly, culture, ethnicity, political orientation, religion, language, and customs mark the internal differences among this group of women. But the immigration process also produces a homogenizing effect: the legal and institutional structures of Canada create certain common conditions, which immigrant women share.

In this chapter, we will examine how, as a result of racist and patriarchal assumptions in our institutions, and the organization of the paid labour force, immigrant women are held 'captive' to their husbands, their families and communities, and their employers. This kind of physical and psychological dependence has implications for immigrant women's physical and mental health, which the term 'adjustment' simply does not fully capture. In adopting a structural approach to understanding immigrant women's experiences, I have deliberately avoided looking at women's 'traditional' roles and the issue of assimilation. By describing women's work as their 'role,' we imply that this is what they are supposed to do 'naturally.' Furthermore, this chapter suggests that if certain conditions persist, immigrant women will not assimilate into Canadian society. While the issue of assimilation is an important one, our focus here is on the institutional and structural barriers that prevent their integration into Canadian society.

In addition to providing a detailed account of immigrant women's situation, we will also examine briefly the historical conditions and present struggle of native women in Canada. Although they also suffer from racism and sexism in our society, the historical and contemporary processes shaping native women's lives are different from those of other Canadian women. We must not make the mistake of equating their circumstances, without empirical investigation.

Finally, this chapter will end on an optimistic note by describing the continuous efforts of native and immigrant women to improve the conditions of their lives and their contribution to making Canada a more democratic and humane society for us all.

Institutional Determinants of Immigrant Women's Experiences

Technically, the term 'immigrant women' refers to women with a certain legal status in Canada – women who are landed immigrants, rather than citizens. This technical definition is deceptive, however. In everyday life, only certain groups of women are seen to be 'immigrant women' by other members of society. They are women of colour, including women from southern Europe and the Third World; women who do not speak English or who speak English with an accent (other than British or American); and women who have certain jobs (for example, a cleaning lady or a sewing-machine operator). In other words, the common usage of the term presupposes class and racist biases.

The purpose here is not to redefine the term 'immigrant women' to include all women who are landed immigrants. We will preserve this common-sense usage. Our aim is to understand *how* this common-sense notion arises. In so doing, we will see that this understanding is rooted in the legal and economic processes of our society, which contain certain sexist and racist assumptions.

To begin this exploration, the first thing to take into account is immigration law and policy. Canada's immigration program has always been designed with the express purposes of directing demographic growth on the one hand, and meeting economic needs and labour market demands on the other.[2] We see this very clearly in our immigration history: people from northern and eastern Europe (for example, Scandinavia and the Ukraine) were encouraged to immigrate to populate and open up the agricultural West; Chinese men were brought in as indentured labourers to build the railway; British and other white European immigrants entered to fill the bureaucratic, professional, and technical strata of the labour force; more recently, South Asians were brought in as farm labourers, and West Indian and Filipino women as domestic workers.[3] While Canada's immigration policy has always been racist, in that white English-speaking immigrants are preferred, non-white immigrants have been allowed to enter the country when there are demands for particular kinds of skills, and as Canada establishes trading relations with non-European nations.[4] Thus, the Canadian mosaic[5] is a direct result of its history as a land of colonialization and immigration. In addition to using immigration as a means to fill gaps in the economy, from time to time Canada relaxes its immigration policy to make room for refugees to enter the country (for example, Jews after the second World War and, more recently, Southeast Asians).[6] But, although controversial, the refugee program is a relatively small part of immigration.

As immigration policy developed historically, efforts were made by the federal government to tie immigration more closely to economic and labour market needs.[7] To this end, a 'points system' was introduced in 1967 as a labour recruitment strategy. Since that time, immigrants have been selected on the basis of points they earn in nine areas such as education, language, and occupation. The points given to occupation, in particular, are constantly revised to reflect economic demands. Immigrants are admitted into Canada under three categories: independent, family class, and business class.

There are two categories of independent immigrants: self-selected workers and assisted relatives. The eligibility of potential independent immigrants is measured by the points system. The former group is granted landed-immigrant status on the basis of the accumulated points for education, work experience, occupation, and economic resources under the points system, which reflects the needs of the economy at that time. Those in the assisted relative category are granted landed-immigrant status after nomination by a relative other than an immediate family member (if they cannot obtain enough points on their own), and the application of the points system. A family-class immigrant is one who cannot qualify to enter Canada under the points system; she or he is granted this status through the sponsorship of an immediate family member who is either an independent landed immigrant or a Canadian citizen. The family class category usually includes the independent immigrant's spouse, children under age twenty-one, or parents over sixty-five. Business immigrants include entrepreneurs, the self-employed, and investors, and are assessed by different criteria.[8] This chapter discusses only the first two classes of immigrants, because it is the relationship between these two groups that contributes to immigrant women's experiences in Canada.

Usually, in an immigrant family, only one member is granted the independent status. In most cases, it is the husband who is so designated, because he is perceived to be the head of the household. The wife is categorized as a family-class immigrant along with the children. In other words, women and men are regarded as different and unequal, an argument used for many years in the legislatures and the courts, as Beverley Baines and Sandra Burt describe in their chapters. This system ignores the fact that the wife may have education and work experience comparable to the husband's and may have made an essential contribution to the family income before immigration. For example, among the industrial workers in Hong Kong and the urban centres of Southeast Asia, which are among the sources of immigrants to Canada, the family of two income earners is the norm.[9] Moreover, once immigrated, the initial financial security of many immigrant families often depends on the labour-force participation of the wife, and only later on that of both spouses. This has to do with the structure of the Canadian labour market, where there are more demands for cheap labour in the marginal sectors of the economy. This, coupled with the increasing necessity for Canadian families to survive on at least two incomes, means that most immigrant wives have to join the paid labour force as wage earners.[10] Yet the assignment of family members according to the classification of 'independent' and 'family class' negates this reality. The official view of the immigrant family, according to immigration procedures, is that of one 'independent' member on whom others depend for their sponsorship, livelihood, and welfare. In this way, the immigration process systematically structures sexual inequality within the family by rendering one spouse (usually the wife) to be legally dependent on the other.

The sponsorship system places many immigrant women in a totally dependent and subordinate position *vis-à-vis* the sponsor, who is legally responsible for her financial welfare for a period of five years. First of all, an immigrant woman's entry into Canada is conditional upon the financial support of her sponsor. If, for some reason, the sponsor should be deported, it is likely that she will be deported also. Thus, prior to an immigrant woman's entry into the country, her legal status as a dependant is already established. This dependence is rooted in the institutionalized (sexist) practices of our legal system, which have tremendous implications for immigrant women's status and self-concept in Canadian society.

Once classified as a dependent immigrant, a whole series of consequences follow, which place a woman in a progressively disadvantageous position. Despite its responsibility for immigration, the Canadian government is minimally involved in the provision of direct services to immigrants. Traditionally, it has relied on the voluntary sector (for example, family networks and ethnic communities) to provide the assistance and services needed by newcomers. Even today, state responsibility for services to immigrants is largely interpreted to mean support for voluntary organizations through funding to community groups and ethnic organizations. Apart from a few statutory services discussed later, social assistance is the responsiblity of provincial governments. As a consequence, eligibility criteria for various programs differ from province to province. In general, family-class immigrants are ineligible for most forms of state assistance during the five-year sponsorship period.[11] They cannot obtain family benefits, welfare, and other benefits unless there is a break in the sponsorship. For an immigrant woman, this may involve proving that she and her husband are legally separated, or, in the case of a relative, that the sponsor is unwilling or no longer able to support her and her children. In any event, the procedure of legally terminating this relationship is degrading and painful for both the woman and her family.[12]

The major statutory service for immigrants is full-time training in one official language and employment training for the household head. These kinds of educational programs are available free of charge. The household head obtains an allowance from the federal department of employment and immigration while taking a program. Since the husband is usually designated as the household head, most immigrant women are denied an important resource, which could potentially open the door for them to better employment and educational opportunities. According to a study conducted in Saskatchewan, many women were told by immigration officials that they did not need to learn English because they were housewives.[13] Yet these women work in garment factories, food processing plants, janitorial and other low-paying, menial jobs while their husbands go to school. Thus, institutional discrimination against immigrant women is built into the statutory services for immigrants.

As 'dependants,' if women wish to take language and job-training programs, then they or their sponsor have to pay. Frequently, the high costs of these programs render them inaccessible to immigrant women. In terms of job-training programs, a minimum of Grade 8 English, or the equivalent, is required. Most immigrant women from the non-English speaking world are automatically excluded by this admission criterion.[14] Thus, in many cases, educational programs are more of a hindrance than a help to non-English speaking, non-white immigrant women. This is how sexist and racist assumptions are manifested in the institutional processes of our society.

Finally, the lack of recognition by Canadian institutions and employers of women's previous education and training is an effective barrier for them to participate as equal members in society. Since immigrant women lack the Canadian work experience required by most employers, gaining recognition for educational levels and professional qualifications acquired in their country of origin is an important step in both seeking jobs in the primary labour market, and in upgrading their training and skills in Canada. The same study from Saskatchewan indicates that, while it is relatively easy for women to obtain recognition for elementary or secondary education, gaining recognition for university, post-graduate, and vocational or professional training is much more difficult. Women wishing to take graduate classes are expected to take some, or all, of their undergraduate classes again. Women with professional degrees and considerable expertise in their fields are denied the opportunities to work until they pass expensive examinations designed to limit the in-take of foreign graduates into Canadian professions.[15]

According to this study, recognition at upper levels was reported by only four out of the ninety-five women interviewed, and they credited this to their previous education in British or American universities. The fact that women who received their educational credentials from Britain and the United States were given preferential treatment suggests racist assumptions in the accreditation process as well as Canada's dominant relation to less developed parts of the world. The findings of this study are corroborated by other studies.[16] As will be seen in next section, these procedures help to keep immigrant women in marginal positions in the paid labour force and contribute to their sense of dependence, isolation, and helplessness.

Immigrant Women in the Labour Force

The legal barriers in our institutions, examined above, have a negative impact on immigrant women's participation in the paid labour force. In addition, the segregation of the Canadian labour market by gender and ethnicity serves to exacerbate their experiences. This is not the place to provide a detailed account of the structure of the labour market. But simply put, the term 'segregated labour market' refers to the fact that some jobs are 'reserved' for women and ethnic/racial minorities, and some for white, English-speaking men.[17]

A review of the status of immigrant women in the Canadian labour force shows that they are concentrated in the upper and lower echelons of the occupational hierarchy, either in highly skilled professional jobs or in job ghettos.[18] (See Table 2.) This characterization is deceptive, however, because it glosses over differences among women who immigrate to Canada. A closer look at these statistics reveals that women holding managerial, administrative, and professional positions are from the United Kingdom and the United States. They are not seen as 'immigrant women' in everyday life. By contrast, women from southern Europe, Asia, and other parts of the globe tend to work in the service, processing, fabricating, and assembly jobs.[19]

In general, non-white immigrants are disadvantaged in a competitive labour market in which Canadian (read, English-speaking) training and work experience are major determinants for entry into higher-paid jobs. Many non-white immigrants, even those in professional and highly skilled technical occupations in their home countries, have to take lower positions because of the lack of recognition by the Canadian government and employers of their qualifications and credentials.[20] Women's experience is made even more difficult because of sex segregation in the Canadian labour market. In her research on the Portuguese community, Boulter found that an immigrant's first job in Canada, usually a low-skilled menial job, is then treated as her Canadian experience and she is subsequently locked into these kinds of jobs.[21] Independent immigrants are at least eligible for state-subsidized educational programs, which may provide them with an avenue of upward mobility. For immigrant women who are 'family class' immigrants, even this alternative is barred to them because of their dependent status. This, coupled with their family responsibilities and obligations, means that their choice of jobs and opportunities is severely limited. They are forced to find paid employment in what economists refer to as the 'marginal' or 'secondary' labour market,[22] and are restricted to a separate and captive labour pool.[23]

Non-English speaking and non-white immigrant women are commonly recruited into three kinds of services and industries. First, they are recruited into private domestic and janitorial service by doctors, lawyers, managers, and the like. Although this kind of employment is usually low-paid and without labour standard protection, it suits the requirements of immigrant women because it can be fitted into their schedule of housework and childcare more easily than jobs with rigid schedules.[24] As well, they do not have to speak English to carry out their work. Increasingly, women from Asia and southern European countries are recruited to do industrial home sewing, doing piecework in isolation in their own homes.[25] Second, immigrant women are found in the lower strata of the service industries, including restaurants, janitorial and cleaning services, and the food industry. Third, they are found in the lower echelons of the manufacturing industries, particularly in light manufacturing such as textile, garment, and plastic factories, and in the retail trade.

Table 2

Occupation by Sex and Place of Birth, 1981 Census of Canada

	Males		*Females*		*Foreign Born Females by Place of Birth*					
Occupational Classification	*Canada*	*Foreign Born*	*Canada*	*Foreign Born*	*U.S.A.*	*UK*	*Southern Europe*	*Other Europe*	*Asia*	*Other*
Total N	5,708,765	1,371,320	3,888,100	908,825	65,195	200,675	179,245	200,810	137,740	125,165
Total Per Cent	100.0	100.0	100.0	100.0	100.0	100.1	100.1	100.0	100.0	100.0
Managerial & Administrative	11.1	11.8	5.4	5.5	7.7	7.5	2.7	6.9	4.6	4.3
Social & Physical Sciences, Teaching	8.7	12.1	10.1	8.2	18.7	9.7	3.2	9.5	6.6	7.0
Medicine, Health, Artistic, Literary	3.0	3.8	10.2	9.7	11.5	10.4	2.9	9.9	12.3	13.9
Clerical	7.3	5.9	37.8	30.2	30.4	40.4	18.7	28.5	28.3	34.9
Sales	9.0	7.2	9.6	8.3	9.3	11.0	6.0	10.8	5.8	5.7
Service	9.2	11.2	15.3	17.6	12.9	13.1	24.2	18.3	18.7	15.6
Farming, Forestry & Mining	9.0	4.1	2.5	2.1	3.2	1.2	1.7	4.1	1.7	0.7
Processing, Fabricating & Assembly	29.4	35.0	6.3	14.7	4.0	4.4	34.6	8.9	18.3	13.8
Transport, Equipment & Other	13.3	8.9	2.8	3.7	2.3	2.4	6.1	3.1	3.7	4.1

Adapted from M. Boyd, 'Immigrant Women in Canada' in *International Migration: The Female Experience*, edited by R.J. Simon and C.B. Bretell (Totowa: Rowman and Allanheld, 1986, p. 55.)

Frequently, they are hired either by small operations owned by ethnic entrepreneurs (for example, small retail stores, supermarkets, delicatessens) in ethnic neighbourhoods, or by large institutions such as factories and hotels that employ over a hundred workers. In the latter case, the size of the industry or business seems to be important in determining whether immigrant women will be hired, because it is essential that the new employees in the workplace speak the same language as the other employees. Apart from businesses run by ethnic entrepreneurs, smaller companies are less likely to hire non-English speaking immigrants because there is less likelihood that they can speak the common language of the workplace.[26]

The jobs open to immigrant women have been described as 'unskilled and dead-end.' But in their study on the organization of job ghettos of immigrant women, Ng and Das Gupta found that in order to procure these jobs, immigrant women must have a variety of general, interchangeable skills, which they have developed from housekeeping and childrearing.[27] They are available on short-term, temporary, or even on an emergency basis. Working hours are also extremely irregular, ranging from a temporary, on-call basis in domestic and kitchen work to shift work in factories and hotels. Very few of them, with the exception of those in the garment and textile industries, are protected by labour standard legislation and union contracts. Fringe benefits, such as medical and pension plans, are not provided.

The story of Maria, a fifty-nine-year-old semi-retired worker, epitomizes the experience of many non-English speaking immigrant women in the 'captive labour force.'[28]

Maria came to Canada in 1955 with her husband and five children. They were tenant farmers in southern Italy and went bankrupt. They were sponsored by Maria's brother to immigrate to Canada. Maria held a variety of jobs after she came to Canada. She got a job in a restaurant washing dishes two days after the family arrived in Toronto. For ten years, Maria started her day at eight o'clock cleaning people's houses. From four in the afternoon until one the next morning, she worked in a restaurant. From her domestic service, Maria acquired cast-off clothing for her children; from the restaurant she brought home left-over food to feed her family. On the weekend she did housework with the help of her eldest daughter, who was responsible for looking after the younger children, as well as the shopping and banking.

Maria did stay home for a couple of years after the birth of her sixth child. Then she went back to work because the family needed the money. At one time, she got a job cleaning in a bank. She would go to work between four and eight o'clock in the morning, before people came to work. She went home just in time for her eldest daughter to leave for school. She stayed home during the day looking after the baby, and went around cleaning houses and offices again at night.

Maria is proud that she now has a nice house and that her children all have had a good education. At the time of the interview, she was still working as a cleaner in a textile factory. "Now," said Maria contentedly, "I go to work because I enjoy it. When I am tired, I go home."

Maria's experience reveals that the 'benefits' that non-English speaking immigrant women receive from their jobs are dependent upon good personal relationships with the employer or supervisor. The wages they earn are inadequate to maintain themselves and their families. As workers, they have few rights, and are completely unprotected and vulnerable to exploitation.

Occasionally, in the garment industry, if a woman shows initiative, works hard, and learns a bit of English quickly, she may become an assistant to the supervisor. But most often, women are confined to operating sewing machines. The more prestigious positions, such as garment cutting and supervisory positions, are usually occupied by men, and women rarely are promoted to these jobs. Thus, although more research on the hiring and promotion policies of business and industries is necessary, the effects of these policies with regard to immigrant women are very clear: they are confined to the bottom layers of the labour force with the worst working conditions and wages. The jobs they occupy are those that other workers are in a position to decline.[29]

When we consider the ways in which immigrant women are locked into a job ghetto, we cannot overlook the role of labour unions in maintaining a segregated labour force. Most of the jobs occupied by immigrant women, with the exception of about 40 per cent of those in the textile and garment industry, are non-unionized. In her study on immigrant women in the labour force, Arnopoulos found that most of the unions covering the textile and garment trade are weak. Some of them have a long history of collusion with management.[30] Apart from the problems of organizing the sectors of business and industry where immigrant women are concentrated, until recently most labour unions have not made a concerted effort either to organize women workers in general or immigrant women workers in particular.[31]

To understand the historical animosity between the labour movement and immigrants, we must refer back to immigration policies. The goals of immigration policies and organized labour have always been opposed. Immigration policies are designed to meet the demands of industries by allowing workers with specialized and general skills to enter Canada, thereby helping to depress wages by increasing the competition for jobs. To protect themselves from excessive exploitation, Canadian workers band together to form labour unions, thereby replacing competition with cooperation. With sufficient numerical strength, organized labour can demand higher wages and better working conditions. In the past, male workers did this by excluding or selectively organizing women, ethnic minorities, and children, thus contributing to the formation of a segregated labour force.[32]

Although there are still gaps in our knowledge in this area, recent published materials begin to shed light on the relationship between the labour movement and women workers.[33] In her study on women in trade unions in B.C. during the first two decades of the twentieth century, Campbell found that, in attempting to protect themselves against competition and employers' exploitation, white Canadian male workers used racist and sexist tactics in organizing to exclude other workers, namely immigrants, women, native peoples, and children from their occupations. These workers were organized into a relatively cheap labour pool, which did not pose a threat to the male labour force. When women were organized into unions, it was done to exclude Oriental workers, thus promoting racism within the union movement. Union practices were sexist in the sense that women's problems were not reflected in union demands. Women workers were consistently paid lower wages than men. The leadership was more concerned about women's morality and health than about bargaining for an adequate living wage on their behalf.[34] As a result of this tradition in our union history, many jobs in the lower echelons of the labour market remain unorganized to this day.

In sectors where organizing efforts have taken or are taking place, union organizers are frequently unaware of the critical needs of immigrant women, whose hesitation and reluctance to participate in union acitivities are interpreted as apathy or a manifestation of traditionalism and backwardness.[35] This does not negate the important contribution of the union movement in bringing about higher wages and better working conditions for immigrant women, but draws attention to the fact that these women have been systematically disadvantaged. There are concrete barriers which curtail the options available to them.

The Organization of Domestic Labour

Women's work in the home – their domestic labour – is often seen to belong to the private domain unconnected to the public work world. It has been undervalued because it does not directly bring in money. Moreover, domestic labour, popularly known as 'housework,' is seen to entail the same tasks for all women. In this section, we will discuss how women's domestic work is *transformed* as a result of the immigration process; it cannot be understood without reference to the social organization of Canadian society and immigrant families' economic circumstances, notably the husband's paid labour outside the home.

While the home may be a place to rest, eat, and relax for the male worker, it is not such a refuge for the woman. This is not to say that the home is not a source of support for her, but to suggest that it also requires a work process that has to be continuously managed and organized. The work of holding a family together is the work of the woman. Her labour produces the material basis for the other family members' enjoyment, from the planning and preparation of meals to the emotional and material support she gives to other members of the household. The labour involved in sustaining a family is, in many ways, common to all women across class and ethnic groups. Susan McDaniel, in her chapter on the changing family, shows that this responsibility has been and still is assigned to women, in spite of changes in female participation in the labour force. What is special about the work of immigrant women is that, when immigrant families come to Canada, the woman's work in the home is intensified. According to a study on immigrant housewives conducted in Toronto, women complained about the difficulties of doing housework properly in Canada.[36] Housework seemed more difficult; life seemed more hectic; there were more worries, from the husband's paid employment to the kinds of troubles that children could get themselves into. Together with this work intensification is a concomitant increase in, and even enforcement of, the woman's dependence on her husband.

How does this occur? The same study discovered that, when immigrant families come to Canada, they become totally immersed in a money economy. This does not mean that immigrant families were untouched by industrialization and a money economy prior to immigration, as industrialization has long disrupted traditional peasant economies. It is precisely the penetration of a wage economy into the farm economy which forces many immigrants to leave their home countries in the first place.[37] The pattern of the worker, who goes from industrial centre to industrial centre in search of wage work, leaving his (and sometimes her) spouse and children in the village or home town, is a common phenomenon in less developed parts of the world. However, in these circumstances, women's work in the home is not fully incorporated into a money economy and appropriated by modern industries. To a large extent, the woman remains in control of the pace of work within the family unit. Her labour is directly visible in the products consumed in the home, such as the bread or noodles that she makes. In many instances, she may also produce a variety of products for home consumption, such as vegetables from her garden or clothes she sews. In a rural or semi-rural setting, the woman's work is indispensable in sustaining the economy of the household unit.

In Canada, the production of family goods has been taken out of the home and appropriated by business enterprises. The immigrant housewife finds herself becoming increasingly reliant on consumer goods, not only because they reduce her work load and make her work easier, but more importantly, because the material conditions in Canada do not lend themselves to the production of subsistence goods within the single family unit. Practically everything that a housewife does or produces can be purchased, from frozen dinners to laundry service. Services available in the city, from dry-cleaning facilities to fast-food outlets, replace the services that once could be obtained only in the home. Eichler has called this process the 'industrialization of housework.'[38] Virtually overnight, then, immigrants are forced to become consumers. At the same time, because many working-class immigrant men work in the lower echelons of the male occupational hierarchy, their wages are not always adequate to sustain the family economy. As a result many immigrant women have to produce some of the basic food stuffs, such as canned foods, themselves. These efforts are sometimes interpreted by other Canadians simply as an exhibition of traditionalism rather than as a way of cutting down costs when family income does not permit the indiscriminate purchasing of processed foodstuffs.[39]

Together with this increasing commercialization of household products is the need for what were previously luxury goods, such as colour televisions, cars, and a paraphernalia of electrical appliances from dishwashers to electric razors. But in Canada these items are not considered luxuries; they are deemed basic to a normal standard of living. Thus, whereas previously only the wage earner was directly tied to a money economy, when the immigrant family comes to Canada, the entire family is immersed in the money economy. Everything now requires money. In addition, immigrants also find themselves absorbed into an elaborate formal credit system, either through buying a house or a car, or simply through the use of credit cards.

In order to acquire the goods and services necessary to maintain a minimum living standard in Canada, immigrants have to work doubly hard in the paid labour force as there is a much greater need for money in the household. Since women's work in the home does not directly bring in a wage, it does not have the same importance either socially or in the family. The family's reliance on a wage puts an immigrant woman in a dependent position *vis-à-vis* her husband, because it is on his wage that she and the children rely for their livelihood. This dependency is a product of the immigration process, in addition to the institutional practices (such as that dictated by immigration law) which created and enforced her dependency. Since the wage is paid to the husband, it obscures the fact that it is not just for him; it is for him to maintain his wife and children. He considers it his money because it is paid to him as an individual, and in this process, the woman's work in the home is seen merely as her private service to a man. At the same time, because of the low-income jobs available to working-class immigrant men, their wages are inadequate to meet all the family expenses, and they have to depend heavily on their wives' services to sustain the family. Clearly, then, the woman's unpaid labour is an essential component in the maintenance of the immigrant worker and the immigrant family.[40]

From this discussion, it can be seen that women's work in Canada is determined *industrially* by the husband's paid work outside the home. Since the husband is usually the major wage earner in the family (because it is he who was recruited into the Canadian labour force), his needs and demands come to dictate and organize the schedule of immigrant women's work in the home. The woman's major responsibility is to ensure his earning power, so that he can return daily to the paid work force. Her work in the home must be oriented to this consideration. If there are other wage earners in the household, then she must cater to their needs and demands as well. Children's activities in schools also are considered part of housework, since the mother in Canada is seen to be responsible for how her children present themselves and perform in school.[41]

As well, there are material differences in circumstance which shape and determine the woman's work. Housework in Canada is privatized in the sense that it is conducted within the confines of the single-family unit. The layout of houses and apartments does not permit the cooperative undertaking of housework among neighbours and friends. While the privatization of basic utilities, such as hot and cold running water and electricity, are meant to and do cut down the amount of labour spent on housework for individual housewives, they also prevent and render irrelevant the cooperative network women have traditionally established in an industrially less advanced setting. The following account by an immigrant woman illustrates this vividly:

"The structure of housework for the women in the peasant neighbourhood, whose husbands have already migrated away to earn a family wage, was far more communal than it could ever be here, if only because of the physical feature of the neighbourhood. When I was growing up, we all lived on a block. And inside the block it was hollow. There was a yard. So there was a yard culture. And everyday, you would do certain things, wash or iron, whatever. Ways were devised for things to be shared. It also had a built-in daycare system. The children had to play in the yard, not on the street. The women would kind of look after the children, informally, you know. You didn't appoint anyone. It just happened. It was a matter of course because that was the place where they would go to do their laundry."[42]

In this regard, the organization of shopping and other facilities also serve to shape women's domestic labour and isolate them from each other. While the centralization of market-places, in the form of supermarkets, may cut down on work for middle class and professional Canadian women, and cut down costs for businesses, it only serves to create more work for immigrant women. This kind of shopping pattern requires and assumes a certain mode of transportation and adequate storage facilities such as large refrigerators and freezers. Large-scale shopping expeditions are certainly not attractive ventures for immigrant women, who do not know the language or the geography of the city and who have to subject their lives to the whims of the public transportation system, sometimes in harsh weather.[43]

Finally, the possession of modern household appliances such as vacuum cleaners and washer/dryers also organize the pace of women's work in determinate ways. All in all, immigrant women's work is organized by the physical set-up of houses, distances to the market and laundry facilities, as well as, and most importantly, by their husband's wage work outside the home. The autonomy which they might have enjoyed previously is seriously undermined. In this setting, they have to become more dependent on the husband, both economically and practically.

The institutional practices, notably as they relate to immigration policy, the structure of the labour market, as well as the social organization of domestic labour, all contribute to immigrant women's dependency and isolation in Canada. But because of their isolation and dependency, their situation is also rendered invisible to other members of society.

Native Women

We cannot discuss the racism and sexism directed at immigrant women without referring to the situation of native women. Together with immigrant women, native women are the most disadvantaged and exploited groups of people in our society. Unfortunately, precisely because of the history of colonization in Canada, much of the past of native people generally, and native women particularly, is lost to us. Since most English accounts of the native peoples were written by whites and are full of racist and sexist biases, we cannot rely on them to provide us with a picture of the role of women in traditional native societies. Recent feminist research has forced a re-examination of past interpretations of the status of native women during early contact periods, and suggests new directions of investigation which begin from the perspective of native women themselves.[44]

It is not the purpose of this chapter to provide a review of the situation of native women. What will be highlighted is the sexism in our legal system which led to native women's disadvantaged positions in Canadian society. As will be seen, although the specific conditions of their oppression are different, the legal, economic, and social processes shaping immigrant and native women's experiences are similar.

Today, a native person is a legal entity. That is, an Indian is defined through provisions set down in the Indian Act established in 1876. Throughout the years, this act has undergone so many revisions in response to political and social changes that descent is no longer a meaningful basis for determining band membership.

Traditionally, native Indians based membership on a number of principles: descent, marriage, residence, and adoption. Among certain bands, membership was very fluid because of intermarriage. With colonization and as more Europeans came to Canada, kinship took on a different pattern, and the meaning of band membership changed. As reserves were set up for native Indians to 'protect' pieces of lands from the occupation of unscrupulous Europeans, there was a need to define band membership more precisely. Beginning in the mid-nineteenth century, the Canadian government developed policies and legislation to cope with problems of defining Indian status.[45]

In order to determine this status, prior to 1941, ethnic origin for an Indian was traced through the mother because many eastern Indian tribes were matrilocal. Thus, children whose mother was Indian were also defined as Indian. Furthermore, Statistics Canada also made a distinction between Indian and 'mixed origin.' In 1941, the definition was changed so that for off-reserve Indians, the father's ethnic status determined that of his children. For those Indians living on the reserve, both the mother's and father's lineages were used as the basis for determining membership.[46]

In 1951, a more complex legal definition took effect: only those individuals who fell under the Indian Act would be classified as Indians. This practice continues today, so that culture and race are no longer criteria for membership. The definition of an Indian is a purely legal one.[47] This is because registered Indians (people who are considered Indians under the Indian Act) are under the jurisdiction of the federal government. They are entitled to certain benefits, such as welfare and education, from the federal government. It is therefore important for administrative purposes to have a precise way of determining membership. Many registered Indians did not challenge this definition because of the limited resources on the reserve and benefits provided to them from the government.[48]

Nevertheless, Indians can give up or lose their status through 'enfranchisement.' It is when we examine the process of enfranchisement that the sexist assumption of the Indian Act comes fully into view. Up to 1960, one way of losing one's legal Indian status was to give it up in order to vote, since Indians were not entitled to vote.[49] Up to 1981, the most common way of losing Indian status was through marriage. Under Section 12 (1) (b) of the Indian Act, an Indian woman who married a non-Indian man automatically lost Indian status for herself and her children. On the other hand, if an Indian man married a non-Indian woman, she and her children legally became Indians. In the case of a native woman marrying a member of another tribe, her name would be transferred to her husband's band list and deleted from her own band.[50]

Ironically, this attempt to exclude women who married out was originally designed, in 1869, to curtail the domination of white men on Indian land. Again, this provision indicates sexist bias in Canadian law: white men married to Indian women were regarded as a threat to the band's resources while white women married to Indian men were not.[51] This law has discriminated against native women and restricted their access to resources provided for other Indians.

Similar to the situation of immigrant women, this legal definition effectively served to cut women off from a host of social benefits available to other members and to negate their cultural heritage. If a native woman married a non-Indian man, she had to leave the reserve. Since native people are under the administrative responsibility of the federal government and resources such as transfer payments and education are provided through the reserves to which they belong, when a woman leaves her reserve she also gives up her rights to these resources. In agitating against the sexism contained in the Indian Act, native women stated emphatically that section 12 (1) (b) of the Act affected them in the following ways: loss of nationality; loss of right to reside where a woman was born; loss of close family ties; loss of a woman's culture and religion; loss of right to family property and inheritance; loss of voting rights; loss of health services; loss of educational rights; and, finally, loss of right to be buried on Indian land.[52]

In the 1960s, various sections of the Indian Act, including Section 12 (1) (b), were again reviewed, in response to the growing militancy of the native movement. However, the section dealing with the status of women did not receive a great deal of attention as native leaders were attempting to prevent a policy proposed by the federal government in 1969, which would terminate all special rights for Indians if it came into effect. Impatient with the indecision of the federal government and confrontation between the bands and the Department of Indian Affairs, two enfranchised women took independent action to challenge the sexist provision of the Indian Act in the courts. They did so without the support of regional Indian associations and against the wishes of their own band councils.[53]

Neither the case of Jeannette Lavell, described by Beverley Baines in her chapter on women and the law, nor that of Yvonne Bedard was supported by the native movement, including status native women. In fact, the National

Indian Brotherhood forcefully intervened in their cases. This division has its historical root in the legal system which provides treaty Indians with special privileges, including their rights to reserves. In the case of the status of women, other status Indians were afraid that their own position and limited resources would be threatened.

These cases, especially that of Jeannette Lavell, did receive a great deal of attention from the women's movement and support from a group called Indian Rights for Indian Women formed by non-status Indian women in 1972. As the issue of the status of Indian women proceeded, both in the court and in the women's movement, it received international attention. In 1978, another native woman, Sandra Lovelace, originally from the Tobique reserve in New Brunswick, took her case to the United Nations Human Rights Committee, arguing that Canada had violated the International Convenant on Political and Civil Rights on the grounds of sexual discrimination.[54]

The agitation by native women, with the support of the women's movement and later the native movement, eventually led to the suspension of Section 12 (1) (b) of the Indian Act in 1981. On February 28, 1985, the Minister of Indian Affairs and Northern Development, David Crombie, announced that legislation eliminating provisions of the Indian Act which were sexually discriminatory would be introduced. He also indicated that the power to control band membership would reside with the Indian First Nation; that is, Indian communities and bands would have the right to determine their own membership.[55]

The struggle of native women is by no means over. Regardless of the pre-colonial situation of the native people with respect to kinship patterns and the status of women, sexist provisions within the Indian Act have re-oriented their thinking. Native leaders have to operate under a climate of limited resources in relation to increasing membership. Time will tell whether and how the status of women will be dealt with in native communities.

Conclusions

While native women are battling for recognition and equality, immigrant women across the country have also mounted similar struggles. They are by no means passive victims of the legal, economic, and social processes we examined earlier in this chapter. Riding on the momentum developed by the women's movement, especially since International Women's Year in 1975, immigrant women in Canada have come together and organized. In the same way native women have demanded their rights, immigrant women are asking for their rights to equal treatment in Canadian society. Today, there are immigrant women's organizations in most major centres across Canada, from lobbying groups such as Immigrant Women of Saskatchewan and service organizations such as Toronto's Immigrant Women's Centre to coalitions such as the Ontario Immigrant Women's Network. In November 1986, out of the second National Conference on Immigrant and Visible Minority Women, a national Advisory Committee was formed. While the precise mandate of the committee will be developed over the next year or so, meanwhile it serves as a central point of reference for immigrant women in Canada.

Within the women's movement, immigrant women, together with women of colour, have begun to challenge the movement's strong middle class and racial biases.[56] They draw attention to the fact that demands from the women's movement in the past, such as equal rights for work of equal value, were defined in terms of white middle class women's perspective and priority. Since immigrant women's locations in society are different as a result of their unequal treatment under the law and in the labour market, their demands have been different. Frequently, these demands are seen to be regressive by middle class women. (For example, 'wages for housework' was at one point a demand by working class immigrant women.) In a recent paper issued by the Advisory Committee on the Status of Women, Estable convincingly pointed out that although immigrant women come from different cultural and class backgrounds, their situation in Canada is determined, to a large extent, by the Canadian legal system. The legal and other barriers must be eliminated before equality can be achieved.[57]

While the debates and discussions of immigrant women with other women and with the government are often heated, they are also positive steps in making visible the special situation of immigrant women. It is through challenging social assumptions and confronting unfair institutional and social practices that we can work toward a more democratic and humane society for all.

Roxana Ng

SUGGESTED READINGS

Arnopoulos, Sheila McLeod, *Problems of Immigrant Women in the Canadian Labour Force.* Ottawa: Canadian Advisory Council on the Status of Women, 1978.

Barndt, Deborah, Ferne Cristall, dian marino, *Getting There: Producing Photostories with Immigrant Women.* Toronto: Between The Lines, 1982.

Boyd, Monica, "Immigrant Women in Canada," in R.J. Simon and C.B. Brettell, eds., *International Migration: The Female Experience.* Totowa: Rowman & Allanheld, 1986.

Campbell, Marie, *Halfbreed.* Toronto: McClelland and Stewart, 1973.

"Ethnicity and Femininity," Danielle Juteau-Lee and Barbara Roberts, eds. A special issue of *Canadian Ethnic Studies* 13, no. 1, 1981.

Estable, Alma, *Immigrant Women in Canada: Current Issues.* A background paper prepared for the Canadian Advisory Council on the Status of Women, March 1986,

Frideres, James S., *Native People in Canada, Contemporary Conflicts.* Scarborough: Prentice-Hall, 1983.

Jamieson, Kathleen, *Indian Women and the Law in Canada: Citizens Minus.* Ottawa: Advisory Council on the Status of Women and Indian Rights for Indian Women, April 1978.

"Immigrant Women," Marguerite Cassin and Jennifer Newton, eds. A special issue of *Multiculturalism* 2, no. 4, (1979).

Ng, Roxana, "Immigrant Housewives in Canada: A Methodological Note," *Atlantis* 8, no. 1, (1982).

Ng, Roxana, and Judith Ramirez, *Immigrant Housewives in Canada.* Toronto: Immigrant Women's Centre, 1981.

"Immigrant Women," Roxana Ng and Himani Bannerji, Joyce Scane, Didi Khayatt, and Makeda Silvera, eds. A special issue of *Resources for Feminist Research* 16, no. 1 (1987).

Chapter Eight

By and About Women

Since 1965, there has been such an explosion in the number of novels and books of poetry by women published in Canada that today it is impossible to derive a sense of the true texture of Canadian literature without looking at the writing by women. Yet this was not always the case. Before the 1960s, the published literature was dominated by male writers, as any university course outline from that period will show. And, of course, this male tradition was a very natural manifestation of the patriarchal culture in which we all live. It is surprising that, in the past, so many fine women writers were ignored; but the female tradition in writing is now getting the recognition it deserves. The amount of material available is such that no short article can include all of the writers who should be respresented. So I have instead chosen to concentrate on a few broad themes that run through the writing in English, and discuss only briefly the experimental writing that is developing out of Quebec and the work of contemporary playwrights.

The portrayal of women by women is not new, but the contemporaneity of the exchange – fact for fiction, fiction for fact – *is*. These authors are writing ourselves and our lives into being, and in the process they bring into focus subjects, such as our sexuality and our experience of aging, which have previously been ignored.

Similarly, a question not always raised when we discuss literature centres on access. Some women writers in our society have voices we rarely hear, so this article will open up the question of women's silencing. Because writing never develops in a vacuum, and because the earlier women writers had little or no recognition, it is important to consider briefly the female tradition in Canadian English literature.

Establishing the Tradition

Writing is something women have always done. In fact, "in the development of modern Western civilization, writing was the first of the arts . . . which it was possible for women to practice."[1] Women write because writing is done in private, usually in the home, and requires little outlay for materials–just a pad of paper, a pen, much courage, and talent. So it should come as no surprise to find that Canadian fiction begins with a woman, indeed with two women.

While visiting Quebec in the 1760s, Frances Brooke wrote the first Canadian English-language novel, *The History of Emily Montague,* published in London, England, in 1769. Then, in 1824, H.C. Thomson of Kingston, Upper Canada, published the first indigenous Canadian novel, *St. Ursula: The Nun of Canada,* by Julia (Beckwith) Hart. The long and complex story had begun. The diaries of Mrs. Elizabeth Simcoe (1791–96) give us detailed information about the lives of the upper class in York (Toronto). This form of writing was used by many of the women who were early settlers in Canada. Diaries and letters, such as the correspondence of Anne Langton (1835–46), later published as *A Gentlewoman in Upper Canada,* are now being recovered and collected by feminist historians, who are also writing the oral histories of older women whose lives span much of this century.[2] In this way we are now establishing the place of women in the literature and in the history of Canada. Sylvia Hamilton, in her article "Our Mothers Grand and Great: Black Women of Nova Scotia," reminds us of an oral tradition stretching back to the 1700s. Carrie Best established *The Clarion* in 1945, the first Nova Scotia newspaper for black people. In doing so, she was following the example set by Mary Shadd Cary, the first black woman in North America to become publisher and editor of a newspaper, *The Freeman* (1853), printed in Windsor, Ontario.[3]

One writer whose work needs no re-establishing is Susanna Moodie (1803–85). She was a prolific writer and her Canadian classic, *Roughing It in the Bush* (1852), has been reissued many times. Moodie's work has taken on a new dimension because of Margaret Atwood's epic poem *Susanna Moodie.* Moodie's sister, Catherine Parr Traill, was neither as graphic (nor as honest) as Susanna when describing the grim life they both experienced in their new country. But then she was less fortunate than her sister: her writing provided the only economic support for her seven surviving children and for her husband, who was never able to adapt to Canada's backwoods. The idealism and optimism in her work is often condemned, but these seem to have been effective characteristics for survival –Mrs. Traill lived to be ninety-seven and wrote her final book at age ninety-two. Anna Jameson, by contrast, did not have to provide for her family with her writing. An early visitor to Canada, she wrote for and about 'the gentry.' In *Winter Studies and Summer Rambles in Canada* (1838) she sets the lives of the civilized colonial garrison against the immense and overpowering wilderness of the Canadian North.[4]

Although Isabella Valancy Crawford (1850–87) was a professional fiction writer (many of her short stories and novellas were published in American magazines) it is as a poet that she is important in the history of Canadian literature. She is a central figure in the male-dominated popular nineteenth-century tradition of narrative poetry, but her poems were largely ignored, uncollected, and only published at her own expense. In the 1970s, Dorothy Livesay, working on the Crawford manuscripts at Queen's University, discovered an incomplete but powerful narrative poem, which has subsequently been published. This act of reclamation brings into focus the continuing need of 're-visionist' work not only to establish the early writing of women in Canada, but also to reassess women's writing that has previously been analysed according to a masculinist tradition. Sandra Djwa, speaking of the new feminine consciousness that was influencing Canadian literature in the late 1950s and early 1960s, tells this anecdote concerning Crawford's status: "Roy Daniels in 1964, when he came to write on Isabella Valancy Crawford for the *Literary History of Canada,* hovered over the adjective 'lady' as descriptive of a female poet and then abandoned it. Crawford was far too good a poet, he judged, to be called a 'lady poet'. No Canadian critic before this time would have shown this distinction."[5]

Two decades after Crawford, we find Sara Jeannette Duncan (1861–1922) tackling her work as a free-lance journalist with audacity and courage. She was a prolific and astute fiction writer, some of whose work has now been reissued in answer to the demands of feminist studies. One of her most important novels, *Cousin Cinderella; or, a Canadian Girl in London* (1908, reprinted in 1971), gives a perceptive analysis of the colonialism directed at an expatriate woman who is extremely conscious of the need for a national identity.[6]

This list of early women writers could continue, for as Atwood says in her introduction to *Roughing It in the Bush* (1986), "when you place the early literature of the Canadas beside that of the United States, a curious thing emerges. It's possible to cover American literature from, say, 1625 to 1900, without spending much time at all on women writers, with the exception of Ann Bradstreet and Emily Dickinson. Attention focuses on the 'great' and overwhelmingly male American writers of the period: Melville, Poe, Hawthorne . . . English Canada produced no such classics at this time – it was settled later – but if you study the literature at all, you can't ignore the women."[7] Atwood suggests that it may be the difference in the dates of settlement (seventeenth century versus nineteenth century) that accounts for the larger proportion of women writers in Canada, but significantly "it's a situation that has persisted until today: the percentage of prominent and admittedly accomplished women writers, in both prose and poetry, is higher in Canada than it is in any of the other English-speaking countries."[8]

But in spite of this, women writers were not acknowledged as part of mainstream writing. This omission was due, in part, to a national hesitancy in recognizing any Canadian literary canon. Sandra Djwa suggests that although "the tide had begun to turn about 1943"[9] with the recognition that we did indeed have a literature that must be acknowledged, this literature was largely ignored by the universities and "up to the middle fifties the tradition was the English (and male) tradition of Milton, Wordsworth" *et al.*[10] So even after CanLit became a recognized field of study, it took special effort on the part of (mainly women) scholars to unearth the early work of women writers and get it reissued.

One writer whose work spans much of the century, and continues as vigorously as ever, is Dorothy Livesay. Her work was ignored for years, but she is in many senses one of the most important foremothers of our writing. Actively engaged in left-wing politics since the 1920s, Livesay has written poetry that is both political and lyrical. She was an early feminist and an ardent advocate of trade unionism, becoming a social worker in order to practise the social justice she believed in.

Livesay has acknowledged the strong and solitary figure of Emily Carr as central in the female tradition. As a visual artist, Carr was totally marginalized and, although she was a contemporary of the Group of Seven, she remained excluded from the Group. Her magnificent West Coast paintings remained relatively unknown until after her death. Her *Journals,* not published until 1966, provide a graphic description of what it means to be woman and artist. Her struggle is confirmed in *The House of All Sorts* (1967), a series of anecdotes about her life as a landlady – a project undertaken in a vain attempt at economic security. Toward the end of her life, Carr wrote *Klee Wyck* (1941), an immediate success that won a Governor General's Award. At least as a writer, Carr was 'acceptable' – writing was something women could do, painting was not. Despite the award, Carr's writing has only received the readership it so clearly deserves since the advent of Women's Studies courses in the 1970s.

In *Klee Wyck,* Carr not only captures the essence of the natural landscape, she also provides portraits of many native women. Until native women themselves broke their silence, as Maria Campbell does in *Half Breed* (1973), Emily Carr's voice was one of the strongest on their behalf. Carr's stories depend on the oral tradition, a tradition absorbed by the contemporary West Coast poet Daphne Marlatt. Like Carr's writing, Marlatt's poetry relies heavily on the Canadian landscape and on the affinity of human and natural cycles.

The 1950s marked a watershed in Canadian writing for both prose and poetry. There was now a growing number of women who were writing innovative and dynamic poetry. Miriam Waddington and P.K. Page were both members of the Montreal group who published in *Preview* during the 1940s. P.K. Page was a scriptwriter at the National Film Board, and her poems in

The Metal and the Flower (a winner of the 1954 Governor General's Award) take both their style and their theme from the kinetic cinematography of her film work. Waddington has an ease and civility in her use of language and metaphor, often turning the mundane into the extraordinary, achieving much the same effect as Alice Munro does in her short stories.

Jay Macpherson, as both teacher and poet, is noted as an early influence on the work of Margaret Atwood and, of course, both women were students of Northrop Frye. Atwood's critical work, *Survival* (1972), depends heavily on Frye's interpretation of the Canadian wilderness as motif and construct in Canadian fiction. The writing in Margaret Avison's *Winter Sun* (1960) has a precision of form and language also evident in Pat Lowther's poetry in the representation of various states and levels of consciousness. Phyllis Webb was also writing in the 1950s, but it is her later work, especially *Selected Poems* (1971), that has influenced many of today's young poets.

Even though we have a fairly extensive tradition of writing by and about women, it would be wrong to assume that women authors have enjoyed a privileged or equitable environment in this country. Rather, in the late 1960s, several cultural and political events coalesced to provide Canadian women writers with a more hospitable, creative environment and an audience eager for their writing. There was a new wave of the women's movement in the late 1960s which focused almost entirely (in its early stages) on the individual experiences of women and derived strength from the consciousness-raising groups, which Naomi Black discusses in her chapter on the women's movement. It was during the 1960s that CanLit came of age, emerging as a *bona fide* field of study.

Writing the Self Into Being

If, in general, there was a new audience for CanLit in the 1960s, then in the 1970s the women novelists enjoyed a rapidly expanding readership.

Margaret Atwood, perhaps the best known writer of this period, warns that:

> writers, as writers, are not propagandists or examples of social trends or preachers or politicians. They are makers of books, and unless they can make books well they will be bad writers, no matter what the social validity of the views . . . Writing tends to concentrate more on life, not as it ought to be, but as it is, as the writer feels it, experiences it . . . [A writer's] work may include the Movement, since it is so palpably among the things that exist. The picture that she gives of it is altogether another thing, and will depend, at least partly, on the course of the Movement itself.[11]

The body of work women writers are producing does indeed record the hopes, dilemmas, failures, and successes of the women's movement, providing the creative counterpart to the political and social changes that are taking place.

The search for individual selfhood, the motivating force of the consciousness-raising groups of the late 1960s, finds its analogue in the writing of the period. A surprisingly large number of these writers choose to explore the emerging self through a writer/protagonist: the woman who writes herself, her story, her life, into being.

Many of the writers discussed here fall under the general heading of realists, though the reality they explore is totally different from that usually portrayed in 'malestream' writing. Women, especially women in the home, live in a subculture in which the norms are closer to abnormal when assessed by external criteria. In order to portray this reality, women writers use different techniques in their writing. They fracture time, as it is constantly fractured in their own lives by countless demands. The narrative voice will vary to include a character talking to herself, or God, or anyone else who will listen. The closures of the novel will alter and break. Whereas the traditional ending of a story often shows the woman protagonist as happily married (or dying of unrequited love), contemporary women writers may alter the closure, leaving the protagonist with ever-increasing options.[12]

Believing in the validity of their own experience sufficiently to write it into being has not been an easy task for women writers. Alice Munro expresses this unease when she describes the mornings she spent, during the 1950s, with a group of house-bound friends. How could she, as writer, transform what she perceived as 'trivia' into the stuff of serious literature? Her experience is told in an 'Appreciation' of Marian Engel's two novels, *Honeyman Festival* and *Sarah Bastard's Notebook*:

> And here was a woman writing about the lives of women at their most muddled, about a woman who can't quite believe in the world of careers, academic strivings, faith in work, and another who is just managing to keep afloat in the woozy world of maternity, with its shocks and confusions and fearful love and secret brutality. You have to remember how shunned, despised, misused, this material was at that time . . . most of us thought there was no way to deal with it except to turn it into the layer-cake fiction of the women's magazines, or hype it up to the manic level of the humour of the professional harried housewives who write newspaper columns.[13]

Munro goes on to explain that it was Engel's bravery and skill in transforming such experience into literature that gave her "that clear glimpse of possibilities which is one of the things a writer is always looking for, and must be most lastingly grateful for, in another writer."[14] It is significant that Margaret Laurence, when interviewed in a 1978 video about *The Fire-Dwellers* (1969), felt impelled to defend what had been discounted by critics as "trivial content."[15] But the world of Stacey McAindra, which Laurence presents in this novel, is one experienced by many women in Canada.

The new thematic material that Munro finds in Engel's work overthrows the established concept of 'universality' and posits a new set of criteria. For instance, much has been written about death and how the heroic male faces it. Death is, of course, universal, and 'great' literature concerns itself with such things. But birth is as universal as death, and until very recently little has been written about the process, or about the cultural and political relevance of birthing.[16] Although everyone experiences birth, women are the only people who can record the reality of giving birth. Women writers are now creating protagonists who choose to remain childless, who accept motherhood with reluctance, or who disengage themselves from the mothering role even after they become biological mothers. In the process, they are recording the radical shift in pattern women's lives may take when the androcentric family institution is challenged and declared invalid. The problem of universality, which takes the masculine norm as its point of reference, annuls the specificity of women's experience, as Lorraine Code observes in her chapter. Women writers have given voice to that specificity, recognizing a commonality in the diversity, the particulars, and the 'trivialities' of women's lives.

Audrey Thomas deconstructs the concept of motherhood and mothering when she deconstructs language: *Birthday.* "Birth Day. The child is told that it's his birthday, but it's the mother who knows."[17] *(M)other.* "Who can see the 'other' in mother?" *Mummy.* "Body of human being or animal enbalmed for burial; dried up body. . . 'This is Anne's mummy.' Mummy . . . All wrapped up in her family."[18] The technique alone releases a new set of truths.

With similar intent, but in poetic form, Dorothy Livesay focuses on both the physical and the mystical aspects of birth:

Faintly insistent
No longer the pickaxe
Desperate to save us
But minute by minute
The terrible knocking
God at the threshold!
Knocking down darkness
Battering daylight[19]

In the ironically titled "Christmas Carols," Margaret Atwood describes yet another aspect of pregnancy that is rarely articulated but is experienced by thousands of women who are caught and controlled in wars fought by men:

Children do not always mean
hope. To some they mean despair.
This woman with her hair cut off
so she could not hang herself
threw herself from a rooftop, thirty
times raped & pregnant by the enemy
who did this to her.[20]

The final section of the poem refers us back to the well-known virgin/whore double standard incorporated into the myths of Mary, mother of God, and Eve, mother of Man.

. . . If mother-
hood is sacred, put
your money where your mouth is. Only
then can you expect the coming
down to the wrecked & shimmering earth
of that miracle you sing
about, the day
when every child is a holy birth.[21]

The title "Christmas Carols" underscores Atwood's comment about the ritualization of society's hypocrisy – a cost demanded of women with sickening regularity.

In *Lives of Girls and Women,* the concept of conventional marriage is questioned as the defining role for women.[22] Alongside this theme, Alice Munro gives us insight into the unique bond/bondage between a mother and daughter; she illustrates the fearful and comic struggle of each to become her own person – growing to potential and yet attempting to retain the links that are life-giving and self-affirming. The narrative of the sexual evolution of Del Jordan is the portrait of the writer as a young girl and, more importantly, it is Munro's realignment of certain social conventions.

Munro uses the writer/protagonist to question the old dispensations. She simplifies the proposition for the reader by making Del Jordan the 'photographer of life' (the apprentice), who knows by the end of her story "that the only thing to do with my life was to write a novel,"[23] which is, of course, the one Munro has written. All of the action is filtered through the narrative "I": in this way Munro explores the changing patterns of women's lives.

Later, in a brilliant short story, "The Office,"[24] Munro directs the reader to what might constrain an older Del, and in the process Munro politicizes the concept of space; in particular, the space that the creating mind requires. The writer/narrator, a wife/mother, demonstrates tenacity and determination to get and hold on to "a room of her own," namely an office. The invasion – almost a rape – of the psychological and creative space transforms the story: the protagonist is forced into a power struggle with a disturbed and disturbing landlord. She must fight for her creative life and, forced out of her office, the story we read is the only evidence that she survives. What Munro noticed in Marian Engel's work, the desperate honesty, the bravado, the subversive wit, and above all the vindication of our experiences and of our lives as women, are all characteristics of her own work.

Writing the self into being is also the main narrative of Laurence's novel *The Diviners*. Laurence uses the snapshot and memory-bank movie sequences as a structure through which Morag 'divines' herself as girl, as woman, and as writer. These images are kept "not for what they show but for what is hidden in them,"[25] and it is the slow, painful, solitary craft of weaving them together, writing them, which Laurence/Morag explores throughout the novel. An anonymous phone call to Morag offers insight into the fear and doubt which accompany every act of writing:

> The woman only wanted to find out . . . wanting the golden key from someone who had five books published and who frequently wondered how to keep the mini-fortress here going and what would happen to her when she could no longer write. Golden key indeed . . . A daft profession. Wordsmith. Liar, more likely. Weaving fabrications. Yet, with typical ambiguity, convinced that fiction was more true than fact. Or that fact was in fact fiction.[26]

Laurence has created a unique community of women in her five Manawaka novels. It is Morag's final movement into the role of novelist that gives added meaning to the struggles (in Laurence's previous books) of each protagonist searching for herself. The many acts of divination are realigned in the final novel, which closes with Morag returning "to the house, to write the remaining private and fictional words, and to set down her title."[27]

The dictionary defines 'divining' as "the act of predicting or foretelling events, or of discovering hidden or secret things by real or by alleged supernatural means; also to find out by inspiration, magic or intuition." This definition of Laurence's title applies as well to all of the authors who frame their novels around a writer/protagonist.

Marian Engel in *The Glassy Sea* (1978) uses the epistolary form as a process of self-discovery. Rita Heber, the protagonist, moves from her life as a single woman into a religious order, out to a marriage, and back again into the communal life. In compiling the novel/letter, Rita is writing herself (and some of her revolutionary ideas) into being. Hers is a story unique in women's writing: Engel/Rita finds practical ways of transforming the comfort and privilege of 'Mother Church' into a communal comfort for all women of all classes. The social and political changes initiated by women in some religious orders are among the most radical of the past decade. Engel, writing in 1976 and 1977, was recording these reforms, which have the potential to change the Church irrevocably. Engel's dedication to her craft, to getting the form and structure absolutely right as the 'container' for such thematic material, is obvious throughout the novel. A letter comprising some 120 pages is a daunting technical challenge, but it is the ideal structure for the necessarily long resolution of the spiritual with the secular.

Intertidal Life (1984) by Audrey Thomas records the complex, convoluted lives of women who are searching for new patterns in their lives. While the book attempts no answers, it is specific in its questioning. Alice Hoyle is Thomas's woman writer, who must not only write her experience, but must also extricate herself from it in order to write it, a problem faced by many women writers. Privacy (space and free time away from domesticity) is essential if she is to write, yet her insistence on privacy makes her suspect to her women friends. She is a woman voyageur:

> But one went on a true quest alone and, except for magical or divine intervention, one fought the terror of the dark wood alone. One didn't bring along three kids, a lame dog and a spiteful cat . . . How many of the men who explored these fog-shrouded coasts and uncharted inlets were actually married? Only Vancouver's gunner on his ship and he didn't bring his family along. Questers have to Pay Attention or they miss the sacred signs.[28]

Alice is a woman obsessed with writing. She does not choose the art; it chooses her. She is a language junkie collecting words, dissecting meaning, spinning connections that in turn create new ideas and act as commentary on the story line. We have already seen how she deconstructs the word 'mother,' and she uses this technique throughout the novel. "*Deliver*. . . Rescue, save and free *from*; disburden (woman in parturition) . . . hand on *to* another" as in marriage; "*deliberare* . . . *liber* free . . . Let no man put ass under."[29]

Here Thomas is de- and re-constructing our concept of womanhood. In fracturing the continuity of the narrative through language, through the shifts from the third- to first-person narrator, through the inclusion of diary entries and children's games, Thomas releases the truth about the fractured life of a woman as writer, mother, friend, wife, divorcée. Alice Hoyle is also portrayed as Alice in Wonderland, forever falling through the gaps in her life made by her trendy husband and discovering an upside-down world in which truth is usually the opposite of reality. She explains: "what's happening to men and women today is just as exciting and terrifying as the discovery that the earth was round, not flat . . . But we all need new maps, new instruments to try and fix our new positions . . . Women have *let* men define them, taken their *names* even, with marriage, just like a conquered or newly settled region.''[30] She concludes that mothers and wives must always be available and ''artists are never 'always there.'''[31] So Alice Hoyle ''housewife'' is crossed out on her divorce papers and Alice Hoyle ''writer'' inserted instead. ''The woman artist has an even harder time . . . if she is to move forward at all she has to develop a layer of selfishness–self-is-ness–that has been traditionally reserved for men.''[32]

Thomas's novel records the shift in relationships that takes place as a woman fixes her new position, and for this writer the transition is complex, difficult, and unresolved. Audrey Thomas, in an interview, says, ''I want to write a really positive novel of women who live without men. I want to do a real quest story.''[33] It is interesting that another West Coast novelist, Ethel Wilson, wrote such a story–*Swamp Angel*–in 1954, but, as Dorothy Livesay points out, her work inexplicably often goes unnoticed.[34]

In *The Handmaid's Tale* (1985) Margaret Atwood depicts her protagonist, Offred, as a writer even though we know that writing is an impossible luxury (and an act of anarchy) in the monolithic Republic of Gilead. Offred not only records her experience as a 'surrogate womb,' she is also recording history for future generations of women. All writing is an act of hope; in this story it is the sole indication of survival. The text we read is evidence of Offred's life beyond the regime: ''By telling you anything at all, I'm at least believing in you, I believe you're there, I believe you into existence. I tell, therefore you are.''[35] Offred's words suggest the power of the creative act and they apply to all of the women protagonists/novelists who are writing our lives into being. There is a new community of women writing and reading which generates its own dynamic. And because we have a literature which is newly inclusive, we are encouraged to explore dimensions of ourselves, such as our sexual needs and our process of aging, which were largely ignored in writing before the 1960s.

Sexuality and Selfhood

In an important book, *Sex, Power and Pleasure* (1985), Mariana Valverde reminds us of the distinction the English language makes between the words 'sex' and 'sexuality.' Sex is ''what we do in bed (or wherever)''; sexuality is ''an ever-present social issue.''[36] She goes on to make two other points, which are relevant to the writing under discussion: first, that ''for the women's movement as a whole, 'sexuality' brings to mind sexual politics: our struggles to equalize relations between men and women, to open up social space for bisexuality and lesbianism.'' Second, what Valverde calls ''sexual pessimism'' – caused by the shadows of violence, guilt and repression – has, she says, become ''a powerful force in the women's movement . . . However, in most women this pessimism is checked and balanced by glimpses of a world in which women explore their sexual desires without fear . . . and by the recognition that if male sexual violence is a serious problem, so is female sexual unhappiness and guilt.''[37] Literary works, in this context, both complement and learn from psychology's new efforts to take women's experiences seriously, which Joanna Boehnert discusses in her chapter.

The guilt and repression that are basic to female sexual unhappiness are subjects that very few writers, men or women, have tackled. And until very recently women have rarely written their sexual fantasies, which are the core of the sexual self. Such fantasies locked in the subconscious become blocking or controlling agents, and only by bringing such inhibitions into consciousness and speaking them, or writing them, do we control them instead of allowing them to control us. So we find that the erotic in literature is a catalyst for the imagination: we envision ourselves in new ways, with empowerment, with a larger sense of ego, and with a sense of new possibilities that heightens our pleasures and adds to our self-knowledge.

In Marian Engel's *Bear* (1976), the erotic and the sexual are dimensions of the psychological and physical self that propel the protagonist, Lou, into change and growth. She is an archivist, a pre-writer, a woman who works in solitude, gathering and documenting facts that do not give her the knowledge she is seeking. Lou has a routine, mechanical occupation that parallels the sex she submits to automatically during her lunch hour, on top of a library table. Moving north to catalogue more archival material, Lou escapes into the primitive world of earth and water, which is the habitat of the bear. While Engel has fun describing this exotic affair of woman and animal, she makes clear that the erotic begins in Lou's mind, in her sexual fantasies. It is emphatically the woman who controls and guides; her needs are gratified, her pleasures fulfilled. This exploration of change and growth through woman's sensuality completely explodes the myth of our sexual passivity. (And on another level it revisions the simple fairly tale of beauty and the beast. Engel transforms beauty, the beast remains just that.) Engel breaks new ground with this novel. Just as Munro saw Engel's early work as revolutionary in legitimizing the mundane aspects of women's experience, here, too, she is daring.

Whereas Engel's novel releases women into new dimensions of self, Atwood's *The Handmaid's Tale* is about the ultimate control of women's sexuality. The novel is a dystopian view of womanhood, which, although futuristic, is grounded in current socio-political trends.[38] Atwood, always aware of the fragility of Canadian identity, warns of a future that is possible for Canadian women as she observes the overall swing to the right in the United States. This book looks forward into an Old Testament world in which patriarchal religion determines that biology is destiny. Here, Atwood analyses the politics of sexuality as dispassionately as she does in her poetry.

The appended "Historical Notes" form a brilliant synopsis, which redefines Atwood's novel according to patriarchal ideology. The notes form a critique, which is a re-enactment of traditional masculinist criticism. The history of Offred (specifically) and of the handmaidens (generally) is trivialized as Professor James Darcey Pieixoto warns against accepting this text as authentic. The appendix is Atwood's statement about the delegitimization and devaluation of women's history and women's writing. The tale/tail of the handmaid are the two sides of the same coin; her profession and her gender are inseparable, and each one marginalizes the other. Pieixoto's call for questions at the end of his lecture is rhetorical: the academic jury has been out and the verdict declared – this handmaid's tale is invalid.

Atwood's poetry returns again and again to these power relationships between men and women, back to the deadly game of sexual politics. The terse and brilliant opening poem in *Power Politics* (1971) encapsulates in four lines the warning sounded in *The Edible Woman* (1969) and fully articulated in *The Handmaid's Tale*:

> You fit into me
> like a hook into an eye
>
> a fish hook
> an open eye [39]

The poem moves from the domestic realm to the savage; the hook in the eye of corset or boot is containing, constricting, but the hook of the hunt is deadly. The images that spin off these lines are all of closure. The eye is filled up, space is obliterated, a living organism dies, the linear invades the circular and destroys it; the I/eye becomes silent/blind. The sardonic, brief four lines effectively leave the page blank, and we realize that here Atwood's poetry is informed by a sexual pessimism which approaches that of Valverde.

While Engel's *Bear* is an exploration of the sensual self, Atwood's writing is driven by an incisive analysis of women's place in the power games of sexuality, which are themselves a deadly reflection of social and cultural realities. *Bodily Harm* (1981) and *Surfacing* (1972) are both novels in which Atwood's protagonists face the traumatic consequences of physical and psychological violation set within the context of sexual politics. In both cases the woman must extricate herself from a relationship with a man before her healing process is possible. Engel's *Honeyman Festival* (1970) provides another dimension. While the story can be read on one level as that of any harassed housewife barely coping with having too many children too close in age, it is the particular characterization of Minn which carries the narrative line. This complex, wacky individual provides Engel with sufficient scope to link the maternal and the sexual in a set of hilarious, yet compelling circumstances.

Margaret Laurence in *A Jest of God* (1966) depicts Rachel Cameron as a profoundly repressed woman who plays out the stereotypical role of spinster; the sexual fears and hypocrisies that cripple her psychologically are manifested in her phantom pregnancy. The double standard of male-female sex roles and the damage accruing to the female psyche is a sub-theme throughout the novel. In Laurence's *The Fire-Dwellers* (1969) we watch Stacey discovering herself as she responds to her own sexual needs. Luke, her lover, is the only male character in the novel who is not locked into the stereotypical masculine role. Luke as symbolic (and actual) healer releases Stacey into a new dimension of self.

Such writing challenges the 'comfortable' roles and traditions that have shored up patriarchal family structures. Because of this, Margaret Laurence came under attack when *The Diviners* (1974) was put on school reading lists. Obviously this woman novelist had gone too far. In writing a protagonist who rejects traditional marriage, controls her own sexuality, opts for single motherhood (by selecting a Métis man to father her child), Laurence became the target of a bigoted right-wing censorship group. Through the characterization of Morag, Laurence challenges the traditional, patriarchal concept of womanhood. In doing so, as Engel says, she creates "one of the few heroines who achieves the apocalypse of knowing what her life has been about, not through the agency of a man, but through her own experience."[40]

The concept of woman as 'generous whore' has been a popular characterization (or caricature) of woman in 'malestream' literature, and during certain historical periods this concept has assumed the proportions of an archetype. In British Restoration comedy no play was complete without such a character, and the trend continues to thrive in the pulp industry across cultures and centuries. Adele Wiseman's *Crackpot* (1978) is a Canadian classic which subverts this myth. The protagonist, Hoda, is a survivor and despite her promiscuity remains an innocent throughout a large portion of the novel. This is the story of a girl/woman who lives on the very edge of society. Marginalized by poverty, ethnicity, and gender, she slips into prostitution very naturally as a means of survival for herself and her father. Throughout her story – even through her pregnancy and her labour – she remains ignorant of her own physiology. Wiseman builds her story so convincingly that we believe in Hoda's innocence, just as we know that in accepting her son as a client Hoda finally confronts her innocence and moves beyond it. Hoda's moment of knowing resembles the reversal point in Greek tragedy when the hero steps into the boundary situation–from which there is no return–and the chorus of commoners (we, as readers) draws back to watch in horror. Hoda steps over the boundary and breaks the taboo of incest. She enters her own knowledge but preserves the innocence of her son, David. Wiseman's novel is not merely about sexuality; it is the story of woman as redemptive agent. The Kabbalistic legend of creation, which prefaces the novel, suggests Hoda's agency. "He stored the Divine Light in a Vessel, but the Vessel, unable to contain the Holy Radiance, burst and its shards, permeated with sparks of the Divine, scattered through the Universe."[41] In the tradition of female writing, Wiseman deflates the grandiosity of divinity by turning her hero into a mere 'crackpot.'

Although many contemporary novelists deal with women's sexuality, and Dorothy Livesay, Betsy Warland, and Gail Scott, among others, are writing erotic poetry, English-speaking novelists are not experimenting with evocative language in the way that Quebec writers are. To write the experience of woman's physicality onto the page not only demands a celebration of the physical, it also requires techniques that subvert 'rational' discourse. The need for such subversive methods is easily understood: the language and stylistics we have appropriated are those of a dominant masculine ideology, which has never interested itself in female-centred eroticism.

Speaking of women's relationship to language, Gail Scott explains that:

> [this] relationship is first formed in our mother's womb as we listen to the rhythms and sounds of her body, and, as women, we continue to develop this largely oral tongue in our continuing relationship and identification with the mother. But at the same time we are developing another relationship to language, that of the 'fathertongue' of education, the media, the law, all of them patriarchal institutions. Consequently we end up with a split relationship to language.[42]

These and Scott's following remarks serve as preface to the methodology of the postmodernist writing in Quebec: "our texts differ as much from those of men as the shape of our sex and its movement towards pleasure differs from theirs." Women's writing, if it is to speak for us, will "reflect the rhythms of our bodies, our minds, more circular, more holistic."[43]

In a perceptive article, Karen Gould describes the task that Quebec feminist writers have set themselves since the mid-1970s as they have 're-visioned' and reconstructed "poetic discourse in an effort to explore the essential physicality of language."[44] Quebec lesbian feminists, such as Nicole Brossard, Madeleine Gagnon, and Hélène Ouvrard, are paralleling the revolutionary work of the current French feminist theorists and writers in claiming the physicality of the female body as the starting point for their creative work. It is in the power of their sexual affirmation as much as in their craft that these post-modernist writers are exciting. They are writing sexual liberation into being. The use of the female body as a "creative force capable of generating new linguistic structures"[45] will, they believe, provide Canadian women with a 'tactile' body of work, which will give new dimensions to selfhood.

But this new writing has been hampered by its poor dissemination. To be useful politically, feminists know that both creative and theoretical work must have a large readership and the primary problem of translation must be addressed. For instance, Nicole Brossard's long poem "Amantes" was written in 1980 but translated into English by Barbara Godard as "Love(h)ers" only in 1986. The lapse of six years between the two publications points to one of the problems faced by Canadian women readers. Our national literature is at times not available to us because of this barrier of language. As well, this new writing demands that a translator be extremely flexible in her feminist theory and linguistic skills. Godard has written a key essay on this subject, "The Translator as She."[46]

But there are other modern writers in Quebec whose work is essential to our understanding of the revolutionary writing of the post-modernists. Women such as Gabrielle Roy, Anne Hébert, Marie-Claire Blais, and Claire Martin have written a literature not of sensuality but of sexual politics. They have catalogued the sexual repression of generations of women, demonstrating how we experience our sexuality when it is a socio-religious construct built upon a schizophrenic ideology of the virgin/mother. These francophone writers have given us the darkest vision of womanhood in Canada, and some of them did so before the social and political movements of the 1960s and in the face of extreme social censure. The sexual pessimism that Valverde speaks of as a spin-off from the women's movement was an early, desperate cry in Quebec literature.

Although the francophone post-modernist work is not as well known as it should be, even by feminists in the rest of Canada, this is not so with the work of Jovette Marchessault. And it is because Marchessault is a dramatist and has had plays translated and performed outside of Quebec that her work is becoming familiar to English-speaking women. Her writing is also more accessible to a larger audience because it does not rely on deconstruction as a basic mode of expression. The ritualistic "Night Cows" (1979) is a celebration of female physicality, and although it is Utopian in vision, it is also gutsy, irreverent, satiric and comic, as the opening lines demonstrate:

> MY MOTHER IS A COW! That makes two of us.
>
> Two beautiful milk cows, butter cows; creators of those sweet oceans

> of magnetic milk which surge through the human body . . . All cows, regardless of race, weight, or colour, are castrated young.[47]

In poetry, prose, and drama, the Quebec writers are introducing a new female tradition, experimental in its technique and revolutionary in its politics.

Jane Rule has not experienced the socio-political and cultural restrictions of the French Canadian tradition, and in an article entitled "Lesbian and Writer," she tells us that she decided to be a writer "because [she] wanted to speak the truth as [she] saw it. To understand and share that understanding."[48] Her critical and creative writing is not wholly concerned with lesbian experience because neither is the world she lives in. Most of Rule's writing falls within the category of social realism, portraying fully developed characters of various sexual persuasions. Anne and Eve, the lovers in *Desert of the Heart,* experience the traditional problems that result from living as women in a patriarchal society, but the fact that they are sexual partners gives them no added power as the story unfolds, nor does it give them any edge on human suffering. This story concerns a search for identity and selfhood:

> If there is no face in the mirror, marry. If there is no shadow on the ground, have a child. These are the conventions the will consents to. But there is a face. There is a shadow. They are simply unsuitable. I'm a case of mistaken identity. . . . So are we all?[49]

Our response is solicited and obtained: so are we all.

It is important to note that because Rule depicts both heterosexual and lesbian protagonists, she is warned by critics from both groups that she risks alienating her readership.[50] Rule is acutely aware of the political aspect of women's lives, not only as it pertains to our sexuality, but with respect to our writing and our publications, too (as her analysis of and support for the feminist presses demonstrates). She is also outspoken on the power that will accrue to us if we listen to our women writers: "They will be our voices if we live up to their intent, severe, humane visions, if we learn to grow with rather than cut down those who have so much to offer us and in our name."[51] Just as sexuality and sexual difference are part of the new writing, so too are the voices of older women.

Old Women at Play

The cult of youth and its sexist bias has roots deeply embedded in Western society. In Canada, the media ignore demographic facts about the increasingly aging population and portray the world as if it consisted only of the young.

However, we are now witnessing the first wave of post-menopausal women who, as a generation, have choices to make, and fruitful lives to live. As feminist research shows, these women ''are often endowed with new energy and vitality, but society perceives them as declining and almost obsolete.''[52] Old women have rarely been portrayed in literature as the resourceful and productive people many of us are. As Barbara Horn notes: ''We need fiction that counteracts ageism. We want stories that present older women as individuals, not as stereotypes . . . to read about spirited, capable, resilient aging females . . . and we should not deny . . . the angers, frustrations, and fears of older females – these are as important to capture as are their courageous acts and hard won pleasures.''[53]

In giving us Hagar Shipley, over ninety years old and ''rampant with memory,'' Margaret Laurence has created one of the best-known Canadian fictional characters and has pioneered the charting of an old woman's psyche. In *The Stone Angel* (1964), we hear the story of the last two days in Hagar Shipley's life. Because the structure of the book is one of recall, we listen as Hagar pulls into the present the events of her life that have made her the strong, angry, stubborn, bitter, and glorious woman she is. Hagar's vision of her life is intensified and clarified in her final hours; such clarity is part of that ironic gift of 'dying well.' *The Stone Angel* is a rare book that explores the subtle and complex relationship between the culturally dictated process of social integration and the responses it elicits from a woman who remains strong and rebellious throughout her life.

Here, Laurence is exploring those aspects of age and womanhood that, traditionally, are not expressed: the destructive and manipulative power often inherent in motherhood; the sexuality of women and the repressive intent of cultural norms; the sexual needs of women into old age; and the isolation and despair that fuel so many 'happy' marriages. Hagar is one of the few tragic heroes in Canadian literature. She is like Lear both in her blindness to her own follies and in her final movement into grace and redemption.

Another astonishing venture into women's old age is *The Book of Eve* (1975) by Constance Beresford-Howe. In it Beresford-Howe touched a previously unrecognized nerve in society. Eva, her comic hero, escapes the ''Eden of marriage'' the day her old-age-pension cheque arrives – she puts on her sneakers and is gone! Naturally, as an old woman without spousal support, what she escapes into is a life of extreme poverty in which sustenance often comes from grubbing in garbage cans. But emotionally and psychologically, the quality of Eva's life improves dramatically. As the victim of marital rape, her own sexuality had been nullified; after her escape she indulges her fantasies and begins to respond to her own sexual needs.

By imagining this Eve into life, Beresford-Howe gives to older women truths about the sexual politics governing their own lives. Although the narrative suggests possibilities that may seem bizarre, they are also seductive. The enormous quantity of mail that Beresford-Howe received from Canadian women in response to this novel suggests the power of art to articulate life.[54]

There is a double standard in the chronicle of aging. For a man, the facial signs of aging, the wrinkles and lines, suggest character. They indicate maturity and celebrate his engagement with life. For a woman, they signify obsolescence. We are all aware that as old women we should be invisible, ashamed that we no longer fit the mold of perfection required of women in our society. Miriam Waddington does not flinch in telling us:

> Old women
> should live like worms
> under the earth,
> they should come out
> only after a good rain . . .
>
> Or be a wood-worm
> that patiently winds
> its journey through
> history's finest
> furniture like those
> old women we see
> in the corridors of
> nursing homes.[55]

Gretel Miles lets her poetry comment on how the media prey on the self-image of women as we age. In "November 1983: Riding the Bus," she asks:

> Would I like to be known
> for my beautiful skin at eighty-nine?
> I think rather
> than gazing down on bus interiors
> in black and white photographs,
> with plunging neckline,
> I would rather be known
> for my poems.
> Or pickled eggs,
> oral sex technique or
> even ancient drunken
> performances, or
> as a fine dancer.[56]

Dorothy Livesay has been writing poetry since the 1930s, but is only now enjoying the popularity and celebration her work deserves. And this is largely due to the women's movement, whose members recognize her commitment to feminism and respond with joy to her writing. Livesay, as an old woman, is unafraid to face her own aging and celebrates her sensuality still. She writes with humour (and in honest anger) about this stage of her life, her poetry growing in strength and vitality. Her writing has the wisdom and compassion that we need to hear as we grow old:

> But I had yet to discover
>   how even in old age
>   a woman moves
>   with freshness
> is a leaf   perhaps
> or a breath of wind
> in a man's nostrils.[57]

Livesay remains acutely aware of the politics of sexuality; she knows the power that accrues to men through their appropriation of women's bodies and the self-doubt that is endemic to womanhood.

> Men have never been
> subjected to physical scrutiny
> as have women
> *What is private?* . . .
>
> For a woman
> *nothing is private!*
> she is invaded
> night after night
> has only the soul's essence
> through which to believe herself
> human, and right[58]

A very different example of a woman's self-creation into old age is outlined in Adele Wiseman's book celebrating the life of her mother, Chaika Wiseman. *Old Woman at Play* (1978), written when Chaika was eighty-two, traces her life and work as a maker of fantastical dolls – thousands of doll couples, who generate their own myths and stories. Wiseman proposes that "what the artist creates is consciousness . . . [an] awareness of our situation, which enlarges creation and ourselves. This sense of enlargement, of augmented power, helps us, even briefly, to imagine that we may somehow become 'better'."[59] Although Chaika created her dolls over a lifetime, using perishable and throwaway stuff like old buttons, tin, plastic, bone, her urge to impose whatever form she found available onto the chaotic experiences of her life gives it a new and vital meaning.

Contemplating Chaika Wiseman's art, most aptly through her daughter's reconstruction of her mother as artist, we realize that the joy of this old woman's play could so easily have been lost. So much of women's history and creativity has been expressed in unpublished material, in letters and diaries, or in lace, embroidery, tapestry, quilts, dolls, and other 'trivia.' In *Old Woman at Play,* Wiseman demystifies and democratizes the creative process. She dislodges art from the concept of fine art, disrupting such male-defined categories. While Canadian women novelists are bringing the total female experience into fiction as a legitimate theme, Wiseman parallels the process by demonstrating that a 'disposable craft,' more an 'old woman's play,' is a creative response to life and is an important artistic statement. Adele Wiseman's suggestion about the sense of empowerment that art brings to life is contained in the figure of the old woman as sage, as soothsayer, as crone – a central and powerful image in ancient female lore.[60]

At one level, Atwood's epic poem "Susanna Moodie" (1970) can be read as a reclamation of this figure. While the story of Susanna Moodie is told with some historical accuracy, Atwood transforms Mrs. Moodie in old age into a strong, defiant, eccentric sage. After her death, her spirit dominates the poem, and this is the aspect of Susanna Moodie that we remember as we close the book. As old woman, she appropriates the land, interpreting it as her element in which we are the neophytes.

> I am the old woman
> sitting across from you on the bus,
> her shoulders drawn up like a shawl;
> out of her eyes come secret
> hatpins, destroying
> the walls, the ceiling.[61]

In modern Toronto, in midtown, her power transforms the city into her own domain. She defies the concrete and the "unexplored/wilderness of wires."

> Turn, look down:
> there is no city;
> this is the centre of a forest
>
> your place is empty.[62]

Mrs. Moodie, as pioneer and as writer, is central to woman's history in Canada, and Atwood's reworking of the story assures her this place. The poem is a clear instance of the female tradition in writing. Marya Fiamengo, within that same tradition, but from her own Slavic background, writes:

> Yes, Tadeusz Rozewicz, I too
> prefer old women . . .
> they give advice
> or tell fortunes,
> they endure . . .
>
> But Tadeusz,
> have you been to America?
> Where we have no old women . . .
>
> Everyone, Tadeusz, is young in America.
> Especially the women
> with coifed blue hair
> which gleams like steel . . .
>
> and I will liberate all women
> to be old in America
> because the highest manifestation of wisdom,
> Hagia Sophia,
> is old and a woman.[63]

This realignment of the wisdom of older women from many cultures is heard increasingly in creative writing.

In Our Own Voice

Even while we are celebrating the number of books by women that are published each year in Canada, we must be aware that, for some women, getting their work published is a minor miracle. While there are no formal structures in society to keep women from writing, there are still countless cultural and political barriers that effectively silence us. If we add the triple bind of race, class, and language to the restraints already imposed by gender, we realize that for certain groups of women the sense of communion, which results from having ourselves 'written into being,' and which empowers us, is not available to them.

Lillian Allen says that concepts such as race and ethnicity are problematic when applied to women and their writing. "The uniformity they presume glides over the intrinsically significant differences that exist within any group."[64] As a black woman, she is immediately seen as speaking for all black women, but, as she goes on to say, there is a "common sisterhood, a common destiny'' that black writers share. Allen identifies the problem of publishing: ''when a black/minority/ethnic writer submits work to publishers, they don't have the tools or frame of reference to make a proper analysis.''[65] But gradually, largely through their own initiatives, and with the help of small presses and journals, this writing is being added to the national literature, giving it a diversity and complexity that reflects the Canadian mosaic.

All writing is a political act, but it is women from the minority groups who have the sharpest political consciousness informing their work. Dionne Brand in her epic poem ''Chronicles of the Hostile Sun'' records her return to Grenada, which coincided with the American air attack and invasion in October 1983. Her description is vivid and riveting: the language in this section of the poem has the kinetic effect of docu-drama. But it is Brand's explicit stance as a black Canadian woman (the outsider to the event) that politicizes the experience and binds us into it. In the same book, the poem celebrating the author's grandmother evokes joy, intimacy, and compassion and binds us again, but in a very different way. Brand's writing runs the gamut from epic to epigram, and her fiction has the same complexity and force as her poetry. Her short story, ''Sans Souci,'' is lacerating in its portrayal of a woman alienated, silenced, and destroyed, yet the tone is never harsh and the imagery is lush, almost seductive.

In the ''Women of Colour'' issue of *Fireweed,* Himani Bannerji echoes the thoughts of Lillian Allen concerning the difficulty of getting into print. Editors, even of feminist journals, have fixed ideas about language, ''they have a particular way of deciding what they'll count as 'saying' and that 'saying' is not how we speak . . . In that sense they are forcing all the most middle class, the most male bourgeois ways of speaking, on to us.''[66]

Bannerji's poetry is uncompromising and diverse, ranging from lyric to polemic. In ''Paki Go Home,'' her voice is raw and honest. It has an immediacy that aligns the reader with the pain, humiliation, and urgency of the poet.

> 3 pm
> sunless
> winter sleeping in the womb of the afternoon
> wondering how to say this
> to reason or scream or cry or whisper
> or write on the walls
> reduced again
> cut at the knees, hands chopped, eyes blinded
> mouth stopped, voices lost . . .

> Now, then and again
> we must organize.
> The woman wiping the slur spit
> from her face, the child standing
> at the edge of the playground silent, stopped.
> The man twisted in despair,
> disabled at the city gates.
> Even the child in the womb
> must find a voice
> sound in unison
> organize.
> Like a song, like a roar
> like a prophecy that changes the world.[67]

Behind the poem is what Bannerji has described elsewhere as "the long train of history" of non-white people, which has been kept suppressed. Many women are now bringing this history to their writing, where it restructures reality and our experience of it.

Claire Harris is one of the finest poets in Canada, but her work is not widely known. She says:

> I am a black woman. Any poetry I write is black poetry. I am not prepared to surrender the truths of my particular personal history. Neither am I prepared to lose the great advantage of those who have historically been denied mainstream participation; those who have been enslaved or savaged by others: the necessary clarity that ensures survival.[68]

Her collection of poetry, *Fables From The Women's Quarters* (1984), speaks about the experience of displacement and of the communities of poor people, worldwide. But, above all, she is speaking for communities of women.

> Now female I stand in this silence where somebody's black girl child jaywalking to school is stripped spread searched by a woman who finds that black names are not tattooed on the anus pale hands soiling the black flesh through the open door the voices of men in corridors and in spite of this yea in spite of this black and female to stand here and say I am she is I say to stand here knowing this is a poem black in its most secret self.[69]

In another poem, she interprets the village experience of elderly Italian women "who crunch their old faith who trail their faint air of the women's quarters past the small shops."[70] By revisioning the fables of women, Harris speaks on behalf of many who do not have a voice and who are still locked into the old customs and practices.

Some immigrant women have to break free of confining cultural traditions before they can establish themselves as writers, but the barrier of language remains the most difficult. The creative voice is born in the unconscious, and to write in a new language requires enormous confidence and faith. Many women continue to publish in their own language in ethnic magazines, but increasingly they are writing in English or their work is being translated.

Maria Adizzi is an Italian-Canadian whose novel *Made in Italy* (1982), analyses the experiences of a traditional protagonist. Adizzi uses the symbol of the cage to reveal the constrictions of a hostile culture and a dwindling community as these affect an aging woman. Similarly, Mary Melfi and Mary di Michele use images of mutilation and paralysis to portray the experiences of silencing and isolation particular to women.

These poets and novelists are writing the history of immigrant people, as Joseph Pivato explains in his article, ''Italian-Canadian Women Writers Recall History.''[71] But they are doing much more than rewriting history. Mary di Michele writes with a feminist consciousness, as do Eleni Albani and Caterina Edwards. Di Michele's poem ''Hunger'' demonstrates the politics of power and the vulnerability of woman as sex object. By juxtaposing images of the high-gloss mannequin disguised as a child with the actual child who is raped and murdered, she underlines the destructive potential of the media as initial seducer and betrayer of women from girlhood to womanhood.[72]

Representing a different community, and a more recent immigrant group, is Marrilu Mallet, a Chilean writer and film-maker living in Canada. In *The Voyage to the Other Extreme: Five Stories* (1985), Mallet uses the first-person narrative throughout the book, but the voice switches from male to female in specific tales. This is an unusual technique for a woman writer, but it gives an immediacy and a validity to Mallet's stories, which record the abuse and torture of Chileans under a fascist regime. Such punishment is not gender-specific, and neither are the effects it produces in its victims after their escape to Canada. There is a grim, Kafkaesque humour in some of these stories, such as ''Blind Alley,'' but nothing relieves the horror that Mallet's characters experience. These stories form part of a new perspective, which is growing steadily in Canadian literature with the influx of political refugees.

In a very different voice, and with a different intent, Greek-born Smaro Kamboureli's, *In The Second Person* (1985) takes the reader on a journey. The poet seeks to reconcile 'the other' in herself – the woman split between two languages and two cultures. The poetry takes its form from the writing of Anais Nin – Kamboureli is reading Nin's earlier journals while writing her own. And the journal form, used by so many women throughout history, is precisely right for the process the poetry records. This is a complex text, which weaves together philosophical and emotional responses to an ancient culture that is discarded even as a new one is explored. Kamboureli's poetry is not about the loneliness and isolation that many ethnic women experience. Instead it is a celebration of the richness and complexity that "a second cultural skin" affords. More, it reflects a sense of empowerment, which comes from the communion the poet shares with such writers as Anais Nin and Virginia Woolf; Nicole Brossard, Phyllis Webb, and Daphne Marlatt.

Joy Kogawa's work displays no such affinity with other authors. Instead, she writes about the effects of silencing, especially of Japanese-Canadian women. Her novel *Obasan* (1982) is an act of exorcism. During the writing Kogawa finds the voice that was doubly repressed by cultural expectation and by political oppression. The diaspora of her people, enforced by the Canadian government during the Second World War, ensured that all communication between them was lost. Kogawa is finally able to ask: "If I could follow the stream down and down to the hidden voice, would I come at last to the freeing word?"[73] The act of writing *Obasan* releases not only the voice of the poet, but also a political self. Since publishing the novel, Kogawa has become the Aunt Emily of her story and is now an insistent voice on behalf of her people and a political activist for the Issei.

After the publication of *Obasan*, Kogawa wrote of the paralysis she was overcoming: "I knew that by silence I would be bowing to the tyranny of fear itself. By silence, I could be a collaborator in chaos, guilty before conscience of inaction where action was required. So I am speaking publicly now about these matters for the first time and with no small terror."[74] Kogawa's reluctance to break her silence is understandable when it is framed by her poetry and prose. In a similar way, native women writers are finally breaking their silence. These women came from an oral tradition in which the rituals of their culture and a sense of communality are basic and essential to the creative act. But they have been denied their culture for almost a century, and in many cases their communion with each other has been disrupted.

Jeanette Armstrong of the Penticton Indian Band started writing by accident: "I started answering back."[75] She began by refusing to be told how her people experienced life, and soon realized that the aboriginal people had much to teach the rest of Canada before it was too late for ecological survival. Armstrong lists the things that have been lost to large parts of the world "through years and years" of colonization: languages, cultures, religions – and most importantly a sense of self that has been denied the individual.[76] Beth Brant, as an Indian lesbian, echoes Armstrong, but she chooses a line by Nicole Brossard to explain her own experience "in order to write one must know that one exists."[77] She, and other Indian writers, are now in the process of creating what she hopes will be a female tradition in native writing. These women express their sexuality in their own words using new and different poetic structures. In the process, they are eradicating the old asexual stereotype of 'woman as squaw.' Beth Cuthand reminds us of the racist "assumption that Indian people don't have the skills to write and that therefore none of us exist." She calls on native women to write in English for greater ease of communication and to write collectively for the strength this imparts.[78]

Maria Campbell and Jane Willis are native women who, in the same year (1973), published their autobiographies. When a writer uses this genre, she is attempting to understand and order the chaotic life experiences, bringing the self into being deliberately and consciously. Campbell's *Halfbreed* reveals the isolation suffered by a native woman who has lost contact with her people, and whose loss of community finds its apotheosis in the figure of her Cree great-grandmother. This figure is Campbell's Cheechum, the traditional old woman/storyteller, who is both prophet and guide. Through her, historic and cultural truths are transmitted and, more importantly, a sense of self is created. This tradition of empowerment through the grandmother is basic in the writing of native women, and it is this matrilineal voice that Barbara Godard analyses in a comprehensive article about the oral tradition in literature by native women.[79] Godard concludes with some interesting speculations on how we might use the oral model to understand the more traditional text (written by women) as a collective, and communal, event.

While there are many fine native poets now in print, it is the strength of the oral tradition that we hear behind the most successful written text. In a similar way, the dramatic monologue by Antonine Maillet in *La Sagouine* (translated 1986) derives its power from an oral culture. This Acadian monologue celebrates the old woman as storyteller – the scrubwoman who "brings from her bucket of water" her culture and her history. In the collective experience of the drama we share most intimately the experience of the woman speaking to us.

Women Playwrights

Margaret Atwood reminds us that the novelist wills into existence a reader for her work: "I tell, therefore you are." But to a much greater degree, the dramatist creates a collaborative text. The ritual of the theatre demands the participation of an audience/listeners who believe in the transforming power of the actor/word/symbol. Each time we are part of successful theatre, we are reminded that theatre and religious ceremony have common roots – the audience/congregation is involved in similar rituals and experiences similar emotional and psychological effects. It is the participatory nature of the drama and the inclusivity of the 'masses' that make them memorable, compared with the solitary stance of reader to text.

Although there are fewer women playwrights than poets and novelists, their output has been augmented by a significant number of adaptations of novels into dramas. Because of this, the total impact of theatrical events by and about women since the late 1960s has been impressive.

The crossover from one artistic form to another has always been popular. Mazo de la Roche's famous *Jalna* saga was one of the longest running theatrical events in London, England, when she adapted her work for the theatre in the thirties. More recently, and using the medium of television, *Anne of Green Gables* (adapted from the novels of Lucy Maud Montgomery) has been performed and acclaimed internationally. Many current women novelists have had their work transferred to screen and stage.[80] Among the most successful adaptations are Constance Beresford-Howe's novel *The Book of Eve,* mounted at the Stratford Festival, her *The Marriage Bed,* re-produced for television, and Margaret Laurence's Manawaka protagonists who were played brilliantly by Norma Edwards in *The Women of Margaret Laurence.* Maria Campbell's *Half Breed* has also been performed as the drama *Jessica.* The protagonist is a Métis woman who is caught between her (almost lost) native culture and her everyday, urban life.

Carol Bolt is an important dramatist, and the production of *Red Emma* (1974) established her as a writer who brings a sharp political analysis to the stage. In this production Bolt brings into the spotlight the life of a woman too often neglected by political historians. Bolt depicts Emma Goldman with compassion and humour, allowing the romantic and idealistic dimensions of the character to develop alongside the anarchic and rebellious. Bolt remains fascinated by the figure of Emma Goldman and is now working on a new drama about an older Emma.[81]

Sharon Pollock chose to retell the Lizzie Borden history/myth in *Blood Relations* (1980), proving that a well-worn tale can have many new perspectives. Lizzie Borden's sexuality had never been considered before, but Pollock's drama reveals a lesbian relationship, which alters many preconceived ideas. The play also explores the darker side of human nature and suggests that most women and men can be murderers, given the appropriate circumstance. Commenting on the way critics review plays, Pollock points up the gender bias inherent in the field: male reviewers went "to some trouble to state that this play *[Lizzie Borden]* has nothing to do with feminism . . . It's only women who see it making a statement about women today. Of course it says something about women . . . about me . . . today."[82] She notes that reviewers who refuse to admit the feminist perspective in her work are lacking in sensitivity or imagination.[83] She has also been accused of preaching to the converted and replies, "Well, it's the converted who make changes. And if the converted come to see the play and are moved to action, or if it endorses them and gives them strength to continue their fight, I don't see anything wrong with that."[84]

In the mid-1970s a group of women who were committed to social and cultural change banded together and formed the Redlight Theatre group. Inspired by the women's movement, the company was determined to write and produce drama by and about women. Diane Grant, an early member of the collective, wrote a series of vignettes that evolved into a fast-paced, hilarious satire, *What Glorious Times They Had* (1974). This is a devastating critique of the men in Parliament who opposed Nellie McClung and her supporters, and in the process Grant underscores the similarities of current and historic gender inequities. The company doubled up in playing certain roles; they researched the characters they performed, helped write and score the music in the play, and encouraged each other as singers. The collective went on to develop other plays, such as *Broom Hilda,* based on the comic strip character, and their collaborative effort continues to give energy and zest to their productions. Other dramatists, and companies, working with overtly feminist material have been successful commercially, proving that there is a viable audience for such plays.[85]

In closing, I want to concentrate on Gwendolyn MacEwen's *Trojan Women* (an adaptation of Euripides' text). While it is not overtly feminist, the many political aspects of the play are impossible to ignore, directing the reader to some of the most basic concerns of contemporary feminism. MacEwen transforms myth into life [86] by ruthlessly paring down the original text. The writing is irreverant, pithy, even colloquial, stripping away the heroic and religious trappings of classical drama. Poseidon is the only god on stage, and his early speech frames the action:

> Family life in Troy was flawless.
> Everyone slept with whomever
> They were supposed to sleep with.
> It was a perfect society.
> Women learned to sew; men learned to kill.
> Honour and glory shone everywhere.[87]

The irony and scepticism of the speech not only sets the tone for the play as a whole, it also mocks traditional family roles, suggesting that the gender bias of 'honour' requires some analysis. Hecuba's opening speech, while picking up Poseidon's observations, introduces the more nebulous concept of piety – the nurturance and preservation of which has always depended on women: "everything is gone . . . /Piety and honesty and honour and glory. /Especially piety.''[88] As the drama progresses, each woman begins to explore the demands of piety as she questions the loss of selfhood that results from the traditional role she has played.

MacEwen achieves an important dramatic effect by cutting out the rhetoric of the glory (or the glory of the rhetoric), which allows her to focus instead on a gender-based concept of honour. This shift in focus in turn dramatizes the specificity of the women's reality, which becomes the true centre of the play. We witness each woman's personal confrontation with the 'self' as she faces her own loss, shapes her own response, and articulates how she will survive even in defeat. Running parallel to this testing of the self along the line of female 'virtue' and masculine 'honour,' is MacEwen's debunking of the glory of war. As the women compare their experiences and question the traditional roles that have trapped them, MacEwen is able to show the empowerment that comes through self-knowledge. The drama becomes a political statement about the use and abuse of power, and it suggests that until women analyse the process they will remain its victims.

In this play MacEwen is working with many of the themes we have traced in both fiction and poetry. Helen is the archetypal 'woman as sex object.' She is ''a woman abducted by violent men!/ And all because of this cursed beauty/ which should have been my glory!''[89] MacEwen shows Helen as a manipulative woman; she remains the quintessential winner of every beauty parade ever held. But what prizes do the 'winners' get? They become just another 'royal possession.' The whole myth of Helen – her birth a result of the divine rape of Leda by Zeus, her 'face that launched a thousand ships,' her self as prize in a game devised by the gods – lies behind MacEwen's drama and is a series of events which, taken together, give us the archetype. Significantly, it is Helen who expresses the loss of selfhood which is the experience of many women: ''We women live beneath the shadows of men . . . /we have no shapes, we have no souls. /We fight among ourselves because we can't locate the enemy. /Is that not so sisters?''[90]

This lack of selfhood, reaches its complete expression in the characterization of Andromache. MacEwen portrays her as the quintessential 'virtuous' woman, a woman who could have stepped out of the pages of Helen Adelin's *Fascinating Womanhood.* These lines describe her role in family life:

> I was a *perfect wife!* I was perfect
>   for Hector's sake.
> There is nothing wrong with being perfect.
> In fact there is everything right with
>   being *perfect.*
> I curbed myself, I never gave in

to the least of my whims.
I stayed at home; I had few friends.
I took care of the house; I knew my place.
I knew when to guide my man
and when to obey.[91]

Hecuba's response to this catalogue of feminine traits is totally in keeping with her characterization throughout the play. She sees through the manipulations necessary in a gender-based hierarchy and speaks as a feminist might:

Oh, your virtues begin to sicken me!
Did you ever possess your *self,* Andromache?
Did you live with Hector, or *through* Hector?
I wonder, I really wonder . . .
You 'perfect' wife, you 'suffocating' mother.[92]

MacEwen portrays a Hecuba who not only guides/goads the other women into self-consciousness, but who also monitors and comments on the cultural realities that have contributed to their victimization. Hecuba is the crone figure who locates the cause of much of our deception; 'malestream' history is "all a web of lies/Where all the gore becomes glory/In the telling and re-telling/Of the lies."[93]

In *Trojan Women,* MacEwen shows that an unquestioning loyalty to a bankrupt culture, especially one built around the paradigm of sterotypic gender roles, is deadly. Through the development of the Hecuba figure MacEwen reveals the process of women's subordination. Through the rage and despair of Hecuba's poetry we make discoveries about the roles of men and women:

Men are beautiful, predictable, utter fools.
They believe, because they must believe
That a single night in their blessed bed
Will turn a normal healthy woman
into their eternal slave![94]

But without men, women are invisible:

When my lord and my sons were killed
I too was nothing
It was as though I had never been.[95]

Hecuba learns that war brings into sharp focus the gender-role paradigm she has been exploring:

I will tell you something I've only recently
learned –

war is blood and blood and blood,
war is babies falling
from the cradles of the sky.
War is the final nightmare.
The last sick page in a long sick story.
War is something that *we* do–
All of us, all of us . . . [96]

Finally the drama comes full circle, back to the opening statement by the god Poseidon: ''Family life in Troy was flawless . . . /Women learned to sew; men learned to kill. /Honour and glory shone everywhere.''

Gwendolyn MacEwen's *Trojan Women* demands a more detailed analysis than is possible here because it demonstrates so clearly the way in which current social and political issues are picked up and incorporated into mythic material, which is then transformed by a great poet/dramatist. This process of transformation, giving the old myth a new authenticity, also releases a sense of collectivity that makes the text exciting reading for a group of women.

This is what the women writers do for us. They make available collective truths that we have rarely shared before and speak at the same time of our individual experiences as women. We are fortunate to be living in an age when we are questioning our roles as women, and we have an incredible resource to help us in this task in the creative writing of Canadian women. Dorothy Livesay should have the last word, because her work has spanned so many years and because she speaks so confidently as a woman. Her words apply to all of our women writers:

Some of us are here
because we were visited
at dawn
were given a third
ear . . .

Some of us are here
as messages
because in the small womb
lies all the lightning.[97]

Shelagh Wilkinson

SUGGESTED READINGS

Aitken, Johan Lyall, *Masques of Morality: Females in Fiction.* Toronto: Women's Educational Press, 1987.

Du Plessis, Rachel Blau, *Writing Beyond the Ending: Narrative Strategies of Twentieth Century Women Writers.* Bloomington: Indiana University Press, 1984.

"The Marian Engel Issue," *Room of One's Own* 9, no. 2.

Fetterley, Judith, *The Resisting Reader: A Feminist Approach to American Fiction.* Bloomington: Indiana University Press, 1978.

Gilbert, Sandra M., and Susan Gubar, *The Norton Anthology of Literature by Women: The Tradition in English.* New York: W.W. Norton, 1985.

Godard, Barbara, "Talking About Ourselves: The Literary Productions of the Native Women of Canada," *CRIAW Papers* 11, July 1985.

Heilbrun, Carolyn G., *Reinventing Womanhood.* New York: W.W. Norton, 1979.

"Margaret Laurence," *Canadian Woman Studies/les cahiers de la femme* 8, no. 2.

"Dorothy Livesay Issue," *Room of One's Own* 5, no. 1/2.

"The Poet Mothers," *Cross-Canada Writers' Quarterly* 8, no. 2.

"Psychology," *Canadian Woman Studies/les cahiers de la femme* 8, no. 4.

Silvera, Makedo, *Silenced.* Toronto: Williams-Wallace, 1980.

Sullivan, Rosemary, ed., *Stories by Canadian Women.* Toronto: Oxford University Press, 1984.

"The Audrey Thomas Issue," *Room of One's Own* 10, no. 3/4.

Walker, Barbara G., *The Crone: Women of Age, Wisdom and Power.* New York: Harper & Row, 1985.

Chapter Nine

The Medical Treatment of Women

In recent years, the popular press has directed a good deal of attention to the medical 'problems' and treatment of women. Headlines have warned about the side-effects of various forms of birth control; articles have detailed the ongoing debate over home versus hospital birth. Caesarian section, mastectomy, and hysterectomy have become household words, as have puberty and menopause. However, the press has not shown an equivalent interest in the medical care meted out to men or to their various physiological processes. This reflects the assumption that man's body is the norm or the given against which woman's is judged. Woman's body is seen as different from man's, more complex in its design and, consequently, more mysterious and challenging in its workings. It is, in Simone de Beauvoir's words, "the other" and as such intrigues, repels, and in general fascinates.[1] But the physical distinctions between the two sexes go beyond the physiological; for many Canadians, they also account for perceived psychological differences as well. As a result, physicians, who for centuries have claimed to be and have been accepted as experts on the body, are given enormous credence when they expound on the potential limitations of the female body and psyche.

This chapter attempts to place the medical treatment of women in Canada in historical perspective, focusing on conventional medical practices from the mid-nineteenth century to the present day. It stresses the historical continuities of issues such as birth control, childbirth, and gynaecological surgery rather than the emergence since the late 1970s of new ones such as toxic shock syndrome, premenstrual tension, *in-vitro* fertilization (discussed in Rona Achilles's chapter), or the new medical 'treatment' of women's aging process. The study emphasizes the role of women as patients and not as health providers, although the two cannot be separated completely. It also only looks at the medical profession as represented by physicians rather than other health care participants. From such an historical overview, three interrelated themes become evident: the relationship between medicine and culture, the medicalization of society, and the interventionist nature of medicine.

Physicians are a product of their particular culture just as any one of us is. They reflect their society's values, and their treatment of women is a concrete representation of those values. A study of the medical perception and treatment of women can tell us much about how the wider society perceives women. However, the repercussions of those perceptions can be very great when held by physicians, since their opinions and views can, and do, have physical and psychic consequences for their patients. Also, because doctors' views do reflect those in the wider society, doctors have not met serious opposition to their attempts to increase their status and expand their influence in society. This expansion has led to the second theme of this paper, what one might call 'the medicalization of society.'

Physicians are members of a profession and, like other professionals, they have made concerted efforts to become experts in a particular field and to enlarge that field. In the twentieth century, they have been very successful as Canadians have increasingly turned to experts for advice on almost every aspect of their lives. People have always looked to experts for guidance, but in the past the experts tended to be religious representatives. With the advent of the scientific revolution, new experts came to the fore, doctors among them. As a result, doctors were able to expand their area of expertise into spheres traditionally deemed non-medical and private and in that way intruded into what had once been the preserve of the family. They have become spokespersons, not only on the health of the body but also of the psyche. They define what it is to be 'normal' in our society and what it is to be 'deviant.' They are present at our birth and increasingly at our deaths. They advise us on what to eat and how much, what we should weigh, and how much exercise we should have. This is a far cry from the mid-nineteenth century when Canadians seldom saw a physician and women generally ministered to themselves.

The medicalization of our society would not be so significant if physicians limited themselves either to giving advice or preventing illness. However, they do not. They want to intervene and cure our ills. Indeed this is their main concern. As one physician has commented, "If we measure interest by activities rather than protestations, physicians have been and are, for the most part, as little interested in health as soldiers [are] in peace."[2] This means that physicians wait until illness strikes and then intervene in a visible and active way by advocating specific therapy, be it medicinal, surgical, or psychological. The teaching methods used in medical schools reinforce this interventionist stance since they focus on the weaknesses of the body, which result in ill-health, rather than on the strengths of the body, which maintain health. Because the medical paradigm views the patient as a passive agent and the physician as the active one, physicians seldom receive opposition to their intervention. The physician defines the best interests of the patient and treats her/him accordingly. But best interests are determined within the context of a particular culture and set of moral and ideological as well as scientific beliefs.

The impact of culture on medicine, the medicalization of society, and the interventionist nature of medical practice affect both women and men. Nevertheless, it is the contention of this chapter that women patients have been and continue to be more vulnerable than men patients to that intervention. This is a result of several factors. The disproportionate number of male physicians means that most physicians have never experienced the normal physiological processes of the female body. When coupled with the tendency to view the male body as the norm, this has often led to the perception that deviation from it is illness. For example, it was quite common in the nineteenth and early twentieth century to refer to menstruating women as 'unwell.' The 1884 *Practical Home Physician,* a popular health manual read by Canadians, even went so far as to blame menstruation for gonorrhoea.[3] Yet viewing the male body as the norm is not the only perspective. As one critic of medicine has pointed out, there are two others. "If the standard of health had been female rather than male, menstruation would have been the norm and men's failure to menstruate the 'physiological peculiarity.' If the health standard had been a human one, neither menstruation in women nor the lack of it in men would have been peculiarities."[4] But neither the female nor the human perspective dominates; the male perspective does.

More significant, however, than using the male body as the norm is that physicians, both female and male, share the biases and views of their own society. If that society perceives women to be other than equal to men, it is not surprising that the medical profession reflects that perception in its treatment of its women patients. This is not an indictment of the medical profession as much as it is a commentary on the values of that society.

Two caveats, however, are necessary. First, the medical profession has never been and is not now a monolith; indeed, some of the best critiques of the medical treatment of women over the last one hundred years have come from within the profession itself. Second, contrary to the standard medical view, patients are not passive and should not be treated as such. They often place pressure on physicians to provide them with the latest treatment, believing that the newest and most technologically intricate must be the best.[5] But if patients are not passive, neither are they equal in their relationships with doctors. In the case of women, that inequality has been particularly apparent.[6]

History of the Medical Profession in Canada

In Canada, physicians have not always been held in high esteem, have not always been well educated, and have not always had a monopoly over the health care system. Traditionally, women in the home dominated health care, and only as the professionalization of medicine occurred did this responsibility lessen. In the mid-nineteenth century, few medical schools existed in Canada. Consequently, many young men apprenticed themselves to a licensed physician for a number of years and then sat a licensing examination. At that point, the newly licensed physician had to face an array of competitors. In addition to regular practitioners like himself, there were the Thomsonians who believed in herbal remedies, the Homoeopaths who believed the more diluted a medicine was the more effective it became, and the Eclectics who practiced a mixture of all systems depending on what they felt would be more suitable for the case at hand. Specific groups, such as the Amerindians, preferred their own traditional healers. Canadians could also seek help from midwives, patent medicine people, or anyone who seemed to have a natural skill for healing. Or they could try to heal themselves, using family nostrums handed down from one generation to another. In an effort to restrict this competition, the regular practitioners pressured authorities to increase the educational requirements for a medical licence. They were particularly concerned about the Homoeopaths and Thomsonians, both of whom called themselves doctors and had their own medical schools. By the end of the century 'orthodox' physicians triumphed when a medical degree from a university became a requirement for licensing. This process, however, was not without opposition from within the profession itself. Increased educational requirements ensured that only the more affluent would be able to practise medicine, and it also meant that young men in rural areas with little access to universities would be forced to go to the major urban areas to study, thus increasing the cost of their training substantially.

One reason for the success of the 'orthodox' physicians in both homogenizing and increasing the training required for medical licensing was that they saw themselves and convinced other Canadians to see them as participants in the great discoveries occurring in scientific medicine in the late nineteenth century, the most important of which was the germ propagation theory of disease. This led to the acceptance of the need for cleanliness on the part of patient and doctor alike when medical care was being provided. It introduced the concept of antisepsis and did much to improve the conditions of health care facilities through the recognition and elimination of germs. The advances made in scientific medicine did not necessarily translate into better care of the patient, but at least the medical profession could explain more of what was wrong than it could before. As a result of the alignment between medicine and science, the profession gained in prestige, which, together with its association with the elite class in society, aided its efforts to acquire a monopoly over health care.[7]

At the same time that the regular practitioners were succeeding in their efforts to monopolize medical practice, the nature of that practice began to alter. Specialities developed which sub-divided the profession. In the late nineteenth century, specialists such as psychiatrists, public health doctors, and gynaecologists emerged. This specialization has only accelerated in the twentieth century. The reasons for this are complex, but it is partly linked to the absolute increase in knowledge available about the human body and the inability of any one physician to comprehend all there was to know. It also reflected the objectification of illness and the division of the body into its component parts. Once physicians accepted that germs caused disease, it became understood that certain germs could cause specific diseases. This resulted in a move away from holistic medicine, that is, from medicine that saw all aspects of a person as interrelated and in need of care in order to treat the diseased part, to medicine that concentrates on the apparent diseased parts only. Once this occurred, physicians could specialize more easily. One result of this specialization was the elaborate creation within the profession of a hierarchy, status usually being linked to the degree of technical intervention required in the specialty. For example, surgeons have more prestige and make more money than general practitioners and, among surgeons, neuro-surgeons have higher status than gynaecological surgeons.

Status within the profession is not only linked to one's area of specialization. It is also linked to gender. Indeed, the fact that most physicians have been and are men maintained the status of the profession in general. Medicine has not been particularly accepting of women, and when it has accepted them it has placed restrictions on them. In the mid-nineteenth century, nursing in Canada was not a field attractive to respectable women. The only exceptions to this were the religious nursing orders of the Roman Catholic Church, which were predominantly, although not solely, located in the province of Quebec. Because lay or non-religious nurses worked long hours for low pay and often in squalid conditions, nursing attracted only the poorest of women, who were unable to obtain other employment. However, as a result of the efforts of Florence Nightingale to establish a training school for nurses in Britain, the situation of nurses entered a new era. In 1874, the Mack Training School for Nurses, one of the first training schools for nurses in North America, opened in St. Catharines, Ontario, and the image of nurses began to improve. Nevertheless, nursing still remained drudgery. Student nurses were a source of cheap labour in the hospital, and when they finished their training, they became private duty nurses with no job security. Needless to say, nurses were trained to be assistants to doctors, subordinate to them in every way. When attempts were made to equalize this situation, doctors tended to respond in a negative fashion. For example, the Victorian Order of Nurses was founded by the National

Council of Women in 1897 to aid women in rural communities who had limited access to physicians. Originally, the scope of their work was to include midwifery. However, the opposition of the medical establishment in Canada was so great to what it saw as an infringement of its prerogatives that the idea was allowed to die.[8]

Similar opposition occurred when some women indicated a desire to practise medicine. At first it was easy to prevent them. To qualify for a licence one had to have apprenticed with a doctor or to have taken a medical course at a university. No self-respecting male physician would take on a female apprentice, and until late in the nineteenth century, no university in Canada would accept women students. When pressure increased on the universities to open their doors to women, university administrators and faculty argued that women were not strong enough, physically or mentally, to complete a medical course of instruction and that the morality of co-education in a field that dealt so intimately with the human body was, to say the least, most questionable. When it became clear that the women were going to insist on being allowed into the profession, rather than giving in with good grace, both the University of Toronto and Queen's University set up separate medical colleges for women in 1883. McGill University was not so generous. It refused to allow women a McGill degree in medicine until 1922.[9]

Although women had gained entry to the profession, the battle was far from over. Internships for women were few and far between, and the normal problems of setting up a practice were compounded when the newly licensed doctor was a woman. So difficult was it for many to get started, that instead of practising medicine in Canada they chose to practise as medical missionaries outside the country.[10] Those who remained still had to face the antagonism of some of their male colleagues, who argued that women doctors should limit themselves to the easier aspects of medical practice.[11] The *Canada Medical Record* in 1890 opportunistically suggested that women physicians could take over midwifery, particularly among the poor, since there was not enough money in it to interest most male physicians.[12] They could also help wean expectant women patients away from the use of untrained midwives in childbirth. Eliminating these women had long been an ambition of regular physicians, since the midwives provided competition for them and also undermined the prestige of the profession by offering a medical service without formal training and for a low fee. The women doctors, themselves, would not be in competition with each other or with male doctors, since medical schools only admitted a handful of women each year.

One last change in the nature of medicine must be mentioned before an examination of its treatment of women can begin, and that is where patients were treated. In mid-century, most Canadians when ill remained at home.

Hospitals existed but they were for the poor who had nowhere else to go or no one to care for them. Canadians viewed hospitals, quite correctly, as places of death. Conditions in them were squalid and the care provided was minimal. Only slowly did they change, aided partly by the improvements in nursing begun as a result of Florence Nightingale's efforts and partly because acceptance of the germ theory of medicine necessitated an antiseptic environment. As medicine developed technologically, hospitals became the logical repositories of new medical equipment and the people trained to use it. Home treatment was inefficient for the kind of medicine practised. Hospitals thus proliferated in the twentieth century and increasingly catered to paying patients. They represented a further success on the part of orthodox medicine for, unlike patients' homes, hospitals were environments doctors could and did control. As a result, health care became less private, less intimate, and less controlled by the family.

Culture and Medicine

For most Canadians, biology is destiny. This concept has its roots in the Aristotelian heritage of Western civilization and focuses on the differences between women and men rather than on their similarities. The persistent effects of this focus are described in other chapters in this book. Lorraine Code discusses its influence in shaping concepts of biological determinism, Joanna Boehnert shows how these concepts affected accounts of the psychology of women, and Beverley Baines discusses the influence of Aristotle's linkage of difference and inequality on legal decisions. For Aristotle, the obvious differences were the physical. The differences were there for a reason, and the reason was to indicate the proper role of women and men in society. Since women were capable of bearing children, the assumption was that they *should* bear children and that the maternal role was primary for them.

Physicians, too, have seen maternity as the main function of women. The result has been a concentration on obstetrics and reproduction to the neglect of other areas of health care for women which would promote their general well-being. The concentration on obstetrics, however, did not reflect a concern for women as whole human beings, but for women as childbearers. Attention within obstetrics focused on the birth and survival of a healthy child over the well-being of the birthing mother. By the turn of the century, physicians had become very concerned about the high rates of infant mortality, but not until the mid-1920s did the profession exhibit equal concern over maternal mortality.

If maternity was woman's natural role, then any interference with that role had to be resisted. In a critique of the rising number of ovariotomies (removal of one or both ovaries from a woman) performed at the end of the nineteenth century, Dr. Hingston of Montreal made it clear that his primary concern was that such surgery interfered with a woman's ability to conceive. This he viewed as "a crime against society" and "the interests of the state."[13] He did not view it as a crime against the woman. Physicians believed that marriage and maternity were ultimate goals for women because of the dictates of their bodies, and if any woman rejected them, the health of her body would suffer as a result. In 1884, a text used in several Canadian medical schools made this clear – spinsters and married women without children were at risk:

> Especially is the liability to the formation of fibromas of the uterus greater in unmarried and nulliparous women than in those who have born children, as if the uterus, deprived of the function of building up a new being, were more liable to use the material for the formation of a tumour.[14]

So convinced were some physicians that the maternal role was natural to women, that they advocated marriage and motherhood as cures for uterine disease.[15]

In a culture that for so long had viewed marriage and motherhood as the proper goals for women, it was difficult to imagine that both might be a burden. Consequently, women who experienced problems with their pregnancies or marriage were blamed for rejecting their natural role. In the 1950s, one physician connected miscarriages to "difficulty in the feminine role," that is, among women who miscarried were those who with "a possessive mother and their underrelatedness to a paternal offset, find femininity, particularly as it relates to motherhood, difficult, if not hazardous."[16] In the same decade, premenstrual tension and even amenorrhoea (absence of menstruation) were attributed to women's unhealthy attitudes towards femininity.[17] In the early 1970s, a young woman whose husband objected to her desire to work was told by her therapist that her husband was correct and that she was at fault for not being satisfied with her wifely and maternal roles.[18] In a manner consistent with the prevailing views of the psychology of women, which Joanna Boehnert discusses in her chapter, women who were uncomfortable with their marital or maternal roles were viewed as deviant, as ill, for their minds were not following the dictates of their bodies. What such women were rejecting, however, was not their bodies but specific social roles which their bodies provided the potential to perform.

The close alliance between social perceptions of women and their health is strikingly evidenced in the medical view of hysteria. Women tend to show their emotions, indeed have been encouraged to do so. Yet this places them at risk of being labelled irrational and hysterical. In the late nineteenth century, physicians viewed hysteria as an affliction "to which every woman is liable."[19]

It was exhibited by lack of control of the emotions, and since women were traditionally viewed as more emotional than men, it seemed logical for physicians in the nineteenth century to assume that the hysteria was simply a natural female characteristic run wild. This would also account for the reluctance to admit hysteria in men. Hysteria in men would be more than pathological; it would be the exhibition of deviant attributes.

The primary cause of hysteria was the physical or biological make-up of women. This was a long-held view dating back to the Greeks, who deemed hysteria as an affliction of the womb and named it accordingly (*husterikos*: of the womb). It was rooted in the very nature of being female. *The Canada Lancet* in 1880 deemed the advice of Dr. Goodell, a noted American gynaecologist, worthy enough to reprint:

> When you are called to treat a young girl with a hysterical attack, there are three things which you had better do. (1) Institute at once firm pressure in the neighbourhood of both ovaries. This is very apt to quiet the patient at once. (2) Administer an emetic. I have found that a woman who is well under the action of an emetic has not the opportunity to do anything else than be thoroughly nauseated . . . (3) And this method of controlling the spasm will often act charmingly – take a good size lump of ice and press it right down upon the nape of the neck. This produces quiet by its powerful impression upon the nervous system.[20]

Fortunately for their patients, Canadian physicians, unlike some American practitioners, seldom prescribed excision of the clitoris for the treatment of hysteria. They were much more conservative about sexual matters and thus were reluctant to propose such surgery to patients who were equally reticent. Nevertheless, cauterization of the clitoris was advised, and one textbook used in Canadian medical schools suggested Battey's or Tait's operation, both of which consisted of removal of the ovaries.[21]

The concentration on controlling women's emotions has only increased over the years. Physicians still tend to view their female patients as suffering more from emotional problems than their male patients. They give almost twice as many prescriptions for minor tranquilizers and, in particular, antidepressants to women than to men.[22] A 1984 report by the Toronto Public Health Department revealed that electroconvulsive therapy (shock treatment) was used twice as often on women as on men, and that this ratio was even higher in other provinces.[23]

Social attitudes not only influence medicine's perception of women's emotional or psychological nature, they also influence its attitudes toward the physical capabilities of women. It has been commonplace in society for years to focus on women's physical weakness compared to men's strength. This is reflected in medicine in the perception that woman's body is prone to disease. Such a belief is not surprising. Gynaecology, the specialty that pays most attention to women, emerged in the latter part of the century when the concept of true womanhood was at its peak. This ideology usually characterized women as different from men mentally, emotionally, morally, and psychologically. In the final analysis these differences were based on and assumed to be caused by physical differences, the most significant of which was the reproductive system. Gynaecology was, and is, predicated on the assumption that woman, that is, her reproductive system, is prone to disease. This view of woman as being somehow weaker than man dominated the nineteenth century and is still present in Canadian society. It is an interesting perspective given the pain of childbirth that women endure and the work that they have historically done either at home or in the work force. To see women as weaker than men contradicts what biologists have long known – that females are more mature than males at birth and that males have a greater incidence of disability and death than females from conception to old age.

Nevertheless, society persists in viewing women as the weaker sex, and physicians reflect this in their perception of women's health. They assume women to be at risk at almost every stage of their lives, beginning with puberty. In the nineteenth century, physicians and Canadians in general believed there were very few biological differences between boys and girls until they reached the age of puberty. At that point, the two sexes separated physically, emotionally, and intellectually. Young girls were urged to cut down on their activities during this time and to rest so as not to over-exert themselves. Doctors believed that the body had only a finite amount of energy, and that during puberty much of a young woman's energy was directed toward the development of her reproductive system. Particularly threatening in their view was education:

> Education has great influence in the development of gynecological diseases. Too great assiduity in study in early youth concentrates the nerve-energy on the brain, and deprives the uterus and ovaries of their share at a time when these organs are undergoing an enormous development, and preparing for the important functions of womanhood and motherhood.[24]

Opponents of higher education for women used such arguments to good effect.[25] Even today, the perception that puberty is a time when young women are at risk has not disappeared.

The danger to women does not decrease as they pass puberty. Adulthood brings with it the likelihood of marriage and with that the dangers of childbirth. Physicians over the decades have argued that women, especially the middle-class women who could afford their services, needed help in giving birth, and the increase in technological apparatus surrounding birth in the present day attests to that view. Even the end of her reproductive life brings no relief to woman in the medical model. Menopause is simply another ordeal that women experience. In the late nineteenth century, menopausal women were viewed as irrational and subject to personality defects. They were liable to "every form of neurasthenia, neuralagia, hysteria, convulsive disease, melancholia," and even insanity.[26] Menopausal women are still ridiculed in contemporary medical literature. In a study of pharmaceutical advertisements between 1966 and 1983, Anne Rochon Ford discovered that menopausal women were depicted as helpless people who could not cope, who were a bother to their families, a nuisance to others, or as one advertisement phrased it, "are beside themselves." They viewed menopause as a time "when women outlive their ovaries," as if this was not a normal physiological process.[27] But while the fact may be physiologically normal, it signifies the end of the perceived social usefulness of women–childbearing. Medicine and culture cannot be separated.

The Canadian medical profession has consistently reflected society's attitudes towards women. This has influenced the way in which physicians have perceived the physical well-being of women and the advice and treatment given to them. Woman's role was to be a mother, and doctors condemned surgical procedures that interfered with or prevented women from bearing children. Canadians saw women as more emotional than men, which confirmed physicians in their historic predisposition to see hysteria as a female disorder. The muscular differences between the two sexes translated into women being perceived as weaker at every stage of their life cycle. Society viewed the higher education of women as unnecessary, and medical practitioners concluded that education undermined the health of young women. Medical practitioners did not create the stereotypical view of women as maternal, emotional, and weak, but provided a medical rationale or support for it. That support has been effective. As one medical historian has explained it:

> When the belief structure of the physician is threatened, even in fields outside of medicine, he often uses his medical expertise to justify his prejudices and in the process strikes back with value laden responses which have nothing to do with scientific medicine. Unfortunately, since he is assumed to speak with authority, his response, perhaps as he intended, has influence far beyond that of the ordinary man.[28]

Medicine is not an objective science (if indeed one even exists). It and its practitioners are caught up with the prejudices and biases of their milieu as much as any one of us is.

Medicalization

Since the mid-nineteenth century, we have seen the increasing medicalization of our society and our lives. This results partly from the esteem placed on learned or formal knowledge compared to experiential wisdom and from the power we give to holders of such knowledge. Doctors have been able to take advantage of this to extend their influence in society by speaking out on traditionally non-medical subjects and linking them to health, that is, medicalizing them. In their efforts to determine the cause of disease in women and in their belief that they have a right and a duty to speak out about those causes and their origins, physicians have expanded their area of expertise. Although they have focused on the physical manifestations of illness, over the years they have pushed their inquiries to expose what they perceive to be the social and moral origins of those manifestations as well. In effect, they have expanded the definition of 'legitimate medical concern,' and in so doing have increased the prestige of the medical profession. This medicalization has affected almost every aspect of women's lives.

One early example was the exercise women should engage in. Physicians argued in the late nineteenth century that exercise was necessary "to secure normal development of the reproductive organs."[29] Of course, they also believed the amount of exercise should be dictated by the needs of the female body and that doctors should be the ones to advise women on what those needs really were: 'appropriate' exercise was consequently defined by doctors' perceptions of the needs of women. Of particular concern was the new craze of bicycle riding. Some feared that it led to ill health. As stated in the *Dominion Medical Monthly and Ontario Medical Journal* in 1892:

> the best saddle does not meet the comforts or requirements of the female pelvis, that aside from the pedal motion that ever tends to provoke erethism the jolt of the machine is not without evil effect upon the uterus and other generative organs, and is especially apt . . . to induce laxity, version, prolapse, with all the concomitants of endometritis, menorrhagia, etc.[30]

Not all agreed. Some physicians believed cycling was good for women as it took them outdoors and made them use their muscles. They believed it would bring about dress reform and, by providing exercise, would aid in the cure of female complaints such as anaemia, constipation, amenorrhoea, and dysmenorrhoea.[31] Cycling was a challenge to the Victorian image of woman. It represented a change that some physicians could accept and some could not. What is significant is not whether they supported bicycling, but that they felt compelled to voice an opinion at all. Whether they disapproved or approved, they were exerting their influence in society to the point that one physician argued that "No woman should ride a bicycle without first consulting her medical man."[32] Even today, in the discussion of whether girls should participate on boys' sports teams, as evidenced in the Justine Blaney case (discussed by Beverley Baines in her chapter), physicians have given testimony about the degree of exercise healthy for girls.

Another area over which the medical profession has extended its competency is the definition of healthy sexuality. For the late nineteenth century and much of the twentieth century, sexual intercourse has been deemed healthy only within the limits of a heterosexual, marriage relationship. Certainly masturbation, until fairly recently, has been censured. Some nineteenth-century physicians argued that masturbation in women led to a dullness in the sensibility of the genitalia and thus weakened the enjoyment of sex. This was a problem, not for the woman, but for her husband who would find his wife cold and indifferent to him.[33] Other commentators maintained it could result in flaccid breasts, deafness, decreasing strength, loss of memory, leucorrhoea, melancholy, nervousness, paralysis, imbecility, and insanity.[34] Central to most discussions on the topic was the role played by motivation. Masturbation was dangerous to health, not because it was a sexual act but because it was a solitary sexual act. The motivation was self-gratification, and the result was individual enjoyment. Marital sex was not dangerous for it was regarded as a moral act, focusing on another human being who was a loved one and engaged in for procreation. It was an altruistic act. The idea that the body could distinguish between types of sexual acts and their motivations suggests that "sexuality [began] to be defined in terms of the mind as well as the body."[35]

By acknowledging that women masturbated (even though they disapproved of it), doctors recognized an active female sexuality. Physicians have always asserted the strength of the male sex drive, but have been more ambivalent in their attitudes toward female sexuality. Women were the child-bearers and child-carers and so it was very important for them to remain virtuous in both mind and body. Nineteenth-century popular wisdom insisted, and some physicians agreed, that a pregnant woman's thoughts and feelings could affect the future moral outlook of her child. Although it was difficult to deny women's sexuality, this sexuality became less threatening for the well-being of the race when physicians linked it to the maternal instinct. The Victorians and many of their descendants believed in a balanced society. The strengths and weaknesses of each sex were offset by the other, that is, each sex complemented the other. Thus if men were rational, women were intuitive, if men had a strong sex drive, women's, by logical necessity, must be weaker. For women to transgress sexually has been and still is seen to be more reprehensible than for men. Sexually active women are believed to be acting against their very nature. It is one of the reasons that being a prostitute has long been a crime in this country, but, until recently, going to a prostitute has not. The men who sought out prostitutes were simply succumbing to their 'natural' drives, whereas the prostitutes were acting in an 'unnatural' fashion. They were the deviants. In the early part of the twentieth century, the medical profession gave support to the idea that most prostitutes were feebleminded – how else could you explain what they did?

Such ideas about female sexuality were slow to change. In World War II, when women joined the armed forces, they were not given either information or prophylactic protection to arm themselves against venereal disease as men were. Again the assumption was that good women did not need that protection for they would not engage in illicit intercourse. In the early years of the war, when a woman did contract VD, she was forced to leave the service, whereas infected men were not. Authorities believed that a woman who had VD was at fault but that male service personnel who had VD were the victims of 'loose' women in the civilian sector.[36]

The tendency of the medical profession to speak out on sexual morality was also evidenced in the 1950s. When the Kinsey Report was made public, some physicians became concerned since its recognition of a strong female sexuality went against the moral standards of society. Most physicians acknowledged the benefits of sex for women, but only if it remained within the marital relationship. Not only was the act to remain within marriage but also discussion of it. Doctors advised wives not to talk about their sexual lives with other women. As Deborah Findlay states in her study of medical attitudes toward women in the 1950s, "This assertion was quite consistent with the doctors' approach to sex as a means of combating the rising divorce rate and bonding a marriage – pro-familial concerns. Not only that, but a good sex life on the part of a married couple was deemed to keep the husband competing successfully at work!"[37]

What is particularly curious about physicians becoming sex counsellors and Canadians accepting it, is that most physicians had no knowledge in this field beyond conventional wisdom. Human sexuality was not part of the medical curriculum for most of this period, and even if it were, medical knowledge about it was not necessarily accurate. Indeed for parts of the twentieth century it was less accurate than in the nineteenth century. Despite the view of Victorian physicians that female sexuality was not as strong as male sexuality, they never denied that it existed. What is more, they knew that female sexuality was centred in the clitoris. As Joanna Boehnert describes in her chapter, once the Freudian revolution occurred, this vital piece of information was neglected and concentration focused on the vaginal orgasm as the epitome of the mature woman's sexual response. It needed the studies by Kinsey, and by Masters and Johnson to centre the female sexual response on where physiologically it provided most pleasure to women.

Another major area which has become medicalized over the years is contraception. At one time, doctors did not really involve themselves with this issue. However, by the mid-nineteenth century practitioners had become antagonistic to the use of birth control and insisted that it was immoral, unnatural, and, therefore, unhealthy. Physicians stated that the use of birth control could lead to nervous disease, insomnia, insanity, and impotence.[38] The practical consequences of these beliefs and attitudes could be cruel. In his text *Lessons in Gynecology,* William Goodell related that he had refused to treat a woman with uterine troubles until she and her husband stopped practising birth control.[39] Yet there was little medical evidence for the medical stance physicians took since the most popular type of birth control used well into the 1930s was coitus interruptus, which has no medical side-effects. Neither did condoms, which have been used since the latter decades of the last century.

The reasons for the medical profession's hostility to birth control were not medical but social. Birth control negated woman's proper role. Goodell mentioned that husbands and wives were constantly beseeching physicians for means to prevent pregnancy but argued that physicians must refuse on moral grounds.[40] Others agreed, arguing that contraception made marriage a form of prostitution. It cheapened sex and dulled sexual enjoyment and so led to unfaithfulness. Doctors were also concerned that contraception was being practiced by the 'better classes.'[41] These were, of course, the women whom the physicians were treating and the ones on whom they depended for their livelihood. Doctors accused women of limiting their families for selfish reasons, such as to maintain their figures or so they could go out in society.[42] The main indicator, however, that the disapproval of contraception was social and not medical was the profession's knowledge of safe ways to prevent conception.

This hostility to birth control gained added support in the early decades of the twentieth century from concerns about racial suicide as immigration from non-English speaking countries increased and altered the ethnic balance of Canada. This was a particular concern of English Canadians, who correctly perceived that native born middle-class English Canadians were limiting their families more than the new immigrants and native-born French Canadians and feared that, as a result, Canada would no longer be an English nation but become a polyglot. Their solution was to encourage a higher birth rate by discouraging birth control. Physicians were at the forefront of this movement, for in it they perceived a way of extending their own sphere of influence. They would become moral arbiters as well as medical arbiters. As one physician explained it, the success of the Roman Catholic Church, especially in Quebec, in dissuading its adherents from limiting family size would then be balanced in Protestant Canada by using the weight of scientific arguments through the medical profession. This could only enhance the position of the latter.[43]

Although the medical profession opposed the use of birth control, many Canadians did not, as demonstrated by the plummetting birth rate since the late nineteenth century. However, birth control had few public adherents in Canada except for some feminists and activists on the left. This changed in the early 1930s when the economic plight of large families became a public concern during the Great Depression. Various groups such as the clergy, business people, and society women were willing to endorse birth control as a solution to economic problems, whereas they had never been willing to endorse it as a recognition of woman's right to control her own body as feminists had and still maintained. The result of this concern was the opening of the Hamilton (Ontario) Birth Control Clinic in 1932 and the establishment of the Parents' Information Bureau in Kitchener, Ontario, in 1933. The latter was begun by A.R. Kaufman, owner of the Kaufman Rubber Company. In 1936, one of Kaufman's nurses, Dorothea Palmer, was arrested for canvassing in favour of birth control in a poor, working class, predominantly Catholic, French Canadian suburb in Ottawa. The trial pitched a French Canadian, Catholic prosecuter, supported by French Canadian Catholic obstetricians against supporters of a more liberalized approach to birth control. The defence witnesses were able to show that birth control, contrary to the prosecution's testimony, did not impair the health of women. Indeed it was an aid in preserving health and thus was deemed to be in the 'public good.' The court found in favour of Dorothea Palmer. This did not change the law against selling and advertising birth control, but it did signal to the police that they would have to step very warily before they prosecuted anyone who did so. Not until 1969 were the selling and advertising of contraceptives legalized.[44] In that same year, doctors were allowed to perform abortions in hospitals if the abortion was approved by a committee of physicians who deemed it was in the interest of preserving the life or health of the woman.

Abortion had been medicalized in the same way as birth control. Up until the mid-nineteenth century, residents of British North American did not perceive abortion as an issue of public concern. Popular convention accepted that there was nothing morally reprehensible with abortion, at least before quickening, the first perceptible movement of the foetus at about the sixteenth to eighteenth week of pregnancy. However, at that point there was some concern, although women who aborted their own foetuses were seldom prosecuted.[45] The real hostility to abortion came from the medical profession, who were the first group to understand the continuous nature of the spectrum from conception to birth and, as a consequence, no longer viewed quickening as a significant biological signpost of a foetus's viability. They were also very much concerned that abortionists were in competition with them, as were midwives and other irregular practitioners. Certainly the fact that abortionists were prosecuted, rather than the women who had requested the abortions, suggested that more than the morality of the act was at issue. As with birth control, physicians originally argued that abortion was a dangerous procedure even though the risks had decreased dramatically by the 1890s.[46] Today, there is more medical danger for many women in pregnancy than in abortion in the first trimester. This 'medical fact' indicates that the control of and opposition to abortion by many physicians continues to be non-medical in nature.

In the 1986 doctors' strike in Ontario, many physicians used women wanting abortions as pawns in their confrontation with the provincial government. Before the strike, some withdrew their services from hospital abortion committees, even though the longer an abortion is delayed the more harmful it is to the woman. After the strike, doctors made it known they would levy certain administrative charges. In the case of abortion, some of those charges totalled $400.[47] The medical profession did not use procedures such as prostate surgery, which affected male patients, as bargaining tools in the same way. These and other actions resulted in the abortion law in Canada being implemented unevenly across the country. One physician pointed out that decisions taken by some therapeutic abortion committees were quite irrational. "Consider, for instance, that a healthy woman with one child was granted an abortion but a 43-year-old Roman Catholic woman with four children and a sick husband was refused. Why was one woman with three girls turned down because her next child might be a boy?"[48] By the end of 1986, no abortions could be performed in Prince Edward Island or Newfoundland as no hospitals had therapeutic abortion committees. This forced women to travel either to the United States or Quebec, to self-induce abortion, or to have an illegal abortion. The minimum estimate in 1984 was that 3,484 Canadian women obtained abortions in the States.[49] This violated one of the four principles of the Consumers Association of Canada Statement on Consumer Rights in Health Care, the right of equal access to health care.[50] The 1988 Supreme Court decision striking down the abortion law acknowledged this very lack of access as a major problem with the law.

Underlying the actions of the physicians opposed to abortion is hostility to women who are rejecting, for whatever reason, the maternal role. Reasons for accepting or rejecting a woman for an abortion are clearly not based on medical grounds. The reasons are linked more to the perceived nature of woman's proper role and morality in which physicians have no more expertise than other Canadians. Yet they are the ones who make the decisions because the law has medicalized abortion with the support of both the medical profession and the public.

The major area of medicalization for women, however, is not abortion but birth. Doctors indicated their desire to exert influence in this field very early on. When anaesthesia in labour was introduced in 1848, most doctors and their patients welcomed it. However, some physicians were uneasy about the effect it would have, not on a woman's health, but on her moral well-being. The American specialist Meigs opposed it, considering the pain of childbirth to be "a desirable, salutary, and conservative manifestation of life force."[51] Tyler Smith in his major text, *Parturition and the Principles and Practice of Obstetrics,* argued that pain was a natural part of childbirth and referred to the morality of that pain. Without it, he feared, woman would descend to the level of the lower animals:

> Provident Nature has, moreover, specially exempted women from the dominion of all passion save that of maternity at the time of childbirth. I believe this exemption and moral superiority arises, in a very great degree, from the physical suffering of parturition. The natural throes deliver woman-kind from those emotions natural to the inferior animals. Here it is that we see more clearly than under any other circumstances, the *morality of pain* . . . The pains of natural labour are hard to bear, . . . but they ennoble the sufferer morally.[52]

Most physicians did not share this fear, for which many of their patients were thankful. However, the opinions expressed by Meigs and Smith do underline the concern of physicians for more than medical well-being and show how willing some were to make judgements in areas outside their expertise. Such judgements were clearly influenced by society's attitude towards women at that time and the desire of physicians to become spokespersons for their society and to extend their influence to non-medical areas.

Doctors were only partially successful in the late nineteenth century in extending their influence over childbirth. Most women were still attended by other women and gave birth in their homes. Traditionally, the only women who give birth in a hospital were the very poor or unmarried women, the latter usually in lying-in hospitals. Gradually, however, physicians began to take over, partially encouraged by the middle class women who could afford them and demanded the most up-to-date treatment. Physicians rationalized the emergence of the male doctor-midwife in the same way men rationalized their control over other areas of economic endeavour. They had the expertise and, according to physicians, this medical expertise was increasingly needed in the management of childbirth. The term 'management' itself suggests an attempt to widen their sphere. They announced widely and clearly that women were no longer fit to have babies without aid. By the turn of the century, increasing numbers of women were attended by a physician during childbirth, although most still had their children at home. As late as 1939 only 41.7 per cent of births in Canada occurred in a hospital. Today it is 99 per cent.[53]

As a result of the increased belief in and use of medical technology, women have seen their control over childbirth decline. It has become an event dominated by strangers in an equally strange environment; an act between patient and doctor, not between woman and woman. Increasing numbers of women have felt alienated from the birth experience. In recent years childbirth has even gone beyond being primarily an act between patient and doctor to being an act between the doctor and the foetus, particularly when new technologies are employed. The mother is treated as merely the foetus's container, upon which the doctor can act at her or his discretion in her or his interest or in the interest of the foetus, not of the mother. The common statement "Dr. So-and-so delivered the baby" indicates how incidental the mother (who actually delivers the baby) has become.

When women tried to regain some control over the process by demanding a more natural childbirth in the 1950s and 1960s, the profession did make some concessions. The introduction of a hospital birthing-room was deemed acceptable by many physicians because they interpreted it as a way of helping the mother respond to parenting and to accept her role in society.[54] However, in recent years, when the women's movement lobbied for reform of birthing practices and when some women opted for home births, various medical societies across the country placed pressure on the doctors to cease attending home births. They also brought criminal charges against midwives in Halifax.[55] This despite the fact that, historically, home births have been the norm and that many studies have indicated that they are as safe as or safer than hospital births.

Medicalization does not stop with act of birth. In the twentieth century, it has also encompassed the childbearing years. Medical practitioners, psychiatrists, and psychologists have been deluging women with advice on the best way to raise children. The most blatant example of the way in which experts have interfered in childrearing was in the 1930s with the birth of the Dionne Quintuplets. So miraculous an event was this that some within the medical profession advised the government of Ontario that the natural parents were unsuitable to raise these children. Instead of helping the family to cope financially and emotionally with the birth of the five little girls, the government removed the children from their parents' custody. Leading child experts, such as Dr. Blatz and Dr. Brown from Toronto, oversaw the Quintuplets' development, using the most up to date psychological and medical knowledge. The sad results of the experts' advice in the adjustment problems experienced by the five girls and their later unhappy lives is only too well known.[56] Yet the advice continues to come. Women are told it is their responsibility to raise a well-adjusted child, and if this does not occur, the mother is blamed. A recent study of American and Canadian journals of psychiatry from 1970, 1976, and 1982 revealed that two-thirds of the articles faulted mothers for the problems of their children.[57]

The result of the medicalization of women's lives and society in general is that physicians have become moral arbiters. This is a responsibility for which they have no training and which many physicians themselves do not want. But by medicalizing so much of our lives, they have extended their influence. This perhaps would not be so worrisome except, as we have seen, medical treatment of women is not unbiased.

Intervention

Medical advances and technology have made it easier for physicians to intervene more drastically in their patients' bodies. All sorts of instruments were invented to 'aid' physicians in examining and treating their patients. The vagina and uterus were particularly prone to being prodded and examined. In the late nineteenth century, physicians had a regular arsenal to choose from: vaginal speculums, dilators, sounds, tents, curettes, and pessaries. In addition, favoured treatment of gynaecological disorders consisted of the use of cauterization, electricity, leeches, vaginal injections consisting of ice, belladonna, laudanum, bromine of potassium, sulphuric and gallic acids, acetate of lead, port vine, carbolic acid, nitric acid, and nitrate of silver. By the end of the nineteenth century, surgical intervention had captured the imagination of the profession. Earlier it had not been resorted to that frequently because infection too often occurred, resulting in an extremely high mortality rate. However, with the acceptance of the need for a clean and antiseptic environment, mortality rates declined. When coupled with the introduction of anaesthesia in Canada, surgery became less of a trauma for both patient and surgeon. However, along with the advantages which accrued, there were disadvantages. Operations became more common, to the point that many within the profession argued too much surgery was being performed. This was certainly the concern of an article in the *Canadian Practitioner* of October 1898, which traced the change the treatment of women had undergone.

> Prior to the dawn of aseptic surgery, the uterus was mercilessly treated to all sorts of applications . . . . Since the introduction of asepsis the abdominal cavity had become the happy hunting ground of the surgeon, and the very impunity with which it may be eviserated or mutilated is a

> strong incentive to the specialist in search of surgical glorification to ply his art. The danger of all specialism is to warp the judgment and contract the mental horizon within the range of its own narrow field of operations.[58]

When the ability to operate safely was linked with the popular belief that gynaecological disorders caused mental instability in women, the result was often unnecessary surgery. A good example of this was the treatment of insane women at the London (Ontario) Asylum at the turn of the century. Believing that gynaecological disorders could cause insanity, the superintendent, Richard Maurice Bucke, introduced gynaecological surgery (varying from simple curettage to complete hysterectomy) into the asylum. When some women seemed to recover their sanity after such surgery, the operation proceeded apace, with the result that as many as 75 per cent of newly admitted women were operated on. As a result, Bucke claimed an increased recovery rate on the female ward of 14 per cent. Critics of the operations pointed out, however, that factors other than the surgery could explain the recovery of the women, for example, the individual care received after the operation. In addition, operations were performed only on those women who had been recently admitted to the asylum, namely those patients whom all agreed had a better chance of recovery even if nothing were done to them. Critics also pointed out that some women died from the operations, while others pointed out that if Bucke was going to operate on his female patients, he should perform similar surgery on his male patients since masturbation in men was considered a cause of insanity. After Bucke's death in 1902 the operations essentially ceased, although Dr. Ernest Hall in British Columbia continued to support them for many years.[59]

Not only was surgery on insane women used when it was not on insane men, in the 1930s it was used on mentally retarded women. In the 1920s and 1930s, doctors and others advocated sterilization as a way of controlling the propagation of the feeble-minded, and two provinces, British Columbia and Alberta, passed sterilization acts for that purpose. Medical supporters of this legislation made it clear that medicine had a particular responsibility since doctors' intervention had caused part of the problem. If left on their own, many of the 'unfit' would not have survived, but medical science had intervened and saved them. Now "medical intervention in the form of sterilization was needed to counter the surge of mental deficiency created by earlier forms of intervention."[60] In a study of the sixty-four cases of persons sterilized from the Essondale Provincial Hospital in British Columbia from 1935 to 1945, fifty-seven were women.[61] In a study of surgery on the native population in Canada in the early 1970s, Dr. Clarence Ekstrand discovered "a surgery rate five times *higher* than the general population, particularly for women and particularly for tubal ligations.''[62] Both in the case of the retarded and in the case of the native people a double standard prevailed. The women of both groups bore the brunt of surgical intervention. Despite the emphasis that Canadian society has placed on the reproductive capabilities of women and the reluctance to intervene with those capabilities, it has been even more hostile to intervention with the sexual/reproductive system of men.

Not surprisingly, the real arena of increasing medical intervention in women's lives is in childbirth. This was a logical step once medicalization of childbirth occurred. At the end of the nineteenth century, forceps were popular, so much so that some physicians argued there was too much intervention with them. In the early part of the century, Caesarians were performed more and more until almost one-third of all births today are through Caesarian section, a much higher rate than in Great Britain and Europe, where midwives are used. The practice of inducing births has become more common as well. A phenomenon once viewed as natural is now viewed as a medical problem and in need of assistance. Over the years, the percentage of births considered normal by the medical profession has been declining, resulting in more intervention. Abnormal births are emphasized in medical literature. Physicans write about their unusual cases; no one wants to hear about the normal delivery. As a result, young medical students graduate with the expectation of seeing problems in the delivery room.

Critics of interventionist childbirth techniques have asked who benefits from it. Caesarians and induction are a medical necessity for a small minority of women. They are also convenient for the scheduling needs of the hospital and physicians, and the number of women undergoing such procedures suggest that it is this convenience that is often of most concern. In addition, making the woman less of a participant places the attending physician at centre stage. It is difficult to assume that patient welfare and comfort was uppermost in the minds of those obstetricians who, after the Ontario doctors' strike, asserted that they would no longer be present at normal deliveries (this may actually decrease the amount of intervention and benefit women) and would no longer guarantee that a woman's doctor would be the one to attend her if she was to deliver after hours and the doctor was not on call. Because we have come to accept childbirth intervention, doctors gain power through the willingness to provide it and through the threat of withdrawing it.

In the late 1920s and 1930s, several studies were made to determine the reason for the high rate of maternal mortality in Canada. The studies pointed to two major causes, one was the weak health of the women because of socio-economic factors, the second was the medical care the women received. The medical profession understandably focused on the second, which eventually led to better pre-natal care and supervision.[63] However, the best care over nine months of pregnancy cannot offset years of poor health. The focus on the maternal role of women led the medical profession and Canadian society to overlook the health needs of women when they were not acting as child-bearers. Instead of encouraging preventive medicine, we depend on doctors' ability to intervene.

Conclusion

The focus of medical treatment of women over the years has been on their reproductive/sexual system. To some degree this makes sense considering that it is one of the factors that distinguishes women from men. However, the male sexual/reproductive system has never exerted the same fascination. This is partly because woman's is more prone to disorder because of its greater complexity, but it is also this complexity that offers the challenge to the medical profession. This perspective is not new. In 1898, one critic of gynaecological operations to cure insanity made it very clear why he believed surgery was more prevalent among women than men.'

> Happy, thrice happy, should man be because of the simplicity of his genital outfit and its meagre attraction for the operation of surgical science. Had nature decreed him to wear his genitals within the abdominal cavity, he, too, might have been compelled to suffer surgical martyrdom for the sake of restoring his reason.[64]

The medical treatment of women has closely reflected the attitudes of Canadians towards women. It reveals how fundamental the differences between the two sexes were and are believed to be. They were rooted in the deepest core of sexual identity and as such exerted a tremendous power over personal identity. Canadians believed that the individual was an organic whole. All parts of the personality – sexual, intellectual, spiritual, biological, moral, and mental – were interrelated. The biological, being more immutable, was the fundamental aspect of personality. Any biological differences between individuals resulted in differences in every sphere.

Has the medical attention focused on women benefitted them? There is no doubt that women are outliving men and have done so since the late nineteenth century. Fewer women die in childbirth than died previously. However, most studies of mortality suggest that environmental factors, such as better nutrition and sanitation, have been more significant in increasing life expectancy than any medical therapeutic.

In recent years, there has been a backlash against the medical care provided women. Women are making themselves more knowledgeable about their own bodies so that they can understand what is happening to them when they are ill. The physical fitness movement attests to the growing awareness among both sexes that good health is based on preventive measures. The increase in the number of women doctors will make some difference to the care given to women. As women, they at least will not view the female body as something divorced from their own. However, it is not only the sex of the physician that stands in the way of sensitive medical care of women. It is medical education itself. Female doctors are trained in the same way as male doctors, and historically there is indication of only slight differences in their treatment of patients. For medical treatment of women to change, medical education will have to focus increasingly on the whole person and not on one aspect of that person. In addition, our society will have to place as much emphasis on preventive medicine as it does interventionist medicine. More significantly, doctors will have to stop using the male body as a norm by which to measure woman's health.

There is still so much we do not know about the medical care of women. For example, we do not have very much information on how the treatment of women varies by class and ethnicity. We are not even sure how much access to health care Canadian women have. We certainly do not have very much knowledge about the way in which nursing care differs from male doctoring. This is unfortunate, for nurses tend to be in closer touch with the patient and base much of their actual activity on their knowledge of the needs of the individual concerned rather than on the more theoretical demands of any specific illness. We also need to appreciate the preventive health care provided by mothers within their own families. After all, it is they who, more often than not, determine whether they or their children even need medical assistance.

Wendy Mitchinson

GLOSSARY

Mastectomy – surgical removal of breast tissue; radical mastectomy consists of the amputation of the breast with wide excision of the pectoral muscles.

Hysterectomy – surgical removal of the uterus.

Hysteria – in the nineteenth century it referred to a state of excitement in which there is loss of control over the emotions.

Antisepsis – prevention of contamination by bacteria by destruction of the infective matter.

Fibroma – a tumor.

Nulliparous – a term to describe a woman who has not given birth to a live child.

Emetic – causing vomiting.

Erethism – excessive irritability or sensitivity to stimulation.

Version – the act of turning, in this case a uterus that has turned.

Prolapse – downward displacement of the uterus.

Endometritis – inflammation of mucous membrane of the uterus.

Mennorrhagia – pain during menstruation.

Dysmenorrhea – painful menstration.

Leucorrhoea – a whitish or yellowish discharge from the vagina or uterine cavity.

Coitus interruptus – when a man removes his penis from a woman's vagina and ejaculates outside her body.

Prostate – an accessory reproductive organ in the male located next to and under the bladder.

Speculum – an instrument for opening or distending a body opening, e.g., the vagina, for visual inspection.

Sound – a slender instrument to be introduced into body passages.

Curette – a spoon-shaped instrument for cleansing a diseased surface.

Pessary – an instrument placed in the vagina to support the uterus or rectum.

SUGGESTED READINGS

Bliss, Michael, ''Pure Books on Avoided Subjects: Pre-Freudian Sexual Ideas in Canada,'' *Historical Papers* (Canadian Historical Association, 1970): 89–108.

Buckley, Suzann, ''Ladies or Midwives? Efforts to Reduce Infant and Maternal Mortality,'' in Linda Kealey, ed., *A Not Unreasonable Claim: Women and Reform in Canada, 1880–1920*. Toronto: Women's Educational Press, 1979.

Buckley, Suzann, ''Efforts to Reduce Infant and Maternity Mortality in Canada Between the Two World Wars,'' *Atlantis* 2, (Spring, 1979): 76–84.

Dodd, Diane, ''The Canadian Birth Control Movement on Trial, 1936–1937,'' *Histoire sociale* 16, (November 1983): 411–28.

Dodd, Diane, ''The Canadian Birth Control Movement: Two Approaches to the Dissemination of Contraceptive Technology,'' *Scientia Canadensis* 19, no. 1, (1985): 53–66.

Lewis, Nora, ''Reducing Maternal Mortality in British Columbia,'' in Barbara Latham and Roberta Pazdro, eds., *Not Just Pin Money*. Victoria: Camosun College, 1984.

McLaren, Angus, and Arlene Tigar McLaren, *The Bedroom and the State: The Changing Practices and Politics of Contraception and Abortion in Canada, 1880–1980*. Toronto: McClelland and Stewart, 1986.

Mitchinson, Wendy, ''Historical Attitudes Toward Women and Childbirth,'' *Atlantis* 4, no. 2, (1979): 13–35.

Mitchinson, Wendy, ''A Medical Debate in Nineteenth Century English Canada: Ovarotomies,'' *Historie sociale* 17 (May 1984): 133–48.

Mitchinson, Wendy, ''Hysteria and Insanity in Women: A Nineteenth-Century Canadian Perspective,'' *Journal of Canadian Studies* 21, no. 3, (1986): 87–105.

Mitchinson, Wendy, ''The Medical View of Women: The Case of Late Nineteenth-Century Canada,'' *Canadian Bulletin of Medical History* 3, no. 2, (1986): 207–24.

Nicholson, G.W.L., *Canada's Nursing Sisters*. Toronto: Samuel Stevens Hakkert, 1975.

Special issue on women and medicine, *Ontario History* 75, no. 1 (1983).

Strong-Boag, Veronica, ed., *A Woman With A Purpose: The Diaries of Elizabeth Smith, 1872–1884*. Toronto: University of Toronto Press, 1980.

Strong-Boag, Veronica, and Kathryn McPherson, ''The Confinement of Women: Childbirth and Hospitalization in Vancouver, 1919–1939,'' *B.C. Studies* 69–70 (Spring-Summer 1986): 142–74.

Chapter Ten

The Psychology of Women

> Psychology has nothing to say about what women are really like, what they need and what they want, for the simple reason that psychology does not know. Yet psychologists will hold forth endlessly on the true nature of women with dismaying enthusiasm and disquieting certitude.[1]

At the time that these words were written by Naomi Weisstein in the late 1960s, the psychoanalytic view of female personality development provided the basis of what was accepted to be the psychology of women. Psychoanalytic theory's relatively comprehensive description and interpretation of the psychological evolution of a girl into a woman was created primarily by Sigmund Freud (1856–1939).[2] Because of the central importance it gave to biological rather than cultural factors in determining personality, Freudian theory was assumed to provide a broad basis for a general understanding of human personality development. In the case of the psychology of women, it provided an explanation (in terms of anatomy) for the fact that the majority of women were wives and mothers with a clearly inferior societal status to men. This particular theory, then, not only supported the societal norms for female behaviour, but also clearly grounded this behaviour in nature rather than in culture.

Since Weisstein wrote these words, many changes have occurred in our conception of the psychology of women. Instead of providing an all-encompassing description of the way in which personality development proceeds and a prescription for how a normal woman *should* feel and behave, the psychology of women today is an active, evolving area of scholarship, teaching, and practise. Its focus is upon a wide variety of psychological issues that previously were either ignored by psychology or presented almost entirely from a male point of view. Now, however, it is possible to find psychologists who are interested in studying varying aspects of events that occur exclusively in the lives of women, such as menstruation, pregnancy, childbirth, and menopause. Others are doing research in areas traditionally assigned to women, such as caring for others or maintaining relationships. It is also possible to find psychologists who are seeking to understand the psychological implications of events that almost exclusively victimize girls and women in our society, such as sexual abuse of children, rape, sexual harassment, or battery. Others attempt to help the victims deal with the often long-lasting consequences of such criminal activities. Some psychologists are providing a new perspective by focusing upon women's experiences in areas that are usually approached from a male point of view, such as achievement, work, leadership, power, and sexuality. Still others are seeking to rediscover the pioneering women psychologists whose names and accomplishments have been hidden from view. And others are exposing the myths and biases that permeate so much of psychology's knowledge of women.

Our understanding of the psychology of women has undergone tremendous changes in the past twenty years. Instead of describing what women are and/or should be like as a result of their 'true nature,' psychologists concerned with this area today are attempting to describe, analyse, and understand the diversity as well as the commonality of the experiences of women that affect their development. Women share the experience of being female in male-dominated societies, but their experiences are also determined by the complex environments within which they live as women. Thus, even though many women are mothers, their experiences of motherhood will be influenced by factors such as their own health as well as that of the child, the practical support in caring for the child they receive from others, the financial resources they have available, the expectations they have for themselves and their child, whether they are lesbian parents, and whether they are the parents of several children. As well, their experiences of motherhood will change with other changes within their lives.

No chapter or book on the psychology of women will say what it means to be a woman, but it may explain why women are still plagued by some of the common beliefs on women's nature and provide another perspective for understanding personal experiences. This chapter will include a discussion of, first, the historical treatment of women by psychology, focusing upon psychoanalytic influences; second, the impact of the feminist movement in evaluating psychology and contributing to changes within the discipline; and finally, some of the innovative interpretations and studies that are contributing to the development and practice of a women-centered psychology of women.

There are, however, some terms that should be explained before looking at the history of the psychology of women. Throughout the chapter reference will be made to psychologists, psychiatrists, psychoanalysts, and psychotherapists. Individuals who identify themselves by any one of these titles may all be involved in providing some kind of psychotherapy (help that involves achieving insight into problems through talking) to people who are experiencing difficulties in dealing with their everyday lives. However, different psychotherapists hearing the same person describe her or his problems may see quite different causes for them and, consequently, may approach the treatment in very different ways. The way in which the problems are understood and treated by the therapist depends very much upon which approach to personality development that therapist embraces.[3]

The specific kinds of professional training psychotherapists receive will also influence the kind of therapy they administer. For example, *psychiatrists* receive medical degrees before embarking upon a residency program in psychiatry. Because of their medical training, they may view psychological problems as illness and use drugs or other medical treatments in addition to or instead of psychotherapy. (Psychotherapists who are medical doctors are the only ones who can prescribe drugs.) *Psychoanalysts* (who may or may not be psychiatrists) have been trained at a psychoanalytic institute to analyse others using techniques to make conscious those unconscious memories, feelings, or desires that are assumed to be the cause of the problems. Some, but not all *psychologists* provide counselling or psychotherapy. Psychologists have generally earned a Ph.D. degree, the program for which has included supervised clinical work. (Many of the psychologists whose work will be referred to in this chapter are not primarily psychotherapists, but are university teachers and researchers.)

All of these professionals as well as others (such as social workers or M.A. psychologists) may be considered to be psychotherapists. Psychotherapy provides the point at which many women encounter psychological beliefs and theories. What the therapist believes to constitute the psychology of women can have extremely important consequences for individual women.

Psychoanalytical Theory

Freud

The psychology of women was, until very recently, assumed to be explained by psychoanalytic theory as developed by Freud and added to by several of his colleagues. The impact of Freud's ideas and work upon psychology generally and psychotherapy specifically has been and continues to be very significant. His ideas have served both as a stimulus for further development and for the creation of opposing interpretations of what it is to be human. Freudian ideas, although controversial, have also been influential in areas such as literature, art, and history, and have been integrated into popular thought.

Freud's work on the psychology of women grew directly out of his conceptualization of the stages of sexual development, which he thought represented a universal pattern for all men and women. Before considering what Freud had to say about women specifically, it is important to look at his general psychosexual stage theory.[4]

Freud postulated that the infant is born with undifferentiated sexual energy, called libido, which becomes organized around different areas of the body as the child matures. What happens at each stage of psychosexual development is seen to have crucial implications for personality development, as well as for the observable physical and behavioural differences between the sexes in puberty and adulthood. The stages are identified by the area of the body which was seen by Freud to be the primary locus of sexual pleasure at that time. During the first year of life, the mouth and the lips are the areas stimulated by feeding and sucking and were seen by Freud to provide sexual pleasure. This period is designated as the *oral stage*. In the second or third year, as the child gains control over bodily functions, the area of pleasure moves. This second phase is known as the *anal stage* of psychosexual development. When the child has achieved mastery over the anal functions in the third or fourth year, the pleasure potential of the genitals is discovered through infantile masturbation of the penis for boys and of the clitoris for girls. This phase of development is referred to as the *phallic stage* and is seen to be especially important for personality development. It is in this stage that the Oedipal complex (the child's sexual desire for the opposite-sex parent) is aroused and, later, successfully repressed through identification with the same-sex parent. The resolution of the Oedipal complex is believed to be more difficult for girls than for boys. According to Freud, the child ceases to display overt sexuality around the age of six and enters the *latency stage*, during which sexual impulses remain dormant until their re-emergence at puberty. During the *genital stage*, which appears at puberty, the libido may be directed toward a member of the other sex, which indicates that the individual has reached psychosexual maturity.

Boys and girls pass through the early stages of psychosexual development in much the same manner with both, according to Freud, engaging in masturbatory acts and connecting them with the ideas of sexual intercourse in the phallic phase. Both are also attached to the mother as the first love object. Freud believed that girls were destined to notice the visible and large penis of a brother or playmate early in the phallic stage, which would lead to their falling victim to envy for the penis and would "leave ineradicable traces on their development and the formation of their character."[5] The little girl comes to believe that she was castrated, which is a wound to her self esteem and leads to a permanent sense of inferiority. And the discovery that all women lack a penis is also the basis for the girl to devalue other women.

She blames her mother for her castration, which causes her to turn away from her mother in hostility, ending the attachment to her in hate. The turning away from the mother paves the way for the attachment to the father to whom she turns with "the wish for the penis which her mother has refused her and which she now expects from her father." The wish for the penis is then transformed in normal femininity to a wish for "a baby from the girl's father, and thereafter is the aim of the most powerful feminine wish."[6] With the transfer of her libido from her mother to her father and the equation of the penis with a child, she resolves her penis envy and is on the course of normal femininity.[7]

In order to achieve sexual maturity, however, she must also renounce phallic clitorial orgasm in favour of orgasm from vaginal penetration. Freud saw other consequences of penis envy in female personality development. In addition to her sense of inferiority, the woman is also left with a residue of penis envy in the form of jealousy, which Freud claimed to be much more prevalent in the mental life of women than men, and leads to their having little sense of justice.[8] Other traits which Freud thought characterized adult women were narcissism (a preoccupation with the self), which was exhibited in a strong need to be loved; vanity (value placed on physical charms), which was compensation for their original sexual inferiority; and shame, the purpose of which was to conceal genital deficiency.[9]

Although it may be difficult to understand today why Freud's views on the psychology of women were taken seriously, it must be remembered that they were taken very seriously. They did have, and continue to have consequences for the lives of individual women. In large part, this was because Freudian theory provided the first 'scientific' explanation based on female anatomy for much of what was believed (and continues to be believed by some) to be generally true of women in Western society. For example, both men and women of Freud's era believed that women were inferior beings; their main goal in life (no matter what else they did) was to marry and have children; they did not get along with other women or with their mothers; they were emotional and, thus, could not make rational decisions; and they were vain creatures who concentrated on their physical appearances. The influence of such beliefs extended well beyond the domain of psychology. It is apparent, for example, in the medical treatment of women, as Wendy Michinson shows in her chapter, and the 'complementarity' thesis, which Lorraine Code discusses in her chapter, gained increased credibility from Freud's views. Because Freudian theory pointed to a natural cause for these effects, there was no need to consider the ways in which women were controlled or restricted by the various institutions of society from the state through the church to the family. It was a theory that reinforced many of the societal beliefs about and practices toward women and did it in a way that was accepted at the time as intellectually and scientifically respectable.

Freud was not the only psychoanalyst who supported an 'anatomy is destiny' theory of women's personality development. His position was (and is) supported by other analysts, at least two of whom (Helene Deutsch and Erik Erikson) achieved popular recognition and made their own contributions to the psychology of women. Helene Deutsch (1884–1982) underwent analysis with Freud, worked closely with him in Vienna before emigrating to the United States, and has been referred to as one of Freud's "dutiful daughters."[10]

Although she did not accept Freud's theory of penis envy, Deutsch did believe that narcissism, along with passsivity and masochism, were essential personality characteristics of the normal feminine woman. All three terms tend to have negative connotations for us today, but Deutsch did not see them as pejorative *per se*. For instance, she saw passivity as the attitude of receptive waiting and expectancy. In trying to give it a positive connotation, Deutsch referred to feminine passivity as "activity directed inward."[11] Healthy narcissism is a loving and valuing of the self, which supports the instinct for self-preservation. And masochism, in Deutsch's sense, is a normal condition for women, who are more attracted to suffering than men, and who, in the normal course of life, experience pain with pleasure in such events as childbirth and defloration. Narcissism and masochism are in balance in normal femininity. The healthy woman is seen to accept discomfort, even pain, associated with her normal functions because of the pleasure that accompanies them, but her healthy narcissism will not allow her to accept too much.[12]

It is ironic that Deutsch, an independent, active woman, who combined marriage, motherhood, and a successful career, embraced and expanded the Freudian (and societal) ideas of what it meant to be a normal woman. Instead of focusing upon the challenges and satisfactions to be derived from breaking down stereotypes and leading an unconventional life as she did, she lent a good bit of her professional prestige to prescribing the traditional roles of wife and mother for the true fulfillment of women.[13] The fact that Deutsch was a woman and her best-known work was entitled *The Psychology of Women* lent scientific and personal validity to the psychoanalytic views of women.

Erik Erikson (b. 1902) is an influential Freudian psychoanalyst who also has supported an 'anatomy is destiny' view of women's development. His psychosocial stage theory of human development expands upon Freud's psychosexual formulation but covers the entire life span, focusing upon developmental crises to be solved rather than simply upon the sexual aspects of development. He acknowledges and emphasizes cultural and historical contributions to personality, but has maintained that the female anatomy, particularly the "inner space,"[14] exerts powerful effects upon women. In 1968 he wrote:

> Am I saying, then, that "anatomy is destiny?" Yes, it is destiny, insofar as it determines not only the range and configuration of physiological functioning and its limitation but also, to an extent, personality configurations. The basic modalities of woman's commitment and involvment naturally also reflect the ground plan of her body.[15]

The filling of the inner space was seen by Erikson as the goal of female development and the emptiness of it as the source of despair by women. And the self identity of a woman was seen to revolve around the man she marries rather than coming from her own interests and achievements. Erikson wrote, "I think that much of a young woman's identity is already defined in her kind of attractiveness and in the selective nature of her search for the man (or men) by whom she wishes to be sought."[16] And later he claimed "womanhood arrives when attractiveness and experience have succeeded in selecting what is to be admitted to the welcome of the inner space 'for keeps'."[17]

How did these particular psychoanalytic views of woman's true nature affect individual women? Even though only a relatively small number of women have ever undergone psychoanalysis, the influence of psychoanalytic thought on western culture since the early part of this century has been considerable. It provided a prescription for what it was to be a feminine woman, which included a number of fairly negative traits, as well as firmly establishing that a woman's goal in life was to marry and have children. With the general acceptance of psychoanalytic theory, norms were established which may have caused individual women (and others) to doubt or question their own normality when they did not conform to the standard. It also has provided labels, often confused as explanations, to apply to aspects of women's behaviour. For example, it is often said that a woman who is beaten by a spouse and stays with him is masochistic. This type of labelling focuses upon the individual, who in this case is a victim, and gives her the responsibility for the fact that someone else is abusing her. Professionals as well as lay people tend to blame female victims for their victimization because they 'know' from psychoanalytic theory that women are subconsciously masochistic by nature.

Two other aspects of psychoanalytic theory that have had particularly negative consequences for individual women are Freud's assertions that, first, the normal, mature female orgasm is vaginal rather than clitoral, and, second, that the girl comes to desire a baby from her father as a result of penis envy. Freud's views on the mature female sexual response were dominant until the careful work of Masters and Johnson in 1966 provided convincing evidence that the clitoris is the primary organ for female orgasm.[18] Before that time, if a woman reported to a doctor or therapist that she did not experience an orgasm during intercourse, she was often told that she was rejecting her femininity and was labelled frigid. The diagnosis comes directly from Freudian theory and again focuses upon woman's nature rather than upon the interaction between sexual partners. If she did not experience orgasm in intercourse she must be unconsciously (if not consciously) rejecting her feminine role. It is likely that many more women, who did not report their lack of orgasm, simply labelled themselves as frigid.

Freud saw the girl on her way to normal adult femininity transferring her attachment to her father and wishing for a baby from him. This aspect of the theory developed as a result of the fact that Freud was told by many of his female patients that they had been seduced by their fathers.[19] However, when Freud did publicly claim in 1896 [20] that infantile sexual experiences figured in the cause of hysteria (a form of emotional disturbance manifested in paralysis, blindness, or other disturbance without a physical cause), it was not well received by the Viennese scientific community. Subsequently he reversed his position and claimed that the reports of seduction were fantasies and were incorporated into his theory as a normal part of development. Our awareness today of the prevalence of the sexual abuse of children emphasizes the enormity of Freud's actions and those of generations of therapists since, in denying that sexual abuse actually took place.[21]

Although the psychoanalytic view of women has dominated psychology, Stephanie Shields[22] has reminded us that the psychology of women as it was extrapolated from sex-difference research did have an active pre-Freudian past. In a pioneering article, which appeared in 1975, she showed how science in the last half of the nineteenth and the first third of the twentieth century played handmaiden to social values and provided 'legitimate' evidence for cataloguing the 'innate' but complementary differences in male and female nature. The 'woman question' entered North American psychology with the incorporation of evolutionary theory into the practice of psychology in the late nineteenth century. The theme of this biological theory as it was applied to the social sciences revolved around the evolutionary supremacy of the Caucasian male. The supplementary, subordinate role of the female was seen as part of this development. Psychological research was directed toward firmly establishing that differences did exist between women and men and concluding that the bases for these differences were biological in origin. It is very instructive to see how societal beliefs were reflected in the work of individual scientists dedicated to providing evidence for the naturalness of women's inferior position in society through research on the female brain, the variability hypothesis (individual differences, particularly as they related to intellectual ability), and maternal instinct. It is also instructive to read that some women psychologists were critiquing this work at the time and pointing out that environmental and social factors alone provided explanations for observed differences. Shields quotes Helen Thompson Wooley's appraisal in 1910 of the quality of research on sex differences as follows:

> There is perhaps no field aspiring to be scientific where flagrant personal bias, logic martyred in the cause of supporting a prejudice, unfounded assertions, and even sentimental rot and drivel, have run riot to such an extent as here.[23]

Freudian views on the nature of women were easily accepted by a profession whose thrust in research on women had been to establish their biological inferiority to men and to understand their position in society as a result of natural rather than cultural factors. Although psychologists claimed to base their conclusions on objective facts, they accepted as fact those things which supported their beliefs. Psychoanalysis, with its comprehensive description of and prescription for the psychology of women, reinforced the conclusions of the earlier sex-difference research and provided a parsimonious explanation of such differences.

Not all psychoanalysts ascribed to Freud's emphasis on biology as the prime determinant of personality development. Some did take issue with his analyses of normal female development. These analysts' views, however, did not receive the kind of popular attention afforded Freudian interpretations. Their positions are not regularly discussed in introductory psychology texts, and it was not until psychology-of-women texts[24] began to appear in the 1970s that undergraduate students were systematically exposed to the ideas of Karen Horney and Clara Thompson.

Karen Horney (1885–1952) was trained as a Freudian analyst and initially saw her work falling within the framework of Freudian theory. She, however, aspired to eliminate the fallacies of Freudian thought, which she thought had their roots in his mechanistic, biological orientation. She believed that female psychology was based on lack of confidence and an overemphasis on the love relationship, but she saw these as having little to do with the anatomy of the female sex organs and much more to do with a woman's interactions within her social environment. As early as 1926 she pointed out that earlier versions of the psychology of women had been considered only from the point of view of men and actually represented a deposit of the desires and disappointments of men.[25] Unfortunately, from her point of view, women had adapted to the wishes of men and accepted that adaptation as representing their true nature.

She also showed how the views of Freudian theory on feminine development mirrored those of the young boy as he becomes conscious of his own genitals as well as those of the little girl. Horney accepted the prevalence of several of the feminine qualities described by Freud, but questioned his interpretation of them. She argued, for instance, that the cultural prescriptions for and restrictions on women were responsible for behaviour that was seen as masochistic. By the end of her career, Horney had broken completely with the Freudian School of psychoanalysis and embraced a vision of the person (female or male), ''whose best energies are affirmative strivings toward knowledge, toward developing spiritual powers and moral courage, toward achievement in all areas, toward the full use of intellect and imagination.''[26]

Clara Thompson (1893–1958) was a psychoanalyst whose work, from the beginning, emphasized the importance of interactions with others, rather than biological attributes for personal development. As an admirer and a friend of Karen Horney, she, too, was concerned with the Freudian views on the psychology of women. She did not question Freud's observations, but pointed out that he saw female development only from a male perspective and overgeneralized from what he observed in his own culture to all women. Writing in the 1940s and 1950s, she emphasized the importance of cultural pressures upon moulding the behaviours and beliefs of women. She not only reinterpreted various Freudian concepts in cultural rather than anatomical terms, but also wrote very perceptively on topics such as working women, female sexuality, and cultural pressures in the psychology of women.[27]

Both Horney and Thompson challenged Freudian interpretations of women's nature as well as the beliefs about women that were prevalent at the time. Although they were active and influential as writers and as analysts, their ideas did not make their way into the popular culture and were not seen as a threat or a corrective to the views about women that dominated psychology and psychiatry (both were also psychiatrists). The *Zeitgeist* (spirit of the times) was such that any interpretations that challenged the androcentric (male-centered) prescriptions for women were not considered seriously if they were heard.

Women had achieved the vote in many western countries by the time Horney and Thompson were writing, and it was widely believed that the franchise would lead to a righting of many of the wrongs that women experienced. But it was not until the 1960s and 1970s, when the far-reaching effects of the present women's movement had begun to sensitize segments of society to the continued, general oppression of women, even in nations that prided themselves upon their liberal ideals of individual freedom, that voices critical of androcentricity in psychology began to be heard. In 1969, when Naomi Weisstein's article, ''Woman as Nigger,'' appeared, there were women psychologists who were beginning to recognize the role which their discipline – not out of malicious intent but through uncritical acceptance of the beliefs in women's inferior nature – had in maintaining and adding to the oppression of women. After the publication of this article, a concerted critique of the way in which psychology treats women began. This critique, which continues today, is extensive and includes analysis of the methods and the knowledge-base of psychology as well as its practices as a profession.

The Feminist Critique

At the center of the feminist critique is the realization that psychology is an androcentric (male-centered) discipline. Androcentrism is reflected throughout the discipline from its research topics, through its language and methods, to its implementation of knowledge in practice. Although Horney and Thompson had identified the male focus as a problem in the psychology of women, it was not until the early 1970s that this bias began to be systematically investigated and exposed. At the same time, women psychologists began to organize in order to further the development of the psychology of women and to lobby for changes within the discipline. They have met with a fair amount of success, and the changes within psychology over the past fifteen years have been impressive.[28]

One of the far-reaching effects of the androcentric bias of psychology is the assumption that the model for human behaviour is the male human being. Using the male as the standard against which females are compared has had many consequences. A few of these are the development of theories of human behaviour that are more descriptive of the lives of men than of women, the valuing of characteristics that are traditionally attributed to men and the devaluing of those attributed to women, and the use of a double standard in evaluating behaviour based on the gender of the individual.

Some general theories of life-span or adult development are based exclusively on the experiences of male human beings. This fact, however, is not always salient in the naming and/or describing of the theories. For example, it has become increasingly obvious that the developmental paths followed by women and men are different primarily because of women's family responsibilities. Women, for example, are more apt to compromise their own career opportunities for their husband's career and their children's needs than are men. Most theories of human development have not included such considerations and, consequently, do not provide a framework for understanding the experiences of a majority of women.

Similarly there are a number of social-psychological theories of social interaction that are based on an image of the rugged individualist striving toward his goals and fulfilling his own needs. When studies have subsequently been done to test implications of these theories, those individuals who showed behaviour that expressed concern for others, for example, were seen as not fitting the model, and, consequently, were evaluated negatively.[29]

The consequence of using the male as the prototype human being is that theories of human behaviour reflect the experiences of men, but not necessarily of women. When measured against this male standard, women are sometimes found to be deviant or aberrant. And individuals who do not measure up to the standard are often seen as less worthy or valuable than those who do meet the standard. Similarly, the characteristics of that deviant individual or group of individuals are also devalued. This devaluing of the female was reflected in Freud's theory (there it was attributed to her lack of a penis) and is common in society in general.

The realization that women were absent from male-based theories of behaviour resulted in early feminist research attempts to add women to existing theories. One area, which generated a great deal of work in the late 1960s and early 1970s, was the theory of achievement motivation. Achievement, as it is generally understood, has traditionally been associated much more with men than with women. Very often women who achieved in the traditional sense of the term were considered failures as women if they were not also wives and mothers. Matina Horner's realization that women were absent from the considerable literature on achievement motivation led her to the discovery of what she called "fear of success." (Fear of success was defined by Horner as a relatively stable personality characteristic, most apt to be shown by intellectually competent women. It was reflected in the expectation of some negative consequences, such as rejection or the threat to one's femininity as a result of being successful.) The work of Horner and many others provided an extensive analysis of the changing factors that influence and/or inhibit achievement strivings and behaviour, and was part of much early research on the topic of women and achievement.[30]

Androcentrism also permeates the language of sex-difference research and is reflected in the differing attributions made for the same behaviour shown by men and by women. Sex-difference research predated Freud's views on femininity and was directed toward establishing scientifically that women had evolved as mothers and as helpmates to men rather than their social, economic, and political equals. At the beginning of the current feminist movement, there were a number of common assumptions about the ways in which men and women differed from each other. In most cases, it was assumed not only that these differences had a biological or natural basis, but also that that was the way it should be, and that it was up to parents to foster these sex-based tendencies. A further consequence of these 'established differences' was that those behaviours or characteristics attributed to boys were implicitly and explicitly seen as 'better' than those behaviours or characteristics attributed to girls. For example, on the average, girls from adolescence on show higher scores on verbal tasks than do boys, while boys, on the average, show higher scores on mathematical tasks. (It should be noted that when talking about sex differences, one is talking about differences between the means [averages] of scores for groups of girls and boys [or women and men]. There are always some boys who score at or near the girls' mean and vice versa. There are often bigger differences among the girls [or boys] than there are between the means of the two groups.) Although we would probably all recognize the importance of both mathematical and verbal skills, some psychologists have minimized verbal abilities, even ascribing them to extensive prior practice rather than to intellect.[31]

In the early 1970s, Eleanor Maccoby and Carol Jacklin examined a large number of studies that tested for sex differences in motivation, social behaviour, and intellectual ability. They concluded that there were only four areas (aggression, verbal, mathematical, and visual-spatial abilities) where one could confidently conclude that there were average differences between males and females. All of the other differences reported in the literature were seen either to have no support or to be inadequately tested.[32]

There have been and continue to be feminist critiques of sex-difference research,[33] and certainly not all feminists agree on the value of continued effort in this area. The critique of the work begun in the 1970s echoed the point made by women psychologists early in the century, as well as by Horney and Thompson. That is, there is no need to resort to biological or anatomical factors to explain psychological or behavioural differences between men and women. The experiences of and expectations for girls and boys from birth on are so great that socialization and cultural factors provide ample reason for any number of differences measured in childhood, adolescence, or adulthood. Parents' expectations for their own and others' infants are so tied up with gender that it is impossible to eliminate this source of influence on a developing person.[34] And schools, churches, and media consciously and unconsciously perpetuate stereotypes of what is appropriate behaviour for boys and for girls. Consideration of many aspects of the sex-difference research leads to the conclusion that there are more similarities than differences between the behaviours of women and men and that women's lives today, like those of men, are characterized by diversity rather than by similarity.[35]

The tendency to hold stereotypical beliefs about individuals based upon their sex or gender[36] leads to a double standard in making judgments about people, which can have very serious consequences. A number of experimental studies and much everyday experience demonstrate that the same behaviour or description of a situation is judged differently depending upon the gender of the person being judged. That is, the explanation given for the behaviour is determined more by whether a man or a woman is (or is believed to be) the actor than by the behaviour itself. One of the early demonstrations of this tendency was by Philip Goldberg.[37] His study showed that female students judged the quality of a written article higher when they believed the writer was a man than when they though the *same* article was written by a woman. Other studies have shown a differential judgment based on gender in a wide variety of situations.[38] As more women do achieve in areas that were almost exclusively male less than twenty-five years ago, experimental results show a weakening of these effects. Yet people still have little trouble recognizing the differential attributions for a businessman and a businesswoman resulting from the same kind of behaviour. For example, while he is seen as good on details, she's picky; he's confident, and she's conceited; he stands firm, but she's impossible to deal with; or he climbed the ladder of success, but she slept her way to the top. Behaviour that earns him praise is the source of criticism and condemnation for her.

The realization that gender is a powerful organizing concept can often help women understand the negative reactions of others toward them, which they may have interpreted as being their fault. That is, independent women, who are characterized as being aggressive, pushy individuals, may internalize these attributions and see them as evidence of a personality flaw. In reality, however, any act of independence or expression of their own view would be seen by some as inappropriate female behaviour and therefore negative. A further consequence of such stereotyping has been that women are not judged as individuals with strengths and weaknesses, but as women who do not and should not fit the male norm still prevalent in psychology.

Psychologists continue to make attributions on the basis of what is seen as gender appropriate. Furthermore, psychologists have a history, as Naomi Weisstein pointed out in her influential 1969 article, of focusing upon the individual and her/his personality characteristics as the *cause* of behaviour, rather than looking to the very important psycho-social environment within which the individual is situated. Weisstein claimed that psychology's focus upon the individual was an important factor in psychology's ignorance of what women are really like.

The importance of context (which includes expectations) for understanding and predicting human behaviour has been well documented in psychology.[39] Yet it was not until the current feminist critique of psychology began that we became fully aware of the way in which women, particularly as wives and mothers, were 'scapegoated' by psychologists. That is, the view of women as primarily wives and mothers was translated into their having full responsibility for the success of their marriages and of their children's development. When things went wrong in either of these areas, women were often seen as not trying hard enough or as possessing personality characteristics that had detrimental effects upon others. For instance, the expressions 'maternal deprivation' and 'schizogenic mother' are integrated into psychological literature and focus attention on mothers as the cause of a host of their children's problems, including schizophrenia. There are no parallel terms for fathers, and the use of the terms alone is often assumed to explain the problems with no further considerations necessary.

Mother-blaming is a common phenomenon, as a 1985 examination of major clinical journals demonstrated.[40] It was found that mothers' activity was blamed for a wide variety of their children's problems and forms of psychopathology by both female and male clinicians, while fathers' activity was cited much less often as a causative factor. Mothers have also been blamed for condoning or driving their husbands to incest.[41] Wives who stay with battering husbands are still believed by some to be showing their masochistic tendencies and be partly responsible for the beatings they receive.[42] Certainly there are circumstances in which the actions of women have been injurious to and/or problematic for their children, husbands, and themselves. But, too often, wives and mothers have been assumed to be responsible for actions of husbands and problems of children *because* they are women, a view that ignores the circumstances within which the interactions take place and the others involved in the interactions. These assumptions about women and their roles have influenced (and continue to influence) the kind of treatment women receive from psychotherapists.

Even psychotherapists who reject psychoanalytic theory have accepted and been influenced by the societal expectations (which are, in turn, influenced by Freudian thought) of what constitutes the adult female role. Since the early 1970s, a number of significant criticisms of psychiatry and psychotherapy have been made, particularly of their effects on women.[43] These analyses have emerged from the stories of women who have turned to the helping professions (psychiatry, psychology, and social work) for aid with problems in living, only to have their complaints turned into symptons of sickness, ignored, and/or used against them, or to have themselves seen as the problem. Others with real physical problems have been treated as if they were 'hysterical' women, whose symptoms are in their heads.

A recurring theme in these analyses is that the continued acceptance by helping professionals of the stereotypes of what it means to be a woman has led them to serve as enforcers of social control rather than as therapeutic agents. Women's problems have often been compounded and aggravated by their therapists' failure to recognize that social expectations, institutions, and interactions, rather than individual personality dynamics, are at the base of their complaints. Phyllis Chesler was one of the first to launch an all-encompassing indictment of psychiatry and its treatment of women in her pioneering and popular book *Women & Madness*. In addition to naming those responsible for the history of abuse of power in the name of therapy, she also suggested the kinds of changes needed to develop a new psychology of women. Others have added to the critique begun by Chesler and have begun to explore what therapy informed by feminist consciousness would involve. A concrete effect of such efforts has been the acceptance of guidelines for nonsexist therapy/counselling with women by the Canadian Psychological Association (CPA).

An examination of these guidelines reveals the kinds of abuses to which women have been subjected in the name of therapy. It also provides a clear demonstration of the ways in which Freudian ideas and societal stereotypes concerning women have been ingrained in therapy. The guidelines are as follows:

(1) The therapist/counsellor is willing to help the woman client to explore alternative life options in addition to the culturally defined gender role. Besides marriage and motherhood, he or she acknowledges the importance of other activities in both creating and solving women's problems.

(2) The therapist/counsellor realizes that women do not bear the total responsibility for the success of marriage and for childrearing.

(3) The therapist/counsellor recognizes the existence of social bias against women, and explores with the client the possibility that her problems may be based on society's definition of women's role rather than entirely within herself.

(4) While respecting the right of the therapist/counsellor to determine the appropriate therapeutic strategy for a client, he or she is sensitive to and avoids the use of theoretical concepts that serve to reinforce the female stereotype of dependency and passivity, or to limit the woman's personal development.

(5) The therapist/counsellor avoids interpreting psychological problems that occur at times of biological change in a woman's life, – e.g., childbirth, menopause – solely in terms of her reproductive/biological functioning.

(6) The therapist/counsellor avoids the use of language implying sex bias, especially sexist jokes and the use of labels derogatory or demeaning to women.

(7) The therapist/counsellor recognizes physical violence and sexual abuse as crimes, and does not encourage the woman client to submit to

them, to accept their legitimacy, or to feel guilty about being a victim. The therapist actively acknowledges that there is no provocation that justifies resorting to physical or sexual violence.

(8) The therapist/counsellor recognizes a woman client's right to have a fully adult role in the therapist-client relationship, without guidance from or deference to a man, and helps her achieve such a role.

(9) The therapist/counsellor considers the sexual activity of the client without employing a ''double standard'' based on gender.

(10) The therapist/counsellor does not treat the woman client as a sex object.[44]

Although making therapy/counselling nonsexist for *all* clients should be a necessary condition for any therapy, feminists do not believe that being non-sexist is enough. They consciously incorporate their feminist beliefs into their practice and employ specific strategies in their work with female clients. Judith Myers Avis has identified a number of strategies used by feminist therapists.[45] They include such things as deliberate efforts to reduce hierarchy between therapist and client; an emphasis and focus on the client's strength; an avoidance of diagnostic tests and labels; the use of therapeutic contracts in order to give women more control over their own therapy; the use of social and sex-role analyses to help women understand the impact of social, cultural, and socialization factors upon their lives; the teaching of skill building, stress management, and assertiveness; and working with women in groups in order to provide support, break down isolation, and increase awareness of the commonality of women's problems and their relation to societal roles and constraints.

Others have pointed out that feminist therapy must be viewed as a perspective that allows for a different way of seeing, understanding, and making connections, rather than as a technique in and of itself. That is, feminist therapy is not another school of therapy but is an approach to therapy that acknowledges the humanity and personal power of both the client and the therapist. The therapist works in a cooperative manner, sharing aspects of her experience rather than remaining aloof while probing and prescribing. Feminist therapists can work within the general framework of a single approach or may be eclectic and use insights and techniques from a number of different kinds of therapy.

In addition to the feminists who provide counselling/therapy in private practice or in private or public hospitals, clinics, or various social agencies, others are developing self-help groups for women outside of the institutionalized helping professions. These self-help groups are founded on the belief that a group of people with a common goal can help and support each other in dealing with problems in living.[46]

Feminists have made some important advances in getting their criticisms heard, setting nonsexist guidelines in place and providing therapy that expands and supports the options of the clients. Yet, much of the training and practice of counsellors/therapists does not take into account the contributions feminists have made.[47]

Another important feminist contribution to psychology has been the critique of the experimental method – the method by which scientific psychology defines itself. Although many psychologists use methods such as questionnaires, interviews, case studies, surveys, and naturalistic observations to gather data, the controlled experiment has been the method most valued by academic psychology. This method provides a way of systematically manipulating a limited number of stimuli or variables while controlling most other factors in the experimental situation. It is believed to be the only truly scientific means by which the *cause* of a particular behaviour can be established. Feminists (and others) have pointed out that the isolation of the individual in the controlled laboratory, stripped of his/her context, greatly limits the usefulness of what is learned.

In spite of the critiques of this aspect of the method, psychologists continue to depend upon this context-stripping methodology, which represents the view that the individual must and can be understood out of context.[48] Although some feminists believe that the experimental method has only limited usefulness in advancing our knowledge of human behaviour, others do not reject it outright. They recognize that it will continue to be used and thus are concerned that researchers become aware of and recognize the potential for sexism at all stages of the research process. In addition to engaging in feminist research, their efforts are directed toward eliminating sexism from all scholarly work regardless of the research method used.[49]

Although there is no one feminst research methodology advocated by feminist psychologists, there are a variety of considerations that inform feminist research into the psychology of women. These considerations include: (1) the acceptance that *all* research is value-laden and influenced by the beliefs and experiences of the researcher;[50] (2) an attempt to be non-sexist at each stage of the research process, from the asking of questions through to the generalization of results; (3) a respect for the subjects of the research, who may be treated more as collaborators in the research than an objects to be studied; (4) the recognition that the understanding and interpretation of psychological phenomena require an interdisciplinary approach with attention to the social, biological, and political context; and (5) the realization of the potential social and political misuses of the research.[51]

The experiences of women are the starting point for research directed toward expanding our knowledge of the psychology of women, thus much of the data in this evolving field are qualitative rather than quantitative in nature. That is, instead of developing a highly structured questionnaire, where individuals' answers are tallied, in-depth interviews often form the basis for beginning to explore an area of concern to women. It is from being immersed in what the participants have said that patterns emerge which begin to provide insights into both the commonalities and the diversities in women's experiences. This kind of qualitative work is seen by some to be the hallmark of feminist research,[52] while others argue that feminists have to use a variety of research methodologies and cannot limit themselves to a single approach. This latter group points out that once the qualitative work has been done, it is necessary to test the implications of that work by using more structured, quantitative methods.

New Directions in the Psychology of Women

The knowledge base of the psychology of women has grown enormously since the late 1960s and continues to expand and evolve. Women's perceived experiences of all facets of their lives constitute the starting point for theoretical and empirical work in this area, with diversity characterizing the questions asked, the methods of investigation chosen, and the analyses of issues offered. It is now possible to see trends as well as some pitfalls in the feminist research in psychology that has been done. Some of the concepts and directions of the pioneering work in the development of a new psychology of women have been seen, in retrospect, to have the same characteristics, such as blaming the victim and focusing upon the individual, that were points of feminist criticism of psychology in general.[53] The continuing development of our understanding of female psychology influences (and is influenced by) feminist scholarship in other areas and is itself continuously informed by the growing consciousness of what it means to be a woman. In broad terms, the development of new scholarship can be traced from a stage where attempts were made to add more information on women to psychology's knowledge base, through a stage of demonstrating the bias and falsity of the accepted wisdom on women, to a stage of focusing upon women's experiences and attributions and learning more about them from a gynocentric (woman-centered) position.[54] Although these trends in scholarship are quite evident, it should be realized that research at all stages is still being done and adding to what we are learning about women. It should also be kept in mind that much of what is being learned is not static, but changes as the social, economic, and political contexts of society change. Although there is no fully formuated woman-based theory of personality,[55] there is an ever-growing amount of information on the psychological aspects of women's lives from birth through to late adulthood.

From the description of the psychoanalytic view of the psychology of women, it might be assumed that feminists would reject all psychoanalytic interpretations as useless. Some do find that "assumptions about the inherent inferiority of women are embedded in the very core of psychoanalytic theory" and that no amount of tinkering can rehabilitate it.[56] Thus, Hannah Lerman does not believe that psychoanalytical theory is useful for the development of a woman-based theory of personality or for understanding the experiences of women generally. Other feminists disagree and have developed analyses that utilize insights from psychoanalytic theory.[57]

Perhaps one of the most ambitious attempts to show how psychoanalysis is relevant to our present-day understanding of the psychology of women was made by Juliet Mitchell.[58] She argues persuasively that Freud's theory provides an analysis of the human condition in a patriarchal society. She points out that psychoanalysis does not deal with biology but with the conscious and unconscious ways we think about biological facts. And she shows how a Freudian analysis, with its emphasis on the unconscious and infantile sexuality, provides fuller understanding of women's inferior role and the feminine personality than an analysis based on cultural conditioning alone. Mitchell (like others who use a psychoanalytically grounded analysis to understand women's situation today) does acknowledge that future cultural changes will be reflected in changed thoughts and attitudes. That is, there is a recognition that the description of human development provided by Freud is not universal as he claimed, but dependent upon the kind of society within which the individual lives. The psychoanalytic interpretations do, according to Mitchell, show how the realities of patriarchy affect development. A more egalitarian society, for example, where both parents nurture and rear children would lead to different mental representations.

The fact that women bear and rear children has long been recognized as a barrier to their full participation in society. Recent adaptations of Freudian theory have explored other consequences of women's mothering and reached the conclusion that a system of parenting in which both men and women actively parent is necessary if sexual inequality is to be eliminated.[59] Nancy Chodorow's thought-provoking adaptation of Freudian theory to explain the pervasiveness of mothering by women claims that "women are prepared psychologically for mothering through the developmental situation in which they grow up, and in which women have mothered them."[60] Her analysis assumes that daughters sense a oneness and continuity with mothers, which enhances and extends the mother-child relationship for girls. The differences, however, that sons feel from their mothers lead to their growing separation from them. Consequently, boys have the need to develop a more differentiated self and experience a growing curtailment of their emphatic tie with their mothers. Chodorow sees the fact that women mother to be a major feature of a sex-gender system, which leads to sexual inequality as we know it. Among other consequences of women's mothering are the creation of a psychology of male domination, a fear of women by men, and the division of the social world into unequally valued domestic and public spheres.[61] As a result of her analysis of women's mothering and its consequences, she advocates a change in our present system of parenting.

Many other feminists have also concluded that a change in our present system of parenting is necessary for women to achieve equality. They have arrived at this point, however, through analyses of societal institutions and the experiences of women, rather than through psychoanalytic insights. (Susan McDaniel offers one such analysis from a sociological perspective in her chapter on the changing family and the impact of feminism on women's lives.) Women are going to continue to want to have children, and more and more mothers of preschool children are going to be in the work-force. The ideal situation of most mothers and fathers sharing equally in the nurturing and care of their children is certainly not yet at hand. But issues and problems around motherhood and childcare will remain important for some time and in the lives of most women.

Let us consider next a group of women, lesbians, who have been greatly marginalized by society and psychology. With a psychology of women, which was directed toward heterosexual attraction, marriage, and motherhood (as was Freudian psychology), lesbianism was seen as pathological and those who embraced it were seen as sick. The feminist and gay movements have led to a greater recognition of life styles that consciously reject the "compulsory heterosexuality"[62] that dominates most if not all societies today. Feminist lesbians are producing an impressive body of knowledge on lesbian existence and identity, which has become a growing part of the disciplinary as well as the interdisciplinary literature on women. Psychology of women texts have generally included information on lesbianism, but the way in which the subject has been treated has changed since the late 1970s. One textbook, which is now in its third edition, has gone from a two-and-a-half-page section on homosexuality within the sexuality chapter in 1977 to an almost six-page section on lesbianism in the sexuality chapter in 1983 to a twenty-three page chapter entitled "Lesbian Identity" in the 1987 edition.[63] Although early definitions of homosexuality revolved around sexual preference for one's own sex, contemporary definitions are much broader. Juanita Williams discusses alternate definitions of a lesbian and points out that even though a final definition has not yet been agreed upon it would include components such as: (1) a woman whose primary bonds, emotional, social, and probably erotic, though not necessarily, are with other women; (2) a woman who identifies herself as lesbian, though she may not do this publicly for reasons related to children, job, friends, and so on; (3) a woman who may (or may not) be part of a lesbian subculture, or community, or simply a group of lesbian-identified women.[64]

Historically, lesbians (like male homosexuals) have been subject to severe penalties ranging from death to imprisonment to social ostracism for their rejection of heterosexuality. Until December 1973, homosexuality was classified as a mental disorder by the American Psychiatric Association. In a review essay of social-science research looking at lesbian indentity and community, Susan Krieger has claimed that:

> the shift that has occurred in the past twenty years may be described as one that moves us from thinking about lesbianism in terms of deviance, narrowness, simple causation, isolated occurrence, and fixed nature to thinking of it in terms of normality, diversity, multiple influence, social context, choice and change.[65]

In her review of the literature she found very little treatment of lesbianism before 1960, but what she did find was based on medical, psychiatric, or psychoanalytic expertise, and depicted lesbians as pathological, that is, sick, perverted, deviant, narcissistic, or masochistic. The influences of Freudianism and the societal myths of normality are clearly evident in the assumptions of these studies. In the late 1950s and early 1960s, work began to appear that challenged the pathological models and suggested that lesbianism was a lifestyle choice closely linked with a sense of personal identity. Krieger claims that the best of the studies published since the mid-1970s views lesbianism as a product of multiple influences, looks at the similarities between lesbians and other women, and considers the lesbian individual in a social context. It also views lesbianism as a matter of total personality identity rather than primarily a sexual condition. The story Krieger hears being told in the social-science literature on lesbianism over the past twenty years is: ‘‘Once we were sick and now we are well.’’[66]

Along with the explorations of lesbian existence, lesbian academics are also pointing out how the institutionalization of heterosexuality dictates not only sexual behaviour but many other areas of our lives. The assumption that heterosexuality is the norm affects lesbians and homosexuals in much the same fashion that androcentrism affects women. Certainly a gynocentric psychology of women must include lesbian existence as a valid choice and consciously work against the heterosexist ideology that influences all levels of human interaction.[67]

Revaluing Women's Qualities

As we saw in the discussion of androcentrism in research, psychologists (and society) have tended to value characteristics such as rationality and independence, which are associated with men, and devalue attributes such as emotionality and dependence, which are often associated with women.

Some of the early work in the new psychology of women seemed to be more directed toward showing that with proper socialization and training girls could be more like boys. Even the early important work on androgyny seemed to lead to the conclusion that 'masculine' traits were still the important ones to have.[68] But a different focus appeared with the work of Jean Baker Miller.[69] Miller, a psychiatrist, draws on a rich background of clinical practice for examples but centers her analysis on the forces she believes affect all women by virtue of their being women. For example, she points out that women in their subservient position to men have been assigned the tasks of providing for bodily needs and comforts as well as the basic emotional connections between individuals. These tasks, which men have seen as humanity's 'lowest needs,' Miller suggests may well be humanity's 'highest necessities.' From their socialization and adult experiences, women have learned a great deal more about men than men often know about themselves, and they have learned how to survive with men. As subordinates they have been allowed to express human qualities such as vulnerability, weakness, helplessness, and emotionality, which are experienced by all people, but whose expression is often denied to men. In a male-dominated culture, these characteristics are not valued, but Miller argues that being able to accept and deal with these aspects of human life are, in fact, *strengths* that women have developed and that humanity needs. Other strengths she attributes to women are their ability to work cooperatively and to be creative in their continual struggle to create a new concept of personhood. She claims that women's strength is also reflected in the organization of their sense of self around being able to make and then to maintain affiliations and relationships with others. This very important aspect of women's being has been recognized by others and is seen to be centrally representative of women's experience and values. As such, it may well characterize a gynocentric psychology of women.[70]

Although caring for others and being aware of their needs and feelings have been, and continue to be, generally devalued by society, Carol Gilligan, like Miller, argues that caring is a source of human strength. Gilligan, a psychologist, was involved in teaching a course on moral development at Harvard with Lawrence Kohlberg, the developer of an influential theory on the stages of human moral development. This theory, however, was based on work done exclusively with boys. In Kohlberg's theory, the highest level of moral judgment is reached when an individual judges moral issues on the basis of self-chosen principles and standards of justice based on universal ethical principles and on the ideals of reciprocity and human equality. At the level below this one, an individual decides moral issues on the basis of maintaining social order and being concerned about the needs and concerns of others.[71] Gilligan's very influential and pioneering work in the area of women's moral development began when she noticed that more women than men were dropping the course she was teaching with Kohlberg. In following up on this observation, she interviewed several of the dropouts and discovered that some of the moral conflicts being experienced by these women did not fit Kohlberg's moral development framework.

She began a series of studies to explore concepts of self and morality and experiences of conflict and choice. In her interviews, she heard what she calls a "different voice" from the one that is emphasized in Kohlberg's work. Although she claims that the different voice is not gender specific, in her work she traces it primarily through what women have to say. The dominant themes of the two different voices she heard are those of responsibilities (care) and rights (justice), which are heard most clearly in the voices of women and men, respectively. Gilligan argues that caring for others is a source of human moral strength. Rather than being a lower step on the hierarchy of moral development, caring, she argues, exists *beside* justice, with moral judgements depending upon the context of the moral problem.[72]

In addition to making audible and revaluing women's voices, Gilligan's research method – using intensive interviews and asking people how they defined moral problems, what experiences they construed as moral conflicts, and asking them to resolve moral dilemmas – clearly provides a model of a feminist research methodology. That is, the participants' experiences and perceptions inform, direct, and provide the context and data for understanding the process of making moral decisions. This qualitative approach to exploring areas in which there is not a great deal known is being used very fruitfully by feminist psychologists to augment our knowledge of women's lives and experiences. (It is this aspect of Gilligan's work that Lorraine Code finds especially innovative in her discussion of *In a Different Voice* in the chapter on feminist theory.) A recently published study (done in a cooperative manner) used such an intensive interview/case study approach with "disadvantaged and forgotten women," who are seldom represented in academic research, as well as with more privileged women. The purpose of the study was "to explore with women their experience and problems as learners and knowers as well as to review their past histories for concepts of the self and relationships with others."[73]

From the portions of the interviews that were designed to elicit information on the woman's assumptions about the nature of truth, knowledge, and authority, the researchers grouped women's perspectives on knowing into five major categories. That is, they identified five different ways that women in their study experienced themselves as knowing. Then they went back to the interviews and provided the context for each of the women in the various categories. The five categories of knowing identified in the study are: (1) silence, a state in which the woman experiences herself as mindless and voiceless, and at the mercy of external authority; (2) received knowledge, a position in which the woman cannot create knowledge on her own but can receive and reproduce knowledge from external authorities; (3) subjective knowledge, a state from which truth and knowledge are conceived of as personal, private, and subjectively known; (4) procedural knowledge, a position in which women are invested in learning and applying objective procedures for obtaining and communicating knowledge; and (5) constructed knowledge, a position from which all knowledge is viewed as contextual, with women experiencing themselves as creators of knowledge, and valuing both subjective and objective strategies for knowing.[74] The analyses of women's ways of knowing using the words and experiences of women are extremely rich, insightful, and moving. The researchers also provide suggestions for educators on how to help women develop their own voices as they learn. They argue that these authentic voices will develop:

> if they [educators] emphasize connection over separation, understanding and acceptance over assessment, and collaboration over debate; if they accord respect to and allow time for the knowledge that emerges from first hand experience; if instead of imposing their own expectations and arbitrary requirements, they encourage students to evolve their own patterns of work based on the problems they are pursuing.[75]

Psychologists and researchers are learning a great deal from listening to women's voices and hearing what it is *they* are saying about their ways of being and doing. At the same time, they are also recognizing the value of women's concern for and connectedness with others and seeing it for the strength it is both for themselves and for their societies. New directions will continue to be charted in the psychology of women and some of the earlier ones will be abandoned. But at this point in time the basis of a psychology of women, which is also *for* women, seems to have been firmly established.

Conclusion

Psychology has progressed a great deal since 1969 when Naomi Weisstein claimed that psychology does not know what women are really like, what they need, and what they want. At that time psychoanalytic theory still provided a description of and prescription for women's development that was based on the fact that they differed anatomically from men. This very restricting formulation, which provided a 'scientific' explanation for societal myths about women, has been and continues to be very influential. Other psychological research on women over the decades has, consciously or unconsciously reinforced the views that women are inferior, aberrant, sick, and/or the cause of a number of problems experienced by their husbands or children. Over the years, voices have been raised against psychology's prevailing views on women, but it was not until the 1970s that the feminist critique of psychology, its methods, and its practices began to be heard and to be translated into concrete policy changes and practices. In the 1970s a new psychology of women began to evolve out of the feminist critique of psychology and renewed interest in research on women. Research on women, feminist psychoanalytic reinterpretations of aspects of women's lives, and debunking psychology's beliefs about women are all part of the knowledge base of what we call the psychology of women. Today, one important concern is to develop a gynocentric psychology of women firmly grounded in women's experiences.

Although there has been a great deal learned from and about women in the last twenty years, it is necessary to remember that it is primarily feminists (who are in the minority within psychology) who are creating, using, and disseminating the knowledge and insights acquired from the new psychology of women. A continuing challenge is to get others to hear the voices of women and learn from what they have to say.

Joanna B. Boehnert

SUGGESTED READINGS

Caplan, Paula J., *The Myth of Women's Masochism*. New York: E.P. Dutton, 1985.

Caplan, Paula J., and Georgina White, "Current Themes in Canadian Feminist Psychology," *Resources for Feminist Research* II, no. 3, (1982): 295–306.

Miller, Jean Baker, *Toward a New Psychology of Women*, (2nd. edition). Boston: Beacon, 1986.

Penfold, P. Susan, and Gillian A. Walker, *Women and the Psychiatric Paradox*. Montreal: Eden Press, 1983.

Stark-Adamec, Cannie, and Meredith Kimball, "Science Free of Sexism: A Psychologist's Guide to the Conduct of Nonsexist Research," *Canadian Psychology* 25, no. 1, (1984): 23–34.

Chapter Eleven

Artificial Reproduction: Hope Chest or Pandora's Box?

Women's dominant role in the reproduction of the species is the source of both their power and their powerlessness. Reproductive autonomy–the ability and right to control fertility–is fundamental to women's health and well-being. Reproductive technologies can enhance or forestall the empowerment of women, depending on how they are used.

Reproductive technology is a very broad term. It can refer to something as simple and user-controlled as a diaphram and at the same time to technologies as complex and physician-controlled as *in vitro* fertilization. Most reproductive technologies fall into three basic categories: those that inhibit the development of new life, those that monitor the development of new life, and those that involve the creation of new life. Those involved in the inhibition of new life are the most familiar - birth control, sterilization, and abortion. Medical advances in the monitoring of new life are more recent and involve techniques such as ultrasound, amniocentesis, chorionic villi sampling, foetal monitoring, and foetal surgery.[1]

Developments in both of these spheres have a tremendous impact on women's reproductive autonomy. Foetal surgery, for example, creates a situation where, potentially, the foetus still in a woman's uterus can be defined as a patient separate from the carrying mother. The capacity to monitor, 'correct,' and artificially sustain foetal life at increasingly earlier stages of pregnancy may, in practice, work against the individual mother's reproductive autonomy. Hubbard documents two instances in the United States where women were forced to undergo Caesarian sections through a court order.[2] The checkered health record of the Pill and I.U.D. further illustrate the extent to which the technological 'hope chest' for reproductive autonomy and choice may become a 'Pandora's box' under the prevailing social, economic, political, and medical conditions. The central question is not simply choice, but choice for whom, and under what conditions?

Feminist efforts in relation to reproduction have largely been devoted to ensure women's right *not* to mother and the right to plan and space pregnancies. The availability of safe and effective birth control and equal access to legal abortion have been major concerns for feminists in the past two decades.[3] More recently, the right to control the conditions of birth and to have access to midwives have emerged as feminist issues. All of these remain important arenas for feminist analysis and action. However, even before these issues are resolved, we are moving into an era that has and will continue to have an unprecedented impact on women's reproductive choice. The developments in the realm of artificial reproduction, those involved in the creation of new life, are the central concern of this chapter.[4]

Artificial insemination, sperm banks, surrogate motherhood, *in vitro* fertilization, frozen embryos, and surrogate embryo transfer are some of the developments in the field of artificial reproduction. This is a field of very rapid medical advances; ten years ago these techniques would have been considered to be the stuff of science fiction. Although the reporting of many of these techniques has moved beyond the medical journals to front-page news coverage, the actual procedures and the implications of their development are sometimes difficult to grasp. The media tend to sensationalize their coverage and label every new form of conception as 'test-tube.' An authentic 'test-tube' baby would require conception, gestation, and birth to occur completely outside of a woman's body – the technical term for which is 'ectogenesis.' The technology for an authentic 'test-tube' baby has yet to be fully developed, although it may not be too far off in the future. The media's inaccurate description of current procedures, however, has sown the seeds for its public reception.

Reproductive autonomy, previously limited to concerns about when, how, or not to mother, is an issue that takes on new meaning through the use of artificial reproduction procedures. New dilemmas, choices and responsibilities accompany their introduction into society. As Lorraine Code notes in her discussion of radical feminists' concern with sexuality and reproduction, Shulamith Firestone, a radical-feminist theorist in the early 1970s proclaimed pregnancy "barbaric" and "the freeing of women from the tyranny of their reproductive biology by every means available" as the first among other structural imperatives for women's freedom.[5] Although Firestone was not lacking in imagination, she did not forsee the complexity and depth of women's role as mothers and its links to both emancipation and domination. In concert with the issues surrounding freedom from motherhood, feminists must now analyse and understand the need to mother expressed by women who will utilize these technologies.

There is a striking absence of social and psychological research on the impact of infertility on either women or men, and infertile women argue that their plight has not been of concern to feminists. Infertility is very simply the inability to reproduce oneself biologically. In the past, the discovery that a wife was 'barren' constituted grounds for divorce, public sympathy, and the woman's social stigmatization. The quest for fertility through artificial reproduction, which is usually taxing emotionally, physically, and sometimes financially, testifies to the strength of the 'motherhood mandate' still pervasive in our culture. Increased participation in the paid labour force and the opening of opportunities for women to enter professions, limited as they may be, have not eradicated motherhood's centrality to women's identity and self-esteem. The reasons for this are complex – family pressures, full adult status, gender identity, and the importance of biological continuity or lineage are some of the factors that induce women (and men) to seek fertility through these costly measures. "It hurts to be infertile," as Barbara Menning states in her defence of *in vitro* fertilization.[6]

Before we can fully comprehend the implications of these procedures for women and for society in general, it is important to understand what they actually involve, who will use them, and for what reasons. Ultimately they will have an impact on all women, although they are currently used only by a small number. One of the questions that needs to be asked in relation to these developments is whether they expand or reduce women's reproductive choices. These technologies definitely do provide the opportunity for some women to bear children who perhaps otherwise could not do so. But they also close down some choices while introducing new pressures and dilemmas for women. A woman confronted with infertility today will likely feel the pressure to pursue every possible avenue to overcome or circumvent her or her partner's infertility. As with the pre-natal diagnostic techniques of amniocentesis and ultrasound, which have become commonplace for many 'high-risk' women, the mere availability of various reproductive technologies may foreclose the option of *not* using them. Furthermore, the causes of infertility may be ignored since they can be by-passed technologically.

Infertility is estimated to affect up to 15 per cent of couples and is considered to be on the increase. At present, approximately one-third of all cases of infertility are attributed to women, one-third are attributed to men, and one-third are either unexplained or shared by both partners. In Canada, infertility is defined as one year of attempting to achieve pregnancy without success. The definition of infertility varies in other countries. In France, for example, the definition is five years of unsuccessful attempts to achieve pregnancy. The definition of infertility itself, therefore, is socially defined and structured. Currently, artificial reproductive technologies are used only to assist couples who have fertility problems or, in some instances, for women without a male procreative partner. However, the potential exists for these technologies to be used for other reasons. For example, a woman or couple might hire another woman to bear their child for a number of reasons–for convenience, economic considerations, or simply to avoid the discomforts and health concerns of pregnancy.[7]

As well as the prevalence of infertility, a number of social factors indicate that the market or demand for these procedures is assured and will likely increase.[8] These include: the decline in availability of children for adoption (particularly healthy white babies); the strong emphasis in our culture on having genetically related children (which is possible with some of these technologies but not with others); late childbearing, which sometimes incurs fertility problems; the use of permanent contraceptive methods such as vasectomies or tubal ligations by individuals who later change their mind about child-bearing;[9] and the increase in genetic counselling, which may forewarn potential parents about possible genetic defects in their offspring. In addition, the increase in single women who want to be mothers and in lesbian couples who want children without contact with a male promises to increase the demand for some techniques such as donor insemination.

Artificial reproduction technologies can be classified into two basic categories – artificial insemination and *in vitro* fertilization. A fundamental technical difference between these two technologies is that conception occurs inside a woman's body with artificial insemination, whereas conception occurs outside a woman's body in a petri dish with *in vitro* fertilization. (*In vitro* is latin for 'in glass.') For each of these two categories there are a number of different procedures, and in some cases they overlap and are used together. Each procedure must be explained and analysed individually.

Artificial Insemination

Artificial insemination is the oldest, least visible, and most widespread of what we now call artificial reproduction technologies. It is arguable, given the simplicity of the procedure, whether it is appropriate to call artificial insemination a technology since it is very simply a replacement for sexual intercourse. Semen, obtained through masturbation, is inserted into a woman's vagina at the time of her ovulation. Sometimes a small cap or diaphram-like device is used to keep the semen in place. Although most artificial insemination takes place in clinical settings, the simplicity of the procedure makes it possible for women to inseminate themselves without the assistance of physicians. Self-insemination groups, who organize the transfer of sperm from donors to women, are springing up in many countries, including Canada.[10] Since conception, gestation, and birth occur through natural processes (or as 'naturally' as pregnancies that occur through sexual intercourse), the term 'artificial' is slightly misleading. Lahey argues that a more appropriate term is 'alternative insemination.'[11]

There are three distinct types of artificial insemination: artificial insemination by husband or male partner (AIH), artificial insemination by donor (AID), and what is popularly referred to as surrogate motherhood.[12] Artificial insemination by husband is used when a man's sperm count is very low. The sperm is concentrated by centrifugal force and inserted into the woman's reproductive tract. This is believed to increase the likelihood of conception. Technically, artificial insemination by donor (AID) is the same procedure. The only difference is that the man who donates sperm is not the recipient's husband or partner.

Artificial insemination by donor is not a new procedure and has a surprisingly long history. The first recorded instance of AID occurred in the U.S.A. in 1884. When a local merchant and his wife were unable to conceive a child, they requested help from a Philadelphia physician, Dr. William Pancoast. After testing both the husband and the wife, the doctor concluded that the husband was infertile. While the woman was anaesthetized, Dr. Pancoast and some of his medical students decided to inseminate the woman with the sperm of "the best looking member of the medical class."[13] The woman became pregnant, but she was never informed about the procedure by her husband or Dr. Pancoast. Arguably, as Corea suggests, this incident was a form of rape.[14] Twenty-five years later, in 1909, a physician, presumably the former "best looking member of the medical class" wrote an article for a medical journal and exposed the whole incident. This aroused an enormous debate in medical journals about the ethics of the procedure. Opponents of the procedure argued that it was against the laws of God and nature; that the use of another man's sperm was adulterous; that the legitimacy of the child was questionable; and that the procedure was dishonest and immoral. Advocates perceived the possibility of improving the quality of the species (an early form of eugenics) and that the source of sperm was irrelevant.[15] Over one hundred years later, we have yet to resolve some of these dilemmas. The Roman Catholic Church, for example, still considers donor insemination to be adulterous. Furthermore, the issue of secrecy is unresolved and the eugenic potential of AID remains problematic.

As there is no regulation or monitoring of artificial insemination, its incidence is unknown. Estimates in the early 1980s in Canada range from 1,500 to 6,000 babies born a year through aritificial insemination by donor alone. Since these estimates were made several years ago and do not include women inseminating themselves outside of clinical settings, the numbers are probably conservative. In the U.S.A. in 1981, it was estimated that there were a total of 250,000 births through AID, with an annual rate of 10,000.[16] Donors are solicited from a variety of sources. A common assumption is that most donors are medical students or medical personnel, but my own study of participants in donor insemination indicates a broader spectrum, varying from postal workers to accountants.[17] Donors are usually paid approximately $25 for time and expenses, which has led Annas to argue that sperm donors are more accurately called sperm vendors. After all, we do not pay blood donors, and there is evidence to indicate that the quality of blood is lower in countries where blood is bought and sold.[18] (The issue of payment for reproductive capacities becomes even more problematic when we look at the practice of surrogate motherhood.) At present, there is no consensus on the number of children one donor can biologically father. The risk of individuals conceived through AID meeting and marrying a half-sibling (unknown to each other as such) increases with the number of AID children produced by each donor. One donor in my study estimated that he had donated approximately 240 times. Another issue concerning donors is the extent of screening for genetic abnomalities or sexually transmitted diseases. This issue is currently exacerbated by the existence of Acquired Immune Deficiency Disease (AIDS).[19] Curie-Cohen, Luttrell, and Shapiro, in their study of artificial insemination practice in the U.S., concluded that screening of donors for genetic diseases was inadequate, that there was little concern for the possibility of matings between half-siblings, and that record-keeping was haphazard.[20]

How the procedure is practised informs us about our attitudes toward it. Although the specifics may vary from physician to physician, the most common practice (which is supported by most legal, medical, and ethical reports) is that donors and recipients remain unknown to each other. Anonymity, it is argued, is essential to avoid emotional complications, to ensure "the stability of the family and the welfare of the child."[21] The fear that conflicting emotional ties might arise if anonymity is not protected is based on the assumption that biologically linked individuals may develop curiosity or feelings about each other which could threaten the coherence of the family unit. For example, AID offspring may become interested in the identity of their biological father, the AID mother might become curious about the man who is the biological father of her AID child, or the infertile husband may feel threatened by the sperm donor who was able to impregnate his wife when he was unable to. Consequently, the recipient(s) usually have no information about the donor, and the donor is generally not told whether a pregnancy or birth has occurred. Frequently there is an attempt to 'match' the physical characteristics of the sperm donor to the AID mother's partner (if present) or to herself. Women using self-insemination (outside of clinical settings) may choose to know or not know their donors.

This, in itself, is a momentous shift in reproductive relations. Although neither marriage nor parenthood have always been based on individual choice – our choices are socially structured in any event – neither to know nor to choose the biological father of one's child is an unprecedented social act. In the case of donor insemination, physicians are choosing the reproductive partner, the man who will be the biological 'father' of an AID mother's child.

The practice of AID is surrounded by secrecy, anonymity, and the confidentiality of the doctor-patient relationship. Most physicians advise the parents that there is no reason to tell the children or any other family members about the child's origins through AID. In this respect, AID anonymity is reminiscent of early adoption practice. Unlike adoption, however, AID anonymity holds out the possibility to heterosexual couples of 'passing' as biologically linked parents. (Single or lesbian AID mothers usually have to explain their child's origin in some way. The explanation of AID may be preferable to the assumption of a 'one night stand.') There is a collusion among participants in the procedure to protect the social father and the couple from the stigma of male infertility as well as an attempt to protect the child from feeling 'different.' However, problems arise for a variety of reasons. In some instances, the offspring of AID find out about their origins and usually not under the best of circumstances. As with most secrets, it is most likely to be divulged during periods of emotional stress and conflict such as marital crises, divorce, or death.

In the United States there is already a group called 'Donors' Offspring' who are asserting their right to know the other half of their biological heritage. This is generally a problem because there is no legal responsibility for the physician to keep records linking the donor, recipient(s), and offspring. Even when records are kept, they are defined as medical records; hence, they are the exclusive property of the physicians. No one in Canada has the right of access to their medical records. In addition, sperm donors participate in AID on the understanding that their identity will remain anonymous. There are, as yet, no laws to protect the participants in AID except in Quebec, where the child is legally considered to be affiliated with the social father, and in the Yukon, where donors are protected from possible legal suits by offspring or recipients. In 1985 the Ontario Law Reform Commission undertook a major study of the legal problems posed by artificial reproduction and proposed amendments to legislation. However, despite the fact that their study purports to protect the 'best interests of the child,' the report agrees with most other reports in viewing donor anonymity as essential to the success of the procedure. Some individuals conceived through AID may have no interest in knowing the identity of their biological father. However, given the current increase in genetic counselling, access to medical information on sperm donors may be considered important by some, and increasingly so by recipients.

Secrecy about a procedure as significant as this can be experienced as a burden.[22] Among the married AID mothers who participated in my study, those who adhered to secrecy all experienced a cost in keeping the donor insemination secret. Although generally described by respondents as 'liveable,' feelings of isolation, a desire to know about the experience of other AID recipients, and painful reminders (usually through comments about physical resemblance of their AID children) were reported. The majority, however, found that secrecy was not feasible and were faced with difficult questions about who, how, and when to tell about their use of AID. For example, one woman's husband had been institutionalized (for mental illness) shortly after the birth of their AID son. Under stress, she had quickly told friends and family that her husband was not the 'real' father. Her son (aged eight at the time of the interview) was now asking questions about this unknown, but somehow 'real' father. Understandably, she was confused and frightened by her son's interest in knowing more about his biological father and was uncertain whether any information could be obtained.

In medical literature, AID is described as a treatment for male infertility. It does not, however, cure infertility but circumvents it through the use of another man's sperm. Ironically, but not surprisingly, it is the fertile woman who becomes the patient. Despite the simplicity of the procedure, when it is practised in clinical settings it is frequently accompanied by other medical procedures to increase efficiency and the success rate. The presumably fertile woman may undergo a series of tests to ensure that she is fertile and that sperm is not 'wasted' on a woman with her own fertility problems. These tests can include, hysterosalpingograms (a procedure in which dye is injected into the fallopian tubes and uterus), endometrial biopsies, drugs to regulate her ovulation, and possibly drugs to sustain the pregnancy. Several AID mothers in my study described the testing as the worst part. In addition, the insemination itself was described as difficult. Finding a physician, arranging to take time off work, and co-ordinating the schedules of up to four individuals (donor, if fresh sperm is used; partner, if present; mother; and physician) to ovulation time was consistently reported as stressful. If pregnancy was not achieved within a few months, the pressure and stress were described as intolerable. Women who choose to inseminate themselves outside of clinical settings avoid additional medical procedures. What all AID mothers share, however, are the legal and social ambiguities arising from this shift in reproductive relations.

Surrogate Motherhood

Surrogate motherhood is a much more socially visible procedure than is donor insemination. This is partially because paternity is a less visible event than maternity. It is also a more controversial social arrangement because biological motherhood is a more complex and involved relationship than biological fatherhood. Therefore, it has captured the attention of the media more than any other artificial reproduction technology. Surrogate motherhood is generally used by couples when the wife is infertile. The husband's sperm is used to artificially inseminate a woman (the surrogate) who agrees (contractually) to surrender the child at birth and who is generally paid a fee for her 'services.' It has the potential, however, to be used by anyone willing and able to pay a woman to bear a child for them for any reason. Surrogate motherhood is actually a misnomer for this arrangement since the 'surrogate' is the biological mother of the child. Another version of surrogacy is when IVF is employed and the 'surrogate' carries a child genetically unrelated to her. Both are extremely problematic practices for the future of all women in relation to reproduction.

Innumerable questions are raised by the practice of surrogate motherhood. It is somewhat reminiscent of wet-nursing, when poor working-class women were used to provide breast milk for babies of wealthier women. By logical extension, it sets the groundwork for some women to become breeders for others – with some surrogates being more highly valued according to the current standards of beauty or intelligence. Margaret Atwood's novel *The Handmaid's Tale* provides a dystopian vision of this possibility. Indeed, as Shelagh Wilkinson argues in her chapter, Atwood, in *The Handmaid's Tale*, is describing the ultimate patriarchal control of women's sexuality and, hence, of their reproductive capacities.

Surrogate motherhood began as an organized practice in the mid-1970s.[23] So far there are no organized surrogate services in Canada. However, media reports indicate that these services exist as an underground practice, and that Canadians are participating in surrogate arrangements (both as surrogates and commissioning couples) through American organizations. In 1984, there were sixteen organizations in the U.S.A. offering surrogate services. In 1987, surrogates were paid approximately $10,000 for their 'services.' The lawyers involved in arranging these services charge approximately the same amount for co-ordinating the arrangement. However alarmed we may be at the idea of women bearing children for a fee, it is the lawyers who really profit.

In contrast to donor insemination, the recipients of surrogate services generally pick their surrogate out of a catalogue and may have contact with her during the pregnancy. (This varies according to the particular organization.) Also, in contrast to sperm donors, who are apparently difficult to find, there is an abundance of women who want to become surrogates. There has been a mixed response from the feminist community about surrogate motherhood, but, whatever the response, it has been strongly stated. On the one hand it is argued that it is exploitation, similar to prostitution or concubinage, and that the surrogate is acting as a surrogate wife to the biological father. On the other hand, some feminists have said, "Why not? Isn't it about time that women got paid for their reproductive labour?"

Any discussion of surrogate motherhood must be grounded in the facts of women's status in the labour force and their role as child-bearers and caretakers. That is, most paid work for women remains low status, low paid, and with little opportunity for advancement. The fee of $10,000 – although less than the minimum wage if calculated on an hourly basis – is still a substantial amount of money, which could alter the short-term economic circumstances of most people's lives. Additionally, some surrogates say it provides "all the magic of pregnancy" without the responsibility of rearing a child.

In order to separate themselves emotionally from the child they will surrender at birth, the surrogates describe themselves as 'vehicles' or 'vessels.' Nevertheless, there is frequently a grief reaction (termed 'transient grief') after the child is given to the contracting couple or individual. There are already self-help groups for surrogates organized to provide support after the child is surrendered. Susan Ince posed as a surrogate applicant to gain insight into the workings of one surrogate organization from the surrogate's perspective. Her documentation of the experience is chilling.[24] She reports the inadequacy of screening procedures (medical and psychological), how she was discouraged from seeking independent counsel, and, in short, the company's complete control over the surrogate.

Although it remains unclear to what extent surrogate arrangements are enforceable in Canada, contracts potentially divest the surrogate of her rights over her body throughout the terms of the contract. This includes extensive controls over diet, lifestyle, and activities. In 1987 in the U.S.A., a surrogate was charged with a misdemeanour for taking drugs during her pregnancy. The surrogate may also be required to undergo medical procedures such as ultrasound or amniocentesis to ensure a 'quality product.' If the foetus is discovered to be 'defective' she may be asked to undergo an abortion late in the pregnancy and forfeit the majority or all of her fee. There is also the question of what happens if the surrogate decides that she does not want to give up the child. In current adoption practice, the birthmother usually has a period of approximately two weeks after birth to make her final decision. There have already been several instances of surrogates changing their minds about surrendering the child after birth. In addition, since the ideal surrogate is married with children of her own (a good track record), what effect the arrangement has on other family members such as her other children, her husband (or partner), and parents is crucial, but remains unknown.

In the New Jersey case of Baby M, the issues that emerged exemplify the dilemmas inherent in surrogate arrangements. The surrogate, Mary Beth

Whitehead, *did* change her mind about giving up her baby. The contracting father, William Stern, decided to fight for custody in the courts, and he won. The trial went on for months and was reported in detail in several media. At the time of the contract, Mary Beth Whitehead was married, a full-time homemaker, and mother of two children; her husband was a sanitation worker. Despite Whitehead's initial claim that she entered the surrogacy agreement because her sister was unable to conceive and she felt "empathy for childless couples who were infertile," the $10,000 must be regarded as a substantial sum for this single-income, working-class family. The Sterns, the contracting couple, were earning an estimated $90,000 between them – William Stern as a biochemist, and Elizabeth Stern as a pediatrician.

The arrangement was transparently class-bound. It is difficult, if not impossible, to imagine wealthy women having babies, fee or no fee, for poorer couples. Beyond the obvious, however, this case was loaded with class issues that stem directly from having or not having money but are less apparent than the capacity to pay $10,000 for someone to bear a child. The Stern's money also bought them knowledge, respectability, and an excellent lawyer. They never gave a press conference without their lawyer present and throughout this highly volatile and emotional case projected a public image as controlled, sensible, and cool. In stark contrast, Mary Beth Whitehead 'spilled her guts' to the media, appeared 'hysterical,' 'out of control,' and hot-headed. She looked 'crazy' – an unfit parent. The Sterns 'looked good' – fit parents. The Sterns might well have been equally hysterical in the privacy of their home but had the 'good sense' not to damage their public image.

The outcome of the case was pre-determined in another dimension, as well. Mary Beth Whitehead cared for her baby for the first four months of her life and named her Sara. The Sterns named her Melissa. When the judge ordered temporary custody to the Sterns (four months after birth and for the duration of the extended trial) the child was named by the court Baby 'M.' Why 'M'? Why not Baby 'S' or more neutrally Baby 'J'? As Annas points out, temporary custody orders almost always become permanent orders.[25] The Sterns had this temporary decision on their side from the beginning of the trial.

As well as the custody of the child, at issue in this case was the enforceability of surrogate contracts. Mary Beth Whitehead signed a contract that required her to undergo amniocentesis at the request of William Stern (which she did against her own and her doctor's wishes), have an abortion if the foetus was deemed by the physician to be "physiologically abnormal," or determined by tests to be "genetically or congenitally abnormal." If she had conceived an "abnormal" child and aborted, she would have received $1,000. If she had refused to abort, Stern's obligation to her would have "ceased forthwith." Judge Sorkow's decision that this contract was valid and binding confirms the

North American belief that 'a deal is a deal,' even when it clearly contravenes social values and legislation against exchange of money for body parts or human beings. Trafficking in humans was outlawed with slavery. The stipulation that Whitehead, like any other surrogate, would receive her $10,000 only upon delivery of a healthy newborn eliminates any doubt about whether payment is for 'services' or for the 'product' – and the product is a child.

Finally, the manipulation of maternal ideology that accompanies the practice of surrogate motherhood and this specific legal precedent is of particular interest. The very success of the procedure is dependent on women conceiving, gestating, and relinquishing their children without any messy emotions like attachment, bonding, affection and/or love. Yet these are precisely the qualities generally required of women to be good mothers; women who leave their child(ren) wear this century's scarlet letter. One mother's virtue, in other words, is another mother's crime. Surrogate motherhood is a practice that challenges these values and it is precisely these values that were re-examined, reneged, and tossed out as outmoded and a 'mistake' in the New Jersey courtroom. Mental health experts, some of whom had written passionately in the 1950s about the importance of maternal bonding, were called to the stand to testify that maternal bonding was really non-existent or not that important after all. Whitehead was reported to play patty-cake incorrectly with her daughter and also (incorrectly) gave Sara teddy-bears rather than pots and pans to play with.

The entire trial is the stuff of a best-seller and undoubtedly several will be forthcoming. Many dramatic scenes were revealed: Whitehead handing her baby out the back window to her husband when the Sterns arrived with the police; Whitehead fleeing to Florida with her baby; the police breaking into her mother's home there and delivering the child back to the Sterns; Stern taping telephone calls from Whitehead in which she threatens to commit suicide and take her child with her; Whitehead's ten-year-old daughter begging the police to be taken away instead of her little sister. Sara/Melissa has already been passed back and forth between her biological mother and biological father and will, no matter who finally gets custody, be labelled for life as a surrogate child.[26] The 'best interests' of this child have already been violated, although her own repsonse to her origins will be unknown for years to come.

In Vitro Fertilization

In vitro fertilization (IVF) is the second major form of artificial reproduction technology. In this method, the process of conception moves firmly into the hands of physicians. IVF is distinct from artificial insemination in that it involves very sophisticated medical technology and medical expertise. The process for recipients is stressful, invasive, and financially and emotionally draining. What we do not read in the newspapers when they report with awe the birth of another IVF child is that the success rate is very low. Approximately 20 per cent of IVF clients achieve pregnancy and fewer than 10 per cent actually give birth to a child – and this may be after several attempts. The history of IVF is short, with the first successful IVF child born in Britain in 1978. Nevertheless, this is definitely a growth industry within the medical profession. There are already nine IVF clinics in Canada, all of which have very long waiting lists, which indicates both the prevalence of infertility and the desperation of couples for their own genetically linked children.

IVF was initially used when the problem of infertility was on the part of the woman, usually because her fallopian tubes were blocked. Yet, there is already evidence of the expansion of its use to couples where the male partner has a low sperm count. Williams, in a preliminary study of IVF candidates, also found IVF being used as a diagnostic tool to define further the source of infertility.[27]

The procedure is not simple. The first step is the retrieval or 'harvesting' of the eggs (note the language of animal husbandry, where all of these techniques were first developed), which involves taking drugs to stimulate egg production, daily blood tests, pelvic examinations, and ultrasound. Then usually, since drugs have been used to stimulate the ovaries to produce more than one egg at a time, between two to six eggs are removed surgically through a laparoscopy.[28] In the second step, the eggs and sperm (usually the woman's partner's sperm, but not necessarily) are joined in a culture dish, where fertilization may or may not take place. If fertilization does take place, the third step is the transfer of the fertilized eggs into the woman's uterus in the hope that implantation and pregnancy will ensue. Usually more than one fertilized egg is transferred to increase the possibilities of implantation. This is why IVF births frequently involve twins, triplets, or quintuplets. If the eggs are transferred back into the same woman from whom they were removed, the procedure is referred to as embryo replacement. If they are implanted in another woman, the procedure is referred to as embryo transfer. Fertilized eggs, technically referred to as *concepti*, may also be frozen and stored for future use by the genetic mother or another woman.

A more recent development in artificial reproduction is called surrogate embryo transfer (SET), which combines artificial insemination with a later stage of IVF, embryo transfer. Similar to IVF, SET is used with heterosexual couples when the probem of infertility is on the part of the woman. With this method, a woman, the surrogate, is artificially inseminated with the sperm of the husband. If conception takes place, the fertilized egg is flushed (also called 'lavage') from the surrogate's uterus and inserted in the uterus of the biological father's wife. At least one birth through this method has already occurred. Although it is argued that this method of artificial reproduction is less invasive than IVF, problems can occur if, for example, the lavage technique is not successful. The surrogate risks an unwanted pregnancy and the decision to abort or carry the fetus to term. If she carries the child to term, conflicts may arise about 'ownership' of the child. Other risks include pelvic infection and ectopic pregnancy, which could potentially result in sterility.[29]

There are a number of medical, legal, and governmental reports that attempt to identify and resolve the problems raised by the use of all these procedures.[30] However, we still know very little about who actually uses them and what their experience is. The legal questions alone raised by these technologies are overwhelming.[31] There is currently a wealth of legal literature that identifies these problems and attempts to resolve them. But the resolution of legal issues will not entirely settle the social problems created by the use of these procedures. Since most of these procedures are still in experimental stages, much is unknown about their short- or long-term social implications. However, at least four social issues can be identified: the further medicalization of the reproductive process; the impact on family; the commercialization of reproductive capacities; and the potential eugenic uses of artificial reproduction technologies.

Medicalization

Among the most obvious social processes involved in the use of artificial reproduction technologies is the further medicalization of women's reproductive experience. Although reproduction requires the biological contribution of both sexes, it is notable that all of these technologies involve women becoming patients, even in the case of AID, where the woman is presumably fertile. Medicalization, as explained by Wendy Mitchinson in her chapter, is the expansion of medical expertise and influence into previously non-medical arenas of society. The medicalization of women's reproductive experience is an ongoing social process. The introduction of artificial reproduction technologies is not a bold leap into Huxley's Brave New World. Rather, it is a significant furthering of already existing social trends. The medical profession is already very involved in making decisions about reproductive matters, including the choice and distribution of most birth control methods, pre- and post-natal care, and birthing, all of which increasingly involve reproductive technologies. The development of artificial reproduction technologies may be perceived as a logical (but extreme) extension of the 'planned parenthood' mentality pervasive in our culture. The further involvement of the medical profession provided by the development of artificial reproduction raises new questions about control and about responsibility and influence. In short, these new techniques may precipitate a host of hybrid social consequences, which reflect, in a heightened manner, already existing social forces.

Society has always attempted to regulate, to some extent, who has sexual intercourse with whom, where, and under what conditions. Informal and sometimes formal sanctions govern sexual behaviour according to, for example, age, race, religion, class, and marital status. Prior to the development of artificial reproduction, conception occurred through the private, intimate interaction of two individuals – sexual intercourse between a man and a woman. All of these technologies separate the act of sexual intercourse from reproduction. This in itself is not necessarily problematic. However, with the exception of self-insemination, artificial reproduction technologies as practised in clinical settings move conception out of the private and into the public realm. Members of the medical profession, in other words, are now deciding who will have access to these services and, therefore, who will or will not become parents. This is not a realm of decision-making for which physicians are trained. Furthermore, the movement of conception into the public realm raises the question of whether every individual has a fundamental right to procreate and whether this right includes access to these services. The potential for discrimination exists on grounds of class (those who can afford to pay for these services), race, marital status, and sexual preference. Most physicians will presumably attempt to uphold the cultural standard that a heterosexual couple are the best possible parents for a child.

Family Structure

The diversity of current Canadian family structures has been documented by Eichler,[32] and is discussed by Susan McDaniel in her chapter in this book. Few Canadian families conform to the presumed cultural norm of a married heterosexual couple who rear their biological offspring to adulthood. Nevertheless, this image/norm of the family persists. When we use the term 'parent,' we generally assume that the biological and social components of the role merge in one person. Exceptions to this are families formed through adoption, foster-parenthood, and step-parenting. In these situations, the term 'parent' is modified by an additional descriptor indicating some deviation from the presumed cultural normal. With adoption, for example, biological parents are referred to as birthparents and social parents are referred to as adoptive parents.

Artificial reproduction technologies make possible further diversity in family configurations. This assortment of parental roles is reflected in the current linguistic and conceptual confusion in describing these roles. With AID, fathering is split into two roles – the generally unknown biological father (sperm donor) and social or rearing father. This family configuration presumes the recipients are a heterosexual couple. If the AID mother is single there will be no rearing or social father. If she is part of a lesbian couple, then the second parent will be another mother (a co-mother) who is not biologically linked to the child.

The role of 'mother' – traditionally the genetic, uterine, and social mother of a child – is potentially fragmented into six different roles through the use of one or a combination of artificial reproduction technologies: (1) an egg donor – a woman who provides an egg but does not carry or rear the child. This is possible through egg donations with IVF and SET; (2) a uterine mother – a woman who provides the gestational environment for a child who is not hers genetically and who she will not rear; (3) an egg and uterine mother (popularly referred to as a surrogate mother) – a woman who is the biological mother but who will not rear the child. (This situation is somewhat analogous to a birth-mother who gives up a child for adoption at birth.); (4) a uterine and social mother – a woman who is the recipient of an egg donation; (5) an egg (or genetic) and social mother – a woman whose fertilized (*in vitro*) egg is carried by another woman who returns the child after birth; (6) a social mother, not genetically related to the child – the recipient of a surrogate motherhood arrangement. This situation is similar to that of adoptive or step-mothers or any woman who raises children to whom she is not genetically related. Although not all of these roles are socially unprecedented, the manner in which they are created is new. The implications of this fragmentation of women's reproductive and mothering experience have yet to be realized.

A child conceived through a combination of these procedures could potentially have five parents – two fathers and three mothers. The two fathers are the sperm donor or biological father and the social father. The three possible mothers are the egg donor, the uterine mother, and the mother who will rear the child (the social mother). Again, these family constellations are based on the presumption that recipients are a heterosexual couple. An even more complex picture of possible family forms emerges when the recipients are single or in lesbian couples.

The practice of freezing eggs, sperm, or embryos, technically referred to as 'cryopreservation', further complicates our common understanding of the process of reproduction. Conception, for example, could occur in a petri dish in Australia. The embryo could be frozen, stored, and transported to Canada where it could be implanted in a woman who (if pregnancy is successful) could give birth to a child, conceived many years earlier, to whom she has no genetic ties and whose genetic parents may no longer be alive. These possibilities alter both our temporal and geographical assumptions about the boundaries of the reproductive process, as well as the common cultural assumption that the parents of a child are genetically linked.

The rights and responsibilities of gamete (sperm or egg) donors, uterine donors, surrogates, and social parents can be legislated. Yet, the image of family as both socially and biologically linked is strong in our culture. The consequences for participants in artificial reproduction procedures, who are linked solely through biological ties, is unknown. The feelings, for example, of a woman who provides an egg, her uterus, or both (as in the case of surrogate motherhood) to create a child she may not have a social relationship with is largely unknown. Anecdotal evidence about surrogate arrangements indicates that in some instances surrogates change their mind about relinquishing their child, some develop a relationship similar to that of an aunt, and others, depending upon the policy of the surrogate agency, have no contact with the child after birth. The feelings of the infertile wife in a couple who utilize a surrogate are also largely unknown. She may feel jealous of her husband's 'surrogate wife,' who can fulfil his need for his own biological child, or the two women may develop a close relationship if the arrangement is successful. A woman who donates an egg for another woman who will carry and rear a child takes on a role somewhat similar to that of a sperm donor.[33] The potential exists, therefore, for women to 'father' children by providing only genetic material, as do men who donate sperm or biological fathers who do not assist in rearing their offspring.

Research on children who are adopted indicates that they frequently desire information about their biological heritage and may search for their biological parents in order to complete their sense of identity. Individuals conceived through one or a variety of artificial reproduction procedures that disassociate their biological and social parentage may react similarly. If accurate records are kept linking biologically related individuals, and if participants have access to these records (both of which are questionable at this time), the bureaucratic and social dilemmas this raises are formidable. Other issues include the unknown responses of other family members such as the biological grandparents of AID or surrogate children (the parents of the donor or surrogate), aunts, uncles, and siblings of children in both the recipient and donor families.

The success of families created through artificial reproduction rests, to some extent, not on the technologies themselves but on our capacity as a society to redefine what constitutes family. In concert with other changes in family forms, artificial reproduction technologies challenge the sanctity and increasingly mythological image of the biologically linked nuclear family as normative. If the emphasis on the blood-tied nuclear family persists, it is likely that a preference will develop for technologies that preserve the genetic links of parents and offspring wherever possible. This could result in the use of more expensive and invasive methods over simpler less costly procedures. For example, in the case of a male with a low sperm count, IVF may be used instead of AID to preserve the genetic link, and when donor gametes are employed, they will likely be used on an anonymous basis. The issues are complex and volatile; the consequences are unknown.

Commercialization

Sperm donors are paid approximately $25 each ejaculate, surrogate mothers are paid $10,000, and surrogates participating in SET are paid approximately $250. Putting a price tag on reproductive capacities has profound social implications. The children created through these technologies will eventually become adults and have to come to terms with their origins. They may feel special and particularly wanted or they may feel like a commodity, bought and sold. In either case, their creation through a commercial transaction is likely to affect their identity and is potentially stigmatizing. Surrogate motherhood has been described as another version of prostitution – the expansion of exploitation of women's sexuality into the reproductive realm.

There are partial social precedents for payment in relation to body parts, organs, and blood. Furthermore, despite legal restriction, baby-selling does exist. Insurance companies establish a 'price' for the loss of an arm, leg, or other body parts. However, all of these analogies are limited since there is a crucial distinction between the maintenance of a life already in existence, the loss of a body part, the use of women's bodies for sexual services, and the payment for reproductive capacities involved in the creation of new life. The result of the latter is a new human being accompanied by new social roles for family members and, consequently, new social responsibilities. Commercialization of reproductive capacities, therefore, although not totally unprecendented, is similar to the issue of medicalization. It is the significant furthering of already existing social trends.

In the U.S.A., a private company is attempting to patent the technology for SET. In a television program ("Hi-Tech Babies," Nova, November 4, 1986), the company's directors reported that egg donors, essential for the success of the company, are available in "cost-effective abundance." The very language used by these entrepreneurs signals a change in our relationship to the reproductive process. Commodification entails a process of evaluating and assessing a human activity or the product of a human activity according to current market forces. It also disguises the presence of the human being involved in the labour required to produce the product. Treating reproductive capacities as commodities, commercializes and brings market values and processes into a realm that has previously been immune to these influences.

Eugenics

The final area of concern is the issue of eugenics. Eugenics is the practice of selective breeding intended to 'perfect' the human species. It is generally distinguished by two different methods–positive eugenics and negative eugenics. Positive eugenics is the attempt to increase the number of children born with 'good' characteristics; negative eugenics is the attempt to reduce the number of children born with 'bad' characteristics. Although a useful dichotomy, an obvious problem arises in deciding what is valued as good or bad, and who is to make these decisions.

At first glance, negative eugenics would seem to be a worthwhile project. Increasingly, genetic screening can detect carriers of diseases such as Huntingdon's chorea, muscular dystrophy, and cystic fibrosis. Decreasing the incidence of these agonizing diseases would seem socially advantageous; however, grey areas abound. Activists in the rights for the disabled movement have pointed out that screening or aborting for 'defects' further devalues individuals considered by society to be 'defective.'[34] One particularly contentious area is the use of pre-natal diagnostic techniques such as ultrasound, chorionic biopsy, or amniocentesis to identify the sex of a foetus, followed by an abortion if the sex does not accord with parental preference. Roggencamp documents the incidence of this phenomenon in India where female foetuses are overwhelmingly aborted.[35]

Although the extent of this practice is unknown in western industrialized countries, we can speculate that wherever males are valued more highly than females, female foetuses would be aborted more frequently. Research on parental sex preferences overwhelmingly indicates a preference for male over female offspring, a view held more frequently by men than women, and particularly in relation to first-borns.[36] The desire for a child of a particular sex is in itself sexist and could potentially institutionalize sexism at a new level, since, for example, first-borns are known to be high achievers. Other concerns include alterations in the sex ratio with fewer females born than males. The consequences of this possibility can only be speculated about and include feminist concerns about gynocide.[37]

Pre-conception sex selection techniques are an example of 'positive' eugenics. These are less invasive methods than post-conception techniques and usually involve theories about the timing of intercourse with ovulation or the separation of X and Y bearing spermatozoa.[38] What was once the substance of folklore is increasingly the subject of scientific study. A U.S. company is marketing a package called "GenderChoice," available over the counter in drugstores, which the manufacturer claims has an 85 per cent success rate. The product relies on the position of sexual intercourse and the proximity of conception to a woman's ovulation time to predict the sex of a child.

The most extreme example of positive eugenics is the existence of a Nobel Prize Winner sperm bank in the U.S.A. from which women or couples of 'superior' intellectual capacities can order sperm. Surrogates and gamete donors may be chosen for socially valued traits perceived as genetically inherited. The underlying assumption is that genetics are the key factor in determining personality traits or capacities such as intelligence, athletic abilities, or musical talents. Australian IVF physicians are already claiming that children conceived through IVF are superior to those conceived 'normally.'[39] Statements such as these neglect to consider the obvious influence of environment–including the particular treatment and care these desperately wanted children most likely receive from their parents.

The twentieth century has seen the rise of experts advising women how to rear perfect children.[40] Artificial reproduction technologies provide the opportunity for a different level of 'quality control' in the parenting process. As well, pre-natal diagnostic techniques provide information about a foetus previously unavailable before birth. A woman in her fifth month of pregnancy may have to choose on the basis of this knowledge whether to have an abortion or carry to term and give birth to a child she knows will be disabled – in a society that devalues the 'imperfect.' This instance of choice posed by the new reproductive technologies is a burden that will be carried largely by women.

The commercialization of reproductive capacities is inextricably linked to eugenic issues. Through commercialization, the child becomes a commodity, the recipient parents become consumers, and gamete donors and surrogates become suppliers. Damaged or defective 'products'–babies who are not 'perfect'–will likely be unacceptable to the consumer. In a surrogate arrangement in 1981, a handicapped child was rejected by both the contracting (presumably) biological father and by the surrogate. Eventually, a paternity test proved the surrogate's husband to be the biological father (this destroyed any validity the contract might have had), and the surrogate and her husband agreed to keep the child. Despite the inevitable increase in the use of reproductive technologies to prevent the likelihood of this situation, other problematic instances are bound to arise in the future.

Social policy already lags far behind these rapidly developing medical advances. As the technologies become more sophisticated, the social dilemmas posed by them become more complex. The crucial question is: Who is going to control these technologies and under what conditions? Medical control over these technologies is already well established and is solidified by recommendations in government reports. Public debate on these issues, at least in Canada, has been quite limited.[41] Since it is unlikely a technology will be withdrawn once it is introduced, all of these technologies are likely here to stay, at least until further technological developments replace them. The project for feminists is neither to embrace nor reject their use. The first crucial step is to monitor and assess the impact of their implementation and lobby for the least abusive practices. In cultivating a critical approach to new reproductive technologies, an important point to consider is that already scarce health resources are being utilized to develop these technologies. As a result, it appears that fewer health resources are being channelled into research concerning the causes of infertility. As with any new social process or technology, we are granted an opportunity to rethink and reorganize some of our most deeply embedded assumptions. Consequently, the alterations in our traditional assumptions about parenting facilitated by artificial reproduction may have a hidden blessing. It has the potential to make us reflect and further our understanding about the meaning and task of parenting. Parenting is, after all, one of the key influences in the reproduction of gender relations over the generations.

Rona Achilles

SUGGESTED READINGS

Arditti, Rita, Renate Duelli Klein, and Shelley Minden, eds., *Test Tube Women: What Future for Motherhood?* London: Routledge & Kegan Paul, 1984.

Bennett, Neil G., ed., *Sex Selection of Children*. New York: Academic Press, 1983.

Corea, Gena, *The Mother Machine*. New York: Harper & Row, 1985.

Corea, Gena, Renate Duelli Klein, Jalna Halma, Helen B. Holmes, Betty Hoskins, Madhu Kishwar, Janice Raymond, Robyn Rowland, and Roberta Steinbacher, *Man-Made Woman: How New Reproductive Technologies Affect Women*. Bloomington: Indiana University Press, 1987.

Holmes, Helen B., Betty Hoskins, and Michael Gross, *The Custom-Made Child? Women-Centered Perspectives*. New Jersey: Humana Press, 1981.

McLaren, Angus, and Arlene Tigar McLaren, *The Bedroom and the State: The Changing Practices and Politics of Contraception and Abortion in Canada, 1880–1980*. Toronto: McClelland and Stewart, 1986.

Roberts, Helen, ed., *Women, Health, and Reproduction*. London: Routledge & Kegan Paul, 1981.

Rothman, Barbara Katz, *The Tentative Pregnancy*. New York: Penguin, 1987.

"Women and Reproduction." A special issue of *Canadian Journal of Women and the Law* 1, no. 2, (1986).

Endnotes

Introduction

1. Frank Denton and Sylvia Ostry, *Historical Estimates of the Candian Labour Force*, 1961 Census Monograph, (Ottawa: Dominion Bureau of Statistics, 1967).
2. Marjorie MacMurchy, *The Woman–Bless Her*, (Toronto: S.B. Gundy, 1916), 20.
3. Canada, Dominion Bureau of Statistics, *Women Who Work, Part 2*, December 1986, 21.
4. Michele Barrett, *Women's Oppression Today: Problems in Marxist Feminist Analysis*, (London: Verso, 1980).

Chapter One

1. Juliet Mitchell, ''Reflections on Twenty Years of Feminism,'' in Juliet Mitchell and Ann Oakley, eds., *What Is Feminism?* (New York: Pantheon Books, 1986), 48.
2. These are the four constant structures of women's oppression designated by Juliet Mitchell in the title essay of her *Women: The Longest Revolution*, first published in 1968. (London, Virago Press, 1984).
3. Marilyn Frye, *The Politics of Reality: Essays in Feminist Theory*, (Trumansburg, N.Y.: The Crossing Press, 1983), 4–5.
4. Nancy Cott draws attention to this paradox in her ''Feminist Theory and Feminist Movements: The Past Before Us,'' in *What Is Feminism?*, 49.
5. *See*, for example, Anne Ferguson, ''Motherhood and Sexuality: Some Feminist Questions,'' and Jana Sawicki, ''Foucault and Feminism: Toward a Politics of Difference,'' both in *Hypatia: A Journal of Feminist Philosophy* 1, no. 2, (1986).
6. From Adrienne Rich's remarks at the Columbia University Seminar on Women and Society, 1976. Quoted by Hester Eisenstein in her *Contemporary Feminist Thought*, (London: Allen & Unwin, 1984), 74.
7. Joan Kelly observes: ''It has been a strength of patriarchy in all its historical forms to assimilate itself so perfectly to socioeconomic, political and cultural structures as to be virtually invisible.'' In Joan Kelly, *Women, History, and Theory*, (Chicago: University of Chicago Press, 1984), 61.

8. *See*: Joan Kelly, "The Doubled Vision of Feminist Theory," in *ibid.*
9. Aristotle, *Politics,* Benjamin Jowett, trans., in Richard McKeon, ed., *The Basic Works of Aristotle*, (New York: Random House, 1941), 1254b.
10. Aristotle, *De Generatione Animalium,* Arthur Platt, trans., in *ibid.*
11. *See*: Judith Hicks Stiehm, "The Unit of Political Analysis: Our Aristotelian Hangover," in Sandra Harding and Merrill Hintikka, eds., *Discovering Reality*, (Dordrecht: Reidel, 1983), 31–43.
12. Plato, *Republic,* Paul Shorey, trans., in Edith Hamilton and Huntington Cairns, eds., *The Collected Dialogues of Plato*, (Princeton, N.J.: Princeton University Press, Bollingen Series, 1961), 455 d–e.
13. *Ibid.* 456b.
14. *Ibid.* 460b.
15. J.S. Mill, "The Subjection of Women," in Alice Rossi, ed., John Stuart Mill and Harriet Taylor Mill, *Essays on Sex Equality*, (Chicago: University of Chicago Press, 1970), 125.
16. *See*: "Early Essays on Marriage and Divorce," (1832) by John Stuart Mill and Harriet Taylor Mill, in *ibid.*
17. Karl Marx, *The Economic and Philosophic Manuscripts of 1844*, (New York: International Publishers, 1964), 96.
18. Frederick Engels, *The Origin of the Family, Private Property and the State* (New York: International Publishers, 1972), 65.
19. For an extended account of the contribution of women to the early socialist movement, *see*: M.J. Boxer and J.H. Quataert, eds., *Socialist Women: European Socialist Feminism in the Nineteenth and Early Twentieth Centuries*, (New York: Elsevier, 1978).
20. Sigmund Freud, *Sexuality and the Psychology of Love*, Phillip Reiff, ed., (New York: Collier Books, 1963), 181.
21. Kate Millet, *Sexual Politics*, (New York: Avon Books, 1971), 187.
22. Noteworthy among texts that approach this task are: Juliet Mitchell, *Psychoanalysis and Feminism*, (New York: Pantheon Books, 1974); Dorothy Smith and David Smith, *Women Look at Psychiatry*, (Vancouver: Press Gang Publishers, 1975); Nancy Chodorow, *The Reproducing of Mothering: Psychoanalysis and the Sociology of Gender*, (Berkeley: University of California Press, 1978); P. Susan Penfold and Gillian Walker, *Women and the Psychiatric Paradox*, (Montreal: Eden Press, 1983); and Hannah Lerman, *A Mote in Freud's Eye: From Psychoanalysis to the Psychology of Women*, (New York: Springer, 1986).
23. Simone de Beauvoir, *The Second Sex*, H.M. Parshley, trans., (New York: Knopf, 1953), 301.
24. *Ibid.*, xviii–xix.
25. Simone de Beauvoir, *Simone de Beauvoir Today: Conversations with Alice Schwartzer, 1972–1982*, (London: Chatto & Windus, 1984), 32.
26. Betty Friedan, *The Feminine Mystique*, (New York: Dell, 1963), 317.
27. *See*, for example, Marion Tapper, "Can a Feminist be a Liberal?" *Australasian Journal of Philosophy.* Supplement to Volume 64 (June 1986). These last points are

paraphrased from Tapper's paper, 47. *See also*: Lorraine Code "Simple Equality Is Not Enough," in the same volume.

28. Some theorists distinguish between Marxist and socialist feminism, arguing that Marxist concerns are more purely economic, whereas socialist feminists are concerned to effect more wide-ranging social reforms. But Josephine Donovan, for example, claims that "contemporary 'Marxist feminism' is more appropriately called 'socialist feminism' to point up that it no longer represents an undiluted Marxism but a Marxism modified . . . by radical feminism." In Josephine Donovan, *Feminist Theory*, (New York: Frederick Ungar, 1985), 66. The term 'socialist feminism' will be used in the rest of this chapter.

29. *See*: Sheila Rowbotham, *Woman's Consciousness, Man's World*, (Harmondsworth: Penguin Books, 1973); and Zillah Eisenstein, "Developing a Theory of Capitalist Patriarchy and Socialist Feminism," in Z. Eisenstein, ed., *Capitalist Patriarchy and the Case for Socialist Feminism*, (New York: Monthly Review Press, 1979).

30. *See*: Susan Sontag, "The Third World of Women," *Partisan Review* 60, (1973).

31. *Cf*: Michele Barrett, *Women's Oppression Today: Problems in Marxist Feminist Analysis*, (London: Verso, 1980).

32. Gayle Rubin, "The Traffic in Women: Notes on the 'Political Economy' of Sex," in R. Reiter, ed., *Towards an Anthropology of Women*, (New York: Monthly Review Press, 1975), 163.

33. This thesis is advanced, for example, by Iris Young in "Beyond the Unhappy Marriage: A Critique of the Dual Systems Theory," in Lynda Sargeant, ed., *Women and Revolution: A Discussion of the Unhappy Marriage of Marxism and Feminism*, (Boston: South End Press, 1981).

34. *See*: Adrienne Rich, "Compulsory Heterosexuality and Lesbian Existence," in A. Snitow, C. Stansell, and S. Thompson, eds., *Desire: The Politics of Sexuality*, (London: Virago Press, 1983), for a superb and extensive radical-feminist analysis of the political implications of compulsory heterosexuality.

35. Heidi Hartmann, "The Unhappy Marriage of Marxism and Feminism," in *Women and Revolution*, 28.

36. Robin Morgan, *Going Too Far: The Personal Chronicle of a Feminist*, (New York: Random House, 1977), 9.

37. There have been significant changes in the workings of this ideology in Canada in the 1980s, largely in response to feminist political pressure. (*See*: Sandra Burt's chapter in this book.) But feminists in Britain continue to express concern at the reluctance of the law to intervene in domestic disputes. *See*: Katherine O'Donovan, *Sexual Divisions in Law*, (London: Weidenfeld & Nicholson, 1985).

38. Mary Daly, *Gyn/Ecology: The Metaethics of Radical Feminism*, (Boston: Beacon Press, 1978), 173.

39. *Ibid.*, 53.

40. *Ibid.*, 1.

41. *Ibid.*, 34.

42. Shulamith Firestone, *The Dialetic of Sex: The Case for Feminist Revolution*, (New York: Bantam Books, 1970).

43. Adrienne Rich, *Of Woman Born: Motherhood As Experience and Institution*, (New York: Bantam Books, 1981), 58.
44. *Ibid.*, 285.
45. Mary O'Brien, *The Politics of Reproduction*, (London: Routledge & Kegan Paul, 1981), 58.
46. *Ibid.*
47. Rich, "Compulsory Heterosexuality," 217.
48. *Ibid.*, 227ff.
49. Perhaps the most accessible of Kristeva's many works to those unfamiliar with the French tradition is *About Chinese Women*, (London: Boyars, 1977).
50. Toril Moi, *Sexual/Textual Politics*, (New York: Methuen, 1985), 160.
51. Julia Kristeva, "Women's Time," *Signs: A Journal of Women in Culture and Society* 7, no. 1 (1981), 21.
52. Hélène Cixous, "The Laugh of the Medusa," in Elaine Marks and Isabelle de Courtivron, eds., *New French Feminisms*, (New York: Schocken Books, 1981), 245.
53. *Ibid.*, 254.
54. Irigaray's two most frequently cited works, *Speculum de l'autre femme* and *Ce sexe qui n'en est pas un*, have been translated into English and published by Cornell University Press.
55. Marks and de Courtivron, eds., *New French Feminisms*, 35. The tools referred to here are those developed by such French structuralists as Jacques Derrida and Michel Foucault, but one might take the reference to apply equally to the entire French intellectual tradition, with its emphasis upon reason and the suppression of the body.
56. *See*: Bell Hooks, *Ain't I A Woman? Black Women and Feminisms*, (Boston: South End Press, 1981), 137ff.
57. Cott, "Feminist Theory," 59.
58. These are Zillah Eisenstein's examples in *The Radical Future of Liberal Feminism*, (New York: Longmans, 1981), 231.
59. Explicit requirements of this sort are less commonly evident than they were prior to contemporary feminist challenges. In 1960, for example, a woman scientist in the United States was told in the early days of her employment, "If you become pregnant, you'll get fired." She reports, "So I got pregnant, and they never knew it. I just wore a lab coat one size larger . . . I came back two days after the baby was born, and I never told a soul there that I had had a child." Vivian Gornick, *Women in Science*, (New York: Simon & Schuster, 1983), 102.
60. Carole Gilligan, *In A Different Voice: Psychological Theory and Women's Development*, (Cambridge, Mass: Harvard University Press, 1982).
61. *See*: Genevieve Lloyd, *The Man of Reason*, (Minneapolis: University of Minnesota Press, 1984). Recent feminist work in philosophy of science endeavours to explain the invisibility of women and 'the feminine' in scientific practice, with its ideals of rational objectivity. *See*: Ursula Franklin, "Will Women Change Technology or Will Technology Change Women?" *CRIAW Papers* (1985); and Sandra Harding, *The Science Question in Feminism*, (Ithaca: Cornell University Press, 1986).
62. In the British newspaper, *The Guardian*, April 1982.

63. This is Mary O'Brien's term, introduced in *The Politics of Reproduction*, and now a widely accepted term in feminist discourse.

64. Work on this project has been made possible by a Strategic Grant from the Social Sciences and Humanities Research Council of Canada, and by a Visiting Research Fellowship from the Humanities Research Centre at the Australian National University in Canberra. I am indebted to Joan Gibson for her perceptive comments on an earlier draft of this chapter.

Chapter Two

1. *Farmers Journal*, 16 July 1828, 4.
2. Veronica Strong-Boag and Anita Clair Fellman, eds., *Rethinking Canada: The Promise of Women's History*, (Toronto: Copp-Clark Pitman, 1986), 2.
3. A term used by Margaret Conrad in her work on Maritime women's diaries, "Sundays Always Make Me Think of Home," in *Rethinking Canada*, 67–81, and "Recording Angels: The Private Chronicles of Women from the Maritime Provinces of Canada, 1750–1950," in Alison Prentice and Susan Mann Trofimenkoff, eds., *The Neglected Majority II*, (Toronto: McClelland and Stewart, 1985), 41–60. Conrad wrote of that separate women's world, with its distinct experiences, values, and identity.
4. For a brief overview of women in New France, *see*, among others, Jan Noel, "Les Femmes Favorisées," in *Rethinking Canada*, 23–44, and Lilianne Plamondon, "A Business Woman in New France, Marie-Ann Barbel, The Widow Fornel," in *Rethinking Canada*, 45–58.
5. Isabel Foule-Delbose, "Women of Three Rivers: 1651–63," in Susan Mann Trofimenkoff and Alison Prentice, eds., *The Neglected Majority I* (Toronto: McClelland and Stewart, 1977), 14–26. She notes that widows remarried within an average of eight months after bereavement. *See also*: Noel, "Les Femmes Favorisées," 25, 33, for examples of remarriage and the legal provisions that accommodated and encouraged this.
6. *See*: Noel. *See also*: Philippe Aries, *Centures of Childhood*, (New York: Random House, 1962); Peter Laslett, *The World We Have Lost*, (Cambridge: Methuen, 2nd. ed. 1979).
7. Noel, "Les Femmes Favorisées," 39.
8. *See*: Noel. *See also*: Plamandon, " A Business Woman in New France," in which the extensive business activities of Marie-Ann Barbel after her husband's death in 1645 are described. *See also*: Louise Duchêne, *Habitants et marchands de Montréal au XVII siècle*, (Montreal: Plon, 1974).
9. Noel, "Les Femmes Favorisées," 32.
10. L. Franquet, *Voyages et mémoires sur le Canada*, quoted in Noel, "Les Femmes Favorisées," 33.
11. For discussion of the legal position of women in New France, *see*: Plamondon, "A Business Woman in New France"; Noel, "Les Femmes Favorisées"; Foulche-Delbose, "Women of Three Rivers."
12. Mary Ryan, *Cradle of the Middle Class: The Family in Oneida County, New*

York, 1790–1865, (New York: Cambridge University Press, 1981), 19, 24. Unfortunately, the history of women in early British North America is woefully incomplete. *See*, however, Marion Fowler, *The Embroidered Tent: Five Gentlewomen in Early Canada*, (Toronto: House of Anansi, 1982); Beth Light and Alison Prentice, *Pioneer and Gentlewomen of British North America 1713–1867*, (Toronto: New Hogtown Press, 1980); Kathleeen McKenna, "Options for Elite Women in Early Upper Canadian Society," paper given at the CHA (Winnipeg, 1986); Naomi Griffiths, *Penelope's Web: Some Perceptions in European and Canadian Society*, (Toronto: Oxford University Press, 1976).

13. Ryan, *The Cradle of the Middle Class*, 20.

14. Barbara Welter, "The Cult of True Womanhood," *American Quarterly* 18, (1966): 150–174.

15. For biographical material on these and other women, *see*: McKenna, "Options for Elite Women"; Fowler, *The Embroidered Tent*; Patrick Brode, *The Bone and the Sinew*, (Toronto: University of Toronto Press, 1986); Kathryn McKenna, "Anne Powell and the Early York Elite," in S.F. Wise, *et al.*, eds., *None was Ever Better*, (Cornwall: Ontario Historical Society, 1984), 31–43.

16. Peter Russell, "Attitudes Towards Social Mobility in Upper Canada," Ph.D. thesis, Carleton University, 1981, 315.

17. McKenna, "Options for Elite Women," 23, 21.

18. This comes from preliminary work I have done with Upper Canadian newspapers 1793–1830. *See also*: Leo Johnson, "The Political Economy of Ontario Women in the Nineteenth Century," in Janice Acton, *et al.*, eds., *Women at Work: Ontario 1850–1930*, (Toronto: Women's Educational Press, 1974); Russell, "Attitudes Towards Social Mobility"; Jane Errington, "The Softer Sex: Rhetoric and Reality of Women's Experiences in Early Upper Canada," unpublished working paper, 1986.

19. Alison Prentice, "The Femininization of Teaching," in *Neglected Majority I*, 52.

20. *Ibid.*, 65.

21. Johnson, "Political Economy of Ontario Women."

22. *See*: P. Malcolmson, "The Poor in Kingston, 1815–1857," in G. Tulchinsky, ed., *To Preserve and Defend*, (Montreal: McGill-Queen's University Press, 1976); S. Houston, "The Impetus to Reform," Ph.D. thesis, University of Toronto, 1974.

23. Sylvia Van Kirk, "The Role of Native Women in the Fur Trade Society of Western Canada, 1670–1830," in *Rethinking Canada*, 61. Van Kirk notes that Indian women made the moccasins worn by all in the West at the time, ensured an adequate supply of pemmican, and were frequently called upon to assist in paddling and steering traders' and explorers' canoes. For a full discussion of the fur trade society, *see*: Van Kirk, *Many Tender Ties: Women in Fur Trade Society*, (Winnipeg: Watson and Dwyer, 1980).

24. Beth Light and Joy Parr, eds., *Canadian Women on the Move 1867–1920*, (Toronto: New Hogtown Press and OISE, 1983), 3. *See also*: Sara Brooks Sundberg, "Farm Women on the Canadian Prairies Frontier," in *Rethinking Canada*; The

Corrective Collective, *Never Done: Three Centuries of Women's Work*, (Toronto: Women's Educational Press, 1974); Linda Rasmussen, *et al.*, eds., *A Harvest Yet to Reap: A History of Prairie Women*, (Toronto: Women's Educational Press, 1976).

25. Marjorie Cohen, "The Decline of Women in Canadian Dairying," in *The Neglected Majority II*, 73.

26. For a brief overview of the impact of industrialization on Canadian society and its women, *see*, among others, Light and Parr, *Canadian Women on the Move*; Acton *et al.*, *Women at Work*; Wayne Roberts, *Honest Womanhood: Feminism, Femininity and Class Consciousness Among Toronto Working Women*, (Toronto, New Hogtown Press, 1976).

27. Alice Klein and Wayne Roberts, "Beseiged Innocence: The 'Problem' and Problems of Working Women," in *Women at Work*; S.M. Trofimenkoff, "One Hundred and Two Muffled Voices," and Graham S. Lowe, "Women, Work and the Office: The Feminization of Clerical Occupations in Canada 1901–1931," in *Rethinking Canada*; Pat Armstrong and Hugh Armstrong, *The Double Ghetto*, (Toronto: McClelland and Stewart, 1984).

28. Joan Sangster, "The 1907 Bell Telephone Strike: Organizing Women Workers," in *Rethinking Canada*; Klein and Roberts, "Besieged Innocence" in *Women at Work*; Roberts, *Honest Womanhood*, Gail Cuthbert Brandt, "Weaving It Together: Life Cycle and the Industrial Experience of Female Cotton Workers," in *The Neglected Majority II*.

29. Veronica Strong-Boag, "Canada's Women Doctors," in Linda Kealey, ed., *A Not Unreasonable Claim: Women and Reform in Canada, 1880s to 1920s*, (Toronto: Women's Educational Press, 1979).

30. Judi Coburn, "I See and am Silent: A Short History of Nursing in Ontario," in *Women at Work*.

31. The progressive age, as it is known in the United States, is ably described in Robert Weibe, *The Search for Order*, (New York: Hill Wang, 1967). For the Canadian context, *see*: Robert Craig Brown and Ramsay Cook, *Canada 1896–1921*, (Toronto: McClelland and Stewart, 1974), and the introduction to *A Not Unreasonable Claim*.

32. Veronica Strong-Boag, "Setting the Stage: National Organization and the Women's Movement in the Late 19th Century," in *The Neglected Majority I*, 88.

33. *Ibid.*, 92.

34. Marie Lavigne, Yolande Pinard, and Jennifer Stoddart, "The Fédération Nationale Saint-John-Baptiste and the Women's Movement in Quebec," in *A Not Unreasonable Claim*.

35. Strong-Boag, "Setting the Stage"; Wendy Michinson, "The WVTU, 'For God, Home and Nationhood': A Study of Nineteenth Century Feminism," in *A Not Unreasonable Claim*.

36. Kealey, ed., *A Not Unreasonable Claim*, 8.

37. *Ibid.*

38. Social feminism in this context is sometimes also referred to as "maternal feminism." *See*: Kealey, *A Not Unreasonable Claim*, 7–8.

39. Susan Mann Trofimenkoff, "Feminism, Nationalism and the Clerical Defence," in *Rethinking Canada*, 136; Lavigne, *et al.*, "The Fédération"; Trofimenkoff, "Henri Bourassa and 'The Woman Question'," in *A Not Unreasonable Claim*, 79.
40. Emily Stowe to Premier of Ontario, 1889, quoted in Wayne Roberts, "Rocking the Cradle for the World: The New Woman and Maternal Feminism," in *A Not Unreasonable Claim*, 20.
41. Strong-Boag, "Setting the stage," 101–103.
42. Carol Bacchi, "Divided Allegiance: The Response of Farm and Labour Women to Suffrage," in *A Not Unreasonable Claim*, 106–107.
43. Roberts, "Rocking the Cradle for the World"; Klein and Roberts, "Beseiged Innocence"; Lori Rotenberg, "The Wayward Worker: Toronto's Prostitutes at the Turn of the Century," in *Women at Work*; Trofimenkoff, "One Hundred and Two Muffled Voices"; Christine Simmons, " 'Helping the Poor Sister': The Women of the Jost Mission," in *Rethinking Canada*; Lavigne, *et al.*, "The Fédération"; Mitchinson, "The WCTU."
44. For the most comprehensive account of the fight for the vote, *see*: Catherine Clevedon, *The Woman Suffrage Movement in Canada*, (Toronto: University of Toronto Press, 2nd. ed. 1974).
45. *See*, for example, Roberts, "Rocking the Cradle," 40–41; Strong-Boag, " 'Ever a Canadian': Nellie McClung, First Wave Feminist," in *Rethinking Canada*; Bacchi, "Divided Allegiances"; Lavigne, *et al.*, "The Fédération."
46. Bacchi, "Divided Allegiances," 102.
47. Michinson, "The WCTU," 159.
48. Strong-Boag, " 'Ever a Canadian,' " 182.
49. Lavigne, "The Fédération," 80.
50. Ceta Ramkhalawansingh, "Women During the Great War," in *Women at Work*.
51. Veronica Strong-Boag, "The Girl of the New Day," in Michael Cross and Gregory Kealey, eds., *Readings in Canadian Social History 4*, (Toronto: McClelland and Stewart, 1985), 169.
52. *Ibid.*; Marilyn Barber, "The Women Ontario Welcomed," in *The Neglected Majority II*; Genevieve Leslie, "Domestic Service in Canada, 1880–1890," in *Women at Work*; Barbara Roberts, "A Work of Empire: Canadian Reformers and British Female Immigration," in *A Not Unreasonable Claim*.
53. Mary Vipond, "The Image of Women in Mass Circulation Magazines in the 1920s," in *The Neglected Majority I*; *see also*: Strong-Boag, "Girl of the New Day."
54. Sylvia Bashevkin, "Independence versus Partisanship: Dilemma in the Political History of Women in English Canada," in *Rethinking Canada*, 254.
55. Roberts, "Rocking the Cradle," 43–44.
56. Bashevkin, " Independence versus Partisanship," 262.
57. Catherine MacLeod, "Women in Production," in *Women at Work*; Anne Woywitka, "A Pioneering Woman in the Labour Movement," in *Rethinking Canada*; Strong-Boag, "The Girl of the New Day"; Gail Cuthbert Brandt, "Weaving It Together."
58. For an account of women in World War II, *see*: Ruth Roach Pierson, "*They're*

Still Women After All'' The Second World War and Canadian Womanhood, (Toronto: McClelland and Stewart, 1986).

59. Pierson, ''Women's Emancipation and the Recruitment of Women into the Labour Force,'' in *The Neglected Majority I*, 144.

60. Bashevkin, ''Independence versus Partisanship,'' 263.

61. Julie White, ''It's Good, It's Bad: The Contradictions,'' in *Rethinking Canada*, 226.

62. Bashevkin, ''Independence versus Partisanship,'' 264.

Chapter Three

1. *Weekend Magazine*, May 3, 1979; ''Womanpoll: Women's Roles and Rights,'' *Chatelaine*, May 1986, 42; Christy McLaren, ''Environment Tops Free Trade in Poll of Canadians,'' *The Globe and Mail*, January 15, 1987.

2. ''Most Say Hubby Should Help at Home,'' *The Toronto Star*, March 10, 1986.

3. Betty Lehan Harragan, *Games Mother Never Taught You: Corporate Gamesmanship for Women*, (New York: Warner Books, 1977); Isabel Bassett, *The Bassett Report: Career Success and Canadian Women*, (Toronto: Collins Publishers, 1985), 282, 288.

4. Indian Rights for Indian Women, Canadian Congress of Black Women, Concerned Farm Women, and Society of Spouses of Military Personnel are a few examples of such groups, which represent most ethnic and occupational groupings of women.

5. The acronyms stand for Realistic, Equal, and Active for Life, and for Alberta Federation of Women United for the Family.

6. Kay Macpherson and Meg Sears, ''The Voice of Women: A History,'' in Gwen Matheson, ed., *Women in the Canadian Mosaic*, (Toronto: Peter Martin, 1976), 71–89; Peggy Hope-Smith and Muriel Duckworth, ''Voice of Women Dialogue,'' *Atlantis* 6, no. 2, (1981): 168–77; Kay Macpherson, ''Persistent Voices: Twenty-Five Years with Voice of Women,'' *Atlantis* 12, no. 2, (1987): 168–76; Candace Loewen, ''Mike Hears Voices: Voice of Women and Lester Pearson, 1960–63,'' *Atlantis* 12, no. 2, (1987): 46–48.

7. Collectif Clio, *L'histoire des femmes au Québec depuis quatre siècles*, (Montreal: Editions Quinze, 1982), 453–58; Azilda Marchand, ''Les femmes au foyer: Hier et demain,'' *Canadian Woman Studies/ Les cahiers de la femme* 2, no. 2, (1980): 15–16.

8. *Chatelaine*, July 1966.

9. Doris Anderson, ''Women's Magazines in the 1970s,'' *Canadian Women's Studies/Les cahiers de la femme* 2, no. 2, (1980): 15–16.

10. Most important among these first-wave groups were the Canadian Federation of Business and Professional Women's Clubs; the Federation of Women's Teachers' Associations of Ontario; the National Council of Jewish Women; the National Council of Women of Canada; the Imperial Order Daughters of the Empire; the WCTU; the YWCA; and the Federated Women's Institutes. *See*: Cerise Morris, '' 'Determination and Thoroughness': The Movement for a Royal Commission on the Status of Women in Canada,'' *Atlantis* 5, no. 2, (1980): 1–21.

11. "Women's March May Back Call for Rights Probe," *The Globe and Mail*, January 5, 1967.
12. Florence Bird, *Anne Francis: An Autobiography*, (Toronto: Clarke Irwin, 1974), 4.
13. There were also two men on the Commission, demographer Jacques Henripin and John Humphrey, a lawyer who had represented Canada at the United Nations' Human Rights Commission for twenty years. Humphrey replaced an initial appointee, Donald Gordon, who resigned after a few months and never played an active role on the Commission.
14. This document was prepared for the organizing meeting of the New Left Caucus, which had just split away from the Students' Union for Peace Action. It is partly reprinted in Sara Evans, *Personal Politics: The Roots of Women's Liberation in the Civil Rights Movement and the New Left*, (New York: Vintage Books, 1980) and more fully in *Women Unite!*, (Toronto: Women's Educational Press, 1972). The citation about "hewers of wood and haulers of water" is from the latter, with changed emphasis, (page 39).
15. Gloria Geller, "The Wartime Elections Act of 1917 and the Canadian Women's Movement," *Atlantis* 2, no. 1, (1976): 88–106.
16. On the Front pour la libération des femmes du Québec, *see*: Veronique O'Leary et Louise Toupin, *Québecoises deboutte!*, (Montreal: Les éditions du remue-ménage, 1968).
17. The Toronto Women's Liberation Group, "Is Feminism Necessary for Women's Liberation?" (Canadian Union of Students, 1969), 3.
18. Charnie Guettel, *Marxism and Feminism*, (Toronto: Women's Educational Press, 1974), 48.
19. Letter from Bonnie Kreps, November 1986.
20. *Report* of the Royal Commission on the Status of Women, (Ottawa: Information Canada, 1970), xii.
21. *Ibid.*, Recommendation 127.
22. New volunteer status-of-women organizations developed in most provinces to pressure for implementation of the recommendations of the Royal Commission. These groups should not be confused with government-appointed Advisory Councils on the Status of Women, which were established at the federal level and in all but two provinces.
23. Naomi Black, *Social Feminism: Theory and Organization in England, France, and the United States*, (Ithaca, N.Y.: Cornell University Press, forthcoming 1989).
24. Gallup poll conducted for the Canadian Abortion Rights Action League (CARAL) in June 1982.
25. Doris Guyatt, "Women in the Canadian Armed Forces: New Directions at last," *The Business and Professional Woman* (Spring 1987): 1.

Chapter Four

1. Peter Laslett, *The World We Have Lost*, 3rd. edition, (New York: Scribner, 1973).
2. *See*: James Dickinson and Bob Russell, eds., *Family, Economy and the State: The*

Social Reproduction Process Under Capitalism, (Toronto: Garamond, 1986); Margrit Eichler, *Families in Canada Today: Recent Changes and their Policy Consequences*, (Toronto: Gage, 1983); Bonnie Fox, ed., *Hidden in the Household: Women's Domestic Labour Under Capitalism*, (Toronto: Women's Educational Press, 1980): S.J. Wilson, *Women, the Family and the Economy*, 2nd. edition, (Toronto: McGraw-Hill Ryerson, 1986).

3. Statistics Canada, *Current Demographic Analysis: Fertility in Canada, From Baby Boom to Baby Bust*, (Ottawa, Minister of Supply and Services, 1984), 122.
4. *Ibid.*, 130–31.
5. Wilson, *Women*, 93–94.
6. Susan A. McDaniel and Ben Agger, *Social Problems Through Conflict and Order*, (Don Mills: Addison-Wesley, 1982), 231.
7. Statistics Canada, *Fertility*.
8. *Ibid.*, 33.
9. B.K. Singh and J.S. Williams, "Childlessness and Family Satisfaction," *Research on Aging* 3 (1981): 218–27.
10. N.D. Glenn and S. McLanahan, "Children and Marital Happiness: A Further Specification of the Relationship," *Journal of Marriage and the Family* 44 (1982): 63–72; G.B. Spanier and R.A. Lewis, "Marital Quality: A Review of the Seventies," *Journal of Marriage and the Family* 42 (1980): 825–39.
11. Ellen Gee and Meredith Kimball, *Women and Aging*, unpublished book manuscript, 1986.
12. Carl Grindstaff, "Adolescent Marriage and Childbearing: The Long-Term Economic Outcome in Canada in the 1980s," *Adolescence*, 1987.
13. Eichler, *Families*, 170–72.
14. Cited by Wilson, *Women*, 102.
15. Meg Luxton, *More than a Labour of Love: Three Generations of Women's Work in the Home*, (Toronto: Women's Educational Press, 1980).
16. Wilson, *Women*, 104.
17. *Ibid.*, 107.
18. Charles Westoff, "Fertility Decline in the West: Causes and Prospects," *Population and Development Review* 9, no. 1, (1983): 99–104.
19. Evidence cited by Wilson, *Women*, 67–69.
20. Martin Meissner, Elisabeth W. Humphreys, Scott M. Meis, and William J. Scheu, "No Exits for Wives: Sexual Division of Labour and the Cumulation of Household Demands," *Canadian Review of Sociology and Anthropology* 12, no. 4, (1975): 424–439.
21. Eichler, *Families*; Luxton, *Labour of Love*; Wilson, *Women*.
22. Statistics Canada, *Current Demographic Analysis: Report on the Demographic Situation in Canada, 1983*, (Ottawa: Minister of Supply and Services, 1984), 22.
23. *Ibid.*, 64.
24. Wilson, *Women*, 22.
25. Eichler, *Families*, 1983.

26. Anne Marie Ambert, *Divorce in Canada*, (Don Mills: Academic Press, 1980).
27. National Council on Welfare, *Progress Against Poverty*, (Ottawa: National Council on Welfare, 1986), 4.
28. Eichler, *Families*, 219; Phyllis Chesler, *Mothers on Trial: The Battle for Children and Custody*, (New York: McGraw-Hill, 1986).
29. Eichler, *Families*, 297.
30. *Ibid.*
31. Letty Cottin Pogrebin, *Family Politics: Love and Power on an Intimate Frontier*, (New York: McGraw-Hill, 1983).
32. *Ibid.*
33. Chesler, *Mothers*.
34. Eichler, *Families*, 236.
35. *Ibid.*, 231; Statistics Canada, *Report on Demographic Situation*.
36. Eichler, *Families*, 236.
37. Sheila Rowbotham, *Women's Consciousness, Man's World*, (Harmondsworth: Penguin, 1973).
38. *Ibid*, 212.
39. Christopher Lasch, *Haven in a Heartless World: The Family Besieged*, (New York: Basic Books, 1977).
40. Dorothy E. Smith, "Women, the Family and Corporate Capitalism," in Marylee Stephenson, ed., *Women in Canada*, (Don Mills: General Publishing, 1973), 22.
41. Linda MacLeod, "Wife Battering in Canada: The Vicious Circle," (Ottawa: Canadian Advisory Council on the Status of Women, 1980).
42. Susan A. McDaniel, "Abortion, Reproductive Technology and Women's Roles as the Barter of the New Right," paper presented at the Ontario Association of Sociology and Anthropology, Waterloo, Ontario, 1985.
43. Margrit Eichler, "The Pro-Family Movement: Are They For or Against Families?" *Feminist Frameworks*, (Ottawa: Canadian Research Institute for the Advancement of Women, 1985).
44. *Ibid.*
45. Susan A. McDaniel, "Women's Roles, Reproduction and New Reproductive Technologies," in Ann Duffy and Nancy Mandell, eds., *The Canadian Family: Feminist Perspectives*, (Toronto: Butterworths, 1988).
46. Margrit Eichler and Jeanne Lapointe, *On the Treatment of the Sexes in Research*, (Ottawa: Social Sciences and Research Council, 1985).
47. Linda Christiansen-Ruffman, Alleyne Morphy, Cannie Stark-Adamec, and Robert Davidson, *Sex Bias in Research: Current Awareness and Strategies to Eliminate Bias Within Canadian Social Science*, Report of the Task Force on the Elimination of Sexist Bias, (Ottawa, 1986).
48. Eichler and Lapointe, *Treatment of the Sexes*; Christiansen-Ruffman, *et al.*, *Sex Bias in Research*; Jill McCalla Vickers, ed., *Taking Sex Into Account*, (Ottawa: Carleton University Press, 1984).
49. Karl King, Thomas, J. Abernathy, and Ann H. Chapman, "Do Adolescents

Believe the Employment of Wives is a Threat to Marital Relationships?'' *The Family Co-ordinator* 27, no. 3, (1978): 231–35.
50. Roland Barthes, *Mythologies*, (Paris: Editions du Sevile, 1957), cited by Eichler and Lapointe, *Treatment of the Sexes*, 13.
51. Ann Oakley, *The Sociology of Housework*, (New York: Pantheon Books, 1974), 27.
52. Eichler, *Families*, 66, 87.
53. Jessie Bernard, *The Future of Marriage*, (New York: Bantam Books, 1973).
53. *Ibid.*, 16–58.
55. Maureen Baker, *Support Networks and Marital Dissolution*, Final Report of Connaught Foundation Project, (Toronto, 1980).
56. Chesler, *Mothers on Trial*,.
57. Eichler, *Families*, 93–97.
58. Cited in Eichler and Lapointe, *Treatment of the Sexes*, 10; cited in Rhoda K. Unger, *Female and Male: Psychological Perspectives*, (New York: Harper & Row, 1979).
59. James A. Doyle, *Sex and Gender: The Human Experience*, (Dubuque, Iowa: Wm. C. Brown, 1985); Susan A. McDaniel, ''Explaining Canadian Fertility: Some Remaining Challenges,'' *Canadian Studies in Population* 11, no. 1, (1984): 1–16.
60. Cited in John Archer and Barbara Lloyd, *Sex and Gender*, (Cambridge: Cambridge University Press, 1985).
61. Wilson, *Women*, 5.
62. Jill McCalla Vickers, ''Memoirs of an Ontological Exile: The Methodological Rebellions of Feminist Research,'' in Angela Miles and Geraldine Finn, eds., *Feminism in Canada: From Pressure to Politics*, (Montreal: Black Rose Books, 1982).
63. Ann Oakley, ''Interviewing Women: A Contradiction in Terms,'' in Helen Roberts, ed., *Doing Feminist Research*, (London: Routledge & Kegan Paul), 1981; Michelène de Sève, ''Prospects for Feminist Research: Towards a New Paradigm,'' *Feminist Perspectives* 3 (1985): 47–60.
64. Evan Stark, Ann Flitcraft, and William Frazier, ''Medicine and Patriarchal Violence: the Social Construction of a 'Private' Event,'' *International Journal of Health Services* 9, no. 3, (1979): 461–93; Chris Huntley Hutchinson and Susan A. McDaniel, ''The Social Reconstruction of Sexual Assualt by Women Victims: A Comparison of Therapeutic Experiences,'' *The Canadian Journal of Community Mental Health* 5, no. 2, (1986): 17–36; D. Herman and L. Hirschman, ''Father-Daughter Incest,'' *Signs: A Journal of Women in Culture and Society* 2, no. 4, (1977).
65. Michele Barrett and Mary McIntosh, *The Anti-Social Family*, (London: Verso, 1982); Dickinson and Russell, *Family, Economy and the State*; Fox, *Hidden in the Household*; Pogrebin, *Family Politics*; Smith, ''Women, the Family and Corporate Capitalism''; Dorothy E. Smith, ''Women's Equality and the Family,'' in A. Moscovitch and G. Drover, eds., *Inequality: Essays on the Political Economy of Social Welfare*, (Toronto: University of Toronto Press, 1981).
66. Michele Barrett, *Women's Oppression Today*, (London: Verso, 1980), 78.

Chapter Five

1. Lisa Peattie and Martin Rein, *Women's Claims: A Study in Political Economy*, (Scarborough: Prentice-Hall, 1986), 37
2. Canada, House of Commons, *Debates*, April 1, 1886, 442.
3. Canada, House of Commons, *Debates*, March 29, 1878, 1512.
4. Sir Joseph Pope, *The Day of Sir John A. MacDonald*, (Toronto, 1920), 138, as cited by Carol Lee Bacchi, *Liberation Deferred? The Ideas of the English-Canadian Suffragists, 1877–1918* (Toronto: University of Toronto Press, 1983), 134.
5. Genevieve Leslie, "Domestic Service in Canada, 1880–1920," in Janice Acton, *et al.*, eds., *Women at Work*, (Toronto: Women's Educational Press, 1974), 75.
6. Veronica Strong-Boag, "Working Women and the State: The Case of Canada, 1889–1945," *Atlantis* 6, no. 2, (1981), 7.
7. Ellen DuBois, "The Radicalism of the Woman Suffrage Movement: Notes Toward the Reconstruction of Nineteenth Century Feminism," *Feminist Studies* 3 (1975), 64.
8. *Ibid.*, 66.
9. Canada, House of Commons, *Debates*, April 11, 1918, 646.
10. Ruth Pierson, "Women's Emancipation and the Recruitment of Women into the Labour Force in World War II," in Susan Mann Trofimenkoff and Alison Prentice, eds., *The Neglected Majority I*, (Toronto: McClelland and Stewart, 1977), 125.
11. *Ibid.*, 145.
12. Nova Scotia, Commission on Hours of Labour, Wages, and Working Conditions of Women Employed in Industrial Occupations, *Report*, December 2, 1918, 7.
13. *Ibid.*, 6.
14. *Ibid.*, 19.
15. Margaret E. McCallum, "Keeping Women in Their Place: The Minimum Wage in Canada, 1910–1925," *Labour/Le Travail* 17 (1986), 53. For an earlier perspective on this legislation *see*: Kathleen Derry and Paul H. Douglas, "The Minimum Wage in Canada," *Journal of Political Economy* 30 (1922): 155–88.
16. There were some indications of changing attitudes in the deliberations about the wording of the amendment. The House of Commons resisted using the phrase "previously chaste," on the grounds that young girls "have not reached that stage of mentality and maturity of character that enables them to come to resolution for their own protection, and to resist importunity not physically but mentally." *Debates*, July 5, 1919, 4635. The Senate insisted that the words be included in the legislation.
17. Veronica Strong-Boag, "Wages for Housework: Mothers' Allowances and the Beginnings of Social Security in Canada," *Journal of Canadian Studies*, 14, no. 1 (1979), 25.
18. *Ibid.*, 33
19. Nellie McClung, "What Will They Do With It?" reprinted in Ramsay Cook and Wendy Mitchinson, eds., *The Proper Sphere*, Toronto: University of Toronto Press, 1976), 322.
20. Keith G. Banting, *The Welfare State and Canadian Federalism*, (Montreal: McGill-Queen's University Press, 1982), 91.

21. Elizabeth Wilson, *Women and the Welfare State*, (London: Tavistock Publications, 1977), 9.
22. Canada, House of Commons, *Debates*, July 25, 1944, 5331, 5336.
23. Canada, Department of Labour, Women's Bureau, Draft of Material for Women's Bureau Section of the Minister's Current Information Book, May 6, 1958.
24. Peter C. Robertson, "Some Thoughts on Affirmative Action in the 1980's," paper prepared for the Affirmative Action Division, Canada Employment and Immigration Commission, March 1980, 9.
25. For a study of the effectiveness of these programs, *see*: Sandra Burt, "Voluntary Affirmative Action: Does it Work?" *Relations industrielles* 41, no. 3, 1986, 541–50. This systemic interpretation of discrimination has now been written into the federal government's definition of affirmative action. Some of the provinces have followed this practice, as well.
26. Canada, Royal Commission on Equality in Employment, *Report*, (Ottawa: Ministry of Supply and Services Canada, 1984), 197.
27. Canada, House of Commons, Neilson Task Force, *Report*, (1987) 109.
28. Canada, Royal Commission on Equality in Employment, *Report*.
29. Canada, Task Force on Child Care, *Report*, (1986), 45, 47.
30. Wilson, *Women*, 165.
31. There is an excellent summary of the history of women's participation in Canadian political life in Jill McCalla Vickers and Janine Brodie, "Canada," in Joni Lovenduski and Jill Hills, eds., *The Politics of the Second Electorate*, (London: Routledge & Kegan Paul, 1981).
32. Thelma McCormack, "Toward a Nonsexist Perspective on Social and Political Change," in Marcia Millman and Rosabeth Moss Kanter, eds., *Another Voice*, (Garden City, N.J.: Anchor Press, 1975), 25.
33. For a review of women's participation in party politics at all levels, *see*: Sylvia Bashevkin, *Toeing the Lines; Women and Party Politics in English Canada* (Toronto: University of Toronto Press, 1985). *See also*: Janine Brodie, *Women and Politics in Canada*, (Toronto: McGraw-Hill Ryerson, 1985).
34. Brodie, *Women and Politics*, 109.
35. *Ibid.*, 3.
36. Sirkka Sirkkonen and Elina Haavio-Manilla, "The Impact of the Women's Movement and Legislative Activity of Women M.P.s in Social Development," in M. Rendel, ed., *Women, Power and Political Systems*, (London: Croom Helm, 1981), 210–14.
37. Interview with Ad Hoc Committee member, March 1983.
38. Una Maclean, "The Honourable Irene Parlby," *Alberta Historical Review* 7, no. 2, (1959): 1–6.
39. Veronica Strong-Boag, "Canadian Feminism in the 1920's: The Case of Nellie L. McClung," *Journal of Canadian Studies* 12, no. 4, (1977): 58–68.
40. Diane Crossley, "The British Columbia Liberal Party and Women's Reforms, 1916–1928," in Barbara Latham and Cathy Kess, eds., *In Her Own Right*, (Victoria: Camosun College, 1980).
41. Canada, House of Commons, *Debates*, November 3, 1970, 842.

42. Canada, House of Commons, *Debates*, April 6, 1936, 1855.
43. Helen Gregory MacGill, *Laws for Women and Children in British Columbia*, (B.C.: Women's Institutes and Local Councils, 1939), 17.
44. John Terry, ''The Gender Gap: Women's Political Power,'' paper prepared for the current issues series, Political and Social Affairs Division, Research Branch of the Library of Parliament, Ottawa, 1984.
45. For a review of this work, *see*: Margaret Conrad, ''The Re-Birth of Canada's Past: A Decade of Women's History,'' *Acadiensis* 12, no. 2, (1983): 140–63.
46. This study was carried out by the author in the spring of 1984, with support from the Social Sciences and Humanities Research Council.
47. Interviews with Bryce Mackasey and Judy Erola, April 1986.
48. The communications between one minister, John Munro, and his Co-ordinator, Martha Hynna, suggest that there was some serious disagreement between them. In one conflict, Martha Hynna objected to the attempt by John Munro to downgrade the position of the Director of the Women's Bureau, Department of Labour. Letter dated April 16, 1974.
49. Interview with Bryce Mackasey, March 1986.
50. Interview with Marc Lalonde, March 1986.
51. This problem appears in correspondence between Sylva Gelber, when she was in charge of the Women's Bureau, Department of Labour, and the Staffing Branch of the Public Service Commission of Canada, July 1969.
52. These are the functions that were set out in the Record of the Cabinet Committee on Social Policy of February 23, 1971. From a letter to Marshall Crowe, Chairman of the Interdepartmental Committee.
53. Interview with Freda Paltiel, Women's Adviser, Health and Welfare Canada, March 1986.
54. This was taken from a briefing document for deputy ministers on status-of-women policy. There is no date on this document, but it was probably prepared in 1976.
55. Nielson Task Force, *Report*, 109–110.
56. For a discussion of this perspective, *see*: Jane Jenson, ''Gender and Reproduction,'' *Studies in Political Economy* 20 (1986).
57. Privy Council Office, Planning Division, ''Situation Report on Canada,'' for planning of Cabinet priorities, September 1971–1972, 11.
58. Memorandum to Cabinet from Pierre Trudeau, 1972.
59. Banting, *The Welfare State*, 172.
60. *Ibid.*,
61. I would like to thank the Social Sciences and Humanities Research Council of Canada for its support of research contained in this chapter.

Chapter Six

1. For accounts of twenty-two of these landmark cases, *see*: M. Elizabeth Atcheson, Mary Eberts, and Beth Symes with Jennifer Stoddart, *Women and Legal Action:*

Precedents, Resources and Strategies for the Future, (Ottawa: Canadian Advisory Council on the Status of Women, 1984).

2. Unless otherwise noted, quotations cited in the discussion of these early 'persons' cases are from the pertinent court reports. *See: In Re Mabel P. French* (1905), 37 New Brunswick Reports, 359; *In Re Mabel Penery French* (1912), 17 British Columbia Reports, 1; *Dame Langstaff* v. *The Bar of Quebec* (1915), 47 cour supérieure 131, affirmed (1915), 25 cour du banc du roi 11; *Rex* v. *Cyr (Alias Waters)* (1917), 2 Western Weekly Reports, 1185, affirmed 3 Western Weekly Reports, 849.

3. Constance B. Backhouse, " 'To Open the Way for Others of my Sex': Clara Brett Martin's Career as Canada's First Woman Lawyer," *Canadian Journal of Women and the Law* I (1985): 37.

4. Karen Berger Morello, *The Invisible Bar: The Woman Lawyer in America: 1638 to the Present*, (New York: Random House, 1986).

5. Margaret Gillet, *We Walked Very Warily: A History of Women at McGill*, (Montreal: Black Rose Books, 1981), 309.

6. *Ibid.*, 305.

7. Marguerite E. Ritchie, "Alice Through the Statutes," *McGill Law Journal* 21, (1975), 702.

8. Eleanor Harmon, "Five Persons from Alberta," in Mary Quayle Innes, ed., *The Clear Spirit*, (Toronto: University of Toronto Press, 1966), 162.

9. Catherine L. Cleverdon, *The Woman Suffrage Movement in Canada*, (Toronto: University of Toronto Press, 1966), 162–63.

10. Sources used in this discussion on the Persons Case include: David Ricardo Williams, *Duff: A Life in the Law*, (Vancouver: University of British Columbia Press, 1984); James G. Snell and Frederick Vaughan, *The Supreme Court of Canada: History of the Institution*, (Toronto: The Osgoode Society and University of Toronto Press, 1985). Unless otherwised noted, quotations used are from pertinent court records; *see*: *In the Matter of a Reference as to the Meaning of the Word "Persons" in Section 24 of the British North America Act, 1867*, (1928), Supreme Court Reports 276; reversed *sub nom Henrietta Muir Edwards et al.* v. *Attorney-General for Canada*, (1930), Appeal Cases 124.

11. Byrne Hope Sanders, *Emily Murphy: Crusader*, (Toronto: Macmillan, 1945), 243.

12. Albie Sachs and Joan Hoff Wilson, *Sexism and the Law*, (New York: The Free Press, 1978), 42.

13. *See*: Mary Eberts, "Sex-based Discrimination and the Charter" and Katherine J. de Jong, "Sexual Equality: Interpreting Section 28" in Anne Bayefsky and Mary Eberts, *Equality Rights and the Canadian Charter of Rights and Freedoms*, (Toronto: Carswell, 1985).

14. Ritchie, "Alice Through the Statutes," 702.

15. Sachs and Wilson, *Sexism and the Law*, 42.

16. Mary Eberts, "The Persons Case," National Action Committee on the Status of Women, *News* 5, (March 1979).

17. Jill Laurie Goodman, "Women, War, and Equality: An Examination of Sex Discrimination in the Military," *Women's Rights Law Reporter* 5, (1979): 246.

18. Unless otherwise noted, quotations used in this discussion of the Canadian Bill of Rights cases are from the pertinent court record.
19. *See*: Special Committee on Human Rights and Fundamental Freedoms, *Minutes of Proceedings and Evidence*, Numbers 1 to 12, (July 12–29, 1960), 641.
20. *R.* v. *Drybones* (1970), Supreme Court Reports 282.
21. *R.* v. *Viens* (1970), 10 Criminal Reports (new series), 363; *R.* v. *Lavoie* (1970), 16 Dominion Law Reports (3d), 647, affirmed (1972), 23 Dominion Law Reports (3d), 364; *R.* v. *Beaulne, ex parte Latreille* (1971), 16 Dominion Law Reports (3d), 657. *See also*: *R.* v. *Patterson* (1972), 19 Criminal Reports (new series), 289; *R.* v. *Obey* (1973), 21 Criminal Reports (new series), 121; *R.* v. *DiPaola and Palatics* (1978), 43 Canadian Criminal Cases (2d), 199; *Hutt* v. *The Queen* (1978), 38 Canadian Criminal Cases (2d), 418; *Westendorp* v. *The Queen* (1983), 32 Criminal Reports (3d), 97.
22. *Attorney-General of Canada* v. *Lavell, Isaac et al.* v. *Bedard* (1973), 38 Dominion Law Reports (3d), 481; *Bliss* v. *Attorney-General of Canada*, (1979), 1 Supreme Court Reports, 183.
23. Kathleen Jamieson, *Indian Women and the Law in Canada: Citizens Minus*, (Ottawa: Advisory Council on the Status of Women, 1978).
24. *See*: *Joseph* v. *Joseph* (1969), 4 Dominion Law Reports 646; *Re Schmitz* (1972), 31 Dominion Law Reports (3d), 117; *Rose* v. *The Queen* (1972), 19 Criminal Reports (2d), 66; *R.* v. *Halliday* (1973), 23 Criminal Reports (new series), 332; *R.* v. *Mackay* (1976), 30 Canadian Criminal Cases (2d), 349, reversed (1977), 36 Canadian Criminal Cases (2d), 349.
25. Special Joint Committee of the Senate and House of Commons on the Constitution of Canada, *Minutes and Proceedings of Evidence*, 32nd Parliament, 1980, 1st session, Issue no. 9, 75.
26. De Jong, "Sexual Equality," 506.
27. Chaviva Hosek, "Women and the Constitutional Process," in Keith Banting and Richard Simeon, *And No One Cheered: Federalism, Democracy, and the Constitution Act*, (Toronto: Methuen, 1983), 289.
28. Penney Kome, "Anatomy of a Lobby," *Saturday Night*, Jan. 1983. *See also*: Penney Kome, *The Taking of Twenty-Eight: Women Challenge the Constitution*, (Toronto: Women's Educational Press, 1983).
29. *Ibid.*
30. Linda Ryan Nye as quoted in Penney Kome, "Anatomy of a Lobby."
31. Quotations used in the discussion of Justine Blainey's case are from: *Re Blainey and Ontario Hockey Association et al.* (1985), 52 Ontario Reports (2d), 225, appeal allowed (1986) 54 Ontario Reports (2d), 513.
32. Margaret Anderson, *Mother was not a person*, (Montreal, Black Rose Books, 1972), 23.
33. *See*: John Sopinka, *Can I Play?: The Report of the Task Force on Equal Opportunity in Athletics*, (Government of Ontario).
34. Helen Lensky, *Out of Bounds: Women, Sport and Sexuality*, (Toronto: Women's Educational Press, 1986).

35. Carol Gilligan, *In A Different Voice*, (Cambridge, Harvard University Press, 1982); Catharine A. MacKinnon, *Feminism Unmodified: Discourses on Life and Law*, (Cambridge: Harvard University Press, 1987); Mary O'Brien, *The Politics of Reproduction*, (Boston: Routledge & Kegan Paul, 1981).
36. ''Women in the Courts,'' *The Toronto Star*, 19 June 1987.

Chapter Seven

1. *See*: Jackie Lay, ''To Columbia on the Tynemouth: the Emigration of Single Women and Girls in 1862,'' in Barbara Latham and Cathy Kess, eds., *In Her Own Right: Selected Essays on Women's History in B.C.*, (Victoria: Camosun College, 1980); B. Roberts, ''Sex, Politics and Religion: Controversies in Female Immigration Reform Work in Montreal, 1881–1919,'' *Atlantis* 6, no. 1, (1980): 26–38.
2. *See*: Warren E. Kalbach, *The Effect of Immigration on Population*, (Ottawa: Department of Manpower and Immigration, 1974); Freda Hawkins, *Canada and Immigration: Public Policy and Public Concern*, (Montreal: McGill-Queen's University Press, 1972).
3. *See*: Alma Estable, *Immigrant Women in Canada: Current Issues*, a background paper prepared for the Canadian Advisory Council on the Status of Women, March 1986; Jean L. Elliot, ''Canadian Immigration: A Historical Assessment,'' in Jean L. Elliot, ed., *Two Nations, Many Cultures: Ethnic Groups in Canada*, (Scarborough: Prentice-Hall, 2nd. ed., 1983).
4. Anthony H. Richmond, ''Immigration and Racial Prejudice in Britain and Canada,'' in *Two Nations, Many Cultures*; Doreen M. Indra, ''Canada Immigration: A Retrospective Look at the Past Ten Years,'' *RIKKA* 4, nos. 3 & 4 (1977): 3–10.
5. John Porter, *The Vertical Mosaic: An Analysis of Social Class and Power in Canada*, (Toronto: University of Toronto Press, 1965).
6. *See*, for example, Irving Abella and Harold Troper, *None Is Too Many*, (Toronto: Lester & Orpen Dennys, 1982); Doreen M. Indra, *Southeast Asian Refugee Settlement in Canada: A Research Bibliography*, (Ottawa: Asian Studies Association, Carleton University, 1984).
7. *See*: Elliot, ''Canadian Immigration: A Historical Assessment.''
8. There are two additional categories of newcomers: the conventional refugees and the designated class of immigrants. The latter group refers to those persons displaced from their homeland, such as the 'boat people' from Indo-China and exiles from some Latin American countries. They are either government-sponsored or privately sponsored (e.g., by the churches or ethnic organizations). Furthermore, people who enter Canada to work on work permits are also governed by provisions in the Immigration Act. Their stay in Canada is tied strictly to a specific job (e.g., domestic work for an identified employer) and they are not considered landed immigrants.
9. *See*, for example, Janet W. Salaff, *Working Daughters of Hong Kong: Filial Piety or Power in the Family?*, (Cambridge: Cambridge University Press, 1981).
10. For a discussion of changing household patterns, *see*: Nancy Jackson, ''Stress on School + Stress on Family = Distress for Children,'' (Ottawa: Canadian Teacher's

Federation, 1983). For the situation of immigrant families, *see*: Roxana Ng and Judith Ramirez, *Immigrant Housewives in Canada*, (Toronto: Immigrant Women's Centre, 1981). For a discussion of the segregated labour market, *see*: Pat Armstrong and Hugh Armstrong, *The Double Ghetto: Canadian Women and Their Segregated Work*, (Toronto: McClelland and Stewart, 1978).

11. As mentioned, the guidelines for social assistance for landed immigrants vary from province to province. For example, in Ontario, family-class immigrants were not eligible for daycare subsidy. In Saskatchewan, all social assistance available to residents of the province was also available to immigrants, with the exception of the Saskatchewan Assistance Plan.

12. *See*: Ng and Ramirez, *Immigrant Housewives*, 49–55.

13. Immigrant Women of Saskatchewan, *Doubly Disadvantaged: The Women Who Immigrate to Canada*, (Regina: Author, 1985).

14. Brenda Janke and Ronnie Yaron, ''A Report on Conditions in the Labour Market and Training Opportunities for Non-English Speaking Immigrant Women in Metro Toronto,'' (Toronto: Working Women's Community Centre, 1979); Roxana Ng and Tania Das Gupta, ''The Organization of the Non-English Speaking Immigrant Women Labour Force,'' a preliminary report to the Wollestonecraft Research Group, OISE, (1980).

15. *Doubly Disadvantaged*.

16. Angela W. Djao and Roxana Ng, ''Structured Isolation: Immigrant Women in Saskatchewan,'' in Kathleen Storrie, ed., *Women – Isolation and Bonding: Readings in the Ecology of Gender*, (Toronto: Methuen, 1987); Estable, *Immigrant Women in Canada*.

17. *See*: Ng and Ramirez, *Immigrant Housewives*, 55–60: Armstrong and Armstrong, *The Double Ghetto*; Paul Phillips and Erin Phillips, *Women and Work: Inequality in the Labour Market*, (Toronto: James Lorimer, 1983).

18. Sheila McLeod Arnopoulos, *Problems of Immigrant Women in the Canadian Labour Force*, (Ottawa: Advisory Council on the Status of Women, 1979); Monica Boyd, ''Immigrant Women in Canada,'' in R.J. Simon and C.B. Brettell, eds., *International Migration: The Female Experience*, (Totowa, N.J.: Rowman & Allanheld, 1986), 45–61

19. Boyd, ''Immigrant Women in Canada,'' 56.

20. Rachel Epstein, Maggi Trebble, and Roxana Ng, ''The Social Organization of Family Violence: An Ethnography of Immigrant Experience in Canada,'' a report to the Non-Medical Use of Drugs Directorate, Health and Welfare Canada, (1979); Djao and Ng, ''Structure solation.''

21. Alison I. Boulter, ''Constituting Ethnic Difference: An Ethnography of the Portuguese Immigrant Experience in Vancouver,'' M.A. thesis, University of British Columbia, 1978.

22. Phillips and Phillips, *Women and Work*.

23. Ng and Das Gupta, ''Nation Builders? The Captive Labour Force of Non-English Speaking Immigrant Women,'' *Canadian Woman's Studies* 3, no. 1, (1981): 83–85.

24. Ng and Ramirez, *Immigrant Housewives*; Ng and Das Gupta, "Organization of Non-English Speaking Immigrant Women Labour Force."
25. *See*: Laura C. Johnson, *The Seam Allowance*, (Toronto: Women's Educational Press, 1982).
26. Arnopoulos, *Problems of Immigrant Women*; Janke and Yaron, "A Report on Conditions in the Labour Market"; Ng and Ramirez, *Immigrant Housewives*, 55–56; Ng and Das Gupta, "The Organization of Non-English Speaking Immigrant Women"; Boyd, "Immigrant Women,"
27. Ng and Das Gupta, "National Builders?"
28. The interview on which this story is based was conducted in connection with the study by Ng and Ramirez, *Immigrant Housewives*, 47.
29. Arnopoulos, *Problems of Immigrant Women*, 57–58; Ng and Ramirez, *Immigrant Housewives*. For an excellent case study of a garment factory, *see*: Charlene Gannagé, *Double Day, Double Bind: Women Garment Workers*, (Toronto: Women's Educational Press, 1986).
30. Arnopoulos, *Problems of Immigrant Women*.
31. *See*: Julie White, *Women and Unions*, (Ottawa: Advisory Council on the Status of Women, 1980); Winnie Ng, "Organizing Workers in the Garment Industry," in *By and About Women*, (Toronto: Women Working With Immigrant Women and Cross-Cultural Communications Centre, 1979).
32. Ng and Ramirez, *Immigrant Housewives*, 58.
33. *See*: White, *Women and Unions*; Cynthia Cockburn, *Brothers: Male Dominance and Technological Change*, (London: Pluto Press, 1983).
34. Marie L. Campbell, "Sexism in British Columbia Trade Unions, 1900–1920," in *In Her Own Right*, 167–86.
35. *See*: Winnie Ng, "Organizing Workers in the Garment Industry." These stereotypes of immigrant women are also prevalent in the women's movement. *See*: Winnie Ng, "Immigrant Women: The Silent Partners of the Women's Movement," in Maureen Fitzgerald, Connie Guberman, and Margie Wolfe, eds., *Still Ain't Satisfied! Canadian Feminism Today*, (Toronto: Women's Educational Press, 1982) 249–56.
36. The study was conducted by Ng and Ramirez for *Immigrant Housewives*. It appeared in an article by Roxana Ng, "Immigrant Housewives in Canada: A Methodological Note," *Atlantis* 8, no. 1 (1982), 113.
37. For a theorization of this relation, *see*: Saskia Sassen-Kobb, "Toward a Conceptualization of Immigrant Labour," *Social Problems* 29, no. 1 (1981): 65–85; F. Frobel, J. Heinrichs, and O. Kreye, *The New International Division of Labour*, (Cambridge: Cambridge University Press, 1980).
38. Margrit Eichler, "The Industrialization of Housework," (Toronto: OISE, GROW Paper, No. 3, 1976).
39. Ng and Ramirez, *Immigrant Housewives*, 28–29.
40. *Ibid.*, 29–30.
41. *See*: Jackson "Stress on School + Stress on Family"; A.M. Cassin and A.I.

Griffith, "Class and Ethnicity: Producing the Difference That Counts," *Canadian Ethnic Studies* 8, no. 1 (1981): 109–29.

42. Ng and Ramirez, *Immigrant Housewives*, 32.

43. *Ibid.*, 39. *See also*: Djao and Ng, "Structured Isolation."

44. *See*: Somer Brodribb, "The Traditional Roles of Native Women in Canada and the Impact of Colonization," *Canadian Journal of Native Studies* 4, no. 1 (1984).

45. Sally M. Weaver, "The Status of Indian Women," in *Two Nations, Many Cultures*, 56–79.

46. James S. Frideres, *Native People in Canada, Contemporary Conflicts*, (Scarborough: Prentice-Hall, 1983), 6–7.

47. *Ibid.*, 7.

48. Weaver, "The Status of Indian Women."

49. Frideres, *Native People in Canada*, 10.

50. Weaver, "Status of Indian Women," 58.

51. *Ibid.*, 59.

52. Information leaflet published by the Native Women's Committee on the Status of Women. For a detailed discussion of the legal ramifications of the law, *see*: Kathleen Jamieson, *Indian Women and the Law in Canada: Citizens Minus*, (Ottawa: Advisory Council on the Status of Women and Indian Rights for Indian Women, 1978).

53. Weaver, "The Status of Indian Women," 62–66.

54. *Ibid.*, 71–74.

55. Press release from the Minister of Indian Affairs and Northern Development, February 28, 1985.

56. *See*, for example, Kathleen Jamieson, "Sisters Under the Skin: An Exploration of the Implications of Feminist-Materialist Perspective Research," *Canadian Ethnic Studies* 13, no. 1 (1981): 130–143; various 1986 issues of the *International Women's Day Committee Newsletter* and *Cayenne: A Socialist Feminist Bulletin*.

57. Estable, *Immigrant Women in Canada. See also*: Immigrant Women of Saskatchewan, *Doubly Disadvantaged*.

Chapter Eight

1. Margaret Atwood, *Second Words: Selected Critical Prose*, (Toronto: House of Anansi, 1982), 193.

2. *See*: Beth Light and Veronica Strong-Boag, *True Daughters of the North: Canadian Women's History: An Annotated Bibliography*, (Toronto: OISE Press, 1980). *See also*: Beth Light, "Recent Publications in Canadian Women's History," *Canadian Woman Studies/Les cahiers de la femme* 3, no. 1 (1981).

3. Sylvia Hamilton, "Our Mothers Grand and Great: Black Women of Nova Scotia," *Canadian Woman Studies/Les Cahiers de la femme* 4, no. 2, (1982).

4. *See*: Clara Thomas, *Love and Work Enough: The Life of Anna Jameson*, (Toronto: University of Toronto Press, 1968 and 1978). *See also*: Clara Thomas, "Heroinism, Feminism and Humanism: Anna Jameson to Margaret Laurence," *Atlantis* 4, no. 1 (1978): 19–29.

5. Sandra Djwa, "The Where of Here: Margaret Atwood and a Canadian Tradition," in Arnold E. Davidson and Cathy M. Davidson, eds., *The Art of Margaret Atwood: Essays in Criticism*, (Toronto: House of Anansi, 1981), 19–20.
6. *See*: Marion Fowler, *Redney: A Life of Jeanette Duncan*, (Toronto: House of Anansi, 1980).
7. Margaret Atwood, " Introduction," in Susanna Moodie, *Roughing It In The Bush*, (London: Virago Press, 1986), xiv.
8. *Ibid.*
9. Djwa, "The Where of Here," 19.
10. *Ibid.*, 16.
11. Margaret Atwood, *Second Words*, 203–204.
12. *See*: Rachel Blau Du Plessis, *Writing Beyond the Ending: Narrative Strategies of Twentieth Century Women Writers*, (Bloomington: Indiana University Press, 1985), for a comprehensive and perceptive approach to this subject. Relevant material is in Ch. 1, "Endings and Contradictions."
13. Alice Munro, "An Appreciation," *A Room of One's Own* 9, no. 2, 32.
14. *Ibid.*, 33.
15. This comment is made on a video-taped interview, "Our Kinda Talk: An Introduction to Margaret Laurence," National Film Board, 1978. *See also*: Margaret Laurence, "Ivory Tower or Grassroots? The Novelist as Socio-Political Being," in Douglas Daymond and Leslie Monkman, eds., *Canadian Novelists and the Novel*, (Ottawa: Borealis Press, 1981), 251–59. Of particular interest, pp. 257–58 on the 'colonial mentality' of women and the responses of Laurence's female protagonists to the dilemma of powerlessness.
16. For a definitive analysis of birthing as a social construct (and the economic and political power that has accrued to patriarchy in its control over birth), *See*: Mary O'Brien, *The Politics of Reproduction*, (Boston: Routledge & Kegan Paul, 1981). *See also*: Meg Luxton, *More Than A Labour of Love*, (Toronto: Women's Educational Press, 1985). This is a brilliant study of three generations of women's work in the Canadian home. Luxton demonstrates, in a sociological analysis, what women are imagining into life. "The Poet Mother," a special issue of *Cross Canada Writers' Quarterly* 8, no. 2, provides an interesting perspective on creativity and birthing.
17. Audrey Thomas, *Intertidal Life*, (Toronto: General Publishing, 1984), 51.
18. *Ibid.*, 136. *See also*: Audrey Thomas, "The More Little Mummy in the World," in *Two In The Bush and Other Stories*, (Toronto: General Publishing, 1981).
19. Dorothy Livesay, "Serenade for Strings (for Peter)," in *The Woman I Am*, (Erin: Press Porcepic, 1977), 19.
20. Margaret Atwood, "Christmas Carols," in *True Stories*, (Toronto: Oxford University Press, 1981), 56.
21. *Ibid.*, 57.
22. *See* "Princess Ida," in Alice Munro, *Lives of Girls and Women*, (Toronto: McGraw-Hill Ryerson, 1971) for the history of Del's mother, as she rebels against the traditional role of woman.
23. *Ibid.*, 203.

24. Alice Munro, "The Office," in *Dance of the Happy Shades*, (Toronto, McGraw-Hill Ryerson, 1968).
25. Margaret Laurence, *The Diviners*, (Toronto: McClelland and Stewart, 1974), 6.
26. *Ibid.*, 25.
27. *Ibid.*, 453.
28. Thomas, *Intertidal Life*. 141.
29. *Ibid.*, 157–58.
30. *Ibid.*, 171.
31. *Ibid.*, 161.
32. *Ibid.*, 173.
33. Audrey Thomas, interview with Ron Graham, *The Gazette* (Montreal), March 29, 1980.
34. Dorothy Livesay, interview, in Bruce Meyer and Brian O'Riordan, eds., *In Their Own Words*, (Toronto: House of Anansi, 1984), 81.
35. Margaret Atwood, *The Handmaid's Tale*, (Toronto: McClelland and Stewart, 1985), 279.
36. Mariana Valverde, *Sex, Power and Pleasure*, (Toronto: Women's Educational Press, 1985), 10.
37. *Ibid.*, 11–15.
38. Margaret Atwood, interview, HER*izons* 4, no. 1, 20–22.
39. Margaret Atwood, *Power Politics*, (Toronto: Oxford University Press, 1974), 1.
40. Marian Engel, quoted in Patricia Morley, *Margaret Laurence*, (Boston: Twayne Publishers, 1986), 133.
41. Adele Wiseman, *Crackpot*, (Toronto: McClelland and Stewart, 1974), 9.
42. Gail Scott, "Shaping a Vehicle For Her Use: Woman and the Short Story," in *In The Feminine*, (Edmonton: Longspoon Press, 1985), 184.
43. *Ibid.*, 185.
44. Karen Gould, "Our Bodies in Writing: Quebec Women Writers on the Physicality of the Text," *Degré Second* 7, (1983): 133.
45. *Ibid.*, 135.
46. Barbara Godard, "The Translator as She: The Relationship Between Writer and Translator," in *In The Feminine*, 193.
47. Jovette Marchessault, "Night Cows," in *Lesbian Triptych*, (Toronto: Women's Educational Press, 1985), 73.
48. Jane Rule, *A Hot-Eyed Moderate*, (Toronto: Lester & Orpen Dennys, 1986), 43.
49. Jane Rule, *Desert of the Heart*, (Vancouver: Talon Books, 1977), 134.
50. Rule, *Hot-Eyed Moderate*, 42–46.
51. *Ibid.*, 24.
52. Leah Cohen, *Small Expectations: Society's Betrayal of Older Women*, (Toronto: McClelland and Stewart, 1984), 10.
53. Barbara Horn, "Beyond Hags and Old Maids: Women Writers Imagine Aging Women," in *Women and Aging: An Anthology by Women*, (Corvallis, Oregon: Calyx Books, 1986), 63–67.
54. In a lecture at Sheridan College, Oakville, (October 1976), Beresford-Howe told

the audience that the mail she received in response to the novel was overwhelming and totally unexpected. She insisted she was "not writing a blueprint for marital break-down–just a story."

55. Miriam Waddington, "How Old Women Should Live," in *Collected Poems*, (Toronto: Oxford University Press, 1986), 324.

56. Gretel Miles, "November 1983: Riding the Bus," *Canadian Woman Studies/ Les cahiers de la femme* 5, no. 3, 31.

57. Dorothy Livesay, "Breathing," in *The Woman I Am*, 81.

58. Dorothy Livesay, "Nothing is Private," *A Room of One's Own* 5, nos. 1 and 2, 67.

59. Adele Wiseman, *Old Woman at Play*, (Toronto: Clarke Irwin, 1978), 59.

60. *See*: Barbara Walker, *The Crone: Woman of Age, Wisdom and Power*, (New York: Harper & Row, 1985).

61. Margaret Atwood, *The Journals of Susanna Moodie*, (Toronto: Oxford University Press, 1970, 61.

62. *Ibid.*, 61.

63. Marya Fiamengo, "In Praise of Old Women," in *North of the Cold Star*, (Ottawa: Mosaic Press, 1978), 90–91.

64. Lillian Allen, "A Writing of Resistance: Black Women's Writing in Canada," in *In The Feminine*, 63.

65. *Ibid.*, 64.

66. Himani Bannerji, "We Appear Silent to People Who Are Deaf to What We Say," *Fireweed* 16 (1983), 11. *See also*: the first issue of *Tiger Lily*, a magazine dedicated to publishing works of minority women.

67. Himani Bannerji, "Paki Go Home," in *Fireweed* 23, (1986), 17.

68. Claire Harris, in *Ibid.*

69. Claire Harris, *Fables From the Women's Quarters*, (Toronto: Williams-Wallace, 1984), 40.

70. *Ibid.*, 10.

71. Joseph Pivato, "Italian Canadian Women Writers Recall History," *Canadian Ethnic Studies* 18, no. 1, (1986).

72. Mary di Michele, "Hunger," in Mary di Michele, ed., *Anything is Possible*, (Oakville: Mosaic Press, 1984), 80–82.

73. Joy Kogawa, *Obasan*, (Toronto: Lester & Orpen Dennys, 1981), Preface.

74. Joy Kogawa, "Is There a Just Cause?" *Canadian Forum*, March, 1984, 24. Paper presented originally to the Canadian Caucus on Human Rights, December, 1983. Dorothy Livesay spoke out on this subject in a documentary poem, "Call My People Home," written for radio, 1950.

75. Jeanette Armstrong, "Writing From a Native Woman's Perspective," in *In The Feminine*, 55. *See also*: Dolores T. Poelzer and Irene A. Poelzer, *In Our Own Words: Northern Saskatchewan Métis Women Speak Out*, (Saskatoon: Lindenblatt and Hamonic, 1986).

76. *Ibid.*, 55–57.

77. Beth Brant, "Coming Out as an Indian Lesbian Writer," in *Ibid.*, 58.

78. Beth Cuthand, "Transmitting our Identity as Indian Writers," in *Ibid.*, 53–54.
79. Barbara Godard, "Talking About Ourselves: The Literary Productions of the Native Women of Canada," CRIAW *Papers* 11, (1985). The article contains useful resources and is one of the very few in-depth studies of the oral tradition in native women's writing.
80. Some of these include: Atwood, Barfoot, Carr, Gibson, Laurence, Munro, and Rule.
81. Carol Bolt, interview, in Robert Wallace and Cynthia Zimmerman, eds., *The Work: Conversations with English-Canadian Playwrights*, (Toronto: Coach House Press, 1982), 270.
82. Sharon Pollock, interview, in *Ibid.*, 123.
83. *Ibid.*
84. *Ibid.*, 122.
85. *See*: Joan Mason Hurley, *Canadian One Act Plays For Women*, (Victoria: A Room of One's Own Press, 1975); Joan Mason Hurley, *Women's Women*, (Victoria: A Room of One's Own Press, 1979); Liberty Jane Carter, *Satin Thigh*, (Toronto: Playwrights' Co-op, 1976).
86. Margaret Atwood has written perceptively about this aspect of MacEwen's work. *See*: "MacEwen's Muse," in *Second Words*, 67–78.
87. Gwendolyn MacEwen, *Trojan Women*, (Toronto: Exile Editions, 1981), 34–35.
88. *Ibid.*, 38.
89. *Ibid.*, 73.
90. *Ibid.*, 72.
91. *Ibid.*, 59. (MacEwen's emphasis throughout.)
92. *Ibid.*, 61.
93. *Ibid.*, 94.
94. *Ibid.*, 60.
95. *Ibid.*, 66.
96. *Ibid.*, 77.
97. Dorothy Livesay, "Why We Are Here," in *The Woman I Am*, 65.

Chapter Nine

1. See Lorraine Code's discussion of de Beauvoir's view of women's Otherness, judged according to a male norm, in Chapter One.
2. Andrew Weil, *Health and Healing: A New Look at Medical Practices–From Folk Remedies to Chemotherapy–and What They Tell Us About*, (Boston: Houghton Mifflin, 1983), 114.
3. Henry Lyman, *The Practical Home Physician and Encyclopedia of Medicine*, (Guelph, 1884), 515.
4. Gena Corea, *The Hidden Malpractice: How American Medicine Mistreats Women*, (New York: Harper Colophon, 1985), 24.
5. An excellent example of this is the introduction of Twilight Sleep as a childbirth treatment in the early twentieth century. It put the birthing mother in "a state of semi-

consciousness induced by morphine and scopolamine.'' This allowed the woman to be conscious during birth, but to forget the pain of birthing. It was a complex procedure and one that women, not doctors, insisted upon. Margarete Sandelowski, *Pain, Pleasure, and American Childbirth: From the Twilight Sleep to the Read Method, 1914–1960*, (Westport, Conn.: Greenwood Press, 1984), 3–26. Of course, one reason that women may have insisted upon the newest techniques, such as Twilight Sleep, is that they had accepted the scientific model, which was based on the supposed rationality and objectivity of scientific investigation.

6. The primary sources used in this chapter are the medical journals published in Canada and the textbooks used in Canadian medical schools, including those published outside Canada. The paucity of Canadian textbooks remained until well into the twentieth century.

7. For further information on the early history of medicine in Canada *see*: Ronald Hamowy, *Canadian Medicine: A Study in Restricted Entry*, (Vancouver: The Fraser Institute, 1984); William Canniff, *The Medical Profession in Upper Canada, 1783–1850*, (Toronto: William Briggs, 1894); John J. Heagerty, *Four Centuries of Medical History in Canada*, (Toronto: Macmillan, 1928); C. David Naylor, ''Rural Protest and Medical Professionalism in Turn-of-the-Century Ontario,'' *Journal of Canadian Studies* 21 (1986): 5–20.

8. For further readings on women in the medical profession *see*: G.W.L. Nicholson, *Canada's Nursing Sisters*, (Ottawa: National Museum of Man, 1975); Suzann Buckley, ''Ladies or Midwives? Efforts to Reduce Infant and Maternal Mortality,'' in Linda Kealey, ed., *A Not Unreasonable Claim: Women and Reform in Canada 1880–1920*, (Toronto: Women's Educational Press, 1979); Margaret Street, *Watchfires on the Mountain: The Life and Writings of Ethel Johns*, (Toronto: University of Toronto Press, 1973); Leslie Biggs, ''The Case of the Missing Midwives: A History of Midwifery in Ontario from 1795–1900,'' *Ontario History* LXXV (1983): 21–36.

9. For detailed descriptions of women's attempts to receive a medical degree, *see*: Carlotta Hacker, *The Indomitable Lady Doctors*, (Toronto: Clarke, Irwin, 1974); Peter Dembski, ''Jenny Kidd Trout and the Founding of the Women's Medical Colleges at Kingston and Toronto,'' *Ontario History* LXXVII (1985): 183–206; Veronica Strong-Boag, ed., *A Woman With a Purpose: The Diaries of Elizabeth Smith 1872–1884*, (Toronto: University of Toronto Press, 1980); Hugh MacDermott, *Maude Abbott: A Memoir*, (Toronto: Macmillan, 1941).

10. Veronica Strong-Boag, ''Canada's Women Doctors: Feminism Constrained,'' in *A Not Unreasonable Claim*.

11. *The Canadian Medical Record* 16 (1888): 239.

12. *Ibid*. 8 (1890): 215.

13. *Canadian Practitioner* 9 (1884): 272. There was a great deal of discussion in the nineteenth century about when to perform ovariotomies. Physicians recognized that removing a woman's ovaries was a serious step and stated that it should only be done when a woman was suffering from debilitating problems, which only a premature menopause could cure. *See*: Wendy Mitchinson, ''A Medical Debate in Nineteenth

Century English Canada: Ovariotomies,'' *Histoire Sociale/Social History* XVII (1984): 133–47.
14. Henry Garrigues, *A Text-book of the Diseases of Women*, (Philadelphia, 1894), 127.
15. Paul Mundé, ed., *A Practical Treatise on the Diseases of Women*, (Philadelphia, 1891), 511.
16. Deborah Findlay, ''Professional Interests in Medicine's Construction of Women's Reproductive Health,'' 8, paper given at the Canadian Sociology and Anthropology Association Meeting, Winnipeg, 1986.
17. *Ibid.*, 10.
18. Interview by the author with the woman (who wishes to remain anonymous), Summer 1977.
19. *The Canada Medical Record* 8 (1880): 237. *See also*: Wendy Mitchinson, ''Hysteria and Insanity in Women: A Ninteenth-Century Canadian Perspective,'' *Journal of Canadian Studies* 21 (1986): 87–105.
20. *The Canada Lancet* 12 (1880): 244.
21. *Canada Medical Journal and Monthly Record of Medical and Surgical Science* 4 (1867): 207; *The Canada Medical Record* 7 (1879): 319; *The Canada Lancet* 15 (1883): 310; *Canadian Practitioner* 14 (1889): 338.
22. Kathleen McDonnell and Mariana Valverde, eds., *The Healthsharing Book: Resources for Canadian Women*, (Toronto: Women's Educational Press, 1985), 19, 112.
23. *Ibid.*, 113.
24. Garrigues, *A Text-book*, 125.
25. *Dominion Medical Monthly and Ontario Medical Journal* I (1893): 68; *The Sanitary Journal* 6 (1894): 56; *Canadian Practitioner* 16 (1891): 261; *The Canada Lancet* 6 (1874): 233; *The Canada Medical Record* 8 (1879): 319; *The Montreal Medical Journal* 25 (1897): 682; Mundé, *A Practical Treatise*, 37.
26. J. Thorburn, *A Practical Treatise of the Diseases of Women*, (London, 1885), 192–93. *See also*: Wendy Mitchinson, ''Causes of Disease in Women: the Case of Late 19th Century English Canada,'' in Charles G. Roland, ed., *Health, Disease, and Medicine: Essays in Canadian History*, (Toronto: Hannah Institute for the History of Medicine, 1984), 381–95.
27. *Healthsharing* 7 (1986): 16.
28. Vern Bullough and Martha Voight, ''Women, Menstruation, and Nineteenth Century Medicine,'' *Bulletin of the History of Medicine* 48 (1973): 66.
29. Garrigues, *A Text-book*, 126; Mundé, *A Practical Treatise*, 36; Alexander Skene, *Medical Gynecology*, (New York, 1895), 23; *The Canada Lancet* 12 (1880): 186–87; William Goodell, *Lessons in Gynecology* (Philadelphia, 1890), 551.
30. *Dominion Medical Monthly and Ontario Medical Journal* 8 (1897): 134–35.
31. *Canadian Practitioner* 21 (1896): 331; *The Canada Medical Record* 24 (1896): 555; *Dominion Medical Monthly and Ontario Medical Journal* 11 (1898): 29.
32. *Dominion Medical Monthly and Ontario Medical Journal* 7 (1896): 501; and 11 (1898): 28, 30.

33. R. Pierce, *The People's Common Sense Medical Adviser in Plain English*, (Buffalo, 1882), 751.
34. *Ibid.*, 749–50; *The Canada Medical Record* 11 (1883): 255; George Napheys, *The Physical Life of Woman* (Toronto, 1890), 35.
35. Mark Poster, *Foucault, Marxism and History: Mode of Production versus Mode of Information* (Cambridge: Cambridge University Press), 132. For a more detailed examination of medical perceptions of female sexuality, *see*: Wendy Mitchinson, "Medical Perceptions of Female Sexuality: A Late Nineteenth Century Case," *Scientia Canadensis* 9 (1985): 67–81.
36. Ruth Roach Pierson, *"They're Still Women After All": The Second World War and Canadian Womanhood* (Toronto: McClelland and Stewart, 1986), 169–214.
37. Deborah Findlay, "Professional Interests," 9.
38. *Kingston Medical Quarterly* 3 (1898): 165; Goodell, *Lessons*, 570, 573; *Canada Medical Journal and Monthly Record* 3 (1867): 226; *Canadian Practitioner* 18 (1883): 296.
39. Goodell, *Lessons*, 566.
40. *Ibid.*, 562.
41. Mundé, *A Practical Treatise*, 43; *Canada Health Journal* 1 (1870): 66.
42. *The Canada Lancet* 4 (1871): 185–86; *Canada Health Journal* 1 (1876): 67.
43. *The Canada Lancet* 7 (1875): 291.
44. For a history of birth control in Canada *see*: Angus McLaren and Arlene Tigar McLaren, *The Bedroom and the State: The Changing Practices and Politics of Contraception and Abortion in Canada, 1880–1980*, (Toronto: McClelland and Stewart, 1986).
45. Constance Backhouse, "Involuntary Motherhood: Abortion, Birth Control and the Law in Nineteenth Century Canada," *The Windsor Yearbook of Access to Justice* 3 (1983): 61–130.
46. McLaren and McLaren, *The Bedroom*, 36.
47. *Kitchener-Waterloo Record*, July 25, 1986, 1.
48. *Pro-Choice News*, Summer 1986, 8.
49. *Ibid.*, 1.
50. J. Storch, *Patient's Rights: Ethical and Legal Issues in Health Care and Nursing*, (Toronto: McGraw-Hill Ryerson, 1982), preface.
51. Walter Radcliffe, *Milestones in Midwifery*, (Bristol: John Wright and Sons, 1967), 81.
52. William Tyler Smith, *The Modern Practice of Midwifery: A Course of Lectures on Obstetrics*, (New York, 1858), 128.
53. McDonnell, *Healthsharing Book*, 62.
54. Findlay, *Professional Interests*, 13.
55. McDonnel, *Healthsharing Book*, 66.
56. For a fuller description of the Dionne quintuplets' lives, *see*: Pierre Berton, *The Dionne Years: A Thirties Melodrama*, (Toronto: McClelland and Stewart, 1977).
57. *Healthsharing* 7 (1986): 18.
58. *Canadian Practitioner* 23 (1898): 579.

59. *See*: Wendy Mitchinson, "Gynecological Operations on Insane Women: London Ontario, 1895–1901," *Journal of Social History* 15 (1982): 467–484.
60. Angus McLaren, "The Creation of a Haven for Humane Thoroughbreds: The Sterilization of the Feeble-Minded and the Mentally Ill in British Columbia," *Canadian Historical Review* LXVII (1986): 128.
61. *Ibid.*, 146.,
62. Robert Morgan, ed., *The Introgenics Handbook: A Critical Look at Research and Practice in the Helping Professions*, (Toronto: IPI Publishing, 1983), v–vi.
63. Suzann Buckley, "Hospital Records and Historians: The Case of Maternal Morality," in W. Mitchinson and J. Dickin McGinnis, eds., *Essays in the History of Canadian Medicine*, (Toronto: McClelland and Stewart, 1988).
64. *Canadian Practitioner and Review* 23 (1898): 580.

Chapter Ten

1. Naomi Weisstein, "Woman as Nigger," *Psychology Today* 3, no. 5, (1969): 20.
2. Sigmund Freud was the creator of the psychoanalytic method by which earlier memories, wishes, and fears hidden from memory are made conscious. He also formed a school around this method which attracted many students, several of whom subsequently broke with Freud and established their own schools of psychoanalysis.
3. Psychoanalytic therapists emphasize the importance of childhood experience in determining personality structures and the power of mental events to determine human behaviour. Their therapy thus focuses on recovering these events from the unconscious mind. Humanistic therapists assume that individuals have great potential for growth, creativity, and spontaneity and are free to make choices. These therapists focus on present behaviour and the individual's ability to change aspects of her/his life. There are more than a hundred different varieties of psychotherapy, each with its own program of treatment and outcome goals.
4. A description of the theory can be found in most introductory psychology textbooks, but the original formulation is in Sigmund Freud, *Three Essays on the Theory of Sexuality*, (1905), (New York: Avon Books, 1965).
5. Sigmund Freud, "Femininity," in *The Standard Edition of the Complete Psychological Works of Sigmund Freud,* Vol. XXII, (London: Hogarth Press, 1964), 125.
6. *Ibid.*, 128.
7. Freud did discuss two other possible, but abnormal outcomes for girls. First, she might have such envy for the penis (and dissatisfaction with her clitoris) that she is led to repress all sexual impulses, thus leading to neurotic problems later in life. Second, her refusal to accept that she has been castrated might lead to a masculinity complex. The fantasy of being a man might then lead to homosexuality and compel her to act as a man. *Ibid.*, 126.
8. *Ibid.*, 134. Freud also goes on to say, "We also regard women as weaker in their social interests and as having less capacity for sublimating their instincts than men."
9. *Ibid.*, 132. Two other articles by Freud that deal specifically with female development are "Some Psychological Consequences of the Anatomical Distinction between

the Sexes," (1925), and "Female Sexuality," (1931), in *Collected Papers 5*, (New York: Basic Books, 1959), 186–96; 252–72.
10. The term was used by Phyllis Chesler, *Women & Madness*, (New York: Avon, 1972), 72.
11. Helene Deutsch, *The Psychology of Women: A Psychoanalytic Interpretation I*, (New York: Bantam Books, 1944), 195. She said about this definition, it "indicates a function, expresses something positive, and can satisfy the feminists among us who often feel that the term 'feminine passivity' has derogatory implications."
12. *Ibid.*, 245–85.
13. *See*: Paul Roazen, *Helene Deutsch: A Psychoanalyst's Life*, (Garden City, N.Y.: Anchor Press, 1985).
14. The inner space is described by Erikson as "internal organs, with vestibular access, leading to statically expectant ova." Erik H. Erikson, "Womanhood and the Inner Space," in Erikson, *Identity: Youth and Crisis*, (New York: Norton, 1968), 271. Erikson developed this concept from a study of children creating play constructions. A recent study seriously challenges the concept and the results of the study. *See*: Paula J. Caplan, "Erikson's Concept of Inner Space: a Data-Based Reevaluation," *American Journal of Orthopsychiatry* 49, no. 1, (1979); 100–108.
15. Erikson, "Womanhood and the Inner Space," 285.
16. *Ibid.*, 283.
17. *Ibid.*
18. W.H. Masters and V.E. Johnson, *Human Sexual Response*, (Boston: Little Brown, 1966).
19. Freud, "Femininity," 120.
20. Freud, "The Aetiology of Hysteria," (1920) in Freud, *Collected Papers I*, (New York: Basic Books, 1959), 183–219. Interestingly, in this article Freud did not once name fathers as the perpetrators.
21. A discussion of Freud's suppression of the truth of the sexual seduction of children is included in Florence Rush, *The Best Kept Secret: Sexual Abuse of Children*, (Englewood, Cliffs, N.J.: Prentice-Hall, 1980), 80–104, and is the focus of Jeffery M. Masson, *The Assault on Truth: Freud's Suppression of the Seduction Theory*, (New York: Penguin, 1985). In Canada, estimates are that 54 per cent of females under the age of eighteen have been sexually assaulted. *See*: Alanna Mitchell, "Child Sexual Assault," in Connie Guberman and Margie Wolfe, eds., *No Safe Place: Violence Against Women and Children*, (Toronto: Women's Educational Press, 1985).
22. Stephanie Shields, "Functionalism, Darwinism, and the Psychology of Women: A Study of Social Myth," *American Psychologist* 30, no. 1, (1975).
23. *Ibid.*, 739.
24. *See*, for example, Sue Cox, *Female Psychology: The Emerging Self*, second edition, (New York: St. Martin's Press, 1981); Juanita H. Williams, *Psychology of Women: Behavior in a Bisocial Context*, third edition, (New York: Norton, 1987); Irene H. Frieze, Jacquelynne E. Parsons, Paula B. Johnson, Diane N. Ruble, and Gail L. Zellman, *Women and Sex Roles: A Social Psychological Perspective*, (New York:

Norton, 1978). Two Canadian contributors to the area are Esther R. Greenglass, *A World of Difference: Gender Roles in Perspective*, (Toronto: John Wiley & Sons, 1982), and Hilary M. Lips and Nina L. Colwill, *The Psychology of Sex Differences*, (Englewood Cliffs, N.Y.: Prentice-Hall, 1978).

25. Karen Horney, "The Flight from Womanhood," in her *Feminine Psychology*, (New York: Norton, 1973), 54–70.

26. Williams, *Psychology of Women*, 77.

27. Clara M. Thompson, *On Women*, (New York: New American Library, 1971).

28. For example, the Canadian Psychological Association (CPA) set up a task force in 1975. Its report, "Report of the Task Force on the Status of Women in Canadian Psychology," *Canadian Psychological Review* 18, no. 1, (1977), contained almost a hundred recommendations, many of which have been implemented. In 1976, an interest group on women and psychology was formed, which became a section of the CPA in 1980. In 1980, guidelines for therapy and counselling with women were introduced. A committee on the status of women was made a standing committee of the CPA board of directors to implement the task force's recommendations, and a psychologist's guide to the conduct of nonsexist research has been published and approved by several CPA bodies.

29. *See*: Jeri D. Wine, "Models of Human Functioning: A Feminist Perspective," *International Journal of Women's Studies* 18, no. 2, (1985).

30. Matina S. Horner, "Toward an Understanding of Achievement Related Conflicts in Women," in Rhoda K. Unger and Florence L. Denmark, eds., *Women: Dependent or Independent Variables?* (New York: Psychological Dimension, 1975). *See also*: David W. Tresemer, *Fear of Success*, (New York: Plenum, 1977), and Martha T.S. Mednick, Sandra S. Tangri, and Lois W. Hoffman, eds., *Women and Achievement: Social and Motivational Analyses*, (New York: John Wiley & Sons, 1975).

31. Cited by Olga E. Favreau, "Sex Bias in Psychological Research," *Canadian Psychological Review*, 18, no. 1, (1977): 56–65.

32. Eleanor C. Maccoby and Carol N. Jacklin, *The Psychology of Sex Differences*, (Stanford: Stanford University Press, 1974). They provide a summary of their results in Maccoby and Jacklin, "Myth, Reality and Shades of Gray: What We Know and Don't Know about Sex Differences," *Psychology Today* 8, no. 7, (1974): 109–12.

33. For example, *see*: Paula J. Caplan, Gail M. MacPherson, and Patricia Tobin, "Do Sex-related Differences in Spatial Abilities Exist? A Multilevel Critique with New Data," *American Psychologist* 40, no. 7. (1985): 786–99.

34. An interesting NOVA program, "The Pinks and the Blues," aired in the early 1980s, provides a wealth of information on this issue. A good discussion is included in Greenglass, *A World of Difference*, 33–46. *See also*: Jeffrey Z. Rubin, Frank J. Provenzano, and Zella Luria, "The Eye of the Beholder: Parents' Views on Sex of Newborns," *American Journal of Orthopyschiatry* 44, no. 4, (1974): 512–19.

35. In her review of sex-differences literature in her CPA presidential address. Sandra Pyke concluded that, "the bottom line with respect to the study of sex differences might well be: never has so much been said by so many about so little." Sandra W. Pyke, "Confessions of a Reluctant Ideologist," *Canadian Psychology* 23, no. 3,

(1983): 125–34. One of the four themes around which Margaret W. Matlin, *The Psychology of Women*, (New York: Holt, Rinehart and Winston, 1987), has written her text is that "women show a wide range of variation from each other in their psychological characteristics, their life choices, and their responses to biological events."

36. The terms 'sex' and 'gender' are often used interchangeably, but those who attempt to make a distinction use 'sex' to refer to the biologically based categories of male and female, and 'gender' to refer to the psychological features associated with the biological status.

37. P.A. Goldberg, "Are Women Prejudiced Against Women?" *Transaction* 5, no. 5, (1968): 28–30.

38. *See*: Inge K. Broverman, Donald M. Broverman, Frank E. Clarkson, Paul S., Rosenkrantz, and Susan R. Vogel, "Sex-Role Stereotypes and Clinical Judgments of Mental Health," in Unger and Denmark, eds., *Women: Dependent or Independent Variables? See also*: Chapter Three in Kay Deux, *The Behaviour of Women and Men*, (Monterey: Brooks/Cole, 1976).

39. *See*: Stanley Milgram, *Obedience to Authority: An Experimental View*, (New York: Harper Colophon, 1974). For the influence of expectations on behaviour, *see*: R. Rosenthal, *Experimenter Effects in Behavioral Research*, (New York: Appleton-Century Crofts, 1966).

40. Paula J. Caplan and Ian Hall-McCorquodale, "Mother-Blaming in Major Clinical Journals," *American Journal of Orthopsychiatry* 55, no. 3, (1985): 345–53.

41. In the introductory textbook, *Psychology Today: An Introduction* (New York: Random House, fifth edition, 1983), 405, and sixth edition, (1986), 342, the mother is implicated in incest because of her inability to fulfill the wife role or for her failure to stop the incest.

42. For a discussion of some of the consequences of this belief, *see*: Paula J. Caplan, *The Myth of Women's Masochism*, (New York: E.P. Dutton, 1985).

43. *See*: Chesler, *Women & Madness*; Dorothy E. Smith and Sara J. David, eds., *Women Look at Psychiatry*, (Vancouver: Press Gang, 1975); Helen Levine, "The Personal is Political: Feminism and the Helping Professions," in Geraldine Finn and Angela Miles, eds., *Feminism in Canada: From Pressure to Politics*, (Montreal: Black Rose Books, 1982); P. Susan Penfold and Gillian A. Walker, *Women and the Psychiatric Paradox*, (Montreal: Eden Press, 1983).

44. "Guidelines for Therapy and Counselling with Women," *Canadian Psychology* 21, no. 4, (1980): 185–86.

45. Judith M. Avis, "Deepening Awareness: A Private Study Guide to Feminism and Family Therapy," *Journal of Psychotherapy and the Family*, (forthcoming).

46. Some of the books written by those who have pioneered in this movement are: Hogie Wyckoff, *Solving Problems Together*, (New York: Grove Press, 1980); Sheila Ernst and Lucy Goodison, *In Our Own Hands: A Book of Self-Help Therapy*, (London: Women's Press, 1985); and Women's Counselling, Referral and Education Centre, *A Handbook for Women Starting Groups*, (Toronto: WCREC, 1984).

47. I recently audited a graduate course in feminist issues in counselling and psy-

chotherapy. I was surprised to learn that the material we read and discussed was new to most of the students. A majority of them claimed that such ideas were never mentioned in their other counselling courses or in their work settings.

48. *See*: Mary B. Parlee, "Psychology and Women," *Signs: A Journal of Women in Culture and Society* 5, no. 1, (1979): 121–33.

49. *See*: Margrit Eichler, *The Double Standard: A Feminist Critique of Feminist Social Science*, (London: Croom Helm, 1980); Cannie Stark-Adamec and Meredith Kimball, "Science Free of Sexism: A Psychologists' Guide to the Conduct of Nonsexist Research," *Canadian Psychology* 25, no. 1, (1984): 24–34; Margrit Eichler and Jeanne Lapointe, *On the Treatment of the Sexes in Research*, (Ottawa: SSHRC, 1985); and Margrit Eichler, *Non-Sexist Research Methods: A Practical Guide*, (Boston: Allen & Unwin, 1988).

50. Some feminists point out that knowledge cannot be value-free, and also claim that it cannot be objective. Others believe that value-freedom can be separated from objectivity and that feminists *must* aim for objectivity in their research. *See*: *Ibid*, 11–14.

51. *See*: Meredith M. Kimball, "Developing a Feminist Psychology of Women: Past and Future Accomplishments," *Canadian Psychology* 27, no. 3, (1986): 248–59.

52. *See*: Jeri D. Wine, "Gynocentric Values and Feminist Psychology," in *Feminism in Canada*, and Liz Stanley and Sue Wise, *Breaking Out: Consciousness and Feminist Research*, (London: Routledge & Kegan Paul, 1983).

53. *See*: Wine, "Gynocentric Values."

54. *Ibid.*, 74–79.

55. *See*: Hannah Lerman, "From Freud to Feminist Personality Theory: Getting Here from There," *Psychology of Women Quarterly* 10, no. 1, (1986): 1–18.

56. *Ibid.*, 6.

57. Two other writers, not discussed here, who fall into this group are: Dorothy Dinnerstein, *The Mermaid and the Minotaur: Sexual Arrangements and Human Malaise*, (New York: Harper Colophon, 1976), and Evelyn F. Keller, *Reflections on Gender and Science*, (New Haven: Yale University Press, 1985).

58. Juliet Mitchell, *Psychoanalysis and Feminism: Freud, Reich, Laing and Women*, (New York: Vintage Books, 1974).

59. Dorothy Dinnerstein's book is one of these, but the more influential analysis was provided by Nancy Chodorow, *The Reproduction of Mothering: Psychoanalysis and the Sociology of Gender*, (Berkeley: University of California Press, 1978).

60. *Ibid.*, 39.

61. *Ibid.*, 218–19.

62. The term was introduced by Adrienne Rich, "Compulsory Heterosexuality and Lesbian Existence," *Signs: A Journal of Women in Culture and Society* 5, no. 4, (1980): 631–60.

63. Williams, *Psychology of Women.*

64. *Ibid.*, 392.

65. Susan Krieger, "Lesbian Identity and Community: Recent Social Science Lit-

erature,'' *Signs: A Journal of Women in Culture and Society* 8, no. 1, (1982): 91–108, (95).

66. *Ibid.*, 93.

67. Jeri D. Wine, ''Toward a Feminist Standpoint for Psychology,'' paper presented at the Association for Women in Psychology conference, New York, 1985.

68. *See*: Sandra L. Bem, ''The Measurement of Psychological Androgyny,'' *Journal of Consulting and Clinical Psychology*, 42, no. 2, (1974): 155–162, and Pyke, ''Confessions of a Reluctant Ideologist.''

69. Jean B. Miller, *Toward a New Psychology of Women*, (Boston: Beacon Press, 1976).

70. Wine talks of relationality which she says ''refers to a consciousness of the necessary interdependence of human beings, to a sense of connectedness to others, to awareness of one's embeddedness in human, social and historical contexts, to the maximization of well-being for all persons, and to commitment to nonviolence.'' In ''Gynocentric Values.''

71. Lawrence Kohlberg, ''The Child as a Moral Philosopher,'' *Psychology Today* 2, no. 4, (1968): 24–30.

72. Carol Gilligan, *In a Different Voice: Psychological Theory and Women's Development*, (Cambridge: Harvard University Press, 1982) and Carol Gilligan, ''Why Should a Woman be more like a Man?'' *Psychology Today* 16, no. 6, (1982): 68–77. For criticisms of the work, *see*: Linda K. Gerber, Catherine G. Greeno, and Eleanor E. Maccoby; Zella Luria, Carol B. Stack, and Carol Gilligan, ''On *In a Different Voice*: An Interdisciplinary Forum,'' *Signs: A Journal of Women in Culture and Society* 11, no. 2, (1986): 304–33.

73. Mary F. Belenky, Blythe M. Clinchy, Nancy R. Goldberger, and Jill M. Tarule, *Women's Ways of Knowing: The Development of Self, Voice, and Mind*, (New York: Basic Books, 1986), 11.

74. *Ibid.*, 15.

75. *Ibid.*, 229. The terms 'connection' and 'separation' in the quote refer to the way in which the individual comes to know the 'truth' about something. For a connected knower, the truth or understanding emerges from putting oneself into the other's position and developing an understanding from immersion in, for example, the play or the problem. There is a relationship of care between the knower and what is to be known. The individual who is a separated knower learns the impersonal procedures for establishing the truth, that is, learns the rules for how things are to be done in a particular subject area. Universities typically emphasize separated learning.

Chapter Eleven

1. Ultrasound involves the use of high-frequency sound waves to produce an image on a video screen of the foetus (or other body parts). Increasingly, particularly in urban centres, it is used routinely in prenatal care and presumed to be safe, although no long-term follow-up studies have been undertaken. Amniocentesis is a prenatal diagnostic

technique used to detect certain chromosomal abnormalities (e.g., Down's syndrome). A needle is inserted into the abdomen of a pregnant woman to extract a sample of the amniotic fluid. Amniocentesis, which cannot be used until the second trimester of pregnancy, is becoming a standard practice for pregnant women over the age of thirty-five. It can be used to detect the sex of the foetus. Chorionic villi sampling (CVS), or chorionic biopsy is a newer, still experimental method of prenatal diagnosis to detect foetal abnormalities, which can also be used to detect the sex of the foetus. A sample of foetal cells are removed through the pregnant woman's cervix. CVS can be performed in the first trimester of pregnancy and the results are obtainable more quickly than with amniocentesis. Foetal monitoring is a method of measuring the foetal heartbeat during pregnancy or labour. Foetal surgery is a form of micro-surgery to correct foetal defects within the womb.

2. Ruth Hubbard, "The Fetus as Patient," *MS*, October 1982.

3. *See*: Angus McLaren and Arlene Tigar McLaren, *The Bedroom and the State: The Changing Practices and Politics of Contraception and Abortion in Canada, 1880–1980*, (Toronto: McClelland and Stewart, 1986) for an historical view of the politics of contraception and abortion in Canada.

4. The typology of reproductive technologies suggested here – the inhibition, monitoring, and creation of new life – is useful to distinguish the variety of reproductive technologies currently available. It is important to note, however, that they are frequently used in combination with each other and are not necessarily distinct. For example, women who conceive through IVF, AI, or surrogate motherhood arrangements may utilize diagnostic techniques such as amniocentesis, ultrasound, or choronic villi sampling, as may women who conceive 'normally.' The focus of the chapter on artificial reproduction is a pragmatic one because of limitations of space. However, other developments, such as the routine use of amniocentesis for women over the age of thirty-five are also important issues in considering new choices available for women in their reproductive and mothering roles.

5. Shulamith Firestone, *The Dialectic of Sex*, (New York: Bantam Books, 1970).

6. Barbara Menning, "In Defense of In Vitro Fertilization," in Helen B. Holmes, Betty B. Hoskins, and Michael Gross, eds., *The Custom-Made Child?*, (New Jersey: Humana Press, 1981), 263–67.

7. For example, in the "Baby M" trial in 1987, the counsel for a surrogate mother attempted to reassert her custody rights on the basis that the contracting mother was avoiding pregnancy for minor or convenience concerns.

8. Furthermore, the causes of infertility may be socially rooted to some extent in occupational health hazards, environmental pollution, food additives, and the use of specific drugs such as DES and devices such as IUDS.

9. A vasectomy is a simple medical procedure in which the vas deferens is cut so that sperm cannot mix with seminal fluid. It can be done in a doctor's office with a local anesthetic. Tubal ligations are more complex procedures (there are several methods) in which the fallopian tubes are blocked or cut so that the sperm and egg cannot join. Usually a general anesthetic is employed.

10. For further information on self-insemination *see*: Nancy Adamson, "Self-

insemination,'' *Healthsharing* 6, no. 4 (1985): 8–9; Francie Hornstein, '' Children By Donor Insemination: A New Choice For Lesbians,'' in Rita Arditti, Renate Duelli Klein, and Shelley Minden, eds., *Test-Tube Women: What Future For Motherhood?*, (London: Routledge & Kegan Paul, 1984), 382–90; Gillian E. Hanscombe and Jackie Forster, *Rocking the Cradle*, (London: Peter Owen, 1981); Cheri Pies, *Considering Parenthood: A Workbook for Lesbians*, (San Francisco: Spinster's Ink, 1985); Susan Robinson and H.F. Pizer, *Having a Baby Without a Man*, (New York: Simon & Schuster, 1985); Joy Schulenberg, *Gay Parenting*, (Garden City, N.J.: Anchor Press, 1985); Kathleen Lahey, ''Alternative Insemination: Facing the Conceivable Options,'' *Broadside* 8, no. 1 (1986): 8–10.

11. Kathleen A. Lahey, ''Reproduction, Male Technology and 'Lifestyle' Conflicts: The Lesbian Challenge,'' paper presented at the Sixth National Biennial Conference of the National Association of Women and the Law, Ottawa, February 1985.

12. *See*: Menning, ''In Defense of In Vitro Fertilization,'' for a description of treatments for infertility that are utilized before artificial insemination is attempted.

13. A.T. Gregoire and Robert C. Mayer, ''The Impregnators,'' *Fertility and Sterility* 16, no. 1 (1965): 130–34.

14. Gena Corea, The Mother Machine, (New York: Harper & Row, 1985).

15. Gregoire and Mayer, ''The Impregnators'': 130–34.

16. G.J. Annas, ''Fathers Anonymous: Beyond the Best Interests of the Sperm Donor,'' *Child Welfare* 60, no. 1 (1981): 161–74.

17. Rona Achilles, ''The Social Meanings of Biological Ties: A Study of Participants in Artificial Insemination by Donor,'' Ph.D. dissertation, University of Toronto, 1986.

18. Richard Titmuss, *The Gift Relationship*, (London: Allen & Unwin, 1970).

19. By the mid-1980s, two Australian AID mothers had already contracted acquired immune deficiency disease through donor insemination.

20. Martin Curie-Cohen, Lesleigh Luttrell, and Sander Shapiro, ''Current Practice of Artificial Insemination by Donor in the United States,'' *New England Journal of Medicine* 300, no. 11, 589.

21. Ontario Law Reform Commission, *Report on Human Artificial Reproduction and Related Matters*, (1985), 103. The Commission was requested by Attorney General Roy McMurtry to ''inquire into and consider the legal issues relating to the practice of human artificial insemination, including 'surrogate mothering' and transplantation of fertilized ova to a third party . . . [and] report on the range of alternatives for resolution of any legal issues that may be identified.'' The legal issues suggested in the terms of reference for the report included: ''(1) The legal status and legal rights of the child and the safeguards for protecting the best interests of the child. (2) The legal rights and legal duties of each biological parent. (3) The legal rights and legal duties of the spouse, if any, of each biological parent. (4) The nature and enforceability of agreements relating to artificial insemination and related practices. (5) The nature and enforceability of agreements respecting custody of the child. (6) The legal rights and liabilities of medical and other personnel involved in performing artificial insemination and other related practices. (7) The legal procedures for establishing and recognizing the biological parentage of the children born as a result of these practices. (8) The applicability of

present custody and adoption laws in such cases. (9) The availability of information to identify the child and the parties involved. (10) Such medical and related evidence as may have a bearing on the legal issues raised in these cases.''

22. The AID mothers who participated in my study included women who were married at the time of insemination, single women, and lesbian couples. Single or lesbian AID mothers consistently adopted an attitude of openness about their AID child(ren)'s origins. The absence of a male partner made it impossible for them to attempt to conform to the conventional image of the family.

23. Anecdotal evidence suggests that women bore children for other women long before the practice became organized and a profit-making enterprise for lawyers and physicians.

24. Susan Ince, ''Inside the Surrogate Industry,'' in Arditti, *et al.*, *Test Tube Women*, 382–390.

25. Annas, ''Fathers Anonymous.''

26. In February 1988, the decision by the higher court, the Supreme Court of New Jersey, was reported. Chief Justice Robert Wilentz overturned all aspects of the earlier court's ruling with the exception of the custody decision. Although the custody decision was not overturned, Mary Beth Whitehead's parental rights were restored which will allow her to seek a new custody hearing. Most significantly, this ruling, which will likely have an impact in other jurisdictions, rules that the contract between Whitehead and Stern was illegal because it violated the state's adoption laws concerning payment for a child. '' 'This is the sale of a child, or at the very least, the sale of a mother's right to her child, the only mitigating factor being that one of the purchasers is the father,' the court said.'' Robert Haney, ''Surrogate Deals For Mothers Held Illegal in Jersey,'' *The New York Times*, February 4, 1988.

27. Linda S. Williams, ''Who Qualifies for In Vitro Fertilization? A Sociological Examination of the Stated Admittance Criteria of Three Ontario IVF Programs,'' paper presented to the Canadian Sociology and Anthropology Association, 1986.

28. A laparoscopy is a surgical procedure requiring a general anesthetic in which eggs are suctioned out through a fiberoptic tube.

29. Robyn Rowland, ''A Child at Any Price?'' *Women's Studies International Forum* 8, no. 6 (1985): 539–46.

30. In Canada, the following reports are available: *Artificial Insemination*, Ninth Report of the Royal Commission on Family and Children's Law, Government of British Columbia, 1975; *Status of Children*, University of Alberta, 1976; *Tentative Proposals for a Human Artificial Insemination Act*, Law Reform Commission of Saskatchewan, 1981; *Storage and Utilization of Human Sperm*, Health and Welfare Canada, 1981; *Report on Human Artificial Reproduction and Related Matters*, Ontario Law Reform Commission, 1985. For the U.S.A., *see*: Ethics Committee of the American Fertility Society, ''Ethical Considerations of the New Reproductive Technologies,'' *Fertility and Sterility*, 46, no. 3 (1986). For Britain, *see*: The Warnock Report on Human Fertilization and Embryology, *A Question of Life*, (Oxford: Blackwell, 1985).

31. Yet to be clarified are the legal rights and responsibilities of all the participants in artificial reproduction. Traditionally, rights and responsibilities for offspring are

assigned to biological parents unless otherwise legislated as with, for example, adoption. In the practice of AID, the husband of the AID mother is named on the birth certificate as the father of the child although the sperm donor is the biological father. Further complications arise from the biological and socially defined differences between maternity and paternity. Is an egg donation, for example, the legal equivalent of a sperm donation? What rights do gamete (egg or sperm) donors have over their genetic material? Who 'owns' the extra embryos that are not implanted? Can physicians, lawyers, or surrogate organizations be liable for inadequate screening procedures or 'damaged goods'? For a discussion of these and other legal issues, *see*: Ontario Law Reform Commission, *Report on Human Artificial Reproduction and Related Matters*, 1985.

32. Margrit Eichler, *Families in Canada Today*, (Toronto: Gage, 1983).

33. The procedure for an egg donation is much more medically invasive than sperm donation, but it is possible that women simply donate extra eggs removed during the initial phase of IVF. In *The Mother Machine*, Corea points out that egg 'donations' might occur unknown to women during surgery.

34. *See*: Anne Finger, "Claiming our Bodies: Reproductive Rights and Disabilities," in Arditti, *et al.*, *Test-Tube Women*.

35. *See*: Jalna Hamner, "Sex Predetermination, Artificial Insemination and the Maintenance of Male-Dominated Culture," in Helen Roberts, eds., *Women, Health and Reproduction*, (London: Routledge & Kegan Paul, 1984).

36. Nancy Williamson, *Sons or Daughters? A Cross-Cultural Study of Parental Preferences*, (Beverley Hills: Sage Publications, 1976); Nancy Williamson, "Sex Preferences, Sex Control, and the Status of Women," *Signs: A Journal of Women in Culture and Society* 1, no. 4, (1976): 847–62; Nancy Williamson, "Parental Preference and Sex Control," *Population Bulletin*, 33, no. 1. (1978).

37. *See*: Neil G. Bennett, ed., *Sex Selection of Children*, (New York: Academic Press, 1983).

38. *See*: Hanmer, "Sex Predetermination," for a more complete discussion of these methods.

39. Fiona Whitlock, "Test-tube Babies are Smarter and Stronger," *The Australian*, May 17, 1984.

40. Barbara Ehrenreich and Deirdre English, *For Her Own Good: 150 Years of the Experts' Advice to Women*, (New York: Anchor Books, 1978).

41. In contrast to Britain, for example, where the publication of the Warnock Report (1985) caused a flurry of public discussion.

Notes on Contributors

RONA ACHILLES received her doctorate in sociology from the Ontario Institute for Studies in Education. Her thesis, entitled "The Social Meanings of Biological Ties," is a study of the participants in donor insemination programmes. She is currently working as a free-lance researcher in Toronto.

BEVERLEY BAINES joined the Faculty of Law at Queen's University in 1974 after receiving her BA at McGill University and her LL.B. at Queen's University. She has taught courses on women and the law, feminist jurisprudence, human rights and property law. She is a member of the editorial board of the *Canadian Journal of Women and the Law*, and takes an active role in issues involving women and the Constitution.

NAOMI BLACK is Professor of Political Science at York University where she has been teaching since 1965, and has served as Women's Studies Co-ordinator (Faculty of Arts) and Adviser to the President on the Status of Women. She has published on international relations theory, foreign policy, feminist methodology, and women's organizations. Forthcoming publications include *Canadian Women: A History* (co-authored as part of the Women's History Collective) and *Social Feminism: Theory and Organization in England, France, and the United States*.

JOANNA B. BOEHNERT has degrees from Lake Erie College, the State University of Iowa, and the University of Toronto. She is an Associate Professor of Psychology and Co-ordinator of the Women's Studies Program at the University of Guelph. Her professional interests include the enhancement of teaching effectiveness and the psychology of women.

SANDRA BURT teaches political science at the University of Waterloo. In her research she focuses on women's organizations and government policy, and she has published articles on the political tactics of the Ad Hoc Committee on the Constitution, the effectiveness of the governments' affirmative action programs, and the origins and activities of contemporary women's groups. She is currently completing a book on the relationship between Canadian women's groups and government.

LORRAINE CODE is a Canada Research Fellow with the Department of Philosophy and the Women's Studies Research Group at York University. In addition to numerous articles in philosophy and in feminist theory, she is the author of *Epistemic Responsibility* (1987, recipient of the Brown University Press First Book Award), and co-editor (with S. Mullett and C. Overall) of *Feminist Perspectives: Philosophical Essays on Minds and Morals* (1988). She is currently writing a book on Knowledge and Gender.

LINDSAY DORNEY is Assistant Professor of English at the University of St. Jerome's College and Director of Women's Studies at the University of Waterloo. She has long devoted her energies to feminist issues in literature and criticisms, in pedagogy and in environmental and social conditions affecting Canadian women. She is a member of the CAUT Status of Women Committee.

JANE ERRINGTON teaches history at the Royal Military College. She has written a book, *The Lion, The Eagle and Upper Canada* (1987), and in addition to carrying on research on women in pre-rebellion Upper Canada, she is completing an illustrated history of Kingston.

SUSAN MCDANIEL is an Associate Professor of Sociology at the University of Waterloo where she has taught since 1976 after completing a Ph.D. in social demography at the University of Alberta. She is the author of two books, *Social Problems Through Conflict and Order* (1982, with Ben Agger) and *Canada's Aging Population* (1986), as well as numerous articles and book chapters on childbearing, adoption, abortion, and women's health issues. As Canada's first Thérèse Casgrain Research Fellow in 1987–88, she is completing a third book, *Childbearing in Change*.

WENDY MITCHINSON is an Associate Professor of history at the University of Waterloo. She is currently working on a study of the medical treatment of women in late nineteenth century Canada. In 1988–89 she will be the Hannah Visiting Professor at McMaster University.

ROXANA NG teaches sociology at the University of New Brunswick. Her research focuses on ethnic and gender relations as they pertain to the experiences of immigrant women in Canada. She has worked with immigrant women's groups across the country since 1976.

SHELAGH WILKINSON is Assistant Professor of Humanities and Co-ordinator of the Women's Studies Programme, Atkinson College, York University. She is founding editor of *Canadian Women's Studies/les cahiers de la femme* and the author of numerous articles on feminist literary criticism and the politics of teaching Women's Studies in patriarchal institutions.